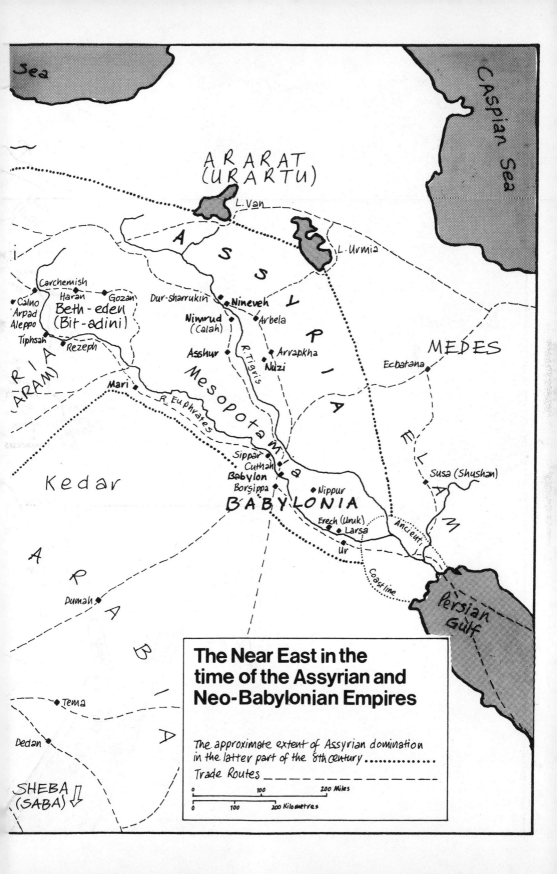

Sea

CASPIAN Sea

ARARAT
(URARTU)

L. Van

L. Urmia

A S S Y R I A

Carchemish
Calno
Arpad
Aleppo
Haran
Gozan
Beth-eden
(Bit-adini)
Tiphsah
Rezeph

Dur-sharrukin
Nineveh
Nimrud
(Calah)
Arbela
Asshur
Arrapkha
Nuzi

MEDES

Ecbatana

R I A
(ARAM)

Mari

R. Euphrates

Mesopotamia

R. Tigris

E L A M

Susa (Shushan)

Kedar

Sippar
Cuthah
Babylon
Borsippa

BABYLONIA

Nippur

Erech (Uruk)
Larsa
Uv

Ancient

A R A B I A

Dumah

Coastline

Persian
Gulf

Tema

Dedan

SHEBA
(SABA)

The Near East in the time of the Assyrian and Neo-Babylonian Empires

The approximate extent of Assyrian domination
in the latter part of the 8th century ....
Trade Routes _____

0   100   200 Miles
0   100   200 Kilometres

KINGDOMS OF THE LORD

*A History of the Hebrew Kingdoms from Saul
to the Fall of Jerusalem*

KINGDOMS
OF THE
LORD

*A History of the Hebrew Kingdoms from Saul
to the Fall of Jerusalem*

by

David F. Payne

WILLIAM B. EERDMANS PUBLISHING COMPANY
GRAND RAPIDS, MICHIGAN

First published 1981 by The Paternoster Press Ltd., England
This American edition published 1981 through special arrangement
with Paternoster by Wm. B. Eerdmans Publishing Company,
255 Jefferson Ave. S.E., Grand Rapids, MI   49503

Library of Congress Cataloging in Publication Data

Payne, David F. (David Frank), 1931-
Kingdoms of the Lord.

Bibliography: p. 295
Includes indexes.
1. Jews — History — 1200-953 B.C. 2. Jews — History —
953-586 B.C. 3. Jews — Kings and rulers. 4. Bible.
O.T. — History of contemporary events. I. Title.
DS121.P39   1981   909'.04924   81-3197
ISBN 0-8028-3559-7   AACR2

TO MY PARENTS

Contents

PART III — THE PROPHETS

PART IV — THE FAITH

List of Illustrations

ACKNOWLEDGEMENTS: The Author and Publishers are grateful to the following for help in supplying illustrations:
The British Museum (1,2,3,4,7,8,9,12,13,14); The Israel Department of Antiquities and Museums (5,6,10); Professor J. B. Pritchard (11,15).

Abbreviations

AB	*Anchor Bible*
AJSL	*American Journal of Semitic Languages and Literatures*
ANEP	J. B. Pritchard (ed.), *The Ancient Near East in Pictures*^{2} (Princeton, 1969)
ANET	J. B. Prichard (ed.), *Ancient Near Eastern Texts*^{3} (Princeton, 1969)
Ant.	Josephus, *Antiquities*
AOTS	D. Winton Thomas, (ed.), *Archaeology and Old Testament Study* (Oxford, 1967)
AV	Authorized Version (King James Version), 1611
BA	*The Biblical Archaeologist*
CBQ	*Catholic Biblical Quarterly*
DOTT	D. Winton Thomas (ed.), *Documents from Old Testament Times* (London, 1958)
ET	English translation
GUOST	Glasgow University Oriental Society, *Transactions*
ICC	*International Critical Commentary*
IDB	G. A. Buttrick (ed.), *Interpreter's Dictionary of the Bible* (New York/Nashville, 1962)
JB	Jerusalem Bible, 1966
JBL	*Journal of Biblical Literature*
JCS	*Journal of Cuneiform Studies*
JSOT	*Journal for the Study of the Old Testament*
JSS	*Journal of Semitic Studies*
Kings	J. Gray, *I & II Kings*^{2} (*OTL:* London, 1970)
LB	Y. Aharoni, *The Land of the Bible* (ET London, 1966)
LXX	Septuagint
MBA	Y. Aharoni and M. Avi-Yonah, *Macmillan Bible Atlas* (London, 1968)
MNHK	E. R. Thiele, *Mysterious Numbers of the Hebrew Kings*^{2} (Exeter, 1966)

NAB	New American Bible, 1970
NBCR	D. Guthrie and others, *The New Bible Commentary, Revised* (London, 1970)
NBD	J. D. Douglas (ed.), *The New Bible Dictionary* (London, 1962)
NCB	*New Century Bible*
NEB	New English Bible, 1961-70
NICNT	*New International Commentary on the New Testament*
NICOT	*New International Commentary on the Old Testament*
OTL	*Old Testament Library*
PEQ	*Palestine Exploration Quarterly*
POTT	D. J. Wisemen (ed.), *Peoples of Old Testament Times* (Oxford, 1973)
RSV	Revised Standard Version, 1946-52
RV	Revised Version, 1881-5
SBT	*Studies in Biblical Theology*
TBC	*Torch Bible Commentaries*
VT	*Vetus Testamentum*
VTS	*Supplements to Vetus Testamentum*
ZAW	*Zeitschrift für die Alttestamentliche Wissenschaft*

Preface

"THERE is properly no history; only biography" (Ralph Waldo Emerson) is a dictum which holds a very large grain of truth when applied to the historical books of the Old Testament; and if the quantity of biographical detail is any guide to relative importance, there can be no doubt that David is the key figure in the history of Israel during the period of the monarchy, and indeed of the whole of the first millennium B.C. The next biblical character to attract equal or greater coverage is none other than Jesus of Nazareth — "great David's greater son".

This book is a survey of the history of ancient Israel from the end of the era of the Judges till the beginning of the Babylonian exile. The political history of Israel is recounted in Part I, while Part II gives detailed attention to the political environment of the period, in a study of Israel's enemies. The prophets are here studied in two ways; in Part I their contribution to Israel's history is assessed, while in Part III the emphasis is rather on the effect which historical events had upon them. Part IV, in a survey of Israel's faith during the relevant period, inevitably looks at the prophetic literature yet again; even so, there is much to be said about the prophets which this book does not attempt to discuss. For introductions to the prophets and commentary upon them, the reader must turn elsewhere.

The reader will find scant attention paid to such questions as the date and authorship of the Old Testament books. These issues tend to be controversial and the arguments about them inconclusive; interested readers must be referred to standard Old Testament introductions and Bible dictionaries. In any case, it is surprising how rarely the answers to historical questions depend on the answers to literary ones.

Bible quotations are taken from the New English Bible except where otherwise stated.

My thanks are due to the writers of many books (not least those of the Old Testament). One is inevitably indebted to standard works such as John Bright's *History of Israel* to a greater degree than one consciously appreciates. My special gratitude is due to my sister, Mrs. R. Z. E. Woods, who typed the whole work from a virtually illegible manuscript; to Mr. B. H. Mudditt of The Paternoster Press for practical guidance and patient encouragement; and last but not least to my wife for her unselfish encouragement at every stage of the work.

D. F. PAYNE

Part One

The Kings

CHAPTER 1

Israel Before the Monarchy

IT was Moses who made Israel a nation; but a nation needs a territory, and it was Joshua who played the leading role in providing that for them. Then, his work done, he died, and the period of the "Judges" began. To some extent, God's promises to Abraham of old had been fulfilled; Israel was potentially the strongest nation in the immediate area, and her people were to be found in varying strengths, in every region allotted to the Israelite tribes. However, much remained to be done to master and to consolidate the territory, and to transform "Israel" into a land as opposed to a people resident in that land. The era of the Judges was therefore to be anything but peaceful; much fighting lay ahead. The Book of Judges suggests, however, that much of the fighting was forced upon the Israelites, who were quite prepared for the most part to settle down as peasants and farmers, and let the political situation find its own level. This rather complacent attitude was in itself almost fatal, as events very soon proved. Various features and factors militated against the political strength and coherence of Israel.

First of all, it is clear that the Israelites were not united. Numbers 32 relates that in earlier days the Reubenites and Gadites had laid claim to territory east of the Jordan before ever Palestine proper had been invaded; but Moses had insisted that they were to give the other tribes full military support in the struggle in Palestine. The situation was different now; each tribe had its own area, and there it remained. Tribal elders were the administrators of the day, and were no doubt jealous of their position, with the result that the tribes were independent of one another. Nor was there any standing army. During the days of the conquest, every able-bodied man had been a soldier; but now they had all dispersed to their farms and smallholdings, and could ill be spared to spend their time fighting. The pruning-hook and the plough-share had displaced the sword and the spear. Thus the Israelite tribes had not the machinery for concerted and effective military action.

A second factor was simply the fact of difficulty of communication. Palestine is no very big country, to be sure; from Dan to Beer-Sheba, the traditional northern and southern limits of Palestine proper, is some 150 miles as the crow flies, while the full east-west extent of the country does not reach half that figure at any point. And there were certainly some reasonably good roads; two famous highways were the King's Highway (cf. Numbers 20:17) and "the Way of the Sea" (cf. Isaiah 9:1), both running south from Damascus, the former through Transjordan, the latter via Palestine proper, leading to Arabia and Egypt respectively. And there were many lesser roads.[1] But speed of travel was very slow; the Gospels give some impression of the time it took to make the journey from Galilee to Jerusalem. It is estimated that the 75-mile journey from Nazareth would have taken something like five days.

It is also probable that the Israelites during the period of the Judges allowed the roads to fall into a state of disrepair. Hitherto they had been properly cared for; in the fourteenth century B.C., a local Palestinian prince had written to his Egyptian overlord, to the effect that he had "made ready all the ways of the king".[2] But the Israelites were new to the ways of settled life, and it took them no little time to catch up with their predecessors in many of the civilized arts. Judges 5:6 testifies that in the early days of the Judges "caravans plied no longer; men who had followed the high roads went round by devious paths".

Presumably messengers were able to make their way reasonably swiftly from one part of the country to another. But in times of emergency, it will have taken an inordinately long while to collect together a body of troops, and then to dispatch it across the difficult terrain of Palestine. When Deborah and Barak had to meet a Canaanite coalition, they mustered as many tribal forces as they could. Evidently some of the tribes they appealed to failed to respond: "What made you linger by the cattle-pens?" Reuben was asked; and other tribes were tacitly rebuked — "Gilead stayed beyond Jordan; and Dan, why did he tarry by the ships? Asher lingered by the sea-shore, by its creeks he stayed" (Judges 5:16f.). Many of the tribes responded nobly; but it is noteworthy that nothing whatever is said about Judah and Simeon, the two most southerly tribes. We must conclude that it was recognised that they

1. See *MBA*, map 10.
2. Cf. Tell el-Armarna Letter 199: 10-13.

were too far away to be of any assistance, and that no appeal was made to them.[3]

But it was more than distances that separated Judah and Simeon from the more northerly tribes. Immediately north of Judah's territory lay the city of Jerusalem and its environs, still inhabited by the Jebusites, a Canaanite clan (cf. Genesis 10:16). Judges 1:21 mentions this fact, and also shows that the Jebusites and Benjaminites could live amicably side by side most of the time. But when further north Canaanites and Israelites were in conflict, there is little doubt as to where Jebusite loyalties would lie, and their stronghold will have constituted a formidable barrier, effectively preventing the two southern tribes from helping their kinsmen to the north. Nor was Jerusalem the only city of strategic position still in Canaanite hands.

The most formidable barrier separating Israelites from Israelites was the Plain of Jezreel, along the northern boundary of the territory of western Manasseh. The Israelites as yet possessed no chariotry, as did the Canaanites, and this meant that they were rarely a match for the latter once they descended from the hills. As a result, few lowland cities were in Israelite hands during the period of the Judges. So while the tribe of Manasseh held the northern part of the hill-country of Ephraim securely, and the tribes of Zebulun and Issachar had consolidated their position in the hills of Galilee, the Plain of Jezreel in between remained largely Canaanite, though allocated to Manasseh.

It is clear, then, that during the period of the Judges the Israelites had no few problems to face. But as if the natural hazards we have listed were not enough, the Israelites made things very much worse for themselves, in several respects. In the first place, inter-tribal jealousies were a constant feature of the Judges period, and indeed beyond, for it was the mutual jealousy and suspicion of Judah and Ephraim that split the Hebrew kingdom into two after Solomon's death. The Ephraimites seem to have been a particularly quarrelsome tribe; they tried to pick a quarrel with Gideon (Judges 8:1ff.), whose soft answer turned away wrath, and they succeeded in provoking Jephthah (Judges 12:1ff.), to their sorrow. The last two chapters of Judges relate how the little tribe of Benjamin fell out with the other tribes, and was almost wiped out in the warfare that followed. On this occasion, fortunately, the other tribes belatedly realized the danger, and declared: "Heirs there must be for the remnant of Benjamin who have escaped! Then Israel will not see one of its tribes blotted out" (Judges 21:17). Such incidents show that while the tribes never quite forgot their kinship and mutual responsibilities, they came very near to doing so at times.

3. For a detailed study of the possible reasons for the absence of mention of Judah and Simeon see A. D. H. Mayes, *Israel in the Period of the Judges* (SBT ii, 29: London 1974) pp. 98-103.

Ringed about as they were by potential foes, such deliberate disunity was the height of folly. But there was a much more insidious danger, which might well have proved disastrous to Israel. We have already referred to the presence of Canaanite cities in the middle of Israelite territory, a matter of no little military moment; but in the event it was not the military danger posed by the Canaanites that proved a major problem, but the attraction of the Canaanite customs and religion. The Israelites were thrown into continuous contact with the Canaanites, and they learned a great deal from them. It is all too easy to condemn the Israelites sweepingly for their apostasy, but one ought to have a certain sympathy with them. Many of us in the Western world of today have inherited a settled, highly developed culture of many centuries' standing; not so the Israelites in 1200 B.C. Of late their only professional training had been as builders, the slave workmen for the Egyptian kings, and the use even of that skill lay a long time in the past. Bezalel, the architect of the tabernacle and its furniture, had been specially endued with skill for such a work, Exodus 31:1ff. relates; for Israel had no trained craftsmen in wood and metal as yet. The arts of war they had learned through dire necessity, under God-given leadership; but who was to teach them the arts of peace? Even where building was concerned they had much to learn; archaeologists have brought to light the fact that the cities destroyed by the invading Israelites were far better built than the Israelite cities erected over their ruins. Solomon, some centuries after the conquest, turned to the Phoenicians for an architect.

We can well believe that as the Israelites turned to farming, they were often grateful for the advice and practical skill of their Canaanite neighbours. Others were less interested in the land, and adopted other trades and professions which brought them into even closer contact with the Canaanites. Maritime trade is a good example of a Canaanite interest adopted on a large scale by Israelites. Deborah's complaint about Dan and Asher noted that they were too busy with their shipping concerns to lend a hand to their fellows (Judges 5:17). Were they perhaps too busy, or simply too indolent? It is perhaps even more probable that they were so enmeshed in trade alliances with the Canaanites that they found it neither politic nor convenient to join in an attack on other Canaanites.

There were relatively few occasions when Israelites and Canaanites found themselves at war, or the commercial and marital alliances formed between them might have proved fatal to Israel's unity. (On the other hand, these same alliances might have undermined Canaanite solidarity too, thus evening things out for both sides.) But there were various other enemies, and against them Israel needed to be united; the friendships with Canaanites were a hindrance to any such communal feeling, for the Israelites found themselves with divided loyalties.

Since they learned so much from the Canaanites, it is not really particularly surprising that many Israelites felt drawn to Canaanite religion as well. Some may have reasoned that Yahweh was the God of the desert, and Baal the god of Palestine. Others may have intended no disrespect to their own faith, but failing to understand that Yahweh was a jealous God, wished to combine both faiths. We may be sure that the spiritual leaders of the nation did their best to disabuse their people of this notion, emphasizing the exclusive demands of Yahweh: "You shall have no other god to set against me" (Exodus 20:3). But the common people had no Bibles, nor any synagogues where they could get frequent instruction, and one wonders how often they heard the accurate facts about their faith. Probably much of the religious knowledge was handed down from father to son — a pattern of behaviour laid down in Exodus 13:8 — and one can well imagine the errors that would creep into such tuition. There is plenty of folk-religion, embodying pagan superstitions, still prevalent within Christendom despite the availability of churches and copies of Scripture.

Thus the merging of the two faiths (technically known as syncretism) was a very natural, if regrettable, development. Another unfortunate factor was that there was considerable superficial similarity between Israel's faith and the worship of the Canaanites. The worship of both peoples centred around sanctuaries; animal sacrifice, with very similar ritual, figured in both faiths; both had their annual agricultural festivals. The two people also used similar sacrificial technical terms, and even the same title for their (chief) deity. The Israelites had but one God, of course, Yahweh by name; but they often referred to him as Baal, which was not primarily a name but the ordinary Hebrew word for "owner", "lord" or "husband". The term Baal was therefore very suitable for describing the relationship in which Yahweh stood to his people; but of course its use led to endless confusion with Canaanite worship. Centuries later the problem was still so acute that the prophet Hosea spoke of a different Hebrew word to denote God's relationship to Israel: "On that day she shall call me 'My husband' and shall no more call me 'My Baal' " (Hosea 2:16). This other word for husband, in Hebrew *ish*, could lead to no such confusion.

One can appreciate something of the ease with which the Israelites fell into Baal worship. For all that, it was to this single factor that the writer of Judges attributed all the disasters that befell Israel at this time:

Then the Israelites did what was wrong in the eyes of the Lord, and worshipped the Baalim. They forsook the Lord, their fathers' God who had brought them out of Egypt, and went after other gods, gods of the races among whom they lived; they bowed down before them and provoked the LORD to anger; they forsook the LORD and worshipped the Baal and the Ashtaroth. The LORD in his anger made them the prey of bands of raiders and plunderers; he sold them to their enemies all around them, and they could no longer make a stand. Every time they went out to battle the LORD brought disaster upon them, as he had said when he gave them his solemn warning, and they were in dire straits.

(Judges 2:11-15)

This was the philosophy of the writer of Judges regarding the Israelite vicissitudes during a couple of centuries. Two questions arise; in the first place, does his philosophy meet the facts, or has he imposed a pattern on the events? And secondly, why was he, in common with other Old Testament writers, so vehemently opposed to Baal worship?

There is good reason to believe that the philosophy of Judges does indeed meet the facts. As we have noted already, alliance of any sort with the Canaanites led to divided Israelite loyalties, and so caused lack of cohesion in the face of various enemies. But religious agreement with them was even more serious, for it struck at the very roots of Israelite unity, which was based on their covenant relationship with their God. So long as they remained faithful to the worship of Yahweh, they remembered their covenant bonds to their fellows; but when they gave their devotion to local Baals, all such ties were weakened, to breaking point.[4] Disaster was not only divine punishment for apostasy; it was indeed the inevitable result of it. But at least disaster had the effect of making the Israelites examine themselves, and ask the pertinent question, "Why are we suffering?" A little thought would reveal that it was Yahweh who had given them the land of Promise, and it was entirely in his hands whether they would keep it. And so time and again they "cried to the LORD", and he "raised up for them a deliverer". In returning to their own sanctuaries, they would rediscover the solidarity they had lost, and the situation would be immediately improved.

The hostility of the biblical writers to Canaanite worship needs no more justification than that Yahweh's demands were exclusive. But they viewed the Canaanite religion with more than disdain, they viewed it with horror. So far we have mentioned only its similarities to the Israelite faith, and said nothing of its clear differences. Even from the Bible, we could work out some of the differences, but of course the Old Testament is not interested in giving posterity a full

4. While not all scholars would date the covenant concept so early there is in recent scholarship a strong tendency to explain Israel's unity during the Judges period in religious rather than political terms. See A. D. H. Mayes, *op. cit.*, especially p. 109.

picture of Canaanite ideas and practices; nowadays, however, it is possible to turn to some documents which give much fuller details of the life and thought of these ancient neighbours of Israel. They are the Ras Shamra tablets.

There was very little material to bring us into direct contact with the Canaanites up till 1928. In that year a Syrian ploughman accidentally unearthed a tombstone in the vicinity of a mound, called Ras Shamra, on the north coast of Syria (opposite the "finger" of Cyprus) and this find led to a thorough excavation of the mound from 1929 onwards. The mound of Ras Shamra, investigation proved, covered the remains of an important city of antiquity named Ugarit, a centre of Canaanite civilization which flourished in the second millennium B.C. All manner of valuable articles and objects came to light, among them a large quantity of inscriptions and tablets of the fourteenth century B.C. Some of the latter are in languages and scripts which were already known to scholars, but a new language and new alphabet figure among the discovered texts, and they have naturally been called "Ugaritic". The Ugaritic language, once it was deciphered and translated, proved to be remarkably similar to Old Testament Hebrew, and has already been useful in clearing up one or two difficulties of meaning in the Old Testament. Two names familiar to readers of the Bible which also appear in the Ras' Shamra texts are Leviathan and Danel (not the hero of the Book of Daniel, but quite conceivably the Danel or Daniel of Ezekiel 14:14).

These tablets give us a much fuller picture of Canaanite worship than we had before Ras Shamra was excavated. As we are well aware from the Old Testament, the Canaanites were polytheists, worshipping a variety of gods and goddesses. The senior god was not Baal, but El; this name seems to have been the common noun for "god" in the Semitic languages, including Old Testament Hebrew. He was thought of as the creator, and sometimes symbolised by a bull. But by the fourteenth century El did not figure very largely in Canaanite worship, for all his seniority, and Baal was the most important deity. (This may explain why the Israelite prophets objected to the title "baal", lord, being given to Yahweh, but accepted without protest the word "el", god, for him.) Baal's father, the texts tell us, was the god Dagan (Hebrew "Dagon") the god of corn, who was adopted by the Philistines when they overran part of Canaan; Ashdod, where a temple to Dagon stood in Samuel's time (1 Samuel 5:2) (and long before and afterwards), was located on the coastal plain of Palestine where much of the corn was grown. There were also temples to Dagon at Beth-shan, at the south-east end of the Plain of Jezreel, and at Ugarit itself.

Baal, properly the title of Hadad, the god of thunder, was the most widely venerated of the Canaanite pantheon. Whereas El was a god of quiet majesty, Baal was the deity who was always actively engaged in warfare against his foes, as befits the god of thunder. His foes were the forces of disorder. But he was also the god of vegetation (which explains his relationship in mythology with Dagon); it was because of this aspect of his nature that he was so important to the Canaanites, dependent as they were on the fertility of the ground. Nowadays, when the preservation and storage of food are relatively simple, we tend to forget how dependent ancient peoples were on good harvests, which could spell the difference between life and death, between prosperity and slavery. Small wonder that the Canaanites revered Baal, and tried by every means to induce him to promote the fruit of the ground year after year. The Canaanite worship, says Professor Gray, represents "man's efforts to enlist Providence in supplying his primary need, his daily bread and the propagation of his kind."[5] This quotation draws attention to the fact that with the fertility of the ground the Canaanites linked the fertility of the womb as well, and attributed both to Baal. Baal worship was in many respects a fertility cult.

The fertility of the ground is of course a seasonal matter. Why was it that Baal produced vegetation every spring and summer, but not in the winter season? The reason for this, the Canaanites averred, was that Baal died every autumn — and came to life again every spring. Baal's resurrection was brought about by a goddess, his consort Anat. After his annual decease, she would go looking for him. He was to be found in the realm of the deity Mot ("death"), and Anat had to defeat Mot before ever Baal could revive; brought back to life, he in turn defeated Mot, showing himself as the god victorious in warfare. And so it came about that Baal was restored to his throne in triumph, and the fertility of the land was secured for another year.

It should be evident by now that the Canaanite conception of their leading deity differed totally from the Old Testament portrait of the Israelites' God. The latter ruled alone, sovereign over all the forces of nature; death was no foe of his, but was his subject. Yahweh was God of nature, but he was not to be identified with it; and the Israelites recognized too that he was Lord over a much wider sphere than just nature, he was the Controller of history as well. Clearly the Israelites had a much superior theology; but one feature of their theology had very important practical results, and that is the fact that Yahweh had no consort, no goddess associated with him. Baal had a consort, Anat — not to mention another one, Athirat (Old Testament Asherah[6]), originally the consort of El — and the

5. J. Gray, *The Canaanites*, (London, 1964), p. 138.
6. The AV, following LXX and Vulgate, translates the word Asherah as "grove", quite wrongly. Cf. 1 Kings 16:33 in AV and RSV or NEB.

marriage of these two was an important feature of the Canaanite mythology, since it was thought to promote the fertility of the ground and its inhabitants. This belief, so different from anything in the worship of Yahweh, expressed itself in an emphasis on sexual relationships; the elaborate temple cult of the Canaanites incorporated "sacred" prostitution. It is certain that the fertility cult practised by Israel's neighbours was a degrading, immoral affair, which proved harmful and demoralizing to its devotees.

Discussing the Ras Shamra tablets, Professor Gray remarks: "These myths give the impression that the Canaanites were very liberal in their religion, seeking by imitative magic in rite and myth to predispose Providence in nature. Their gods were like the Greek gods, glorified human beings, contentious, jealous, vindictive, lustful, and even, like El, lazy . . . there was no moral purpose in the fertility cult."[7] The Canaanites, in fact, created their gods in the image of man, literally and figuratively; the contrast with Yahweh-worship is patent. The God of the Old Testament is wholly moral in character and action, not arbitrary and whimsical, and moreover he demands morality from his worshippers.

Baal worship, then, tended to be degrading, with an abnormal emphasis on warfare and sensuous love, promoting in its adherents hatred and lust, to which types of lack of self-control man is only too prone in any case. Perhaps the readiness of the Israelites to accept Canaanite ways led to some of the mutual jealousies between Israelite tribes which we have already mentioned. It is certain that those of weaker moral fibre will have found the Baal cult a more pleasant and comfortable religion. The last five chapters of Judges, which do not make very pleasant reading, may serve to demonstrate how thoroughly the defects of quarrelsomeness and lust had permeated Israelite society before the era of the Judges ended. The writer's final comment, "Every man did what was right in his own eyes", is a very apt description, summing up neatly both the political and the moral situation.

Can nothing be said on the credit side? To get an accurate impression of the situation one must study the other side of the coin. In the first place, it does seem that the Israelites never lost completely their sense of mutual relationship; the covenant bond was a reality to which they were prepared to return when reminded of their obligations. Secondly, we may well believe that the custodians of many of the sanctuaries (even if some of the latter were tainted by Canaanite customs and concepts) will have reminded their fellow-tribes of their duties at the annual festivals, when all were to present themselves before the Lord. Thirdly, we may surmise that there were faithful souls, not very vocal and not seeking

7. *Ibid*, p. 136.

the limelight, who steadfastly refused to lose or to modify their belief in Yahweh and their loyalty to him. In a similarly black situation a century or two later the prophet Elijah, thoroughly despondent and pessimistic, was assured by God himself that no less than 7000 in Israel would refuse to bow to Baal (1 Kings 19:18).

Even so, it is safe to say that Israel did nothing during this period to deserve its election, which is a mystery indeed.

The forces tending towards weakness and disintegration were thus very strong indeed, and it is something of a miracle that Israel survived. The attacks of various enemies might well have meant the end of the new nation; yet Israel did survive, and not long after her lowest ebb became for a short while the strongest nation in the Near East. How is this to be explained? Did a military genius arise from somewhere, and change the whole pattern of history? Did a group of fanatics, patriotic or religious, get control of the nation's affairs? Some of the "Judges" were doubtless able generals, and some of them were clearly devout; but the Book of Judges lays no stress on either of these facts. The salvation of Israel was due to the fact that God raised up men and clothed them with his Spirit; he and he alone was the real Deliverer of Israel.

CHAPTER 2

Prelude to Monarchy

THE problems of Israel's own making were very real, as we have seen, but the immediate dangers were due to the pressure of her neighbours on all sides. Archaeology has shown clearly that between 1200 and 1000 B.C. many Palestinian cities were burned and ravaged, some of them more than once; Bethel, for instance, was severely damaged at least three times. So even without the evidence of the Book of Judges, it is plain that the promised land was the scene of no few battles between the days of Joshua and David. The Book of Judges, however, goes further than excavations do, and reveals the names of the enemies of Israel, and gives some account of the reason for their hostility. There were three main causes, in fact: the Canaanites, as the dispossessed people, tried on occasion to put back the clock and recover lost territory; the Philistines were imperialists, and wanted to extend their control, making their neighbours their vassals; and the Midianites and others were nomadic raiders who had no aims beyond emptying the barns of other people in order to feed themselves.

One of the early narratives of the Book of Judges (3:12ff.) throws light on the situation which developed in south Transjordan. The Israelites' predicament was occasioned by the territorial expansion of the Moabites, who were ably marshalled by their king Eglon. The Moabites were distant relatives of the Israelites and were their neighbours throughout their history.[1] Immediately east of the north end of the Dead Sea was located the tribe of Reuben, occupying territory once owned by Moab (although it was not the Israelites who had dispossessed them), and no doubt the Moabites, south of them, eyed the Reubenite land covetously. Also bordering on the

1. See below, chapter 14.

Reubenites were the Ammonites, closely akin to the Moabites, and the Israelite tribe found itself the victim of a pincer movement from the south and north-east. Without a king and without support from other tribes, Reuben was overrun.

Eglon found himself master of the land between the Dead Sea and the great desert to the east. Most of it is a plateau some 3000 feet in altitude; the mountains rise steeply from the Dead Sea well over 4000 feet below. The plateau is cut by occasional streams and gorges; the most notable river is the Arnon (modern Wadi Mojib), which had formed the boundary between Moab and Reuben. The soil is reasonably fertile, but the region has always been devoted chiefly to sheep farming; Deborah was soon to chide Reuben with tarrying among the sheep-folds (cf. Judges 5:16, RSV). The Dead Sea is a natural, well-named barrier to the west; by overrunning Reuben, Eglon gave himself the opportunity for further expansion westwards, just north of the Dead Sea. Just across the Jordan from here lies the city of Jericho; though the city itself lay in ruins, the oasis which had created the city was a valuable prize for Eglon. By now he was expanding at the expense of the Benjaminites; and not only did he take some of their territory, he took tribute from them.

But it was his greed for tribute that indirectly led to his downfall. The very man who brought it one year was able to assassinate him. This man was Ehud, who swiftly rounded up a small army of his fellow-tribesmen, who then came down from the hills west of the Jordan and stationed themselves at the fords across the river. The death of their king threw the Moabites into a panic, and they obeyed the natural impulse to make their escape homewards — straight into the hands of the waiting Israelite force, who were not slow to take advantage of the situation.

This exploit by Ehud effectively put an end to Moabite domination of Benjaminite territory, but the biblical record leaves us to guess what happened to Reuben, east of the Jordan. The Moabites may have left them alone for the moment, but the former were not long inactive, and it is certain that the Reubenites were never a force in Israelite affairs hereafter.

This whole episode had clear political implications, for those who had eyes to see. The Moabites' success revealed plainly the value of effective leadership; it was not until Ehud took matters into his own hands and showed himself an able leader that the Israelites had any hope of ejecting the Moabites. It is also noteworthy that the closely related Moabites and Ammonites joined forces to achieve their ends; whereas Reuben and Benjamin took no concerted action whatever, from first to last, apparently.

The Moabites were a small nation, and could never have dominated the whole of Israel; at best they could only have whittled away a peripheral piece of territory. In due course Israel was to lose much of its original domain, without losing its own identity, so it is clear that the Moabites could have done little lasting damage. But had the Canaanites ever really combined to attack Israel, the Israelites would have been hard put to it to defeat them. The nearest approach to a full-scale Canaanite attack was the campaign headed by Sisera, and had it proved successful, the very heart of Israel would have been subjugated, and Israel as a whole might well have disintegrated.

The story of this campaign is told in ordinary historical narrative in Judges 4, and in a triumphant poem in the following chapter; naturally the approach of the two accounts is quite different, and it is not easy to piece together all the details. At times the compiler of the Book of Judges has, for brevity, telescoped events, giving the impression that two campaigns were one; and Judges 4 may be one such abbreviated narrative. However, assuming that there was one campaign and not a series, we gather that the man who set it afoot was Jabin, king of Hazor, a great Canaanite stronghold north of the Sea of Galilee. This city had been destroyed and burnt down by Joshua not so long before (Joshua 11:10f.), but evidently the Canaanites had retaken the site. It lay within Naphtali, not far from the north-east boundary of Israelite territory; and its strategic importance was later recognised by Solomon, who fortified it afresh (1 Kings 9:15). The site is now an uninhabited mound, which has recently been excavated by Israeli archaeologists.

The tribe of Naphtali was inevitably involved in the fighting that eventually took place; like neighbouring Zebulun, we read, they "risked their very lives" (Judges 5:18). But if Jabin was the moving spirit behind the confederacy, the man who led it into battle was Sisera, and the scene of conflict was not Hazor, but the Plain of Jezreel away to the south. As we have seen, the Plain was not commanded by the Israelites, but formed a barrier between Manasseh to the south and Zebulun and Issachar to the north. Here Sisera, with his nine hundred iron chariots, was long unassailable and "oppressed Israel harshly" (4:3). (The Iron Age was just beginning in Palestine, and the Philistines' use of this metal, and their determined efforts to hold the monopoly of it, gave them a great advantage in warfare.) It is evident that the confederacy was not limited to the Canaanites, for the name Sisera is not Canaanite, and the city of which he was king was called Harosheth-ha-goiim, "Harosheth of the (foreign) nations". His people were probably distantly related to the Philistines. From the Plain of Jezreel, Sisera was able to impose his will on the Israelites south of him, as well as north; it is noteworthy that not only Manasseh but Ephraim and even Benjamin, far to the south, responded to the call to arms when it came.

This grave threat to Israel's independence was eventually met, fittingly enough, by united action on the part of Israelite tribes north and south of the Plain. The leading figures were the prophetess Deborah, who hailed from Ephraim, and Barak, whose home was in Naphtali; north and south indeed! The battle was pitched in Sisera's territory, and the Israelites were obliged to muster a huge army in order to counteract the enemy's chariotry. As long as he could, Barak kept to the hills, where the chariots would be of little use; his final camp was on Mount Tabor,[2] the highest hill rising in the Plain itself. However, he need have had no anxiety about the fearsome chariots, for nature itself rendered them useless; the battle took place beside the Kishon, and a sudden downpour caused the river to run high, with the result that Sisera's chariots were bogged down in the mud. His army was routed, and he himself fled, finding it quicker to travel by foot, apparently. He soon suffered the indignity of meeting death at a woman's hand.

It is considered likely that Sisera's defeat took place c. 1125 B.C.[3] Thereafter the northern tribes were untroubled for some time. The next danger was of a different sort, although once again Manasseh figured largely in the story. This time the aggressors were the Midianites, aided and abetted by the Amalekites and other nomadic groups; coming from the fringes of the desert to the east of Palestine, they travelled swiftly on their camels into more fertile country, and took what plunder lay to hand. Shrewd and cunning as desert raiders have always been, they knew precisely when the various fruits and crops were harvested, and timed their raids to perfection. The livestock, too, fell prey to them.

Once again, the Transjordanian tribes were conspicuous by their inaction. The people of Gad and eastern Manasseh must have been the first victims of the Midianites, and the fact that the raiders moved in force into the Plain of Jezreel, west of the Jordan, indicates that the Israelites east of the river were no danger to them. It also suggests that the Midianites had already made the most of the pickings in Transjordan, and were looking for more fruitful fields to plunder.

The situation at the home of Gideon, somewhere in the hills south of the Plain of Jezreel (Ophrah cannot be identified with any certainty), is also revealing. Gideon's own father, of the tribe of Manasseh (the western part of the tribe), had an altar to Baal on his property, although it must be said in his defence that he was not very concerned about it when his son pulled it down (Judges 6:30f.). So

2. Tabor has since the fourth century been identified as the Mount of Transfiguration; but on the whole, probability is against this identification.

3. Cf. J. Bright, *A History of Israel* (OTL: London, 1972) p.172; S. Herrmann, *A History of Israel²* (London, 1975) pp.117f. A. D. H. Mayes, however, wishes to date the conflict much later in the Judges era; cf. J. H. Hayes and J. M. Miller, *Israelite and Judaean History* (OTL: London, 1977) p.314.

much for the religious situation; as for the Midianite threat, it appears that the only defence against it which was so far resorted to was to match cunning with cunning, and to hide away the food and livestock. So we first meet Gideon "threshing wheat in the winepress", of all places (Judges 6:11).

No longer were the opposing sides Israelites and Canaanites; the whole settled population, however varied their ancestry, were forced to unite against the nomadic raiders. It was also inevitable that if the Canaanites were not to be exterminated, they would be ultimately integrated into Israel. But if the Israelites and Canaanites were to fight on the same side, it must be under Yahweh's banner; so Gideon's first move was to destroy the Baal altar, and to erect one to Yahweh. Not till that was done were the necessary military steps taken.

The details of the battle need no re-telling. It was certainly not weight of numbers that defeated the Midianites, nor did a cloudburst cause their discomfiture. Perhaps they were already unsure of the outcome (if we may judge by the dream one of them had on the eve of the Israelite attack), and the element of surprise was sufficient to overwhelm them. Gideon and his loyal band, together with reinforcements from Naphtali and Asher, pursued the raiders as they fled eastwards from the Plain of Jezreel. But just as the men of Ehud had seized the fords across the Jordan to the north of the Dead Sea, and thus prevented the Moabites from escaping unscathed, so now Gideon had made sure that the fords to the south of the Sea of Galilee were controlled; the tribe of Ephraim supplied the troops required for this manoeuvre. Even so, a considerable body of Midianites escaped across the river.

Gideon felt that it was not enough to chase the marauders back across the Jordan, and he sought to follow up his initial success by a campaign east of the river. Now was the opportunity for the settled population of Transjordan to play their part in squashing the Midianite threat, and Gideon invited the help of the two cities there, Succoth and Penuel. But apparently the local citizens felt that it would be imprudent to offend the raiders, who might return all too soon, once Gideon and his men had withdrawn to the far bank of the Jordan; and they refused even to provision Gideon's small army. None the less, Gideon achieved a second success against the fleeing raiders — and returned to bring down retribution upon the two cities.

The Abimelech episode (Judges 9) serves to show something of the state of affairs in central Palestine during the first half of the eleventh century B.C. In and around Shechem, in southern Manasseh, the Israelites and Canaanites were making common cause, and were endeavouring to organize an efficient system of government, but at the expense of the purity of the Israelite religion. The attempt was far from successful, for two reasons: in the first place, the situation gave scope for unscrupulous adventurers; and secondly, jealousies between Israelites and Canaanites were only dormant, not dead. In the first flush of enthusiasm consequent upon the defeat of the Midianites, the people of Manasseh had invited Gideon to become their king, and if he refused the position,[4] it is evident that his family did exercise some sort of authority in the locality. Abimelech saw the opportunity of playing on Canaanite sympathies; as a son of Gideon, he enjoyed the respect given to his family, and as a Canaanite on his mother's side he was able to win full support from that section of the population. For three years he was king of Shechem, after he had killed off the full Israelite members of his father's clan. But he himself was Israelite in part; and cannot have pleased the Canaanite citizens of Shechem any too well, for presently a certain Gaal, presumably a Canaanite, was able to move into the city behind Abimelech's back, and win over the citizens to his cause. Abimelech took strong measures, and emerged victorious — but was mortally wounded in the process.

The Ammonite attack finally beaten off by Jephthah (Judges 10f.) in many ways paralleled the earlier Moabite campaign. Once again, the Gileadites (i.e. the Israelites in Transjordan) were easily overrun, and once again territories west of the river were affected. But for once the Gileadites found the will and strength to resist, through the agency of Jephthah, a man whom they had earlier driven into exile, and who had gathered round him a band of marauders to the north of Ammon. The Ammonites were soundly defeated and thrust back into their own territory.

Thus during 150 years, from the time of Joshua[5] till the early eleventh century, various Israelite tribes were harassed by enemies on the north and the east. But the worst threat to Israelite independence was still to come, from the south west: the Philistines. Hitherto the tribes of Judah and Dan had been remarkably free from the troubles that befell other tribes. Shamgar's exploit against the Philistines (Judges 3:31) was probably an isolated incident, for the Philistines had arrived in Palestine at about the same time as the Israelites, and no doubt needed some time to establish themselves before attempting to expand at the expense of others. Like the Canaanites, the Philistines engaged in a good deal of commerce by sea. In industry too, they were skilled; excavations have unearthed a number of their furnaces for smelting iron. Iron was not unknown in

4. The suggestion that Judges 8:23 is to be interpreted as Gideon's politely veiled *acceptance* of the royal position is intriguing but not altogether convincing.
5. 150 years if Joshua lived in the mid-thirteenth century as is generally held. However a fifteenth century date is not impossible in the light of the researches of J. J. Bimson, *Redating the Exodus and Conquest* (JSOT Supplement 5: Sheffield, 1978).

Palestine before the Philistines arrived, but it was they who introduced its use on a large scale. Iron-working was a skill they brought with them, but of course they needed the raw materials as well as know-how, and this requirement may have been one of the first motives that led them to extend their territory. As early as 1150 B.C., they began to expand to the south-east, into the arid region of the Negeb; copper and iron ore were plentiful down towards the head of the Gulf of Aqaba. Meanwhile the Israelites were making little use of this new and superior metal; by the time of Saul, moreover, the Philistines had ensured that they held the monopoly of the iron industry, which put the Israelites at a great disadvantage in the warfare between them.

The Philistines were not a political unity in south-west Palestine, but they were capable, both psychologically and in organization, of effective united action, as the Canaanites and Israelites rarely were. Each of their five chief cities, Gaza, Ashkelon, Ashdod, Ekron and Gath, was ruled by a *seren* or "lord" (possibly comparable with the Israelite "judges"); but these five chiefs acted in council when concerted action was necesary. As a result, their fighting machine was highly efficient and as well organized as it was well armed.

The most southerly of the Israelite tribes, Simeon, may have suffered when the Philistines expanded to the south east, though Scripture is silent on this point; Simeon was never a major tribe, and its territory gradually became virtually incorporated into Judah, its big northern neighbour. At first Judah, immediately east of the Philistines, escaped lightly, for the simple reason that she occupied a very hilly region; no doubt there were border incidents, however. But the tribe of Dan, north of Philistia, was not so fortunate; much of Dan, like Philistia, was situated on the coastal plain, and was without natural defence of any kind. No doubt the Philistine pressure developed gradually — there was no sudden "blitzkrieg" invasion. But it was very real for all that.

The only Danite who emerged as a "judge" was the colourful but not altogether admirable figure of Samson. Notable as his exploits were, it is significant that they never included leading an army against the foe; he acted single-handed, and his best efforts can have occasioned little more than minor set-backs for the Philistines. The Book of Judges notes that "the dead whom he killed at his death were more than those he had killed in his life" (16:30). He was an uncomfortable person to have in the vicinity, nevertheless, and we can well understand the Philistine endeavours to eliminate him.

The account of his death (16:23ff.) rings true in several details. The picture of the Philistines making merry is particularly credible, for beer-mugs have been unearthed time and time again by excavators of Philistine sites. Archaeology has also thrown light on the architecture of the house which Samson pulled down about his own head; the larger Philistine houses frequently had a number of pillars supporting the upper part of the buildings.

But once Samson was dead, the tribe of Dan was left without a champion and without an army capable of withstanding the Philistines. No doubt many of them were overrun or driven out, becoming incorporated in Judah. One band of 600 men, with their families, however, had the wisdom to realize that discretion was the better part of valour, and they emigrated to the far north of Palestine, passing through many other tribal territories *en route*. North of the Sea of Galilee lies a plain (known as "The Finger", because of its shape) some 25 miles long, through which flows the Jordan at the start of its journey south; at the north-eastern edge of this plain, at the foot of the slopes of Mount Hermon, lay the unsuspecting Canaanite city of Laish, and upon it the Danites descended. Destroying it, they rebuilt the city and renamed it "Dan"; it became the traditional northern outpost of Israel, in the common phrase, "from Dan to Beersheba".

The Philistines and related groups mastered the whole of the coastal plain, as far north as the Carmel range. Then following the great road which led to Damascus, they turned inland, through the pass of Megiddo, and into the Plain of Jezreel, and so extended their control as far as the Jordan near Beth-shan. Thus they cut off the central tribes from those in Galilee, and indeed encircled the southern and central tribes on three sides. This in itself was a serious enough situation for Israel, but the Philistines were not satisfied; they meant to make the hill-country theirs too, and master the whole area west of Jordan. (In one sense they succeeded permanently, for the term "Palestine" commemorates their name to this day.)

This unhappy state of affairs is the background situation to 1 Samuel. Despite their extremity, the Israelites do not seem to have undergone a change of heart towards their God, but they did focus their attention on the central shrine, Shiloh, in the territory of Ephraim, where Eli was in charge, attended by Samuel. A strong Philistine army marched into western Ephraim, and at the first encounter at the edge of the coastal plain, defeated the Israelites soundly. The Israelites regrouped, but felt that there must be some way of ensuring victory. Their minds cast back, and recalled that when they marched from victory to victory under the leadership of Moses and Joshua, the ark of the covenant had gone into battle with them. Very well, it should now serve them again, as a talisman. But the ark, unattended by the Divine Presence it symbolized, proved a broken reed; the Israelite army was decimated, and the sacred ark captured, at the disastrous battle of Aphek (1 Samuel 4:1-11), *c.* 1050 B.C.

However, in the event the ark of the covenant brought the Philistines no pleasure, and before long they returned it. Even so, they may have retained general supervision over it. It is very probable that they then proceeded to attack Shiloh and destroy the sanctuary there. While it is true that recent excavations have left the date of Shiloh's fall in some doubt,[6] the total silence from now on about this important sanctuary strongly suggests that it suffered destruction at the hands of the Philistines. At the very least the sanctuary would seem to have been abandoned, due to Philistine pressure.

6. Cf. M. L. Buhl and S. Holm-Nielsen, *Shiloh* (Copenhagen, 1969), pp.61f., where it is suggested that Shiloh may have fallen to the Assyrians, some three centuries later.

CHAPTER 3

The First King: Saul

SAMUEL survived the débâcle, and indeed was able to rally his people to drive the Philistines back, as 1 Samuel 7 records. But it is evident that he himself was not the man to lead troops into battle. He managed to instil fresh hope and courage in his countrymen, and he was able to win the support of the non-Israelite population; but all this was but a postponement of the problem, not a solution to it. The Philistines remained a constant menace, and waited patiently for their opportunity. As Samuel aged, no obvious successor to him was apparent, and the tribal elders became very anxious, and with good reason, for the Philistines began again to encroach on the hill country and to install garrisons there. If Israel was to survive, some drastic step seemed necessary.

That Saul became the first king of a united Israel is a matter of historical fact; but the circumstances in which this took place are involved, and have been much debated. A casual reading of the biblical data leaves one with the impression that, viewed politically, Saul's reign was a success (at the beginning, at any rate), but a disaster from the religious point of view. We may well believe that the matter was more complex than this, however. Political motives, religious motives, and indeed personal feelings, must all be taken into account. It used to be fashionable to over-simplify the issues, arguing that the passages in 1 Samuel 8-12 which are hostile to the monarchy were late and unhistorical; but it is significant that two of the most important recent works on the history of Israel[1] recognize fully that opposing viewpoints were represented in ancient Israel.

---

1. M. Noth, *The History of Israel*[2] (London, 1960); J. Bright, *A History of Israel*[2] (London, 1972). In his recent discussion of the topic, A. D. H. Mayes finds little reliable historical information in the relevant chapters except for 1 Samuel 11. This viewpoint is based more on literary than historical arguments, and does not seem to be demanded by the evidence, cf. J. H. Hayes and J. M. Miller, *Israelite and Judaean History* (OTL: London, 1977), pp. 324f.

"Monarchy", remarks Professor Bright, "was an institution totally foreign to Israel's tradition".[2] For 200 years Israel had existed without kings, even though most of her neighbours had long ago adopted the system of monarchy, and those Israelites of a conservative outlook will have felt that the election of a king would be an unwarranted and unhappy innovation. Israel was a brotherhood, and this revealed itself by sturdy independence of mind in every village and in every tribe. A centralized government and administration might have far from beneficial effects for the ordinary citizen, and it would certainly take a great deal of power out of the hands of local elders. On the tribal level, there was good reason to fear that a powerful tribe like Ephraim might become the aristocracy round the king, and assert its supremacy over smaller tribes.

Political inertia, then, will have said, "Let well alone". But there were powerful factors working in the opposite direction; first and foremost, of course, the dire necessity of keeping the Philistines at bay. Cohesion of the tribes was clearly essential, and this demanded central administration, with a strong hand controlling it. It was finally a deputation of tribal elders who demanded a king; evidently they were willing to submerge their personal feelings and submit to a king — better to submit to an Israelite king than to a Philistine overlord.

A second factor was the example of Israel's neighbours. The Canaanite system of goverment was the city-state pattern, with a king at the head of each. Just as Canaanite culture attracted many Israelites, so too Canaanite methods of administration appealed to some. Israel's judges had some of them gained great prestige through the victories they achieved, and others had no doubt found their judicial positions a good basis for acquiring power, and several of them had been virtually monarchs, in a limited area. Gideon's family has already been mentioned in this connection; Jephthah had demanded a permanent position as "head" in Gilead as the price for his leadership in battle (Judges 11:9ff.); and one of the "minor" judges, Jair, seems to have held a position of more than ordinary eminence (Judges 10:3f.). It was therefore not an entirely novel request that the elders put to Samuel: "Appoint us a king to govern us, like other nations" (1 Samuel 8:5). At the same time, it must be remembered that the Canaanite kings did not wield authority over a very wide area; each city had its own king. So the demand for a king over all Israel was certainly novel in the scope it envisaged. But even for this there had been something of a precedent, in the attempt of Abimelech to impose his authority over a group of cities; he started as king of Shechem (Judges 9:6), but later he transferred his capital

2. J. Bright, *op cit.*, p. 182.

elsewhere, and installed an officer, Zebul, as ruler of Shechem (9:28ff.).

It may well be that Abimelech's very endeavour to become king on a rather more grandiose scale had led to his unpopularity. But a more recent precedent, again to a limited extent only, was to hand, in the person of Samuel himself. He exercised authority as a judge over a considerable area for many years: after the fall of Shiloh we find him active in Bethel, Gilgal, Mizpah and his native Ramah (1 Samuel 7:15ff.). He claimed no kingly prerogatives, to be sure, but it is evident that the elders of Israel were afraid that his authority might descend to his sons, whom they had good cause to mistrust; he had already made them judges in Beersheba (8:1ff.).

So much for political considerations; but strong religious feelings were held too. Since the days of Moses, the Israelites had always viewed their God as their King: the Song of the Sea ends with the words, "The LORD will reign for ever and ever" (Exodus 15:18); Gideon's reply to the suggestion that he become king in Israel was, "I will not rule over you . . . the LORD will rule over you" (Judges 8:23). To many a devout Israelite it will have seemed deliberate apostasy to seek to set a man in the place of God. On the other hand, it became evident that God's seal of approval was upon Saul; "the spirit of God suddenly took possession of him" (1 Samuel 10:10), and those who were cynical about Saul's capabilities are dismissed as "scoundrels" (10:27). Thus in the religious sphere too, there were conflicting opinions about the project.

The general biblical perspective is not that a king as such was a breach of the divinely appointed order — there was no religious objection to David's kingship. But kings had to prove themselves worthy; and in the eyes of the Old Testament writers this is where Saul ultimately failed. The Israelites' demand for a king, however, was not based on Saul's virtuosity, but on their unwillingness to accept the human leadership God provided for them from time to time by placing his spirit on one man and another. Their demand for a king was therefore against God's wishes, and was thus a token of their rejection of his own sovereignty over them. Their request was nevertheless granted, but it could bring them little permanent pleasure.

A practical result of the accession of Saul was the divorcing of political leadership from religious leadership. Samuel retained the voice of authority in the latter sphere; all was well so long as Samuel and Saul agreed, but that happy state of affairs did not long continue.

Saul's reign began auspiciously enough. He was a man of outstanding physique and handsome appearance; without any seeking the crown on his part, it was freely offered to him, while Samuel, who might well have shown jealousy at losing his own position as national leader, gave him full support; and finally he found in himself fresh and unsuspected capabilities, as he experienced the visitation of the spirit of God. A ceremony at Mizpah, in his home territory of Benjamin, showed him that he had both divine and national support. Apart from his own winning appearance, there were two factors which no doubt influenced the Israelites to make him king, in spite of any previous reluctance: firstly, there was the fact that his tribe was small and insignificant, so that there was no danger that Benjamin would ever lord it over the other tribes; and secondly, the unequivocal support Samuel gave Saul must have surprised and impressed many.

Meanwhile, what were the Philistines doing? It may seem surprising that they should have stood by and permitted this significant, and for them ominous, change in Israelite administration. One can only think that they were unable to hinder it. They were only just beginning to move back into the hill country, and the nature of the terrain prevented them from achieving the control they could have wished. The mountainous area west of the Jordan is dissected by numerous valleys, rendering swift military movement difficult; and in such country, the local inhabitants, with their intimate knowledge of the terrain, always have a big advantage over invaders, however skilled.

Mizpah lay at the summit of an isolated hill some eight miles north of Jerusalem. It is possible to visualize what happened: Mizpah, on a secure hill-top, was far enough away from the Philistines to enable a representative group of the Israelites to carry out the ceremony of making Saul king without fear of interference; but immediately afterwards Saul speedily dispersed his subjects to their own homes, he himself returning quietly to his native Gibeah, only a few miles from Mizpah. The time was not yet ripe for confonting the Philistines in battle. For the moment therefore, both towards the enemy and towards those Israelites who refused to accept him as king, "he held his peace" (1 Samuel 10:27, RSV). We next find him quietly farming, which can have done nothing to reassure those Israelites who were sceptical about him; after all, a tall frame, a handsome appearance, and an ability to prophesy in trance-like fashion, do not necessarily make one an able leader in battle.

But an opportunity for swift and effective action soon presented itself, and Saul immediately showed his mettle. A city of northern Transjordan called Jabesh-gilead was suddenly besieged by the Ammonites, who were obviously completely confident of success. The city itself was too small to be able to drive them off, and the Ammonites must have felt morally certain that in view of the severe pressure on the Israelites west of the Jordan, the city would get no help from more powerful tribes. But Nahash, the Ammonite king, made two mistakes: he overlooked the fact that the city he was attacking had a long standing friendship with the tribe of Benjamin, and he failed to reckon with Saul. Issuing truly royal commands, Saul rapidly mustered an army on the western side of the river, and from there descended on the Ammonites, who were overwhelmed and put to flight.

Jabesh-gilead was no great distance from the Philistine-held fortress city of Beth-shan, which lies at the south-east end of the Plain of Jezreel, where the Plain runs into the Jordan Valley. It is probable that the speed with which Saul acted prevented any possibility of the Philistines' intervening at Jabesh-gilead; but apart from that consideration, it must be remembered that between Beth-shan and Jabesh-gilead lay the river Jordan, the most natural geographical boundary in Palestine. "The Jordan depression", Dr. J. M. Houston has written, "is unique among the features of physical geography. Formed as a result of a rift valley, it is the lowest depression on earth".[3] On either side of this deep valley rise lofty mountain ridges, all the way from the Sea of Galilee to the Dead Sea. The actual floor of the valley is arid and desolate, but next to it, on either side, is the well-named "jungle of Jordan" (*cf.* Jeremiah 12:5, RSV). Through this formidable valley the river itself winds about almost incredibly; its actual length is more than twice the distance as the crow flies between Galilee and the Dead Sea. It is therefore understandable that the Philistines, capable soldiers that they were, saw the dangers of crossing the Jordan before they fully controlled the territory west of it. We have already seen how both Moabites and Midianites came to grief as a result of venturing across the river.

The victory over Ammon not only raised the morale of all Israel, but also gave Saul such prestige that the whole nation rallied behind him; those who had stood aloof were now silenced or won over. A fresh ceremony, almost spontaneous, took place to ratify Saul's royal position. It occured at Gilgal, a Benjaminite city very close to the Jordan, a site well away from Philistine territory, and at the same time conveniently near to Transjordanian soil — it is highly probable that the Gileadites had been particularly slow to recognize Saul as king, in view of their security from the Philistine threat.

And now the moment could no longer be delayed; Saul must take action against the major foe. He divided the tribal forces into two parts, himself leading one of them, his son Jonathan the other. It was Jonathan, a man of remarkable enterprise and daring, who struck the first blow, by killing the Philistine prefect at Geba, only three miles from his father's home and capital, Gibeah.[4] 1 Samuel

3. J. M. Houston, "Jordan", in *NBD*, pp.654ff.
4. It is not certain whether Jonathan killed a prefect or defeated a garrison (cf. 1 Samuel 13:3, RSV). Nor is it certain whether the scene of the incident was Geba or Gibeah itself.

13:4 relates that in consequence "the name of Israel stank among the Philistines", and we can well believe it. Electing a king and killing a Philistine officer were scarcely marks of submission. The Philistines responded by bringing up the full might of their army and occupying Michmash, a strategic Benjaminite city to the north of the Israelite forces, and cutting the route into Benjamin from Ephraim. The sight of the well-equipped Philistine army, and the knowledge that reinforcements from the northern tribes could not get through to them, thoroughly dismayed Saul's meagre force, so "they hid themselves in caves and holes among the rocks, in pits and cisterns. Some of them crossed the Jordan into the district of Gad and Gilead". Saul held firm at Gilgal, but "all the people at his back were in alarm" (1 Samuel 13:6f.).

In such frightening circumstances, Saul felt desperately in need of God's blessing on the forthcoming battle, and he waited a full week and more for Samuel to come and offer sacrifices appropriate to the occasion. As Samuel still delayed, Saul grew impatient; we can sympathize with his feeling, but in fact the delay was all to the good, for had he marched into battle with a small, ill-equipped and demoralized army, he would surely have been cut to pieces. At last, Saul took it upon himself to offer sacrifice, and had scarcely done so when a very irate Samuel arrived on the scene; and so the first breach between the two leaders of Israel took place. Meanwhile Jonathan, almost single-handed, had altered the situation completely. Entirely unaccompanied except for his armour-bearer, he showed himself to the Philistine garrison at Michmash, who naturally assumed that he was but one of an Israelite force, and went out to engage them in battle. But Jonathan skilfully chose a narrow point on a steep ascent, and he and his batman were able with ease to kill off their attackers one by one. This simple ruse was sufficient to defeat a whole garrison! Still under the impression that they were being attacked by a body of troops, the Philistines suddenly realized how many men they were losing, and panicked. As they started to take to their heels and even to fight each other, Saul arrived on the scene with his small army, and the panic became a rout. Those Israelites who had previously deserted speedily found their lost courage, and joined gleefully in the pursuit. As for those Israelites who had been traitors to date, throwing in their lot with the Philistines, they too saw which way the wind was blowing, and changed sides without delay.

So the Philistines were bundled out of the hills, defeated not so much by force of arms as by Jonathan's intimate knowledge of the hill country (not to mention his personal daring). Saul knew how to turn a situation to good account, and he never let up the pursuit until the army were driven back to the coastal plain. They for their part did not give up so easily, and for the rest of his reign Saul was obliged to fight them constantly. However, they were unable to reoccupy the hill country so long as he reigned, which gave Saul full independence and freedom of movement.

Nor were the Ammonites the only group to attack the Israelites on other frontiers. In Transjordan, the Moabites and the Aramaeans put pressure on Reuben and eastern Manasseh respectively, and in the south Judah and Simeon were harassed by Edomites and Amalekites. But at last Israel was able to take a united stand against such enemies, and we read that Saul dealt effectively with all these raids and inroads, one after another. Saul probably reached the pinnacle of success and prestige with his early defeat of the Philistines, but these frequent campaigns were sufficient to maintain his prestige throughout his reign. It must not be forgotten how dependent Saul was on the loyalty of his subjects; there was no precedent in Israel for royal position, and one sound defeat might well have cost him his throne. The excavations at Gibeah have shown that Saul's court was not one of oriental luxury by any means, but rather of almost rustic simplicity; nevertheless, the maintenance of armies throughout his reign will have entailed the financial support and forced service of all the tribes, which would not be calculated to make any administrator popular. Inter-tribal jealousies, and the desire for independence, were always near the surface.

For these various reasons it is evident that Saul's position was none too secure, and of this fact he must have been keenly aware. But at the beginning he did not have to rely on prestige alone, for he had the full support of Samuel. The first encounter with the Philistines had weakened this bond, as we have seen; and the Amalekite campaign was to create a permanent breach between the two men, knocking the prop of religious support from under Saul. The Amalekites were an ancient foe of Israel, and one that was viewed as particularly treacherous (cf. Deuteronomy 25:17ff.); the command was therefore that none who were captured should be spared. A sacred vow to this effect was made. Yet Saul, purely for his own pleasure and advantage, took it upon himself to break this solemn oath. This was the second occasion on which Saul had flagrantly disobeyed the divine command given him through Samuel, and his actions made it clear that there was another king in Israel besides Yahweh. The judges had all been subservient to the spirit of Yahweh, which had dominated their actions; the king was an autocrat, already proving the maxim that power corrupts.

Samuel did not mince his words. He advised Saul outright that just as he had rejected God's commands, so God had rejected him; as far as God was concerned, Saul was no longer king. Saul was genuinely distressed by this pronouncement, as well he might be, but the aged prophet was adamant. The two men parted; "and

Samuel never saw Saul again to his dying day'' (1 Samuel 15:35). In his personal life too, Saul lost touch with God; never again did he find himself possessed by God's spirit. All that he had left were his natural skill and experience, together with the fickle loyalties of his subjects. It is easy to understand why he became subject to fits of depression which grew more and more severe, till in the end he was not a rational man, but appeared morose, irritable, and suspicious of all around him.

We first meet the youthful David as a shepherd boy on his father's farm at Bethlehem, a city of Judah only about ten miles south of Saul's city, Gibeah. Samuel anointed the lad to be Saul's successor as king over Israel. We may take it for granted that Saul knew nothing of this episode. He first met David as a harpist; when it became apparent that music soothed Saul's fits of depression, David was recommended to the king as a skilled performer, and soon entered the royal service in this capacity. But if David's harp had a soothing effect on Saul, David himself was soon to have a very different effect on the king. The hands that could charm music from the strings of a harp soon proved their skill with a very different instrument, one of a lethal kind.

Every reader who ever attended a Sunday school knows all about David and Goliath,[5] but it may be worthwhile to note one or two of the background details of the story. The scene of the duel was in the foothills of western Judah, where they rise from the coastal plain of the Shephelah; the Philistines marched in force into these hills, and the Israelite army was obliged to counter the threat, and block the passes leading up into the mountains. But the Philistines had no intention of attempting a pitched battle, and they resorted to a method of warfare common in the ancient (and mediaeval) world, but far removed from the total warfare of our own day; the battle was to be settled by a single combat of a selected champion from each side. The victorious champion in such duels won great prestige for his side; the element of prestige is very clear in the account of David's encounter with Goliath (1 Samuel 17), both in the insulted reaction of the giant Philistine to the youthful and inexperienced aspect of David, and in the discomfiture and flight of the Philistines once their hitherto invincible champion was dead. Once again, they returned to their home on the plain in a hurry.

Saul had been hard put to find an Israelite champion, and he had held out two glittering prizes to any volunteer — marriage to the king's daughter, and permanent freedom of taxes for his family (17:25). Little did he imagine that his youthful court harpist would be the man to claim them. It is not surpising that he instituted fresh

5. For problems connected with the biblical narrative, cf. D. F. Payne in *NBCR*. p. 318.

enquiries about David's family and antecedents; one likes to know as much as possible about one's future in-laws, and as the king's son-in-law David would be an influential figure in Israel. Nor was David's victory in single combat a flash in the pan; Saul put him fully to test, and was so impressed by his ability that he gave him a high-ranking military position. And David did all that could be asked of him, going on from success to success.

From the point of view of the welfare of Israel, David's arrival on the scene was opportune, and the populace was duly grateful to him. But from Saul's personal point of view, David's growing reputation was a threat to his own position, which was, as we have seen, based to a considerable extent on prestige. Saul's reputation against the Philistines was not forgotten, but the women in the streets made it clear who was the man of the moment: "Saul has slain his thousands, and David his ten thousands." Comparisons are odious, runs the saying — and Saul would have agreed heartily.

David's reputation might have been more tolerable to Saul if the younger man had had less charm of character. If David had been a boor, or conceited, Saul would have had less reason to fear him, for no opposition group of any consequence would be likely to grow round an unpopular figure, however great his military reputation. But the fact was that David had an unusually winsome and attractive personality; all Israel loved him, including members of Saul's own family. Jonathan might well have hated David as a potential rival, yet the friendship between the two is proverbial. Indeed, in his more rational moments Saul himself was won over.

One can have a certain sympathy with Saul's feelings; the defection of Samuel must have been a bitter blow, and the rise of this influential and to Saul enigmatic figure must have seemed the last straw. One wonders if it ever came to Saul's notice that Samuel had anointed David as the next king of Israel; he may at least have suspected that Samuel supported David. Be that as it may, one can see that Saul had good reason to view David as a potential rival; but on the other hand, David never gave him the slighest cause to question his loyalty. Even when Saul was openly seeking to kill him, David could not bring himself to lay a hand on Saul when the opportunity presented itself, for the king was Yahweh's anointed.

Before long Saul's dark suspicions got the better of him, and David was obliged to flee from the court to save his life. His first move was to go to Samuel in Ramah for sanctuary, pursued by Saul; David's very contact with Samuel may have confirmed the suspicions of the king. From Ramah David wandered from place to place in the south of Palestine, and presently made his headquarters at Adullam, in the hills of Judah, not so very far from Philistine territory (only twelve miles or so from the city of Gath). It was here that David's supporters increased one hundredfold; till now he had with him only two or three servants, but when he left Adullam he commanded 400 men.

A number of those who joined David were his own kinsfolk, but the majority of the 400 consisted of "men in any kind of distress or in debt or with a grievance" (1 Samuel 22:2). This sounds very much like the motley crew who had constituted Jephthah's band, described in Judges 11:3 as "idle fellows". But we are not to suppose that all David's men were typical malcontents, social misfits who rebel on principle against established law and order, though of course some of them may have been. The group who joined David at the cave of Adullam were welded into a highly efficient military unit, which later formed the nucleus of the royal troops when David became king, and to whose loyalty and skill David was to owe a great deal. Men of such calibre cannot have been totally irresponsible citizens. There is every probability that a good many of David's men had a legitimate grievance against Saul or against his administration. It would be surprising if the king, in his deteriorating mental condition, had not offended some of his subjects. A number of biblical passages suggest that there were occasions when Saul would brook no argument from anybody, but acted with despotic forcefulness. We know from 2 Samuel 21:1f. that, for some reason, he slaughtered some of the Gibeonites, a non-Israelite group whose cities were incorporated in Benjamin and who were in close treaty relationship with Israel; years after the death of Saul, this act of his had been neither forgotten nor forgiven.

Another clue to the reasons for Saul's unpopularity in some quarters may be found in the phrase "in debt"; debtors may have no-one but themselves to blame, but on the other hand they may be a symptom of something wrong with the economic structure, or the administration of justice, of the state concerned. It may therefore be significant that no few debtors were to be found among David's supporters.

There was one man at the cave of Adullam whose motives for joining David are transparent. This was Abiathar the priest, who afterwards officiated, with Zadok, at the sanctuary in Jerusalem. When David had left Samuel in Ramah, and fled south towards the wilderness of Judah, he had been granted temporary shelter by the priesthood of a city called Nob. The priests had acted in innocence, intending no disloyalty to Saul; but for all that, Saul descended upon them and slaughtered not only the priests but the ordinary citizens of Nob. Abiathar, however, managed to escape, and got away safely to David's camp. There is reason to believe that Nob had functioned as the chief sanctuary after the abandonment of Shiloh; one can imagine the horror felt by all devout, God-fearing Israelites at Saul's wanton brutality there.

If Abiathar and the debtors in David's camp are any guide to the situation, we may conclude that faults in Saul's judiciary system and his heedlessness of religious proprieties may have caused a good deal of the discontentment of his subjects. It is apparent that by now there was a complete breach between the king and the custodians of the religious welfare of Israel. The political administration and the religious organization stood opposed, or at least out of harmony; and very probably the administration of law fell between the two. The law was primarily a religious function, stemming as it did from Israel's covenant with God; the first laws had been the stipulations or obligations of the Sinai covenant, and the written law was always deposited in the sanctuary, just as the Ten Commandments had been placed in the ark of the covenant. During the Judges period, the wilderness ideal of a single sanctuary was lost (with not altogether happy consequences for Israel's faith), but law was still administrated in the tribal sanctuaries. Samuel himself, we read, "went on circuit to Bethel and Gilgal and Mizpah; he dispensed justice at all these places, returning always to Ramah. That was his home and the place from which he governed Israel" (1 Samuel 7:16f.).

When Israel took to itself a king, inevitably some changes must have taken place in the legal system; if nothing else occurred, the king certainly became the highest court of appeal. It would be very interesting to know what exactly Samuel put in writing when he "explained to the people the nature of a king, and made a written record of it on a scroll which he deposited before the LORD" (1 Samuel 10:25).[6] If David himself, who had the happiest relations with the religious authorities during his reign, was not altogether successful in his administration of legal affairs,[7] then it is certain that this aspect of Saul's governmental machinery was less than satisfactory.

In the light of these considerations, the details of 1 Chronicles 12:1-22 become more plausible than many biblical scholars will allow. The Chronicler relates that the trickle of men who joined David at Adullam became a flood before Saul's reign was over: "from day to day men came in to help David, until he had gathered an immense army" (1 Chronicles 12:22). We may well believe that the dissatisfaction with Saul's regime increased as his reign progressed. Saul's own tribe, Benjamin, remained loyal for the most part — as the Chronicler concedes (12:29) — but he claims that even some of them went over to David. This detail seems the more probable when we remember that both Gibeon and Nob were in Benjamin.

6. The late Professor Robertson suggested that the law-code promulgated thus by Samuel was the Book of Deuteronomy. Cf. E. Robertson, *The Old Testament Problem*, (Manchester, 1950).

7. See below, pp. 51f.

David no doubt drew much encouragement from the support he received at Adullam, but the numerical strength of his friends brought its own problems. In the first place, a lone fugitive can often secrete himself completely, especially in the barren wilderness of the southern hills of Judah; but an army of 400 men cannot easily be hidden. Furthermore, a band of able-bodied men 400 strong needs both an occupation and a livelihood; it was scarcely possible to settle to till a fertile valley when Saul was organizing a systematic and thorough search of the whole area. However, before these problems became acute, an unexpected opportunity presented itself; still menacing the foothills of Judah, the Philistines attacked a certain city called Keilah, a short distance south of Adullam. After some brief hesitation, David and his men marched to relieve Keilah, and were able to drive the Philistines off. This exploit provided David's troops with food and shelter for the time being, and incidentally served to maintain David's reputation as the champion of Israel against the Philistines; but inevitably the news of David's movements got to Saul's ears, and the royal armies descended upon Keilah. David's band of men narrowly escaped, and afterwards found themselves obliged to keep to the more barren areas. The southeastern hills of Judah have always been remote and sparsely populated (it was hereabouts that the Dead Sea Scrolls lay undiscovered for almost 2000 years), and here the fugitives had plenty of space in which to hide themselves; but they were forced to approach farms and towns for supplies, and so gave away their position time and time again. It was equally unfortunate that they had little to offer in return for provisions, and began to give the impression that they were preying on the local farmers. Nabal (1 Samuel 25) was in all probability not the only farmer to rebuff David's men.

Eventually, after one or two narrow escapes from Saul, David realized that there was no future for himself and his guerrilla band (now 600 strong) within the confines of Saul's kingdom, and he determined on a bold step. He, who had done so much to hinder the Philistines in the past, now marched into their territory and offered his services to the king of Gath, Achish! The Philistines might well have cut them to pieces, but Achish had a better plan. While Saul had been obsessed with his pursuit of David, he had had little time to organize an anti-Philistine campaign with his previous efficiency; this state of affairs well suited Achish, and he thought he might perpetuate it by installing David and his men on the very borders of Judah, where he still might draw Saul's fire, so to speak. As it happened, Saul wrote David off as soon as the latter went to Gath, but Achish was not to know that, for David maintained the pretence that he and his men were harassing the border towns of Judah. In point of fact, they were attacking the Amalekites and other semi-nomadic tribes of the northern Negeb.

During the sixteen months that David was at Ziklag (the city given them by Achish), he was able to weld his band into a formidable fighting force. We may hazard the guess that this period also gave him the opportunity to observe the Philistines' military organization, and perhaps get possession of some Philistine weapons too. At any rate, he was later to prove a far more effective general against the Philistines than Saul ever was, and Saul was no mean soldier. It is doubtful if the Israelite army was ever particularly well armed and equipped before David's reign; most of their iron weapons will have been booty taken when the Philistines were worsted in battle.[8]

And now the sands of time had run out for Saul. The Philistines determined to put their full military strength into the field, and challenge Saul to the pitched battle they themselves had avoided for so long. Even David's army was pressed into service, for by now Achish trusted him implicitly. The Philistine forces marched north, making no attempt to fight their way into the hills of Judah or Ephraim, and came into the Plain of Jezreel. Their intention, presumably, was to cut off Saul from his northern tribal territories. Beth-shan, the Philistine outpost at the eastern end of the Plain, lies not five miles from the Jordan, and the Philistine army could quickly have reached the river, occupied the Jordan valley up to the Sea of Galilee, and truncated Saul's kingdom at one blow. This manoeuvre forced Saul to leave the mountains, and fight them on level ground of their own choosing; he must block their advance across the Plain of Jezreel. So the Israelite armies made their headquarters at the city of Jezreel itself, blocking the approach to Beth-shan and there awaited the Philistine assault.

The Philistines paused to review their troops at Aphek, before making their way through the pass of Megiddo. It now transpired that the other Philistine leaders did not share Achish's faith in David's men, and insisted that they be sent back to Ziklag; after all, if the Philistines were to suffer a slight set-back in the battle, these men of doubtful loyalties might change sides and turn a retreat into a rout. David protested vigorously — did he perhaps hope he would find some opportunity of turning the tide of battle against the Philistines? — but to no avail, and he turned back to Ziklag, anxiously waiting for news from the battlefield.

The result of the battle was no surprise. On level ground the Israelite army was no match at all for the Philistines, and was soon dispersed in headlong flight. They tried to head for home, south into the Gilboa range of hills, and it was there that most of them were overtaken and killed. Here Saul was so badly wounded that his capture was certain, and he took his own life rather than suffer such

8. Cf. 1 Samuel 21:8f.

humiliation. Jonathan was another who died in battle. Next day the victors found their bodies, and the bodies of two more of Saul's sons, and proceeded to display them on the walls of the city of Beth-shan. It was the final humiliation that their corpses should remain unburied.

But while the remnant of the Israelite army fled in terror, one group of Israelites acted with presence of mind, courage, and a proper sense of gratitude. A few miles away, the other side of the Jordan, lay the city of Jabesh-gilead, which Saul had rescued from the Ammonites at the start of his reign. The citizens organised a party to creep up to the walls of Beth-shan during the hours of darkness and rescue the royal bodies. And so Israel's first king was interred at Jabesh-gilead, while all Israel mourned. It was left to David to put it into words:

"How are the mighty fallen, and the weapons of war perished!"

CHAPTER 4

David's Rise to Power

THEIR victory at the battle of Gilboa (*c.* 1000 B.C.) left the
Philistines for the moment very much in control of the situation.
Indeed, it must have seemed to many an Israelite that the whole
reign of Saul had been nullified; the enemy were back in the
position they had held when Saul first took office. Once again the
Philistines sent their garrisons into the heart of the hill country, and
virtually dominated the territory west of the Jordan. They had no
desire to push the Israelites out — they were not numerous enough
to take over for their own use all this territory. Nor did they capture all the cities; they contented themselves with stationing their
garrisons.

Meanwhile there were two Israelites who tried to pick up the
pieces. One of them was David, who was back at Ziklag, south-west
of Judah, when news of the battle reached him. The other was Saul's
close relative (cousin, probably) Abner, who had served as the
commander-in-chief of Saul's armies. One son of Saul survived the
battle, and Abner determined to make him the next king of Israel.
The young man's name was Eshbaal,[1] and he was acclaimed king
by the northern and Transjordanian tribes. Abner no doubt had
every intention of being the power behind the throne, and in making
Eshbaal king seems to have acted on his own account. There was no
religious support for this move, but it was natural enough that Saul's
son should succeed to the throne; the hereditary principle was
common all around Israel if there was as yet no real precedent in
Israel (if we exclude Abimelech from consideration). The majority of
the tribes acquiesced, therefore; but it is noteworthy that the royal

1. This, the original form of the name, occurs in 1 Chronicles 8:33; the usual
biblical form is Ish-bosheth, a later modification designed to avoid the use of the
name "Baal".

headquarters was located not in Benjamin, but across the Jordan, at Mahanaim, out of Philistine reach. It is doubtful if Eshbaal's kingship ever meant much in practice to the Israelites west of the river.

Meanwhile, far from Eshbaal's capital, David was acting with rare skill and diplomacy. To an impartial observer, his chances of ever taking Saul's place as king of all Israel must have seemed thin indeed. His recent position as a Philistine vassal might easily have stamped him as a traitor in the eyes of Judah; Saul's persistent hostility to him in recent years might well have established him as a *persona non grata* in the eyes of Benjamin and all who had supported Saul; and whatever he did now, he must not offend his powerful overlords, against whom he had no River Jordan to serve as a natural defence. The fact that David succeeded in establishing good relations with all the tribes of Israel, without forfeiting Philistine goodwill until he was ready to do battle with them, is a clear indication of his diplomatic genius.

As far as Judah was concerned, he had already succeeded in part in offsetting his defection to the Philistines, by his policy of attacking the enemies of Israel to the south, notably the Amalekites. In the last few days of Saul's life, the Amalekites gave him a fresh opportunity to achieve a reputation at their expense; as soon as the Philistine armies, David and his men with them, had marched north, the Amalekites had descended upon the now unprotected settled peoples in the south — upon the territory of Judah and the Philistines alike, and in particular upon David's own city of Ziklag. But David's men, dismissed by the Philistines, returned to Ziklag much more rapidly than the Amalekites could have expected, and the upshot was that the Amalekites were caught unawares and suffered heavy casualties. This speedy and effective punitive action against the Amalekites will have made David popular with Judah and the Philistines equally; but David proceeded to share out the plunder with a number of cities of Judah, thus underlining his kinship with them.

Having thus paved the way, he returned to the centre of Judah. In the city of Hebron he was anointed king over his own tribe, and so began his long reign. Presumably by now the tribe of Judah was used to a monarchy, and wanted a king; Saul, however, had proved a disillusionment, and his son's rule was centred too far away to be of any use to them. David, on the other hand, was one of themselves; he was known as a soldier of ability, and his earlier popularity was not forgotten; and he was on the spot. The Philistines, for their part, must have been persuaded that David was still their vassal; and in any case it will have pleased them well enough to see an opposition kingdom to that of Eshbaal. A divided Israel, at war with itself, will have suited them admirably. So they permitted David to rule Judah for them. They were thus relieved of the necessity of placing garrisons in Judah; and this in turn must have pleased the men of Judah admirably.

David thus gained political support from both Judah and the Philistines; nor must we forget that he had considerable religious support from his own people, whereas Eshbaal had none. Abiathar and some of the priesthood had long accompanied him in exile, and David was careful to consult the sacred oracle before making important decisions. So now, before making for Hebron, he "inquired of the LORD" (2 Samuel 2:1), and was directed to that city. Hebron was only two miles south of the shrine of Mamre, and here no doubt the anointing ceremony took place — a religious rather than a political ceremony. We read of no prophet or priest taking part in this coronation,[2] to be sure, but Samuel's designation of David was no doubt recalled. Later on, at any rate, David not only showed great concern for religious proprieties, but also emphasized the religious aspects of his royal position; it is therefore more than likely that he did so from the first.

In his dealings with the other tribes of Israel, he was careful to show no disrespect for Saul, but he tacitly assumed that he was the proper successor to Saul, ignoring Eshbaal as far as he could. The man who brought him word of Saul's defeat and death related that he had actually given the wounded king the *coup de grâce*; this temerity earned him execution from David, who could thus claim to have avenged, in some measure, the death of Saul. There was not the least exultation in David's camp at the death of a rival and persecutor; David led his whole people in genuine lamentation at the death of a champion of Israel. The elegy he composed remains a testimony to his sincerity, recorded for posterity in 2 Samuel 1:19ff.

When further news reached him, to the effect that Saul's body had been retrieved and given decent burial by the people of Jabesh-gilead, David sent them a warm message of commendation (2 Samuel 2:5ff.). In this message he also conveyed the fact that he was king over Judah, and made promises to "do good" to the citizens of Jabesh. By such means he ensured that he would not appear as the leader of a rebel faction, hostile to Saul and all he stood for. But of course Eshbaal cannot have regarded David as anything but an interloper, and David was obliged to view him as an enemy.

It is doubtful whether David took much direct action against Eshbaal; only one clash between the two opposing armies is recorded, and it is not clear who precipitated it. It took place at Gibeon, on Benjaminite soil, so it is clear that the men of Judah had left their home territory; on the other hand, Eshbaal's men were a

2. It is this fact that leads Noth to maintain that this coronation was "a purely political act" (*op. cit.*, p.183).

very long way from their base in Transjordan. This single encounter, in which David's men came off best, was a fight between selected champions, so little bloodshed resulted; the victory will have increased David's prestige, without giving him the reputation of massacring Israelites. Indeed, any bitterness resulting from the fight seems to have been on the victor's side, for Joab, soon to be if not already David's chief general, lost a brother in the Gibeon encounter, killed by Abner in person, and he never forgave his counterpart at Eshbaal's court. The opportunity for revenge soon arrived.

Conceivably David tried to put pressure on Eshbaal by surrounding his territory with enemies. He must have been on good terms with the Moabites, for he had placed his parents there for safe-keeping during the days of Saul's persecution. At some period, too, he made a treaty with the king of Ammon (cf. 2 Samuel 10:1f.). And one of his wives at Hebron was the daughter of the king of Geshur, a Syrian city not far north of the Transjordanian tribes, which presumably must also have been an ally of David. It is no wonder that Eshbaal, hedged about by Philistines, Syrians, Ammonites and Moabites, not to mention Judah itself, found his cause crumbling.

It may well be that Abner saw which way the wind was blowing, and sought an excuse to desert his protégé. At any rate, he acted in a way that could only imply that he planned to displace Eshbaal as king of Israel, and when Eshbaal challenged him, took the greatest offence, and immediately began to treat with David. Since Abner was Saul's cousin, his defection to David meant that David was now receiving support from the house of Saul itself. David demanded, moreover, that Abner should bring with him Saul's daughter Michal, whom Saul had long ago betrothed to David.

Abner's arrival in Hebron might well have signalled an Israelite landslide in support of David, had not Joab chosen this singularly unfortunate moment to take his personal revenge. With the murder of Abner, Joab not only avenged his brother, he also ensured that Abner should not be made commander-in-chief of David's armies in preference to himself; but his personal gain might well have been David's loss, for Abner's death would scarcely have given any confidence to supporters or relatives of Saul who were thinking of bringing their support to David. It is clear that David was dismayed at Abner's death, and he did all in his power to clear himself of any complicity in the assassination. He roundly cursed Joab, and insisted on full court mourning for Abner; he himself acted as chief mourner at the burial.

But Eshbaal's cause was by now doomed, in any event. The end came swiftly: two of his own army officers treacherously murdered him, and brought his head to David at Hebron, fully expecting to be praised and rewarded. David once again made it clear to all that the enemies of Saul and his family were his own enemies, and the two assassins were summarily executed. But their deed could not be undone, and the northern tribes found themselves without a leader; the figurehead had gone, and so had the able general who had been the power behind the throne. Few of Saul's family remained alive — the nearest in line to the throne was but a seven-year-old boy, and a cripple at that. There was only one man to whom they could turn if they wanted a king, and his name was David. Without further delay, a deputation of all the tribes came to Hebron, and David was once again anointed king, this time over the whole of Israel.

David's position at this stage of his career was remarkably similar to that of Saul at the beginning of his reign. Both men found themselves enthroned over a united Israel, receiving wholehearted support in some quarters, accepted as a necessary evil in others. Both faced the immediate prospect of fierce and prolonged warfare with the Philistines. An early defeat by this formidable enemy would have brought about the downfall of either man. Saul had one advantage over David; he came from a small tribe, and so occupied a neutral position in inter-tribal rivalries, whereas David came from the powerful Judah, and must therefore have been viewed with not a little suspicion by Ephraim in particular, the most important northern tribe. But potential jealousies were no immediate problem to David, for all the tribes were in perfect agreement as to the necessity of defeating the Philistines once and for all. In two respects David was better off than his predecessor: he himself was already an able and experienced soldier, whereas Saul had had no battle experience at all when he became king; and he commanded a professional army, well trained and well equipped, as against the tribal levies which Saul had led.

Warfare with the Philistines was inevitable; the phase of diplomacy was over. As an opposition force to Eshbaal, David had served the Philistine cause well, but as king of a united Israel he stood between them and their objective, full control over Palestine west of the Jordan. 2 Samuel 5 does not say when their attack came,[3] but we can scarcely doubt that it took place very quickly after David's acclamation by all the tribes. The Philistine strategy is plain; they marched in force inland towards the city of Jerusalem, which, with several other non-Israelite cities, separated Judah from Benjamin and the northern tribes. In other words, they aimed to prevent a united Israel becoming a practical reality; if his kingdom was not to fall apart again, David was forced to dislodge them from their vantage point in the valley of Rephaim, just south of Jerusalem. Here they had found level ground in the mountains, and were able

---

3. The chapter gives the impression that David's capture of Jerusalem took place before the Philistine attack but it is almost certain that the writer was not following chronological order.

to deploy their forces, and await David's attack on terrain of their own choosing. But this advantage was offset by the fact that David was thoroughly conversant with their battle methods, and had a well-trained and flexible army (whereas Saul had been obliged to rely on sheer weight of numbers). It appears that in the first battle David attempted no ruses, but met them in a head-on clash, and defeated them; but 2 Samuel 5:20 gives all too few details.

A single reverse did not deter the Philistines, whose strategy had been sound enough, and in due course they re-grouped, presumably in greater strength, and reoccupied the valley of Rephaim. At some stage they even captured Bethlehem, as 2 Samuel 23:14 reveals. This time David decided to employ a stratagem, making use of his better knowledge of the locality. All the Philistines' attention was concentrated towards the south, naturally enough; but David was able to lead his army round their rear, and attack from the north. A second victory resulted, and this one was much more decisive than the first had been. The Israelite forces followed up their success by driving the Philistines headlong from the hills once again. The pursuit was not halted till the very borders of the Philistines' own territory.

We are not told whether the Philistines made any further attempts to march into the hills of Judah; if they did, they must have been driven back equally competently. More probably they reverted to their earlier tactics of harassing Israelite towns in the foothills, such as Keilah, which David had relieved when in exile from Saul.[4] Later on David carried the war into their own camp, but for the moment he was no doubt content to have repulsed them. The Philistine threat was permanently broken.

One effect of the Philistine strategy in occupying the valley of Rephaim was to underline the fact that geographically (not to mention any other respects) David's kingdom was not a unity. The piece of Canaanite territory lying between the tribal areas of Benjamin and Judah had long created a barrier between Judah and the northern tribes, and David's administration of the northern territories was bound to suffer so long as this state of affairs remained. Now that the Philistine threat was removed, David determined to eliminate this hindrance to the internal security of his realm. Mustering his army, he marched on Jerusalem, the most important Canaanite city in this region.

Jerusalem already had a long history. Signs of occupation of the site date from the third millennium B.C.[5] Egyptian records as early as the nineteenth century B.C. mention the city by the name of Urushalim; so it is clear that the name "Jerusalem" belonged to the city long before it came into Israelite hands. Through most of the

4. See above p. 33.
5. It is reported that newly discovered documents from Ebla mention Jerusalem as early as the twenty-fifth century but relevant texts have yet to be published.

second millenium B.C. Jerusalem was a city-state, ruled by its own kings, like many other Palestinian cities. Genesis 14 introduces us to one of these kings, Melchizedek, a contemporary of Abraham. In about 1500 B.C., Egypt assumed control of Palestine, and the petty kings there became vassal rulers. One of the kings of Jerusalem of this period, by name 'Abdu-Kheba, wrote to his Egyptian overlord, asking for assistance against invaders. His letters are still extant, among the Tell el-Amarna Letters.[6]

The next king of Jerusalem whose name we know was Adoni-zedek, who led a confederacy of Canaanite[7] kings against Joshua (Joshua 10:1ff.). By now Jerusalem was in the hands of a Canaanite tribe called Jebusites (cf. Genesis 10:15f.), and despite Joshua's victory over Adoni-zedek, it remained in Jebusite hands, and was apparently called "Jebus" after its occupants. Judges 1 relates that at one time Judah defeated the Jebusites (verse 8) and that the Benjaminites lived for years side by side with the Jebusites here (verse 21); but evidently the Canaanite tribe maintained the actual fortress of the city, strongly fortified against attack.

It was therefore no easy task that awaited David's men; the city lay on a well-fortified hill, and the Jebusite garrison obviously considered it impregnable, taunting David with the words "Never shall you come in here; not till you have disposed of the blind and the lame" (2 Samuel 5:6). Perhaps their over-confidence contributed to their downfall; Joab found a way into the city, and the fortress was in Israelite hands before the Jebusites realized what was happening. This route may well have been a water-shaft; the perennial problem of Jerusalem was its lack of a good water supply within the city walls. But the precise meaning of 2 Samuel 5:8 is uncertain as a comparison of the Revised Standard Version with the New English Bible will show; the parallel in 1 Chronicles 11:6 says nothing of the means by which the capture was achieved.

The capture of Jerusalem was but the first step in David's plans for consolidating his realm and uniting his people. He had at one stroke eliminated the Canaanite barrier cutting Judah off from the other tribes; now he proceeded to turn this hitherto alien territory into the very centre of his kingdom. In the first place, he no doubt recognised its strategic value; just as it had served as a major barrier to the full unity of the tribes of Israel, so now it should serve as Israel's most easily defensible stronghold. The deep ravines which

6. El-Amarna is the modern name of ancient Akhetaton, the capital of Egypt during the reign of Akh-en-aton (mid-fourteenth century B.C.). The Amarna tablets, first discovered in 1887, consist of diplomatic correspondence of his reign and that of his predecessor.

7. In this book the term "Canaanite" is used in its wider sense, of the preIsraelite indigenous inhabitants of Canaan". More strictly the Jebusites and their neighbours were Amorites. See now also J. A. Soggin in J. H. Hayes and J. M. Miller, *Israelite and Judaean History* (OTL: London, 1977) pp. 353-356.

enclose the city on three sides give it admirable natural protection; but there were some weak links in the defences, obviously, or Joab's men would not have captured it so swiftly, and David soon gave some attention to strengthening the fortifications (cf. 2 Samuel 5:9).

Jerusalem not only replaced Adullam as David's stronghold, it also replaced Hebron as David's capital. The jealousy of the northern tribes towards Judah has already been mentioned, and it was a shrewd diplomatic move to transfer the capital out of the territory of Judah. Jerusalem lay on the border between Judah and Benjamin, without ever having been incorporated into either tribal territory. It is widely believed nowadays that David's realm was never an integrated kingdom, but a joint kingdom linked only in the person of the king;[8] one might perhaps compare the union of England and Scotland in the person of James I (James VI of Scotland). If that view of the matter is correct, there will have been all the more reason for David to find a neutral capital. David did all he could to preserve its neutrality, moreover, taking care not to flood the city with Judaean retainers. He made it the royal city, "the city of David". His palace builders were neither Judaean nor Israelite, but Phoenicians, and his personal bodyguard was largely drawn from Philistine ranks. Many Jebusites probably continued to live in Jerusalem, too; it was a Jebusite, Araunah by name, who owned the site of the future temple (2 Samuel 24:16).

David's Jerusalem, therefore, was from the purely secular point of view a very different capital from Saul's Gibeah.[9] But it is not the secular advantages of Jerusalem which have made it the most sacred city on earth to Jew and Christian alike, and the third most holy city in Muslim eyes. David was king in Zion — a name which came to symbolize all the spiritual and religious aspects of the city. The original meaning and application of the name Zion are no longer known for certain, but before long the name became used for the temple hill, and signified the religious capital and centre of Judah, and indeed of all Israel till the kingdom broke into two. It would appear that Zion was the name of the stronghold, the fortified part of the city, at the time of David's capture; but it was not long before David transformed his capture into the holy city, the city of the sanctuary.

Jerusalem had had sacred associations long before David's time.

---

8. This view was first put forward by A. Alt in 1930 and has since gained wide currency; but see G. Buccellati, *Cities and Nations of Ancient Syria* (*Studi Semitici*. 26: Rome, 1967) pp. 48-154, for persuasive counter-arguments and useful bibliography. The present writer is even more doubtful about Alt's arguments for viewing the kingdom of Judah itself as a twin kingdom (Jerusalem over against the rest of Judah), and the Northern Kingdom as yet another twin unit (the city of Samaria over against "Israel").

9. It is possible that Saul made the important city of Gibeon his capital at one time; the evidence is not really conclusive, however. Cf. J. Blenkinsopp, *Gibeon and Israel* (*The Society for O.T. Study Monograph Series,* 2): Cambridge 1972, pp. 63f.

It has sometimes been doubted whether the Salem of Genesis 14:18 is identical with Jerusalem,[10] but there is good reason to think they were indeed one and the same. Jerusalem had a long history of devotion, then, to 'El 'Elyon, "God Most High", whom the Canaanites worshipped and whom Israel recognised to be none other than Yahweh (cf. Genesis 14:22). No Israelite could reasonably object to David's choice of Jerusalem to be his religious capital, since it contained the shrine where Abraham had welcomed and received the blessing of God Most High.

But David was not content merely to take over the Jebusites' sanctuary as it stood. While his people undoubtedly venerated the ancient shrine where their ancestors had worshipped, they possessed a sacred object which probably meant even more to them, linked as it was with their constitution as a nation under Moses — the ark of the covenant. The ark seems to have been virtually neglected during Saul's reign, and it still lay in the obscurity of a little town on the borders of Judah and Benjamin called Kiriath-jearim (1 Samuel 7:1f.) or Baale-judah (2 Samuel 6:2);[11] it could not have been restored to Shiloh, in any case, if indeed that lay in ruins. David accordingly made due preparations, and brought back the ark to Jerusalem, where he installed it in a tent especially pitched for it. 2 Samuel 6 emphasizes the fact that all Israel joined with David in thus setting up a new central sanctuary for the nation, and describes the joy with which everyone, from the king down, celebrated this event. Only the memory of Uzzah's carelessness and death and the boorish attitude of Saul's daughter Michal to her husband David marred the occasion in any way.

To have charge of the shrine David appointed two priests, Abiathar and Zadok. The former had supported David in times of adversity, and we may see his appointment as a just reward for his loyalties; but it was also only proper that the continuity with the old Shiloh priesthood should be preserved. Abiathar was the obvious choice. Zadok's name is the more famous, since he was the father of the line of Jerusalem high-priests for many generations; not until 174 B.C. was the high-priesthood finally removed from the house of Zadok.[12] Nevertheless, the reason why David appointed him to serve alongside Abiathar is something of a mystery. One suggestion is that he was already functioning there, as the Jebusites' chief priest, and that David merely confirmed him in office. To have done so would have helped to cement relationships with the Jebusites, it is true, but it seems improbable that David, diplomat though he was, can have

10. An alternative possibility is to link it with the "Salim" of John 3:23; but the Salem of Psalm 76:2 is undoubtedly Jerusalem.
11. Or perhaps Baalath-judah (= NEB), for which the Baalah of 1 Chronicles 13:6 would be a natural abbreviation in Hebrew.
12. Cf. F. F. Bruce, *Israel and the Nations* (Exeter, 1963), p. 137.

felt any urgent need to give the Jebusites equal treatment in such a fashion. It seems much more probable that Zadok was already a well-known priest in Israel; he may have acted for a time as Saul's priest, or he may have been in charge of the important sanctuary at Gibeon.[13]

But even if Zadok had no previous links with Jerusalem, David by no means neglected the earlier traditions of worship in that city. There is a striking difference between 1 Samuel 13 and 2 Samuel 6; King Saul had offered sacrifice at Gilgal and been sternly rebuked for it by Samuel, but King David did no less in Jerusalem without any word of censure arising. The reason for the contrast is that Saul had no priestly rights in Gilgal, and had usurped Samuel's prerogative by seizing them; but David, far from usurping anyone else's rights, was merely exercising the age-old prerogatives of the king of Jerusalem. To David and his line the oracle ran as follows: "You are a priest for ever, in the succession of Melchizedek" (Psalm 110:4). Melchizedek had been king and priest in Jerusalem; David similarly appears to have exercised both functions, although he may well have delegated some of his priestly duties to his sons (cf. 2 Samuel 8:18).[14] It appears from 1 Chronicles 15f. that David's own chief services to the shrine lay in the realm of organization of the sacred personnel, and especially of the musical enrichment of the order of worship.

The capture of Jerusalem was thus a most significant event in Israel's history, and indeed in the history of civilization and of faith. It was the genius and insight of one man that brought this about. From a purely military point of view, the city's capture was but one step in the process of mastering and consolidating David's kingdom. Though the Bible nowhere records the fact, David must have gone on to take possession of all the non-Israelite cities within the confines of Israel. The Jerusalem enclave had been one Canaanite obstacle to Israelite unity; Israel's other major defensive weakness, which the Philistines had so recently exploited with great success, was the Plain of Jezreel. Such cities as Megiddo and Beth-shan had been independent too long for Israel's good, and there is no doubt that David made them part of his kingdom; they were certainly in Solomon's hands at the start of his reign (cf. 1 Kings 4:12). Possibly some of these cities tried to oppose David, but it is probable that most were shrewd enough to realize that if even the Philistines were no match for David's armies, they themselves had no choice but to

13. See the discussion by J. Mauchline, "Aaronite and Zadokite priests", *GUOST* 21(1965-6), pp. 1-11. A point to be borne in mind is that Zadok was of Levitical stock, according to 1 Chronicles 24:1-6.

14. The Hebrew text of 2 Samuel 8:18 states unequivocally that they were "priests" (there are no adequate grounds for alternative renderings), but it has been argued that originally the text read "administrators". Cf. G. J. Wenham, *Were David's sons priests? ZAW* 87 (1975) pp. 79-82.

submit. Megiddo suffered destruction at about this period, so it
would seem that it was one city which did try to resist David.[15]

As for the Philistines, David evidently believed in the adage that
the best form of defence is attack, and he asserted his supremacy
over them in further victories. He temporarily wrested one of their
five major cities, Gath, from their control, according to 1 Chronicles
18:1. But for the most part he was satisfied that they should pay him
tribute (cf. 2 Samuel 8:11f.).

In the three centuries or so that separated Moses from Solomon,
no major power was in a position to impede either the Israelite
occupation of Palestine or her rise to power. In this fact the Jew and
Christian alike may well see the hand of God overruling in history.
The nearest potential enemies of any size were Assyria and Egypt —
the Hittite empire, based on eastern Asia Minor, had collapsed
about 1200 B.C. Assyria, however, was at a low ebb throughout this
period, due to pressures from the mountain peoples to the north and
east of Assyria, and more particularly from the Aramaeans, to the
west of them, who swarmed into what we know as Syria. The
Assyrians were thus far too busy keeping their own territory intact to
pose any threat to Israel as yet. Egypt, which had previously
dominated Syria-Palestine, grew weak about 1200 B.C., due very
largely to internal problems and pressures, and by David's time its
kings were only too glad to seek alliances and friendships with
smaller Palestinian states. Thus the small states of Syria-Palestine
were left free to pursue their own policies, and David made the best
possible use of his opportunities. We do not know what precipitated
most of his campaigns, but the details provided in 2 Samuel 10
regarding the outbreak of David's war with the Ammonites give us
some insight into the general picture. The Philistines, the
Aramaeans, and the Israelites were engaged in a power struggle;
and smaller states no doubt formed alliances with one or another of
these. Ammon at one time supported Israel (cf. 2 Samuel 10:2), but
the day came — probably after the Philistines were defeated —
when her king, Hanun, began to suspect David's intentions. He
therefore gratuitously insulted David's envoys, and at the same time
took the precaution of making alliance with several Aramaean
kingdoms. The result was that David became involved in a war of
considerable dimensions, from which he eventually emerged the
victor. Ammon was captured, and the Aramaeans subdued and
forced to pay tribute.

The campaigns against Moab and Edom may have started in
somewhat similar fashion. During Saul's reign, David had been on

15. Cf. Y. Yadin, *BA* 33 (1970), p. 95. We may further note the very plausible
suggestion that David implemented the instructions of Joshua 21 regarding Levitical
cities, many of which were now frontier cities or places of strategic importance; cf. J.
Gray, *Joshua, Judges and Ruth (NCB:* London, 1967) pp. 174f.

good terms with the king of Moab, for he had sent his parents there (1 Samuel 22:3f.). David's own great-grandmother, Ruth, had been a Moabitess (Ruth 4:13ff.). So his conquest of Moab and his subsequent savage treatment of the Moabites (2 Samuel 8:2) suggest that they must have broken faith with him in some particularly treacherous fashion. We can only guess, but it is at least conceivable that they took the opportunity to attack him when he was engaged in the life-and-death struggle with the major foe, the Philistines.

The casual reader of the Bible no doubt gets the impression that the Philistines were a single political unity, and that the Syrians (or Aramaeans) were too. We have already noted that on the contrary the Philistines were divided into five major units; but it is at least true that the Philistines seem to have co-ordinated well, and for practical purposes may be viewed as a political entity. The Aramaeans were more fragmented; a century or two later, the Aramaean state which played a continuous part in Israel's affairs was the kingdom of Damascus, and when the Old Testament speaks of "the Syrians" without further definition, it is nearly always Damascus that is intended. In David's reign, several small Aramaean kingdoms were drawn into alliance with the Ammonites, and yet another, Damascus, came to the aid of one of its neighbours, Zobah (2 Samuel 8:5f.). All were alike defeated by David. But one Aramaean kingdom, Geshur, is not mentioned in this connection. Earlier in his career, David had married a princess of Geshur, who bore him Absalom (cf. 2 Samuel 3:3). This will have been a "diplomatic" marriage, and it probably served to keep Geshur neutral during David's wars with the Aramaean states. There is no evidence that David indulged in wanton aggression on all his weaker neighbours. For all we know to the contrary, some provocation lay behind all his campaigns. Nevertheless one can see why the courtiers of the Ammonite king had their suspicions of David's motives.

At any rate, the result of David's wars was that he dominated an area, to the east of his own territory, which extended from the Red Sea (the Gulf of Aqaba) in the south up as far as the Euphrates. In the semi-wilderness south of Judah the Amalekites and other nomadic tribes were subdued (cf. 2 Samuel 8:12), and on Judah's west flank the Philistines were submissive. To the north-west lay the territory of the Phoenicians, centred round the cities of Tyre and Sidon. With them, David entered into a treaty relationship, apparently on a friendly basis, although it is clear that it was David who dictated the terms. The Phoenicians were great maritime traders, and they were content to expand by colonization overseas; otherwise this survivor of the old Canaanite civilization might well have proved troublesome to Israel in later years.

CHAPTER 5

David's Later Years

THUS by the middle of David's reign, the ancient covenant promise to Abraham had been fulfilled: "To your descendants I give this land from the River of Egypt to the Great River, the river Euphrates" (Genesis 15:18). David ruled, directly or indirectly, all the territory between the Wadi el-Arish and the upper Euphrates. In the second half of his reign he had only to consolidate his realm. There is no doubt that he must have brought in a great many administrative changes and innovations, quite apart from the new capital, Jerusalem, and all that it meant to Israel and Judah. Saul had left a kingdom in name, which was still not very much more than a loosely-knit confederacy of tribes; David must have done much to break down the tribal system, not least by incorporating Canaanite cities and communities into Israel. Of the details of his administration, however, we know remarkably little, apart from two lists of his chief officials (2 Samuel 8:16ff., 20:23-26). The census recorded in 2 Samuel 24 was no doubt intended to provide information which could be used both for tax purposes and as a basis for conscription to the army. In the days of the Judges, the various leaders of Israel had been content to summon smallholders from their farms when battles were necessary; but David's victories could not have been achieved nor his conquests maintained without a standing army, which then as now lays a burden on a country's economy.[1]

The census did not take place without disaster; even Joab was opposed to the measure, and it seems fair to assume that the blame for the ensuing pestilence was laid at David's door by many of the

---

1. For other details of David's administration that may be deduced from the biblical material, cf. J. Bright, *op. cit.*, pp. 201ff.

1. Shalmaneser III in his chariot

2. Jehu, 'son of Omri', bows before Shalmaneser III. From the Black Obelisk of Shalmaneser III

people; had not the king himself confessed to sin and folly (2 Samuel 24:10)? No doubt too there were those who clung to the memory of Saul, and viewed David as a usurper; the fate of Saul's family recorded in 2 Samuel 21 will have angered such people, although David's treament of Saul's grandson Mephibosheth (2 Samuel 9) may have done something to mitigate their bitterness. It is clear, however, that David tried to keep too much of the judicial administration in his own hands, a mistake which caused a certain amount of frustration and discontent (cf. 2 Samuel 15:3ff.). However, these factors by themselves would have come nowhere near toppling David from his throne. The threat to David came from within his own family.

In nearly every respect David showed himself an abler, shrewder and more devout ruler than Saul — with one glaring exception. Saul, so far as we know, had only two wives, and those not necessarily simultaneously; but David can scarcely be said to have observed the warning of Deuteronomy 17:17. His early marriages, at least, were an act of policy: Michal linked him with the house of Saul, Abigail and Ahinoam (1 Samuel 25:42f.) brought him into wealthy land-owning families in both the south and the north of the land, and Maacah (2 Samuel 3:3) gave him a treaty relationship with the kingdom of Geshur. What inspired most of the other marriages we do not know; but subsequent events suggest that the only woman David married for love was Bathsheba, and where she was concerned lust, adultery and murder began the story of their liaison.

The story of David and Bathsheba needs no re-telling. No modern writers could hope to match the skill and effectiveness with which Nathan the prophet pointed the moral (2 Samuel 12). If anyone is tempted to take an "objective" standpoint, and talk about the general moral standards of the ancient world and its rulers, it is sufficient to reply that Israel's sacred statute books promulgated much higher standards — and that David himself made the solemn confession "I have sinned against the LORD" (2 Samuel 12:13). The Second Book of Samuel represents the Bathsheba affair as the turning point in David's career; from now on he was to encounter problem after problem. R. A. Carlson has summed up David's career from this point on as "David under the curse."[2]

There was a very practical reason why David's latter years were far from happy. By building up a considerable harem, he invited palace intrigues, which could only intensify with the passing years, as his sons grew to manhood. There was as yet no precedent in Israel for the smooth transition of power from one king to the next, and it looks as if David never took the step of nominating a crown prince.

2. R. A. Carlson, *David, the Chosen King* (Uppsala, 1964), Part Two, *passim*.

He favoured Solomon, Bathsheba's son, but it is significant that at
the very end of his reign, Bathsheba admonished him, "Did you not,
my lord the king, swear to your maidservant, saying, 'Solomon your
son shall reign after me'?" In other words, David's oath to that
effect had been a private and personal one to Bathsheba alone.

Solomon was by no means the eldest son. If Michal had ever given
birth to a son, he would have had a special claim to the throne, as
Saul's grandson and David's son; but Michal never had a child (cf.
2 Samuel 6:23). David's first-born was Amnon, and five other sons
were born to him before he transferred his capital from Hebron (2
Samuel 3:2ff.); and if the list of 2 Samuel 5:14ff. is in chronological
order, Solomon was not even the first son born in Jerusalem. In
terms of normal inheritance, therefore, Solomon's claim to the
throne was slender. During Israel's previous history, however, the
men who had claimed leadership were recognised not for any noble
lineage but because they showed themselves to be men of ability and
courage and action. This had been true of the "Judges", of course,
but of Saul and David too. The Judges had also been recognised as
men of God's appointment; they had demonstrated that they were
governed by the Spirit of God, and some at least had had the
unequivocal support of priests and prophets. In such circumstances
of background and environment, therefore, any ambitious son of
David might seek to win the crown by setting out to attract popular
and prophetic support.

Whether or not David's eldest son, Amnon, was at all ambitious,
there is no doubt that the third son, Absalom, had every intention of
securing the throne for himself. Possibly the second son, Chileab,
died in childhood or adolescence; at any rate, he took no part
whatever in the succession struggle, and only Amnon seems to have
stood in Absalom's way. Absalom accordingly took steps to remove
the obstacle Amnon presented. Amnon for his part seems to have
been no very attractive character, and he certainly gave Absalom
every reason to hate him. David's example of sexual promiscuity
was followed by Amnon, who raped and humiliated his half-sister
Tamar — Absalom's full sister. It now became apparent that another
fault of David's was over-indulgence of his children, for although he
was extremely angered by Amnon's conduct, he did nothing at all to
punish the wrongdoer. But in the Bathsheba affair, David had set
another bad example, that of suborning to murder; it was Absalom
who proceeded to follow that precedent, apparently feeling no
conscience about it nor fearing punishment for it.

It took Absalom two full years to lay his plans and put them
into effect. A carefully-arranged festal gathering at Baal-hazor gave
him the opportunity to assassinate Amnon. Apparently he had all
his brothers and half-brothers at his mercy, but only Amnon lost his
life; it looks as if Absalom did not consider Solomon a potential

rival. In any case, Absalom was in no hurry, and went off into self-imposed exile at his mother's home, the royal court of Geshur. Absalom's resolve only hardened with the passage of time, but he was shrewd enough to realise that his father's temperament was different, and that in time David would be prepared to let bygones be bygones. And so it turned out; three years after Amnon's death, David needed little persuasion to invite the fratricide home again, once Joab, his commander-in-chief and long-standing adviser, applied a little pressure. Absalom returned to Jerusalem, accordingly, only to find that David had some sort of punishment in mind for him after all — to deny him a place in the royal court. There is no doubt that Absalom found it a very severe punishment; that the crown prince (in his own estimation, at least) should be denied every court privilege was a humiliation he could not brook. He endured it in silence for two years, and then set about rectifying the matter in a most high-handed fashion. He challenged his father to put him on trial, but he knew well enough David would do no such thing. Whether he knew it or not, however, Absalom had made a bad enemy; Joab was not the man to forget or forgive the wanton destruction of his property (2 Samuel 14:28ff.).

If David thought the incident closed when he welcomed Absalom back to court, he was sadly mistaken. The way now lay open for Absalom to claim the crown when his father died; but with feelings of bitter resentment towards his father, the young man saw no reason to wait so long. Four years later he staged a *coup d'état* which all but succeeded; it is certain that it would have been completely successful if Joab and his troops had not remained devotedly loyal to David.

One can with little difficulty put oneself in Absalom's position and understand — without approving — why he acted as he did. The puzzle is why and how he managed to win such a following. Naturally enough, there were those who like Shimei (2 Samuel 16:5ff.) clung to the memory of Saul and felt hatred towards David. There were also those who had reason to be discontented with David's administration — and 2 Samuel 15:1ff. indicates how Absalom played on such feeling and sought to win such people to his side. Nor must we discount Absalom's personal attractiveness and persuasive qualities. Moreover, since he was David's eldest surviving son, there was every chance that the general populace would accept the new *status quo* readily enough once David had been put out of the way. It is clear that Absalom hoped to achieve his goal by speed and surprise. But when all that is said and done, it still remains almost certain that Absalom must have drawn considerable support from other quarters. His army was no small one; a figure of 12,000 is mentioned in 2 Samuel 17:1 and in the final battle 20,000 are said to have fallen (2 Samuel 18:7). Nor can these have been professional soldiers, for the army remained loyal to David.

It is difficult sometimes to decide whether Old Testament references to "Israel" mean the whole nation including Judah, or account.[7] The exact details given in 2 Samuel 18:19ff. suggest that we are reading the words of a participator in the events, and this in the revolt. But what about Judah, David's own tribe? In view of the fact that it was at Hebron, in Judah, where Absalom first raised the standard of revolt, we cannot exonerate Judah. It is also significant that once Absalom was dead, the elders of Judah showed themselves extremely embarrassed by the whole affair (cf. 2 Samuel 19:11). One gets the impression that Judah was quite stongly pro-Absalom, while the northern tribes were more divided on the issue. Conceivably Absalom adopted different tactics in the two regions, exploiting administative deficiencies in the north, and patriotic feelings in the south. (Had not David "abandoned" Hebron, and gone out of his way to court the northerners?) 2 Samuel 17:14 strongly suggests, moreover, that Absalom had restored the tribal elders to a position David had in effect taken from them.[3] It has also been suggested in the light of 1 Chronicles 22:8 and 28:3 that David had gained a reputation for ruthlessness and bloodshed, perhaps largely because of the many battles he had had to fight, and that this was the major cause of the widespread disaffection.[4]

Whatever his tactics, Absalom succeeded in mobilizing a large army against his father without arousing any suspicions beforehand: no mean feat. Far from being forewarned or forearmed, David had little enough time to organize his own escape, as 2 Samuel 15 makes clear. Flight was the only course open to him for the moment, and probably there was only one compass direction, the east, which offered any safety. To the west lay little military strength, and David could scarcely flee to the Philistines now, as he had done in earlier days. To the north lay Ephraim, the most powerful of the northern tribes, and David had no time to attempt to gauge the degree of its disaffection. The southern road was out of the question, for Absalom was already marching along it towards Jerusalem. But to the east lay the Jordan, and beyond it safety. In Transjordan, there was plenty of difficult terrain, which could (and in the end, did) test Absalom's untried soldiery. David seems to have known that he could rely on the loyalty of the Transjordanian tribes; they were much more open to attack from outside than other parts of Israel, and they no doubt appreciated and valued the security David had given them. Rich landowners like Shobi and Machir and Barzillai (2 Samuel 17:27ff.) had profited from the peace and security David had brought them, and they were prepared to pay heavily to maintain David in power.

3. Cf. Y. Aharoni, *LB*, p. 274.
4. Cf. J. Weingreen, *VT* 19 (1969), pp. 263-266.

Another factor was that many of David's loyal troops were already stationed in Transjordan, simply because that was the part of Israel most open to enemy attack; once he reached Mahanaim, David was soon able to muster a competent army.

Thus we find David taking the road east out of Jerusalem, across the Kidron ravine and passing Olivet, then downhill all the way to the Jordan some twenty miles away. Absalom could not hope to cut off this route, for between the southern and eastern roads out of Jerusalem lay the barren and uninviting hills of the wilderness of Judah. Absalom's real hope of lasting success lay in swift immediate pursuit of David, but the young usurper was not shrewd enough as a strategist to appreciate the fact.

David's capital was abandoned to Absalom; even the royal concubines were left behind. In the brief interim before Absalom arrived in the city, it was left to individuals to make their own decisions whom to support. It is no surprise that Benjaminites and relatives of Saul like Shimei seized the chance to vilify David, whom they regarded as a usurper. Possibly even Mephibosheth was tempted to desert David; his servant Ziba accused him of this, and though Mephibosheth later denied it, he was clearly in no position to prove his innocence, and it looks as if David was uncertain whose story to believe (cf. 2 Samuel 19:29). Ziba, we may well believe, had his eye on the main chance; in that case, it is interesting to note how swiftly he decided to support David, not Absalom.

Valuable support for David's cause came from the priesthood (15:24), apparently unanimously. David insisted that they should remain in Jerusalem, but they would there serve to undermine Absalom's cause and to provide an information service for David. Even more valuable were the services rendered by Hushai, who had the very difficult task of offering Absalom bad advice and of making it sound like good counsel. This he achieved brilliantly.

If Absalom had little or no support from the religious authorities, he had one adviser who had a reputation for remarkably sagacious counsel, as reliable as that which could be obtained from God himself through the priesthood (16:23). His name was Ahithophel.[5] Absalom knew beforehand that he could count on Ahithophel (15:12). We are never told Ahithophel's motives for turning against David; if indeed he was Bathsheba's grandfather, it may be conjectured that he had conceived a hatred of David for bringing shame on Bathsheba.[6]

Ahithophel's advice to Absalom was not in the least ambiguous or halfhearted. First, Absalom must burn his boats behind him; by

---

5. On the role of Ahithophel, see W. McKane, *Prophets and Wise Men* (SBT 44: London, 1965), pp. 55-62.
6. Cf. E. R. Dalglish, *IDB* I, p. 74 (s.v. "Ahithophel"). Ahithophel had a son Eliam (2 Samuel 23:34), and Bathsheba's father bore the same name (2 Samuel 11:3).

publicly appropriating David's harem, he would put himself in a position from which there could be no turning back. This was shrewd counsel, for if Absalom had ever had second thoughts and been reconciled to David, no doubt he would have been forgiven; but his followers would then have found themselves in a very invidious position. Hushai raised no objection to this counsel; perhaps he felt that David's cause would be best served if Absalom took a step from which there could be no turning back. Absalom took the advice (16:20ff.), and thereby fulfilled Nathan's prediction to David (cf. 12:11f.).

Ahithophel's military advice was equally practical and unequivocal; David must be pursued immediately, before he could reorganize, and be killed. Once David was dead, further opposition to Absalom would be pointless, for who could support a dead king? Ahithophel offered to organize the pursuit himself. The shrewdness of this counsel was self-evident, and Hushai was convinced that this plan must be scotched, if David were to survive and regain the throne. His counter-proposal was that Absalom should muster the biggest army possible, and overwhelm David by sheer weight of numbers; he knew full well that this would take time, and time was what David badly needed. Hushai used every artifice of emotive language and appealed to Absalom's vanity, with the result that his plan of campaign was adopted. The shrewd Ahithophel did not need to wait to see what would happen; he went straight home and committed suicide (17:23f.).

Undaunted by the loss of his best adviser, Absalom put Hushai's policy into effect, and presently marched at the head of a very big but inexperienced army into Transjordan, where he could do nothing but allow David to select the battleground. What experience of battle Absalom's commander Amasa had, we do not know; but he was no match for Joab and David's seasoned troops. The battle was joined in wooded country, and the brief statement of 2 Samuel 18:8 is eloquent: "the forest took toll of more people that day than the sword". Absalom himself was one victim of the forest; in his haste to elude some of David's men, he directed his mule carelessly, and was left helplessly dangling in mid-air when his luxuriant hair became entangled in an oak tree. David had given the strictest instructions that Absalom's life was to be spared, but the ruthless Joab saw the folly of any such unwarranted clemency, and himself ensured the usurper's death. Apart from any long-term advantages in Absalom's death, Joab saw clearly that it would immediately end the revolt just as Ahithophel had anticipated that David's death would quell opposition to Absalom. Too many men had already been killed in the battle, and Joab was able to pull back his troops as soon as Absalom was dead (18:15f.).

The story of how David heard the news of his rebel son's death, and of his reactions to it, is told with a pathos and realism that affects every reader. It is widely held, even by those who are in general fairly sceptical about the historical accuracy of Old Testament books, that in these chapters we have a scarcely-edited eye-witness account.[7] The exact details given in 2 Samuel 18:19ff. suggest that we are reading the words of a participator in the events, and this would very probably be Zadok's son, Ahimaaz. The whole of 2 Samuel 9-20 and 1 Kings 1f. may derive from him, for Zadok and his family must have been well placed to know what went on in the palace.

It appears that David was so beside himself with grief over Absalom's death that he was in danger of letting the situation slip. Absalom's defeat and death paved the way for David to take firm control of his kingdom once again, but strong and effective action was necessary. Joab evidently feared that anarchy would soon overtake the realm, and he urged David in typically blunt and brutal terms to get control of himself and his affairs. David responded to Joab's exhortations, although he was already too late to prevent something of a breach between Judah and the northern tribes. The situation compelled him to make a special appeal to his own tribe Judah, and any hint of favouritism was bound to cause annoyance and jealousy to the northern tribesmen, particularly if their loyalty to David had been less divided then Judah's. But David dared not lose the support of Judah, and he had to risk northern resentment. It is partcularly surprising to see that he appointed the rebel commander-in-chief as his own leading military officer, displacing Joab; it is difficult to decide whether the chief reason for such a move was political necessity, the wish to conciliate, or simply spite towards Joab.

Judah was successfully wooed by David, whose family continued to reign in Judah for more than three centuries. Most of the men of the north pocketed their pride and allowed David to resume his control over them; he had after all brought security and a measure of prosperity, and there was no viable alternative. Nevertheless there was an abortive attempt to detach the northern tribes from David. This second rebellion was led by a Benjaminite, Sheba by name, who unlike Absalom endeavoured to appeal to inter-tribal jealousies: "What share have we in David? We have no lot in the son of Jesse. Away to your homes, O Israel" (20:1).

Probably we should not take the statement "the men of Israel all left David" (20:2) too literally. We may well believe that many took the line of least resistance, and waited to see what would happen;

7. R. N. Whybray is a rare exception; see his *The Succession Narrative (SBT* ii, 9: London, 1968), pp. 10-19. See now J. A. Soggin in J. H. Hayes and J. M. Miller, *Israelite and Judaean History* (OTL: London, 1977), pp. 337f; D. M. Gunn, *The Story of King David* (JSOT Supplement 6: Sheffield 1978).

but it is at any rate clear from the sequel that Sheba gained very little active support. None of the garrison cities opened their gates to him; despite a false start, David's troops speedily pursued him to the northern limit of Israelite territory, the city of Abel of Beth-maacah, which lay very near Dan (the traditional northern outpost). Thanks to the intervention of a wise woman of the city, which appears to have been renowned for sagacity, not even a battle was necessary, and it would appear that the only man to lose his life was Sheba himself. Similarly the only recorded casualty on David's side was the commander-in-chief, Amasa, and he was killed not by Sheba's troops but by the ruthless and efficient Joab, who thus resumed his position as David's general.

David's rule was not again threatened, and on the surface all seemed as it had been before Absalom's revolt. But not only was David himself a different man, never now to be free from palace intrigues; his kingdom had lost its inner unity. If he had been politically neutral in earlier years, he was now firmly aligned with Judah, at least in people's minds. The seeds of dissension were there, and would spring up and come to fruition half a century later.

For the rest of David's reign, we have no record of events; perhaps there was in any case little to record, but the biblical writer limits his interest to the question of the succession. When we next meet David, he is an old and failing man (1 Kings 1:1).[8] He had nominated Solomon to succeed him, but had taken insufficient care to ensure a smooth succession, and his eldest surviving son, Adonijah, saw a chance to seize the throne. Like Absalom before him, he laid careful plans; but where Absalom had relied chiefly on popular support, secrecy and speed, Adonijah saw the value of powerful and influential friends. Joab was the most notable military figure in the land, and Abiathar the senior representative of the priesthood; it is a testimony to Adonijah's personality that he was able to win the allegiance of them both. They had both served David's interests loyally for many years.

With the full support of the army and the religious authorities behind him, Adonijah's cause could not have failed; but in fact he had neither. If Abiathar sided with Adonijah, his colleague Zadok did not, and neither did the outstanding prophet of the time, Nathan. Of more immediate practical importance, however, was the fact that Joab shared the military power with Benaiah, and the latter was opposed to Adonijah. On paper, Joab was the senior officer; but Benaiah, the commander of David's personal troops (cf. 2 Samuel 20:23), was in the position of having loyal soldiers on the spot, and it was their presence which tipped the scales in Solomon's favour.

8. The last four chapters of 2 Samuel present a series of episodes drawn from earlier periods of the reign of David.

The climax came when Adonijah, who had made no secret of his aspirations (cf. 1 Kings 1:5), decided that the time for action had arrived and made preparations to hold a sacrificial meal at En-rogel, just outside Jerusalem. There is no doubt that is own coronation was to have been the ''grand finale'' of this meal. His neglect to invite Solomon and others (1 Kings 1:10) showed that he had no intention of ''peaceful coexistence'' with them, as Professor Gray puts it,[9] and Solomon's supporters, who had obviously been waiting for Adonijah to make a rash move, immediately went into action. David was easily persuaded to make Solomon his co-regent, and Adonijah was adroitly out-manoeuvred.

Ancient Jerusalem had only two natural sources of water, both of them located just east of the city, outside the walls. The more southerly of the two was En-rogel, today's ''Job's Well'', beside the village of Silwan, at the southern end of the Kidron Valley; it was there that the abortive coronation of Adonijah took place. Solomon's party, with David's blessing, held their ceremony at the other spring, Gihon (now commonly known as ''the Virgin's Fountain''), which lay rather nearer the city, but was yet within earshot of En-rogel. 1 Kings 1 relates how the pomp and ceremony of Solomon's procession from Gihon back into the city was audible to Adonijah and his guests; their consternation may be imagined.

These events had their sequel; most notably, they led to the removal of Abiathar from the joint priesthood, which left Zadok and his successors in sole possession of the high priestly office. But that did not occur till after David's death.

We do not know how long the co-regency lasted — a year or two at most, one would think, for David was already very old and infirm when Solomon's coronation took place. David's days of forceful action had passed, but he was still capable of sagacious advice, as we see in his final charge to Solomon, recounted in 1 Kings 2:1ff. Much of this was unexceptionable: ''Be strong and show yourself a man, Fulfil your duty to the LORD your God; conform to his ways, observe his statutes and his commandments, his judgements and his solemn precepts, as they are written in the law of Moses, so that you may prosper in whatever you do and whichever way you turn, and that the Lord may fulfil this promise that he made about me: 'If your descendants take care to walk faithfully in my sight with all their heart and with all their soul, you shall never lack a successor on the throne of Israel' '' (verses 2-4). This advice Solomon should have heeded carefully. But David went on to show a vindictive spirit, very different from the clemency he exercised throughout his reign. One can understand his feeling towards his old enemy Shimei, but nobody had served David more loyally than Joab, whose recent

9. J. Gray, *Kings*,[2] p. 84.

espousal of Adonijah's cause showed his opposition to Solomon, not his disloyalty to David. David's hatred of Joab no doubt dated from the death of Absalom, but till his senility the king kept such unworthy thoughts in check. In extenuation, we may observe that David probably wished Solomon to have a more trouble-free reign that he had himself experienced and accordingly urged him to give short shrift to potential trouble-makers. At any rate, whatever the morality of it, the advice was shrewd, and Solomon not only accepted it but built upon it.

CHAPTER 6

The Reign of Solomon

JOAB was promptly struck down, even though he had sought sanctuary at the altar (1 Kings 2:28ff.). Shimei was forced to move his home to Jerusalem, where his activities could be observed, and he was forbidden to leave the city on pain of death; one single and evidently harmless breach of this royal edict resulted in his summary execution (1 Kings 2:36ff). Nor was Abiathar's support of Solomon's rival overlooked; he was promptly dismissed from the priesthood, which thereby lost its last link with the old priestly line at Shiloh (1 Kings 2:26f.); Abiathar's retirement to private life left Zadok without any rival. It is not recorded that David recommended Abiathar's dismissal, and it is hard to believe that he would have wished it.

Finally, what of the pretender to the throne, Adonijah himself? David gave Solomon no instructions about him either, and one imagines that David would have been as lenient with him as he had been with Absalom. Evidently Solomon took no action against his elder brother until David had died, because the pretext for Solomon to have Adonijah killed was the latter's request to marry Abishag, who was David's concubine at the end of his life (1 Kings 1:1ff.). Quite possibly Adonijah was genuinely attracted by the beautiful Abishag, but the fact remained that to appropriate a king's concubine was tantamount to a claim to the throne, and one may suspect that Adonijah still had hopes of ousting Solomon. Solomon, at least, chose to see his brother's request in this light, and immediately instructed Benaiah to have Adonijah executed (1 Kings 2:13ff.).

The Bible puts it in a nutshell: "Thus Solomon's royal power was securely established" (1 Kings 2:46). Indeed it was; and it is interesting to compare his position now with that of his two predecessors, Saul and David, at the start of their reigns. Both had faced a measure of suspicion or opposition from their own countrymen; both had met this problem by resolute action, coupled with understanding and leniency. Solomon, however, eliminated his rivals and potential enemies swiftly and ruthlessly. Saul and David had been forced to woo their subjects and win their loyalty, in order to face the major threat posed by the Philistines; Solomon had no similar need for diplomacy, since no foreign power now menaced the realm, and his high-handed actions towards Adonijah and his associates seem to have set the keynote for his reign, to judge by 1 Kings 12:4.

A more striking and more obvious contrast is to be seen in the political situations inherited by Saul and David on the one hand, Solomon on the other. Both Saul and David had come to the throne in circumstances of severe Philistine pressures, and both had had to fight to maintain their positions; but Solomon inherited a large — too large for easy administration — and relatively peaceful realm, and his task was that of organization and consolidation. Israel needed a sound administration and a sound economy.

The Bible offers us some interesting and informative details of Solomon's economic measures. If Israel had relatively little in the way of mineral resources,[1] she was exceptionally well-placed for trade and commerce. Solomon controlled an area which separated the Mediterranean from the great Syro-Arabian desert to the east; overland trade between Arabia and Asia Minor, between Egypt and Mesopotamia, could be carried out only with his good will. Solomon saw lucrative possibilities here, for himself and for the state, and 1 Kings 10 describes, among other things, some of the more exotic and costly treasures which were brought into his court — "gold, silver, ivory, apes and monkeys" (v.22). The final paragraph of the chapter tells how he acted as a middle-man in large-scale trading in horses and chariots. The details of this enterprise are not entirely clear, but it seems likely that he acquired his supply of horses from Cilicia (in south-east Asia Minor), and the chariots from Egypt.[2]

It is in the same context of trade and commerce that the story of the Queen of Sheba is to be read. The story (told in 1 Kings 10:1ff.) has caught the imagination of countless readers, and it has become much embellished in legend,[3] but that should lead no-one to suppose that the original narrative is just a fairy-tale. The queen supplied

1. Modern Israel is aware of many more mineral resources than ancient Israel would have appreciated.

2. Kue (NEB "Coa") was in Asia Minor, and so was Musri, which is probably the original reading in v.28 (instead of Hebrew *mitsroyim*, "Egypt"); but perhaps "Egypt" should be retained in v.29. See J. Gray, *Kings, ad loc;* W. F. Albright, *Archaeology and the Religion of Israel*[3] (Baltimore. 1953), p. 135.

3. Not least in Ethiopia; cf. E. Ullendorff, *Ethiopia and the Bible*, (London, 1968), ch.3.

Solomon with gold, spices and precious stones, in return for which he gave her "all she desired, whatever she asked"; undoubtedly her trade mission resulted in a commercial alliance profitable to both parties. Whether the "Sheba" from which she came was the well-known territory in South Arabia or a smaller kingdom in the northern part of the Arabian peninsula is not certain.[4]

Nor was Solomon's trading confined to overland routes; he had a fleet of ships built at Ezion-geber from which an important maritime trade in the Red Sea could be conducted (1 Kings 9:26ff., 10:11f.). David's conquest of Edom, opening the route to the Gulf of Aqaba, was thus turned to good account.

One natural resource from which Solomon profited to a limited extent was the copper abundant in the Negeb, in the far south of his realm. In this area some copper mines were exploited, and no doubt some of the copper was exported from Solomon's Red Sea port of Ezion-geber (the Elath of later times).

N. Glueck, who first excavated Ezion-geber, described it as the "Pittsburgh of Palestine",[5] but more recent assessment of the site indicates that it was not in fact a refinery, although refining was carried out near the mines, and metal work in Ezion-geber.[6] 1 Kings 7:46 mentions a foundry, further north, between the Sea of Galilee and the Dead Sea; if the ancient Greek translation of this verse is to be believed, a process of sand casting was employed here.[7] Archaeological evidence suggests that Solomon did not employ his country's mineral resources so thoroughly as he might have done.

Two major trade alliances were concluded, with Egypt and Phoenicia. Solomon married an Egyptian princess, and reaped an immediate advantage, for the dowry proved to be an important city, Gezer, which lay between Jerusalem and the Mediterranean coast. Even David had never wrested it from the Canaanites, but the Egyptian king had recently attacked and captured it (1 Kings 9:16). No doubt Solomon went on to reap many commercial benefits from the alliance with Egypt. No such political marriage was necessary in the case of Phoenicia, for the king of Tyre, Hiram, had been on treaty terms with David and remained so with Solomon.[8] Hiram must have gained considerable commercial profit from the alliance, but Solomon benefited even more, since he was able to call upon Phoenician skills as yet undeveloped by the Israelites, in particular seamanship and architecture.

So much for the credit side of the ledger; there is no doubt that

4. See J. Gray, *ad loc.* Yet another possibility is the "Horn" of Africa.
5. N. Glueck, *The Other Side of the Jordan* (New Haven, 1940), p. 94.
6. See Y. Aharoni, *LB*, p. 274n.
7. So JB. See F. F. Bruce, *op cit.* p. 36, for other possible meanings of the verse.
8. Cf. F. C. Fensham, *VTS* 17 (Leiden, 1969), pp. 71-87.

Solomon achieved a state income undreamed of by Saul or even David. He had inherited peace, and he took every opportunity to turn peace into prosperity. In the early and middle years of his long reign he must have achieved this aim; yet he left a largely bankrupt kingdom to his son. The trouble was that his income was exceeded by his expenditure. Much of the expenditure was necessary and legitimate, but much besides was wanton personal extravagance. He and all his court despised silver, we are told, while where his many building projects were concerned, he denied himself nothing (1 Kings 10:21; 9:19). The description in 1 Kings 10 of the magnificence of his court includes no moral comments; the details speak for themselves.

Solomon's most famous building project was the temple at Jerusalem, though it may be doubted whether it was his greatest architectural feat; it took nearly twice as long to build the royal palace adjoining the temple. He also enlarged the city considerably, and repaired its fortifications. Both buildings required an enormous amount of materials and workmanship from the Phoenicians, and Solomon could not afford to pay full costs; he had to detach twenty cities of Galilee from his kingdom and donate them to Hiram — who clearly felt he had got the worst of the bargain (1 Kings 9:10-13).[9] The royal palace was the last word in luxury; and Solomon's harem was of no less luxurious dimensions (1 Kings 11:1ff.). Even in his maritime trading ventures he found himself dependent on Phoenician skills and co-operation. Long before his reign ended, Solomon was obliged to rely heavily on taxation and on forced, unpaid labour (*corvée*). David's wars had ensured a good supply of slave labour, for so prisoners-of-war were regularly employed in the ancient world; but Solomon fought no wars, and he was forced eventually to raise a levy of 30,000 free-born citizens of Israel (1 Kings 5:13). It would seem from the sequel (1 Kings 12) that he took steps to impose a lesser burden on his own Judah than on the other tribes.

Thus the state revenues suffered and the citizenry suffered from Solomon's excesses. Nor was that all; in his anxiety to achieve good terms with his neighbours, he showed a religious tolerance towards them which, in the biblical writer's view of the matter, amounted to prostrating himself before their gods (1 Kings 11:33). Indeed, he went so far as to build idolatrous shrines in and around the holy city itself (1 Kings 11:4ff.). It is probable that he also built a number of shrines outside Jerusalem dedicated to the God of Israel, to judge by the temple recently excavated at Arad.[10]

9. 2 Chronicles 8:1f. suggests that subsequently Solomon retrieved this lost territory; see J. M. Myers, *2 Chronicles,* (*AB*: Garden City, 1965), p. 47.

10. Cf. Y. Aharoni in D. N. Freedman and J. C. Geenfield, *New Directions in Biblical Archaeology* (Garden City, 1969), pp. 28-44.

Yet we cannot fault him for building the temple, nor for his administrative endeavours to bring order and stability to his kingdom. The twelve administrative districts he organised are listed for us in 1 Kings 4:7-19. Their primary purpose, however, was "to improve the efficiency and intensity of tax collection",[11] so Israelite citizens must have viewed the greater administrative efficiency with mixed feelings. Solomon's military measures, again, must have cost a pretty penny, even though their aims were good and their planning shrewd. Strong fortresses were established at strategic intervals throughout his kingdom, from Ezion-geber in the south to Hazor, north of the Sea of Galilee, and in them he stationed his 1,400 chariots and 12,000 horses (1 Kings 10:26). Solomon was as determined to avert internal revolts as he was to discourage invasion from outside his realm.

Before the end of Solomon's reign, however, the empire David had skilfully created showed signs of breaking up. We read of Solomon's "adversaries" in 1 Kings 11. It is not entirely clear what they accomplished, and the role of the kingdom of Egypt is particularly uncertain, but between them they must have been a thorn in Solomon's side, to say the least. It was vital to Israel's economy that the trade routes with the south should be maintained and kept open, but they were all too vulnerable along the 150 mile stretch between Beersheba and Ezion-geber. The mountainous Edomite region offered sanctuary to those who were of a mind to harass the caravans, and the natives of Edom had no love for Israel, especially since the massacres by Joab in David's reign. At that time a royal prince of Edom, Hadad, by name, had escaped to Egypt but at the very start of Solomon's reign he returned home and stirred up trouble. Undoubtedly Solomon managed to hold his activities in check — even after Solomon's death and the breaking up of his kingdom, Judah was able to dominate Edom for several generations.

Damascus became another centre of disaffection. The Aramaean states had probably never been controlled by David or Solomon in the same sense that Edom or Moab were; it may well be that many of them were happy to benefit from the commercial network Solomon had organized, and so were amenable to Solomon's "influence". At any rate, one less well-disposed Aramaean, Rezon by name, saw his chance to take control of Damascus. Solomon never dislodged him, evidently, and Rezon went on to found a long-lived dynasty, which in process of time came to pose a major threat to the very existence of Israel. But at the present juncture, we know only that Rezon and his band of men caused Solomon some trouble.

Nor is the trouble caused by Jeroboam to be discounted, even though it was not till after Solomon's death that he achieved

11. Y. Aharoni, *LB,* p. 277.

anything like success. He plotted revolt, clearly, and if the rising proved abortive,[12] the very fact that it happened indicates some of the tensions that were building up in the heart of Solomon's homeland. Jeroboam's connexions were with the important central tribes of Ephraim and Manasseh, where he was probably in charge of the compulsory labour system,[13] and it is interesting, to say the least, that he had prophetic support and incitement.

Jeroboam fled to Egypt in the final years of Solomon's reign, after the death of the Egyptian king who was Solomon's father-in-law. The new king, Shishak (935-914), was establishing a new dynasty (the 22nd) in Egypt, and his intentions towards Israel were not friendly. But it was the previous king, Solomon's father-in-law, who had offered asylum to the Edomite Hadad, and one wonders just how well disposed to Solomon he really was. Was his capture of Gezer purely for the purpose of donating the city to Solomon (1 Kings 9:16)? Professor Aharoni argues that David had conquered Gezer, and that the Egyptian attack on the city was part of an attempt to wrest the Philistine area from Solomon's kingdom. If so, Solomon was strong enough to resist the Egyptians, and retrieve Gezer.[14] On the whole, however, this seems an unlikely interpretation of the evidence.[15] At the very end of his reign it is beyond doubt that Solomon felt the need for first-rate southern defences, and strongholds such as Gezer and Arad were well fortified and well garrisoned.

The "golden" quality of the Solomonic era was clearly not unalloyed, any more than Solomon's famed wisdom extended to all his deeds. It is worth noting, perhaps, that his wisdom resided very much in his words, not his deeds. He exhibited it in conversation with the Queen of Sheba, in his tongue-in-cheek judicial decision in the case of the two claimants to the one child, and most notably in the many proverbs he created and fostered — fully three thousand, we are told (1 Kings 4:32). He could "speak" admirably of trees, flora and fauna (1 Kings 4:33); but his deeds did not always match the wisdom of his words.

The least adulterated "gold" of his era, it would seem, was the flourishing literature. Since the time of their wilderness wanderings, the Israelites had had all too little peace, all too little opportunity to devote themselves to the arts. Solomon's reign of forty years (the figure may or may not be a round one) at last allowed the possibility of great Hebrew literature, and we need not doubt that some of the finest narrative material in the Old Testament dates in its polished

12. The Septuagint gives many more details, of uncertain reliability, than does the Hebrew Bible; English Bibles follow the Hebrew text.
13. Noth expresses doubt about this, p. 206n. See also J. Gray, *Kings,* pp. 154ff.
14. Cf. *MBA*, p. 72.
15. See K. A. Kitchen in *NBD* (s.v. "Egypt") for a more probable view.

form, based on earlier records to be sure, from the Solomonic era. "Wisdom" activity, too, culminating in books such as Proverbs and Ecclesiastes, was first fostered in Israel by him; it was to continue for many centuries, into inter-testamental times.[16]

16. E.g. the Apocryphal books Ecclesiasticus, Wisdom of Solomon. The Book of Proverbs was of course not completed in Solomon's reign, as the reference to King Hezekiah proves (Proverbs 25:1).

CHAPTER 7

The Early Divided Monarchy

IT has been widely held, since A. Alt first argued the position,[1] that David and Solomon, unlike Saul, ruled not a single united realm, but a twin kingdom; in other words, Israel and Judah were quite separate political entities, united only in the fact that each acknowledged the same man as king. If, therefore, the two kingdoms should ever decide to offer allegiance to two different men, very few links would need to be broken; Israel and Judah would quite naturally fall apart.

Despite such tenuous political bonds, Israel and Judah had been united now for fully a century, if we ignore the two year reign of Eshbaal, and it is clear that Solomon's son and successor Rehoboam did not envisage any political disaster when he went to Shechem for his second coronation service (so to speak). Equally, it seems that the men of the northern tribes had no thought of doing other than ratifying his kingship over them (1 Kings 12:1ff.). Their request for more lenient treatment than they had been experiencing under Solomon was a fair one, even if Solomon's old enemy Jeroboam had returned from Egypt and put in a good deal of propaganda. But Rehoboam's foolish response was all that the situation required to divorce the two political units. Rehoboam was of the tribe of Judah; very well, Judah was welcome to him. The king's crowning act of folly was his choice of mediator — Adoram or Adoniram, who had supervised the forced labour levies, and who must have been the most unpopular man in all Israel. The fact that Adoram was summarily stoned to death is in itself indicative of the hatred Solomon's measures had caused.

1. Cf. A. Alt., *Essays on Old Testament History and Religion* (Oxford, 1966), pp. 205-237. Alt's original article (in German) was published in 1930.

Rehoboam made one final attempt to remain master of his inherited domain; he mustered a fair-sized army and was on the point of marching into the seceding territories when a prophet unexpectedly intervened. The prophet, Ahijah, a northerner, had some years earlier recommended to Jeroboam the division of Solomon's kingdom; now Shemaiah, a southern prophet, took exactly the same line, and found no difficulty in persuading Rehoboam's troops to go quietly home again (1 Kings 12:22ff.). Whether Rehoboam could have achieved anything by military force is in any case dubious; if southern troops had shed northern blood, it would scarcely have helped to heal the breach, plainly. The breach was irrevocable, but at least there was no large-scale warfare between Rehoboam and the seceding tribes. The "continual fighting" to which 1 Kings 14:30 refers was not an attempt at conquest by Rehoboam, but rather an effort to stabilize a secure frontier between the two states.

The failure of Solomon to unify his kingdom, the social injustices he had tolerated if not actually fostered, and now the incredible stupidity of Rehoboam, turned an empire of moderate dimensions into two small, second-rate states. The conquests achieved by troops and diplomacy were lost overnight, with the sole possible exception of Edom. To the west, the Philistines broke free from their tributary status. Other areas which had been dominated by Solomon were separated from Rehoboam's control by the sheer geographical fact of the existence of the new state of Israel, the northern kingdom. The only bonus for Rehoboam was that the tribe of Benjamin linked itself firmly with Judah, though the wording of 1 Kings 12:20f. may imply that Benjamin did so perforce and not of free choice. The fortress of Jerusalem on her very borders may have put an irresistible pressure on the Benjaminites.

At least Rehoboam had the benefit of a firmly-established personal position in Judah and Benjamin, and of an existing administration there. The new kingdom, Israel, on the other hand, had to create everything from scratch. It is evident that they aped Judah in every way possible; to begin with, they decided to continue with a monarchy, and did not revert to the old "Judges" structure of earlier days. The man they elected to take office, at the instigation of the prophet Ahijah, was Jeroboam. In his very name we may see other deliberate conformity with Judah. Many a reader of the English Bible must have found the names Jeroboam and Rehoboam confusingly alike; they are equally alike in Hebrew, and also in their meanings, "May the people increase!" and "May the people expand!" respectively. We know that at least two Hebrew kings had throne-names,[2] and it may well have been common practice;[3] very

2. See 2 Kings 23:34; 24:17.
3. Cf. A M. Honeyman, *JBL* 67 (1958), pp. 13-25.

probably, then, Jeroboam deliberately chose a name like his rival's.

For a capital, Jeroboam chose Shechem, a city of central position and long-standing importance. From the political aspect, it could well rival Jerusalem, but Jeroboam was well aware that David had given Jerusalem a religious status second to none, and Solomon's temple, containing the unique ark of the covenant, could well have continued to attract devout worshippers from the north. Jeroboam felt it was not enough to organize a closely similar culture and ritual, quick though he was to do this; he decided he must find religious rivals to Jerusalem, and his choices were Dan, on his northern boundary, and Bethel near his frontier with Judah (or rather, Benjamin). There may have been strategic reasons behind his choice; certainly he could build upon ancient traditions in both cases. The sanctuary at Dan had links with Moses himself,[4] while that at Bethel dated back even further, and was closely associated with none other than Jacob, forefather of the Israelite tribes.[5] Accordingly, Jeroboam made Dan and Bethel royal shrines; that is to say, he sought to make his own position secure within the liturgies of those shrines, in the same way that the. Davidic kings' rule was guaranteed in the liturgy and traditions of the Jerusalem temple.[6]

These various policies of Jeroboam had their effect, and he held the throne of Israel till his death, without apparent difficulty. Presumably his subjects accepted Dan and Bethel readily enough. But the worship at both sanctuaries was very quickly corrupted, 1 Kings 12:32 relates, and the whole sacrificial system of the northern kingdom is characterized as "a sin in Israel" (v.30) by the Old Testament historian. It is true that in his view of the matter all sanctuaries outside Jerusalem were *ipso facto* unacceptable to God; but he had good historical reasons for this attitude, in view of the syncretistic and idolatrous practices which regularly affected the worship of Yahweh at such shrines. What offended the Bible writer most about Jeroboam was his installation of golden images, of bull-calves, at Dan and Bethel. Now it could be true, as W. F. Albright suggested,[7] that these images functioned in precisely the same way as the cherubim of the Jerusalem temple, i.e. as pedestals or supports for the "throne" of Yahweh. But this possibility scarcely tells the whole story. Why, it may be asked, did Jeroboam choose bulls instead of cherubim for this cultic adornment? And must they not have been more visible and accessible to the general public than were the Jerusalem cherubim? For the latter never gave rise to

4. Cf. Judges 18:30; the AV reading "Manasseh" is incorrect, though based on an ancient Jewish alteration to the Hebrew text.
5. Cf. Genesis 28.
6. See especially 2 Samuel 7: 1-16.
7. Cf. W. F. Albright, *From the Stone Age to Christianity*[2] (Garden City, 1957), pp. 298-301.

idolatrous worship, to our knowledge; but Jeroboam's bull-calves were immediately reminiscent of the Canaanite religion, in which the senior deity, El, was actually worshipped as a bull on occasions.[8] It is probable that Jeroboam was deliberately permitting, indeed inviting, pagan rites to take place, no doubt with the intention of keeping all his subjects happy. The Dan sanctuary, as we know from Judges 18:31, had a long history of idolatrous practices, and Jeroboam was not the man to offend a majority of his subjects by a religious purge. On the contrary, he felt he could afford to let priests and worshippers whose standards were higher abandon their possessions and go south to Judah (cf. 2 Chronicles 11:13ff.).

It is perhaps worth recalling in this connexion that since the conquest of Canaan the Israelite people had always had a multiplicity of shrines; Bethel and Dan were no innovations. During the whole period of the monarchy Judah no less than Israel had its various sanctuaries, one of which, at Arad, has been excavated in recent years. The Arad temple is in most respects a perfect replica of Solomon's temple in Jerusalem, though on a smaller scale.

From this point on, the writers of Kings and Chronicles give us far less detail about the lives and careers of the Hebrew kings; the biblical historians were much less interested in purely political events than we are, and at times their omissions tend to surprise modern readers. The next major event in the history of Palestine illustrates this point very well. 1 Kings 14:25f. relates it thus: "In the fifth year of Rehoboam's reign Shishak king of Egypt attacked Jerusalem. He removed the treasures of the house of the LORD and of the royal palace, and seized everything, including all the shields of gold that Solomon had made". 2 Chronicles 12:2ff. adds some details of the size of the Egyptian force, and mentions that "the fortified cities of Judah" were captured. Questions immediately spring to our minds. Why did Shishak attack? Was this a punitive raid, or an endeavour to secure Jeroboam's throne for him (after all, Jeroboam had been Shishak's recent protégé)? With just the biblical data to hand, we might have come to the conclusion that the last suggestion was correct; it sounds plausible, and would also explain conveniently why the Egyptians returned and took no further active interest in Judah for some years afterwards. But in fact such a theory is totally ruled out by other evidence; Shishak's chief target was not Rehoboam at all, but Jeroboam and his newly-acquired kingdom! We may instead hazard the guess that Jeroboam failed to keep certain promises he had made to his former protector.

Our evidence that Jeroboam was also attacked comes from an Egyptian temple inscription. In the Amun temple at Karnak,

---

8. The alternative to Albright's hypothesis is accordingly that Jeroboam's bulls were intended as images of Yahweh.

Shishak (or Shoshenq) himself recorded in remarkably full detail the events of his campaign in Palestine (although there are difficulties both in reading and interpreting the inscription).[9] Shishak's troops captured towns as far north as Megiddo and Shunem; the Egyptians must have bypassed Bethel and Shechem by a very narrow margin — indeed, one wonders if Shechem bought Shishak off, as Jerusalem did, or if it was perhaps captured (there is a gap in the inscription just at this interesting point). Shortly, in any case, Israel chose a new capital, Tirzah (cf. Kings 15:21).

Shishak's campaign seems to have been connected in the main with trade-routes; he asserted Egyptian domination over the major highway through Palestine — up the Philistine coast, and through the pass of Megiddo into the Plain of Jezreel. Then he turned south and apparently destroyed Solomon's fortress at Ezion-geber, in order to damage Judah's Red Sea trade.[10]

The biblical writers were in general more interested in Judah than in Israel; apart from that, they wished to emphasize how far Rehoboam fell in a mere five years. He had inherited an empire; five years later, master of a small state, he could protect his capital itself only by denuding his palace of its treasures. Solomon's court had despised silver; his son's court had to be content with bronze! The biblical writers were not slow to point the moral.

Rehoboam used the twelve years that remained to him after Shishak's invasion in building secure defences for his state. Details are given in 2 Chronicles 11:5ff., which make it clear that the king of Judah was enough of a realist to retract his southern and western frontiers to defensible lines, abandoning some of the key fortresses of Solomon's era.[11] Interestingly, however, he drew no northern frontier, and it may be that he never gave up his dream of becoming king of all Israel one day.

Rehoboam predeceased Jeroboam by a few years;[12] his son Abijah (also called Abijam) continued the border strife with Israel, and was able to inflict a heavy defeat on Jeroboam, as 2 Chronicles 13 relates. Jeroboam lost many men and some miles of border territory — Bethel included. Before this victory, the frontier lay a mere eight miles north of Jerusalem — one can understand the anxiety of the kings of Judah — a distance Abijah was able to double. Abijah's reign was short; his successor Asa inherited the benefits of the victory, and was able to maintain this frontier until after Jeroboam's

9. For details, see B. Mazar, "The campaign of Pharaoh Shishak to Palestine", *VTS* 4 (Leiden, 1957), pp. 57-66; Y. Aharoni, *LB* pp. 283-290; *MBA* map 120; K. A. Kitchen, *The Third Intermediate Period in Egypt* (Warminster, 1973), §§252-258.

10. Shishak's inscription breaks off before Ezion-geber is mentioned, but the excavations there have shown that the fortress suffered destruction at about this period.

11. See *MBA*, map 119.

12. Variously computed; see the tables on pp. 293f.

death. Jeroboam's son, Nadab, soon embarked on a campaign against the Philistines, besieging Gibbethon — a campaign which is probably again to be interpreted as a border dispute, in much the same general area as the Israel-Judah dispute. While engaged in this siege, Nadab lost his throne and his life to a man of Issachar named Baasha, who like Jeroboam had prophetic support in claiming the crown. Thus the very first "dynasty" of Israel terminated swiftly after the death of its founder, a precedent which would be followed all too often.

By about the year 900, then, we find Asa as king of Judah and Baasha as king of Israel, with the border feud still continuing. Till that time this had been a private quarrel, but the situation was now to be complicated by outside interference. First there came another invasion from Egypt, probably under the command of Shishak's son and successor Osorkon I;[13] on this occasion Judah was the target. Asa, unlike his grandfather, proved equal to the occasion, and this time the Egyptians were repulsed with heavy losses; it was a long day before they interfered in Palestinian affairs again. It seems likely, however, that the effort involved in meeting and defeating this serious challenge from the south weakened Judah, because soon afterwards Baasha succeeded in retrieving all the border territory lost by Jeroboam, and in pushing Judah's frontier back south of Ramah, a mere five miles from Jerusalem. He proceeded to fortify Ramah against Asa's troops. Asa felt that this was an intolerable situation, but he was not strong enough to throw the Israelite troops back by frontal assault. A diversionary tactic was called for; his father, no doubt with the same possibility in mind, had made a treaty with the former king of Damascus (Tabrimmon), and Asa now renewed it, suggesting to the present king of Damascus that he should invade Israel from the north, so relieving the pressure upon Judah. The Syrian ruler, Benhadad I, was happy to oblige; he swiftly captured a number of Israelite cities of importance, such as Dan and Hazor, and probably also overran the northern part of Israelite Transjordan at this juncture. From Judah's point of view, all this had the desired effect. Baasha — previously in treaty relationship with Damascus himself — had to return to his capital to organize his northern defences, and he was forced to draw troops away from his southern frontier. Asa then pushed that frontier northwards once more, and established secure fortresses at Mizpah and Geba, utilizing the building materials from Baasha's abandoned fortress at Ramah. This new frontier was little different from the line inherited by Abijah; two generations' struggles in that area thus achieved little but the ultimate stability of the frontier, and of course served to weaken both kingdoms not a little. The swift rise of

13. The Bible calls him Zerah the Ethiopian (2 Chronicles 14:9).

Damascus to a position where it could threaten and embarrass Israel was certainly due in no small measure to the folly of Rehoboam and to the strained relations between Israel and Judah which inevitably ensued.

The border hostilities between Israel and Judah gradually died out, either of their own accord, or (more probably) because of the foresight and diplomatic skills of a new king on the throne of Israel, Omri by name. His son Ahab is far better known to posterity, not because he was more able than his father, but because the biblical writer has given us far more information about him; that fact in turn is due to the fact that Ahab was the contemporary of an outstanding Israelite prophet, Elijah the Tishbite.

Omri's name (as also Ahab's) perhaps suggests some Arab ancestry;[14] be that as it may, he certainly fell short of the high religious standards set by the writer of 1 Kings. Moral and religious questions apart, however, he was a man of no little political acumen and achievement; it may be no accident that in later years the Assyrians referred to Israel as "the house of Omri", even after the fall of his dynasty. Omri gained the throne within a year or two of Baasha's death. Baasha's son, like Jeroboam's before him, was able to hold the throne no more than a year or so, before falling victim to a *coup d'état*. No fewer than three army officers contended for the crown: first Zimri captured it, then he lost it to Omri, from whom Tibni endeavoured to wrest it unsuccessfully. Needless to say, Baasha's son (Elah), Zimri and Tibni all lost their lives in the struggle. How long these struggles lasted is difficult to say; Zimri's "reign" lasted seven days, according to the Hebrew text of 1 Kings 16:15, but the Greek text makes it seven years (improbably). Between Tibni and Omri, however, there was a measure of civil war, and no indication is given how long it lasted; some scholars calculate that the two men reigned over different parts of Israel for four or five years.[15] By 875 B.C., in any case, Omri held the throne of all Israel quite securely. In all, including the period of civil war, he reigned only twelve years, but in them he gave Israel a new strength and stability. It must have been he who established the friendly relations with Judah which his son Ahab found valuable (cf. 1 Kings 22:1 ff.). It was he, too, who renewed the good treaty relations between Israel and the Phoenicians, thereby giving to his kingdom west of the Jordan stability, security, and some economic advantages besides; on the debit side, however, he also gave his kingdom a future queen who was to prove notorious, for undoubtedly it was Omri who engineered the diplomatic marriage

14. On Omri's name and background, see J. Gray, *Kings,* pp. 364f.
15. E.G. J. Begrich and E. R. Thiele; but W. F. Albright places the civil strife within one single year (876 B.C.). See pp. 293f.

between Ahab and Jezebel, daughter of the king of Tyre. He also provided his kingdom with a measure of glory; 1 Kings 16:24 relates how he appropriated the site of Samaria and made it his capital, while excavations have revealed something of the magnificence which he and his successors gave it.[16] In some ways, clearly, Omri was a second Solomon.

Unlike Solomon, however, Omri was prepared to take military initiative where he thought it necessary. The steady increase of the power of the Syrian kingdom of Damascus must have caused him some concern, though evidence is lacking that there was any direct conflict between him and Benhadad. What is certain is that Omri sought to give greater strength to his Transjordanian possessions by reconquering Moab, which had been lost to Israel on Solomon's death. A Moabite inscription, known as the Moabite Stone or Mesha Stele, testifies to this: "Omri, King of Israel" — it reads — "he oppressed Moab many days",[17] and goes on to mention briefly the fact of Omri's conquest.

Omri's reign was not a long one, perhaps only seven years as sole ruler (or so a comparison of verse 23 with verse 29 of 1 Kings 16 suggests). On his death, his son Ahab succeeded to the throne, and reigned in Samaria for more than twenty years, the contemporary of Jehoshaphat of Judah. The Bible tells us more about Ahab than about any other ruler of the Northern Kingdom, but even so we could wish that the details were fuller! The documentary sources for Ahab's reign utilized by the author of 1 Kings seem to have been primarily concerned with the prophets of the day, notably Elijah, and so Ahab's doings are reported only where they led him into conflict with the prophets.

It is clear, at any rate, that he continued his father's policy of good relations with Phoenicia to the north and Judah to the south. He was married to Jezebel, the king of Tyre's daughter, and he arranged a marriage between his own (and presumably Jezebel's) daughter and Jehoshaphat's son. Both these marriages had disastrous consequences, as will be seen; but at least they secured Israel's northern and southern defences. Such security was vital, because it was now that the Syrians really became a power to be reckoned with, and a hostile power at that. The king of Damascus, Benhadad,[18]

---

16. A large number of ivories were found at Samaria; cf. 1 Kings 22:39. There may well have been ulterior motives behind the creation of this new capital. It may have been intended to serve the non-Israelite sector of the population and therefore housed a temple to Baal instead of Yahweh, cf. J. H. Hayes and J. M. Miller, *Israelite and Judaean History* (OTL: London 1977), pp. 402f.

17. Cf. *DOTT*, p. 196.

18. It is not clear whether this was the same king that had invaded Israel in Baasha's reign or a son and successor bearing the same name (or title). Cf. K. A. Kitchen in *NBD*, s.v. "Benhadad". This (?second) Benhadad is called Adad-idri (i.e. Hadad-ezer) in Assyrian records.

was a capable soldier and administrator, who appears to have been bent on empire, for he was able to enforce his will over smaller Syrian states; 1 Kings 20:1 relates that thirty-two lesser kings supported his invasion of Israel; within a year he had removed them from office (verses 24f.). It was not always easy to assess the purpose of invasions of ancient times; we do not know whether Benhadad was seeking to add Israel to his territory, or whether he was endeavouring to force Ahab into alliance with him, to face a greater foe, Assyria. It is fairly clear at least that this was not a mere plundering raid, or he would not have taken the time and trouble to besiege Samaria, which soon proved by its defensibility what a good choice of capital Omri had made.

This invasion by the Syrians, and the siege of Samaria, seem to have taken Ahab by surprise. Subsequent events show that his forces were far from negligible, in numbers or competence. Archaeological discovery has confirmed this fact: at Megiddo alone, Ahab had a fine chariot city.[19] Nevertheless, Ahab's response to the invasion was initially weak-kneed; he was prepared to go to almost any lengths to placate Benhadad, as 1 Kings 20:1ff. reveals. However, once Ahab was prompted to retaliate — by Benhadad's overreaching himself, by the advice of Ahab's counsellors, and by a prophet's favourable predictions — a heavy defeat was speedily inflicted on the Syrian army. Benhadad needed the winter to reorganize; then in the spring he invaded again. This time Ahab was ready for him, and the battle was joined near Aphek, a little south of the lake of Galilee.[20] Although the terrain was of the Syrians' own choosing, and despite their greater numbers, they once again suffered a heavy defeat; Benhadad himself was captured. The prophets, who were growing to be a force in Israel to be reckoned with, maintained that Benhadad should not have been released, and the sequel showed that the Syrian king was not to be trusted; but no doubt at the time Ahab felt that he was getting favourable terms, when Benhadad covenanted to restore territory wrested from Israel, and to permit Israelite bazaars to be established in Damascus itself. Ahab would have preferred good trade to constant warfare.

Ahab was not to escape warfare, however. In recent years a major nation of the upper Tigris region, Assyria, had embarked on a policy of aggression and expansion. During David and Solomon's era, Assyria had been quiet and inactive, but from the end of the tenth century the Assyrian kings found themselves more free to pursue their own designs. The city of Tyre, now Ahab's ally, had been one city forced to pay tribute to the Assyrian king Ashurnasirpal II

---

19. Cf. Y. Yadin, "Megiddo of the Kings of Israel", *BA* 33 (1970), pp. 66-96.
20. A different Aphek from that mentioned in connection with the Philistines in 1 Samuel 29:1.

(883-859 B.C.), whose armies had been able to reach the Mediterranean coast. None of the small or relatively small states of Palestine, Syria, or eastern Anatolia (i.e. Turkey) could fail to take warning; and when Asshurnasirpal's son and successor Shalmaneser III marched westwards in 853 B.C., he found that a coalition of major dimensions had been formed to resist him. (See plate 1 facing p. 48.) Ahab and Benhadad had made a truce (cf. 1 Kings 22:1), and were leaders of this league, together with another Syrian king, Irhuleni of Hamath. Ahab supplied 2,000 chariots, 10,000 infantrymen; Benhadad 1,200 chariots and 20,000 men. Even Egypt sent a token force of 1,000 men, while an Arabian king supplied 1,000 camels. It is interesting to note that none of the Phoenician cities joined the coalition, perhaps out of prudence; and neither did Jehoshaphat of Judah.

The battle was joined some distance north of Hamath, at Qarqar on the Orontes. All our information about it — for the Bible mentions nothing but the truce between Samaria and Damascus — comes from Shalmaneser's own record, a monument called the Kurkh Stele, now in the British Museum. We need not doubt Shalmaneser's veracity (in general terms) when he lists the names of his foes and the size of their armies, but something of a question-mark arises in one's mind on reading his account of the outcome of the battle. He claims a handsome victory: "They came directly toward me in close battle, but with the superior aid which Ashur the lord had given, and with the mighty weapons which Nergal, my leader, had gifted me, I fought with them. From Qarqar to Gilzau I defeated them. I smote 14,000 of their men with weapons, falling upon them like Adad pouring down a hailstorm. I flung their bodies about, filling the plain with their scattered soldiery."[21]

But if a victory it was, it was to say the least a Pyrrhic one. Two facts seem to speak louder than Shalmaneser's boastful words. In the first place, it is on record that far from following up his alleged victory, he did not send his armies so far west again for four years or so. Secondly, Ahab and Benhadad felt free, within a very short time after the battle of Qarqar, to resume their own petty quarrels.

The final event of Ahab's reign, which must have taken place within three years of Qarqar, and probably very soon after the battle,[22] was Ahab's attempt to recapture the Israelite city of Ramoth-gilead. It is clear that Benhadad had either never fulfilled his promise to withdraw from Israelite territory in Transjordan, or else had encroached once again during the period of truce with

---

21. *DOTT,* p. 47.
22. Qarqar gives us the first absolute date for the history of the Israelite monarchy. In any case, Ahab died within three years of Qarqar (cf. 1 Kings 22:1), i.e. no later than 850 BC; but since the next Assyrian invasion came in 841 BC, when Jehu was king, and since we have to fit in the twelve year reign of Jehoram (cf. 2 Kings 3:1) in the interval, it seems tolerably certain that Ahab died in 852 BC at the latest.

Ahab. Taking the advice of most of his prophets, Ahab marched on Ramoth-gilead, an important city which lay on one of the major routes through Palestine-Syria, "the King's Highway." It was however the one prophet he chose to ignore, Micaiah ben Imlah, who told the truth: Ahab would fall at Ramoth-gilead. Despite the king's precautions in disguising himself, a chance arrow found a weak point in his armour, and he was mortally wounded. He displayed considerable courage at the last, allowing himself to be propped up in his chariot all day, so that his men should not panic at the news of his fall. It was probably loss of blood that killed him. His courage saved a rout; but his death signalled the end of the campaign, and Ramoth-gilead remained in Syrian control.[23] Further south in Transjordan, the Moabites took heart from the Israelite failure at Ramoth-gilead, and proceeded to reassert their independence and to retrieve lost territory.

Jehoshaphat, as was noted above, was not amongst the confederate kings who fought the Assyrians at Qarqar; but he was Ahab's willing ally at Ramoth-gilead. Indeed, his willingness was so unreserved that it is sometimes suggested that Jehoshaphat was Ahab's vassal. Other biblical data rule out this possibility, however; both Kings and Chronicles make it clear not only that there was no warfare at any time between Ahab and Jehoshaphat, but also that Jehoshaphat was a reasonably strong king in his own right. Jehoshaphat's declaration to Ahab, "What is mine is yours; myself, my people and my horses", is somewhat reminiscent of Ruth's pledge to Naomi — "Your people shall be my people, and your God my God" — which nobody could say was a pledge extracted from her under duress. A further parallel is that Ahab and Jehoshaphat were related by marriage, just as Ruth and Naomi were.

Jehoshaphat's strength was largely shown in the fact that his neighbours left him well alone, according to 2 Chronicles 17:10f. He brought security to his kingdom by means of well-planned military and administrative measures, as the same chapter relates. Y. Aharoni sets out[24] in map form the twelve administrative districts which it is widely thought that he instituted in Judah. In the south of his realm, he was able to control Edom and deny it a king of its own (cf. 1 Kings 22:47). He sought to utilize the port of Ezion-geber to the commercial and economic advantage of Judah, but a storm apparently wrecked his merchant fleet.

23. It should be mentioned that there is a tendency among present-day scholars (contrast Gray's first and second editions of *Kings*) to deny that "the king of Israel" of 1 Kings chapters 20 and particularly 22 was Ahab. It is true that Ahab's name is rarely mentioned in these chapters, and could be attributed to a late editor; but Jehoshaphat — Ahab's contemporary — is named with some frequency in chapter 22, and no convincing alternative possibility to Ahab has been suggested.

24. *MBA*, map 130. See also his discussion, in *LB*, pp. 297-304. The information from which the map is drawn is found in Joshua 15: 21-62.

Jehoshaphat's alliance with Ahab also brought him into conflict with the Moabites and their allies. It is difficult to be sure when exactly the Moabites embarked on their campaign to achieve their independence, and to carry the war into the enemy's camp. That Jehoshaphat was involved in the fight with Moab is beyond doubt, but it is not certain whether the Moabite revolt began before or after the death of Ahab. The Moabite king, Mesha, who ultimately emerged victorious, set up a triumphal stele which was discovered in the area in 1868, and which gives us full details of his campaign. The relevant parts of it read as follows: "Omri . . . oppressed Moab many days . . . And his son succeeded him and he too said, 'I will oppress Moab!' In my days he spoke thus, and I saw my desire upon him and upon his house."[25]

If we take the reference to Omri's "son" literally, we must conclude that it was Ahab who bore the brunt of Mesha's attack, presumably at a time when Israel was fully stretched in holding the Syrians at bay. But in ancient Near Eastern literature, "son" was often used loosely for "descendant" or "successor" (even an unrelated one), so that one cannot be certain that Mesha's inscription really intended a reference to Ahab. (It is certainly impossible to take literally this inscription's reference to "forty years" of Israelite domination by Omri and his sons, since the whole dynasty of Omri reigned scarcely forty years!) On the other hand, the Bible's very concise remark that Mesha revolted after Ahab's death (2 Kings 1:1, 3:5) is not necessarily decisive; it may mean no more than that serious Israelite military operations did not take place till after Ahab's death, even though Mesha may have stopped paying tribute and started on his policy of expansion some time previously. At all events, whatever the precise chronology may have been, it is clear from 2 Kings 3 that the struggle with Moab lasted well into the reign of Ahab's son Jehoram; Ahab was briefly succeeded by his son Ahaziah, who apparently achieved little of note during his short reign except to fall out of an upper window, injuring himself fatally, and leaving the throne to his brother Jehoram.

Mesha's first move was undoubtedly to stop paying the high annual tribute demanded of him — 100,000 lambs and the wool of 100,000 rams (2 Kings 3:4). He then set about retrieving lost territory, and pressing northwards, overran some of the territory of the Israelite tribe of Gad. The Israelite residents of Transjordan thus found themselves in danger of being crushed between Aramaean pressure from the north, and Moabite expansion from the south. The king of Israel was forced to take action eventually.

Jehoram laid his plans well; first of all he made it a joint campaign, utilizing like his father the new friendly relationship with

25. Cf. *DOTT,* p. 196.

Judah. Jehoshaphat was once again willing to offer troops, and his vassal, the king of Edom, was also pressed into service. The plan of campaign was equally shrewd; the allied force attempted to surprise Mesha by attacking his rear — marching right round the south of the Dead Sea, and invading Moab from the south. This was Edomite terrain, and the presence of an Edomite contingent was no doubt very valuable. The allied campaign proved initially successful; but when the Moabite king took the drastic step of offering his own crown-prince in sacrifice to the Moabite god Chemosh, the superstitions of the troops of Jehoram and his allies overcame their valour, and they withdrew, fighting a final battle at Horonaim, as the Moabites pursued their advantage.

Apparently the Moabites decided on reprisals against Judah; 2 Chronicles 20 records that they in turn mustered a confederate army and invaded, followed an unexpected route, almost certainly fording the Dead Sea at its narrowest point to reach the western shore some miles south of En-gedi. From En-gedi they marched toward Jerusalem; Jehoshaphat was ready for them, and marched to give battle near Tekoa. However, it appears that the confederates fell out among themselves, and Moabites, Ammonites, and "men of Seir" attacked each other savagely. Thus the danger to Jerusalem was averted; and Jehoshaphat took good care to scotch any future surprise attack of this sort by establishing forts at En-gedi and on Masada (a natural vantage-point dominating the ford which the Moabites must have used).[26]

Of Jehoshaphat's successors, his son and his grandson, little need be said. It is unfortunate that they bore the same names as Ahab's two sons who succeeded to the throne in Samaria — though they reigned in reverse order! In Jerusalem, Jehoram reigned before Ahaziah, in Samaria Ahaziah reigned before Jehoram![27] Jehoram of Judah proved less able than his father, and he lost control of Edom, and with it the lucrative southern trade-routes. On his death, his wife Athaliah — Ahab's daughter — continued to exercise a dominant role in the state; evidently the queen-mother often held an important position in state affairs.[28] In any case, Ahaziah's reign was to be cut short very quickly, as we shall see.

The Israelite Jehoram lost control of Moab, as we have described. But it appears that he may have had some slight success on the Syrian front, because we read in 2 Kings 9:14 that the Israelites, by

26. Masada is best known nowadays because of its association with the final episode of the Jewish revolt against the Romans, AD 66-70. Masada was such an impregnable fortress that it held out against the Roman armies for a further three years or so.
27. In 2 Kings 8:16-29 the Israelite king is called "Jehoram", the Judaean king "Joram" (an abbreviated form of the same name), to distinguish them, but these spellings are not used consistently.
28. Cf. R. de Vaux, *Ancient Israel*[2] (London, 1965), pp. 117ff.

the end of his reign, were defending Ramoth-gilead instead of attempting to capture it. The story of Naaman of 2 Kings 5 belongs to the reign of Jehoram; the story itself is too well known to need repeating here, but its political background is worth noting. The Israelite girl in Naaman's employ had been captured in a Syrian raid on Israel, we are told. But it is clear that there was no full-scale warfare between the two nations, at least at the time when Naaman could visit Israel — a Syrian general, carrying a ''letter of commendation'' from the king of Damascus to the king of Israel! On the other hand, Jehoram's rather worried reaction (2 Kings 5:7) indicates how tense relations still remained. Indeed, it may be that at some stage in his reign Samaria suffered yet another siege, which brought the city to the verge of starvation; but it is perhaps more likely that the narrative of 2 Kings 6:24-7:20 relates to a later date (and to a later Benhadad).[29] Be that as it may, hostilities broke out at Ramoth-gilead late in Jehoram's reign, and like his father before him, he put in a personal appearance at the battlefront; history again repeated itself when he was wounded, but there the coincidence ends. Unlike Ahab, Jehoram's wound was not fatal, and he retired to Jezreel in order to recuperate. His days were nevertheless numbered, and his throne in danger; but apparently there was little hint of the disaster to come, or else we may be sure that the king of Judah, Ahaziah, would have kept well out of the way. Instead, he paid a visit to Jezreel, and put his own head in a noose thereby. A whirlwind *coup d'état* eliminated both kings at one stroke.

If the *coup d'état* was swift and sudden, the forces that motivated it had not by any means materialized overnight. It is clear that the author of the Books of Kings considered the two prophetic figures of Elijah and Elisha as of considerably greater consequence than Omri and his successors on the throne of Israel. True, the biblical writer's interests were primarily religious, but the fact was that quite apart from these prophets' religious importance, both Elijah and Elisha were far from negligible as political figures in Israel. To a large extent, in fact, the fall of Omri's dynasty was due to their activities. But we must retrace our steps to the early years of Ahab's reign to see how the quarrel between king and prophet built up.

Perhaps the beginning of the conflict can be traced to a single event, the political marriage between Ahab and the Phoenician princess, Jezebel. Such unions for political advantage were no novelty in the ancient (or more recent) world; David himself had set the precedent in Israel. But the position of queen was a position of power and influence, for those who cared to take advantage of it, and Jezebel must have been a particularly strong character. One

---

29. See below, p. 154.

imagines that Ahab can scarcely have been a weakling, but in the biblical records Jezebel emerges as the dominant partner. Ahab, for his part, though we may well doubt whether he was ever notably devout, was quite content to observe the traditional worship of his own people, even if he did bow the knee to Baal as well when it suited him. His courtiers included prophets of Yahweh, and his two sons who succeeded him both bore names which incorporated the name of Israel's God (Ahaz*iah* and *Jeho*ram).

That Jezebel should wish to retain her own religion is not particularly surprising, and again there was precedent for that, in the provision made in Jerusalem for Solomon's Egyptian queen. But Jezebel was not content with a private chapel, nor with her husband's readiness to pay lip-service to Baal; she meant to dethrone the God of Israel, and make her Baal the chief deity and her faith the official state religion. There has been some discussion as to which "Baal" she revered,[30] but it would seem highly probable that the god of Tyre, known an Melqart, was the deity whose worship she sought to promote. Whether her militant advocacy of this foreign cult was for purely religious reasons is not so certain; it may be that much of her motivation derived from the fact that the prophets of Yahweh limited by constitutional right the powers of the king — and queen. In either case, she encountered the opposition of the Israelite prophets, and responded vigorously. Some were massacred, and at least 100 of them driven into hiding (cf. 1 Kings 18:4). Jezebel can have been in no doubt that she had won.

The abrupt appearance of Elijah heralded the fact that she had won no more than the first battle, even though his message to Ahab had no apparent bearing on the religio-political situation. He simply predicted a long drought (17:1), intimated that only he — as God's agent — could end it, and disappeared as abruptly as he had come. We find him — though Ahab could not! — in Jezebel's own home territory, Phoenicia, before long. There is magnificent dramatic irony here; in Phoenicia and in Israel alike, the official deity, Melqart, was shown to be powerless to control the elements, while the God of Israel could sustain his prophet, and others besides, as easily in Sidonian Zarephath as on Israelite soil. But of all this Ahab knew nothing; and he chose to ignore the fact that the drought was Yahweh's doing — so far as he was concerned, it was Elijah and Elijah alone who was the troubler of Israel.

The long drought (attested by the Greek writer Menander, so Josephus records)[31] must have caused ordinary citizens no little hardship and distress, and made them at least dimly aware that *some* deity was letting them down. Melqart was equated with Baal in

30. See D. R. Ap-Thomas, *PEQ* 92 (1960), pp. 146-155.
31. *Ant.* viii, 13, 2.

3. Tiglath-pileser III

Israel — the god of the weather. Where was he? Elijah's sarcastic challenge to Jezebel's prophets (1 Kings 18:27) will have struck a ready response in Israelite ears. No few of the ordinary citizens will also have resented Jezebel's rough handling of the prophets of Yahweh.

Thus the scene was set for the second round of the struggle. The contest took place on Mount Carmel, a wedge-shaped range of hills near the Mediterranean coast; the fine city of Haifa today lies on its lower slopes. It was renowned for its beauty and fertility, but presumably Elijah had other reasons than these for choosing it for his battleground. Indeed, it is not clear why it was chosen; there was good reason for Elijah to keep out of Jezebel's way, to be sure, but then neither Dan nor Bethel was at all close to the capital, and either would have served equally well from that point of view. Both Dan and Bethel were corrupt shrines, on the other hand, and probably Elijah wanted nothing to do with them. But the Carmel altar had been abandoned, and by repairing and using it Elijah would avoid giving any appearance of supporting an adulterated Yahweh-worship. We do not know when it had been abandoned, however, and it may be that Jezebel's recent policies had been responsible for its destruction, if 1 Kings 19:10 offers any clue; if so, Elijah's choice of Carmel may well have been symbolic. The choice may also have been strategic, for Carmel lay very close to the border with Phoenicia; the discomfiture of the prophets of Melqart on the very borders of his proper domain would speak for itself.

Many explanations of the miraculous fire which consumed Elijah's sacrifice have been proffered — none more ingenious (and improbable) than the suggestion that the "water" which doused the sacrifice was in reality naphtha! Lightning would still seem the most probable solution.[32] However sceptical of miracles some modern readers may be, it must at least be beyond doubt that something startling occurred, to give Elijah the unanimous popular support which enabled him to exterminate the idolatrous priesthood. Nor could the whole chapter be dismissed as legend, for it would leave far too little basis for the great reputation which clung to Elijah's name ever afterwards.

Probably Elijah hoped that his Carmel victory would force Jezebel's hand, since it would show the strength of popular resistance to the religion she was seeking to enforce, and since the cultic officials had been decimated. But possibly he would have been better advised not to shed blood, despite the provocation, for then the feud that arose between the court and himself and his followers might

32. There has been some discussion of the possibility of lightning from "a clear blue sky". But the fact that the sky was clear when Elijah went to the summit (verses 42ff.) does not necessarily imply that it had been clear all day.

have been avoided. It may not be without significance that the biblical writer does not suggest that the Lord instructed Elijah to slaughter the Baal-prophets.

Whatever might have been, the reality was that Elijah did resort to bloodshed, following Jezebel's precedent, and she responded promptly with a threat on his life. Elijah fled; clearly he placed no confidence in the popular support he had just elicited at Carmel. His wilderness encounter with God (1 Kings 19) taught him the power of the spoken word. He was instructed, we are told, to "anoint" a new king in the Syrian kingdom of Damascus, a new king in Israel, and finally a new prophet, Elisha, to be his own successor. It has often been pointed out that he did not literally obey any one of these three instructions; he did appoint Elisha, though not by anointing, but he left it to Elisha to carry out the other two commands. However, we should not be too literalistic in our reading of the passage. The point was that Elijah, the rugged individualist, was from now on to adopt a different policy; hurricane, earthquake, drought and lightning, devastating though they may be at the time, do not carry the same power of conviction as the quiet word of reason and persuasion. From now on Elijah must ensure continuity and co-operation in building up a popular front, headed by Elisha and the prophetic bands ("the sons of the prophets"), against Ahab and his court, and even influence the affairs of Damascus, as opportunity presented itself, with the same objective in view. A show-down must come, in which many lives would be lost; in that sense Elisha wielded a sword as much as did Hazael of Damascus and Jehu, the future king of Israel.[33]

The prophetic bands were well placed to preach to the populace, for they were located at sanctuary-cities like Bethel (cf. 2 Kings 2). But their message was not limited to religious considerations; the foreign gods of Jezebel could not be divorced from the foreign ways she sought to introduce. The marked difference between her conception of royal rule and the traditional ways of Israel was high-lighted by the Naboth affair (1 Kings 21). Nowadays, of course, Naboth would have lost his vineyard by compulsory purchase order, as H. L. Ellison has aptly remarked,[34] but apparently under Israel's laws Ahab could do nothing to circumvent Naboth's curt refusal to sell the property which adjoined the royal residence in Jezreel. Ahab was content to sulk; the law was the law. Jezebel was incredulous: "You make a fine king of Israel, and no mistake!" (1 Kings 21:7, JB), she exclaimed. There were other laws about property, such as the one that made an executed criminal's holdings forfeit to the crown, and

---

33. For a useful discussion of 1 Kings 18, see H. H. Rowley, *Men of God* (London, 1963), pp. 37-65.
34. *The Prophets of Israel* (Exeter, 1969), p. 31.

before long Jezebel saw to it that Ahab gained the piece of land he fancied. The ordinary citizen was not safe while Jezebel controlled affairs in Samaria, though perhaps many failed to realise the fact, in view of the apparent legality of Naboth's trial and execution. But Elijah took a hand. While his denunciation and threats made no difference in the short term, they served two immediate purposes: they brought the Naboth affair to public notice, and they made it clear that Elijah championed the cause of the ordinary citizen. It took time, but eventually there were fully 7,000 in Israel who repudiated the worship of Melqart, and with it the rule of Ahab and his queen.

Elijah could never have settled at court, if only because Jezebel would not have tolerated it, but his successor Elisha acquired a house in Samaria, where he could be in contact with the court. He must have worked subtly and secretly for the overthrow of Omri's dynasty, meanwhile claiming the right exercised from the very beginning of the Hebrew monarchy for prophets to have an official voice at court. Much of his ministry, it appears, was not in itself political, but consisted simply of helping ordinary folk in time of trouble, so demonstrating God's love and power; for those who chose to consider the implications, however, it was a reminder of the powerlessness of the gods of Jezebel, and a call to worship Yahweh, to whom alone their national covenant obligations were due.

At last Elisha found that the time had come to act decisively. The king of Damascus, who had achieved little against Israel in recent years, fell ill. Elisha immediately went to Damascus, and put it into the mind of Hazael, a mere palace official or courtier at the time, to seize the Syrian throne. So Hazael became king; the Assyrians disparagingly termed him "a son of nobody",[35] but his lack of royal blood was more than compensated for by his military ability. He at once put strong pressure on the Israelite army at Ramoth-gilead. The Israelite forces there, we may safely assume, were "demoralized by Israel's long and costly war with Damascus, dissatisfied with the weak leadership of Joram, and resentful of the luxurious indolence of the court in Samaria."[36] The Israelite king, true, was prepared to leave his court and grace the battlefield, but he was wounded and retired to Jezreel to recuperate. That left the way open for the army's discontent to mature; and Elisha again moved decisively, sending a young prophet to anoint a high-ranking army officer at Ramoth-gilead, Jehu by name, as the next king of Israel. Jehu required no second bidding, and his speed of action more than matched Elisha's. Enjoining secrecy, he pursued Jehoram to Jezreel as fast as he could.

35. *Cf. ANET*, p. 280.
36. E. W. Heaton, *The Hebrew Kingdoms*, (London, 1968), p. 90.

Jehoram must have been astonished to see troops approaching his Jezreel residence, and even more so to see that Jehu had deserted his post at Ramoth-gilead. Probably fearful that the city had fallen to Hazael, he enquired urgently whether all was well. But Jehu, deliberately misinterpreting the question, responded that all was far from well as long as Jezebel — Jehoram's mother — was alive and active, and he thereupon killed the king with a single arrow. The king of Judah, Ahaziah, who had been visiting Jehoram, was quick to flee, but the blood-thirsty Jehu ordered his death too; in fact, the small party from Judah escaped, but not before Ahaziah received a wound from which he died only a few miles away. It is difficult to see what advantage Jehu hoped to gain from his death, unless he feared that Ahaziah would seek to avenge his near relative's death. Jehu's next victim at Jezreel was Jezebel, who at least met her end with courage. Having thus superintended personally the deaths of the king and the powerful queen mother, Jehu proceeded to engineer from a safe distance the massacre of all Ahab's surviving kith and kin in Samaria. So perished the dynasty of Omri, and soon afterwards the last vestige of the foreign idolatrous cult was eradicated. The prophets had won the day — or had they?

CHAPTER 8

Syria Rampant

FROM the religious point of view, Jehu was raised up to punish
and to outroot the idolatry fostered in Israel by Omri's successors
and Jezebel in particular. So much had been the word of the Lord
to Elijah. But Jehu himself was not one of the prophets, and at the
moment of time when he organized the death of the last members of
Ahab's family it was by no means self-evident what he represented, apart from his own personal ambitions and interests. Jehu
was in full control, with the army's backing, and it remained to be
seen what his policies would be. It was clear to him that the previous
dynasty's downfall had been due to their willingness to embrace
foreign ways of life; very well, he would ally himself with the most
conservative elements in Israelite life. He therefore sought out
the leader of an extremely conservative, indeed extremist group,
the Rechabites. We know from Jeremiah 35 that these folk still pursued the nomadic ideal, refusing to live in houses or to enjoy any of
the fruits of civilization, and served Yahweh with a zeal that
bordered on fanaticism. They would have no qualms about bloodshed in what they considered a good cause. But in making alliance
with them, Jehu seems to have by-passed the prophets, probably
deliberately.

Reaching his capital, Jehu announced that he meant to support
the foreign Baal cult of Jezebel, which was a credible pose, and so
succeeded in assembling together every priest and devotee of
Melqart. He then slaughtered every man of them without
compunction, and ensured that this form of idolatry could never
recur by destroying and desecrating the temple of Melqart and every
article sacred to it. "Thus Jehu stamped out the worship of Baal in
Israel" (2 Kings 10:28).

By these means Jehu eliminated every rival (his dynasty was to last much longer than any other in Israel) and sought to enlist the support of the conservative elements of the population. It soon became apparent, however, that his support of Yahweh-worship was for political ends only; as the author of Kings puts it, ''Jehu was not careful to follow the law of the LORD the God of Israel with all his heart'' (10:31). In the situation of the time, nobody would have expected him to spare potential enemies, and his attack on Ahab's successors had had the divine blessing pronounced upon it in advance; but Jehu showed a ruthlessness and blood-lust that was unforgivable by any standards. 2 Kings 10 records how he slaughtered the nobility and the friends of the previous court, and also a fresh group of men of Judah who chanced to make an innocent visit to Jezreel. The prophets could not condone this sort of wanton brutality, and a century later one of their number still recalled with horror the murders committed at Jezreel.[1] We cannot even credit Jehu with a desire to put right the social wrongs and religious syncretism which had developed in recent years.

If Jehu had secured his own position inside Israel, he had done untold harm to the international position of his kingdom. He had deserted his post at Ramoth-gilead, and left the king of Damascus free to overrun all the Transjordanian territories: ''In those days the LORD began to work havoc on Israel, and Hazael struck at them in every corner of their territory eastwards from the Jordan'' (2 Kings 10:32f.). He had lost every ally the previous dynasty had won; if Phoenicia could have overlooked the death of Jezebel, Judah would certainly not readily forgive the death of her king, Ahaziah. Meanwhile in Samaria itself, every statesman and administrator of ability and experience had been killed off.

No king can afford to weaken his realm in order to strengthen his own position, but Jehu did just that. If he had nobody he need fear in Israel, there were those outside Israel's frontiers whom he had every reason to fear, and this grim truth was very quickly brought home to him. He came to power in 841 BC; that very year he was utterly humiliated by the Assyrians, who were still ruled by Shalmaneser III. Under Ahab, Israel had acquitted herself reasonably well twelve years earlier, at the battle of Qarqar; the kingdom of Damascus, now under Hazael, was as able to hold out against the Assyrian armies as she had been at Qarqar, and indeed it may have been due to Hazael's relative strength that the Assyrians decided to turn their attention westwards.[2] But Jehu could not offer the slightest show of strength, and he had no option but to pay the tribute imposed upon him by Shalmaneser. The tribute was not

1. Cf. Hosea 1:4f.
2. Shalmaneser claims that he besieged Damascus, but he did not take the city (*ANET*, p. 280).

large, as it turned out: "silver, gold, a golden bowl, a golden vase, golden cups, golden buckets", with one or two other other items, are listed. (The source of our information is a limestone obelisk found at Nimrud, the biblical Calah, on which Shalmaneser records some of his military successes.) Perhaps Jehu made light of it; but the fact remains that his humiliation was recorded in visible form for all time. The same Assyrian monument[3] depicts Jehu kneeling prostrate before the Assyrian monarch. We know of no other contemporary representation of any king of Israel or Judah; Solomon in all his glory is left to our imaginations; Jehu in all his humiliation is graven in the rock for ever. (See plate 2 facing p. 49.)

The Bible is silent on this episode, and Shalmaneser's record is laconic in its brevity; hence an alternative interpretation must be allowed, namely that Jehu voluntarily paid tribute to the Assyrians, in an effort to secure their help against Hazael. If so, the Assyrians did nothing to help, and on the whole it seems more likely that Jehu had no option in the matter. Excavations at Hazor in upper Galilee seem to show that Shalmaneser now attacked and destroyed it, which would obviously mean that Jehu tried to resist the Assyrians. But even if he paid tribute of his own free choice, his humiliation was none the less for that.

In passing, it is intriguing to note that the Assyrian king set up his royal monument at a place on the Mediterranean coast called Ba'li-ra'si, which has been identified with the Mount Carmel headland.[4] So here where through Elijah Yahweh had achieved a signal victory a few years before, the Assyrians now demonstrated to both Phoenicia and Israel who was the most powerful human ruler in the whole region. However, after token tribute and the symbolic act of erecting this monument, Shalmaneser marched back to Assyria with his armies, and left Phoenicia, Israel, and Damascus to their own devices.

Meanwhile what of Judah? It is strange how frequently the history of one Hebrew kingdom mirrors that of the other. Jehu's *coup d'état* in Samaria was followed by a double *coup* in Jerusalem. However, there is a clear and direct connection between the two events. In the Northern Kingdom, as we have seen, the bloodthirstiness of Jezebel was replaced by that of Jehu. In the south, the primary factor in the chain of events were the bloodthirstiness of Jezebel's daughter, Athaliah, and the typically bloodthirsty intervention of Jehu.

Athaliah had married the crown prince of Judah during the reign of Jehoshaphat to cement the newly-forged alliance between Israel (ruled by Ahab) and Judah. She was Ahab's daughter, we know, but

---

3. The Black Obelisk is now in the British Museum. For the text, see *DOTT,* p. 48.
4. Y. Aharoni, *LB,* p. 310.

it is nowhere recorded that Jezebel was her mother. J. Bright[5] has shown reasons for doubting that Jezebel was her mother, but it seems hard to imagine that anyone other than Jezebel's daughter could have been such a replica of the Phoenician queen in both creed and conduct. Like Jezebel in Samaria, Athaliah sought to introduce idolatry in Jerusalem itself, probably the same cult of the Phoenician god Melqart, and would brook no opposition. Her husband Jehoram gave her no trouble when he came to the throne; and on his death Athaliah as queen-mother was in a powerful position to dominate her son, the new king Ahaziah. He, however, had a very short reign, since he was murdered by Jehu, as we have seen. We do not know who might have succeeded him in the normal course of events; the royal line of Judah had suffered tragedy of late. First, Jehoram, Athaliah's husband, had eliminated every potential rival to the throne; secondly, a raid on Jerusalem by Philistines and others had swept away most of Jehoram's own family (cf. 2 Chronicles 21:16f.); and now Jehu had murdered not only Ahaziah but some forty-two of his "kinsmen" (2 Kings 10:12ff.). Athaliah now determined to compound this iniquity, by taking the throne herself and murdering all the survivors of the royal line of David. Presumably she had no sons of her own;[6] and she meant no sons of any other queen to survive. The line of David almost came to an abrupt end in this fashion, but unknown to Athaliah there was a single survivor, a baby boy, Joash by name, who was rescued by his aunt and hidden away by the priests in the temple of Yahweh. Athaliah's partisans had no respect for the temple, and broke into it to ransack its treasures to enhance the Baal cult; but they never suspected the existence of Joash, and he remained unharmed, brought up safely by the chief priest, Jehoiada, who happened to be the husband of the boy's rescuer.

Athaliah must have ruled with an iron hand, but there was no lasting strength in her position. We may guess that her supporters were either time-servers or foreigners. The ordinary citizens of Judah had no love for her, and must have resented much that she had done, but they were in a dilemma. By now the line of David was part and parcel of the constitution of Judah, and there appeared to be no survivor of the dynasty — undoubtedly the very existence of Joash must have been the best-kept secret — while Athaliah was by legal right the queen-mother. So law-abiding citizens seemed to have no alternative but to endure Athaliah. Even the prophets were silent.

Six years passed uneventfully, though evidently during this time Jehoiada sought to build up some sort of opposition to Athaliah.

5. *op. cit.*, p. 238 n. 41.
6. But see 2 Chronicles 24:7 (NEB).

Finally, when he judged the time to be ripe, he made sure he had sufficient military strength to win the day.

The dramatic story of the overthrow and death of Athaliah is told in detail in 2 Kings 11, retold in 2 Chronicles 23. This *coup d'état* was very different from Jehu's in the north. It was inspired not by the prophets but by the chief priest; it was carried through with a minimum of bloodshed; and far from displacing and destroying a dynasty, it replaced on the throne a true son of David — the seven-year-old Joash. There was popular rejoicing: "the whole people rejoiced and the city was tranquil" (2 Kings 11:20).

But the sorry chain of events had weakened Judah as much as Israel. The whole region between Egypt and the northern Euphrates had broken up into small, mutually hostile or suspicious kingdoms. Judah had not only suffered a raid on Jerusalem itself by Philistines and others, she had lost control of Edom, and with it her access to the Gulf of Aqaba and her port of Ezion-geber; Joash could do nothing to reverse this loss, and his kingdom was thrown back on its own limited resources throughout his reign.

The Syrian kingdom of Damascus, however, was able to profit by the weakness of the states to the south. Once the Assyrians had withdrawn, the king of Damascus, Hazael, built up his army afresh, and embarked on a policy of conquest. He swept the Israelite forces out of Transjordan, and there is evidence to show that he also made himself master of the territories of Moab and Edom further south in Transjordan. Undoubtedly the purpose behind this activity was to control the important trade routes with Arabia. West of the Jordan, too, the Israelite forces were hard pressed by Hazael's attacks. Philistines and Ammonites seized their opportunity to plunder their Israelite neighbours, as the Book of Amos indicates.[7] Jehu went to his grave after a twenty-eight reign which can have brought him and his subjects little joy. His son Jehoahaz (814-798) had scarcely succeeded to the throne when the Syrian inroads reached their peak. The fortress city of Hazor, which had so recently fallen to Shalmaneser's armies, was now destroyed once more, as excavations have shown, and it can be assumed that this disaster for Israel was accompanied by the utter defeat of her army. Hazael could, if he had wished, have deposed Jehoahaz, but he preferred to reduce Israel to a dependency, leaving Jehoahaz as a puppet king. Israel's chariotry, so powerful half a century earlier, was reduced, on Syrian instructions, to a mere ten in number (2 Kings 13:7). Hazael intended invading Judah as well, though no reasons are given, but Joash was able to buy him off by paying a handsome tribute. The Philistine city of Gath (perhaps still under the control of Judah) also felt the weight of the Syrian armies.

7. See M. Noth, *op. cit.*, p. 249 for details.

Hazael's successor Benhadad III[8] showed no signs of relenting when he came to the throne of Damascus in c. 806 B.C.; the prophet Amos brackets him with his father as an aggressor against Israel (Amos 1:4).[9] Nevertheless the day of retribution had come for Damascus, because "the LORD appointed a deliverer for Israel" (2 Kings 13:5). The biblical writer does not trouble to specify who the deliverer was; but Assyrian records unfold the story. Shortly after Benhadad's accession, the reigning king of Assyria, Adad-nirari III, brought Assyrian armies into Syria once again, and this time the power of the kingdom of Damascus was permanently broken. Israel and other small states had to pay the Assyrians tribute once again, but at least they were spared the devastation caused by armies marching through their lands. Benhadad had no such relief; the Assyrian campaigns against him culminated in his abject surrender, as in his own captured palace he had perforce to pay over a very heavy tribute.[10]

Once again the Assyrian armies withdrew to their own territory, allowing the smaller powers of Syria and Palestine to draw breath. The armies of Benhadad were not the formidable war-machine they had been, however, and other states set about reaping the advantage. Another Syrian kingdom, Hamath, started to expand at the expense of Damascus, and slowly the two Hebrew kingdoms also began to retrieve their fortunes.

8. Or perhaps Benhadad II; see p.154, note 4.
9. It is perhaps at this point in time that the siege of Samaria described in 2 Kings 6f. took place. Cf. J. Gray, *Kings,* pp. 517ff. See above, p
10. *ANET,* p. 281.

CHAPTER 9

New Prosperity

THE eighth century B.C. thus opened with a dramatic reversal of the fortunes of both Israel and Judah. New kings came to both thrones within a year or two of 800 B.C. Joash of Judah in his later years had rebelled against his priestly upbringing, thus making enemies; and his kingdom's weakness, coupled with some social unrest, probably increased a feeling of discontent with his régime. A Syrian invasion at the end of his reign increased popular feeling against him to such an extent that he was assassinated. There was no *coup d'etat,* however; his 25-year-old son Amaziah succeeded to the throne without opposition, just a year after the death of Jehoahaz of Israel. The new king in Samaria was Jehoash,[1] son of Jehoahaz and grandson of Jehu.

The all-too-brief account of the reign of Amaziah given in 2 Kings 14 tells of the quarrel between the two Hebrew kingdoms, which led to a temporary set-back for Judah. But we may infer from the fuller details given in 2 Chronicles 25 that at the start of their reigns, Jehoash and Amaziah repaired the alliance which Jehu had breached two generations earlier. The two kingdoms appear to have made common cause in the reconquest of the territories east of the Jordan. In northern Transjordan, Jehoash achieved three signal victories over the Syrians (at the expense of the kingdom of Damascus); Judah's attention was of course focussed on the Edomites, who must be reconquered if the trade routes with Arabia were to be exploited once again. In central Transjordan, the Moabites and Ammonites were left alone for the time being.

In preparing for his assault on the Edomites, Amaziah at first

---

1. A longer form of the name ''Joash''. Both ''Joash'' of Judah and ''Jehoash'' of Israel are in fact spelled in both fashions in the biblical records.

planned to supplement his own forces by the use of troops from
Israel. But in the event, due to prophetic advice, he decided against
using these mercenary troops. He had already paid for their
services, but since they could have profited to an even greater extent
from booty taken in the campaign, they set out for home in no very
good mood. Their resentment boiled over, and they took their booty
from cities of Judah[2] instead, killing and looting on a large scale at a
time when the armies of Judah were fully occupied in their campaign
against Edom.

Amaziah's campaign went well, and Judah successfully re-estab-
lished control over the northern part of Edom. Returning to his
capital, flushed with victory, Amaziah was infuriated to discover the
damage caused by the Israelite mercenaries, and immediately
declared war on Israel. Jehoash could scarcely be held responsible
for the mercenaries' behaviour, and he had no wish to quarrel with
Amaziah; his words to Amaziah "You have defeated Edom . . . and
it has gone to your head" (2 Kings 14:10) were true enough. But the
contemptuous tone of Jehoash's message was not calculated to
placate the angry king of Judah, and warfare inevitably resulted.
Jehoash made good his boast; the armies of Judah were routed in
battle at Beth-shemesh, and the Israelite troops proceeded to capture
Jerusalem itself. Jehoash was content to raid the royal and temple
treasures, and to break down the northern fortifications of the city.
as a reminder that he could recapture the city any time he chose.
Having thus demonstrated conclusively that Israel was much the
stronger of the two kingdoms, he withdrew — he had no wish to sub-
jugate Judah.

Jehoash died not long afterwards, and was succeeded by his son
Jeroboam II, who was to have a long and prosperous reign. It
appeared that Israel had at last found stability, and a dynasty
capable of holding on to the throne, though time was ultimately to
prove otherwise. Judah, on the other hand, had dynastic stability,
but nevertheless showed considerable discontent with individual
rulers. Amaziah, like his father before him, died by assassination.
The cause of the conspiracy is not recorded; the defeat by Israel
cannot have been the immediate cause, since that disaster occurred
more than fifteen years before the assassination, but it may perhaps
have been one of many reasons for Amaziah's unpopularity. There
was tension between the court and the priesthood at this period; and
there may well have been those who never forgave him for his execution of his father's assassins. He took no reprisals against the latter's
children; perhaps he paid for his leniency.

---

2. 2 Chronicles 25:13 is puzzling — the Israelite soldiery would scarcely have
attacked their own capital, Samaria. Probably some other name, similar to
Samaria, stood in the original Hebrew text.

However, under Amaziah's son and successor, Judah too found new prosperity. According to 2 Kings 15:2 he reigned for fifty-two years, though the figure probably includes a co-regency at each end of his reign.[3] He is called both Azariah and Uzziah in the Bible; it has been reasonably conjectured that the former was his personal name, the latter his throne-name.[4] By the end of his reign he appears to have become more powerful and influential than the Israelite king, but there is no hint of any further conflict between the two kingdoms. Evidently after the débâcle at Beth-shemesh Judah was content to let Israel well alone, and it was already Israel's policy to avoid molesting Judah. So, on amicable terms if not linked by formal treaty, the two kingdoms drew strength from each other's stability and influence, and, in effect, set about re-assembling David's empire.

Jeroboam II must have been one of the ablest kings Israel ever had, though we know all too little about his achievements. The prophet Jonah makes a brief appearance in the Books of Kings (2 Kings 14:25), to predict Jeroboam's victories in Transjordan. There Moab and Ammon were conquered once again, while the Syrians of the Damascus kingdom were not only driven out of all Israelite territories, but indeed made subject to Israel in their own homeland. The northern Israelite frontier was extended to the region of Hamath once again, just as it had been in David's time.

Strangely enough, the Books of Kings tell us even less about Uzziah's achievements, which are summed up in a single statement: "He built Elath and restored it to Judah" (2 Kings 14:22). This simple detail in fact implies the thorough subjugation of Edom — an achievement his father had begun, and one which Uzziah must have completed. Beyond that, we have to turn to 2 Chronicles for a list of Uzziah's successes and policies. In 2 Chronicles 26: 3-15 we read that he built up "a powerful fighting force" with which he defeated or overawed Philistines, Arabs, Meunites and Ammonites.[5] Philistine territory was overrun as never before; he not only captured existing Philistine cities but built new Judaean cities in their territory. The damage done to the fortifications of Jerusalem by Jehoash of Israel was put right, and he strengthened the defences of the southern wilderness region. He fostered new departures in military methods, and took a keen interest in agriculture: "he loved the soil", we are told. There is evidence that his "many cisterns" in the wilderness included some at Qumran, where centuries later the community which produced the Dead Sea Scrolls was to establish itself. The whole Negeb was settled and peopled as never before.

3. If E. R. Thiele's calculations are correct, he was sole ruler for no more than seventeen years (767-750 BC). See tables on p. 293.

4. See discussion in *IDB* iv, p. 742 (s.v. "Uzziah", by H. B. MacLean).

5. For details, cf. J. M. Myers, II Chronicles (AB: Garden City, 1965) *ad loc.*

The mention of "Ammonites" in 2 Chronicles 26:8 is of special interest. The accuracy of this reference has often been doubted; Ammon, after all, traditionally came within Israel's sphere of influence rather than Judah's, and — as we have seen — Uzziah provoked no quarrel with Israel while it was ruled by the equally powerful Jeroboam II. It is tempting to follow the Septuagint which again reads Meunites[6] (a people of the Edomite area) as in the previous verse. However, there is adequate reason to take the Hebrew text seriously. Uzziah presently contracted leprosy, or some serious skin disease,[7] and had to leave many of his official duties to his son Jotham (cf. 2 Kings 15:5); but there is evidence that till the end of his life he remained very much in control. The Assyrian armies reappeared west of the Euphrates at the very end of Uzziah's reign; the Assyrian king Tiglath-pileser III in 743 B.C. began a series of campaigns in the west, and some of the endangered states of Syria-Palestine quickly formed a coalition against him. The leader of the coalition, according to the Assyrian Annals, was "Az-ri-a-u" of "Ia-u-da-a", and it seems likely that this was none other than Azariah of Judah, unless the similarity of name is a mere coincidence.[8]

Jeroboam II had died two or three years before this coalition confronted the Assyrians, and at his death his kingdom had broken up into near-anarchy. His son Zechariah was assassinated after six months' reign, and the assassin (Shallum) achieved no more than a month's reign before yet another usurper (Menahem) unseated him. Menahem managed to restore order sufficiently to hold the throne for some years, but in reality Israel was now a spent force,[9] and there was no longer any rival to Uzziah as regards power and influence. Hence he was not only the organizer of the coalition in northern Syria, he was also free to dominate and take tribute from the Ammonites, who had formerly been subject to Israel. The squabbling contenders for the throne in Samaria were in no position to give strong leadership to the satellite states around. Just as Jehu's usurpation had destroyed the authority of Israel built up by Omri's

6. In Hebrew, "Ammonites" and "Meunites" are extremely similar words, which could have been very easily confused in scribal transmission.

7. As the NEB margin indicates (2 Kings 15:5), it is clear that what the English Versions have traditionally rendered "leprosy" must in fact have included a variety of skin diseases.

8. Opinions have always been divided about the identity of Azriau; cf. *DOTT*, pp. 54ff. for text and brief discussion by D. J. Wiseman. More recent studies have deleted the place name "Yaudi" (?Judah) from consideration, thus reducing the coincidence of names to one; cf. J. H. Hayes and J. M. Miller, *Israelite and Judaean History (OTL:* London 1977) pp. 424f. Even so it seems unnecessary to postulate some unknown individual as leader of the coalition, so long as Azariah of Judah remains a possibility.

9. There is some likelihood that Menahem was not able to bring Transjordan under his control, and that Pekah (the future king of Israel) held that territory after Jeroboam's death. Cf. E. R. Thiele, *MNHK,* p. 124.

dynasty, so now in turn Jehu's dynasty's achievements were nullified abruptly by internal weakness and usurpation. There seems very good reason to believe that, as H. Tadmor has argued,[10] Judah became natural heir to Israel's domains on the death of Jeroboam II.

The statement of 2 Chronicles 26:8 accordingly testifies not only to Judah's prosperity and power under Uzziah, but also to the sudden and disastrous weakness of the Northern Kingdom. The Books of Kings go a long way towards explaining the reasons for the downfall of Omri's dynasty, but since so little is said of Jeroboam's reign, we are less able to account definitively for the fall of Jehu's dynasty and for the subsequent anarchy. To be sure, there was an inbuilt dynastic weakness in Israel, and the personal ambitions of such men as Shallum, Menahem and Pekah undoubtedly played a big part in the events that followed Jeroboam's death. But a conspiracy requires some sort of motivation, and none of the three would have succeeded but for the existence of a large measure of discontent with Jeroboam's regime.

The documentation of Israelite discontent is available to us not in the historical books of the Old Testament but the prophetic. Both Amos and Hosea prophesied in the Northern Kingdom during the reign of Jeroboam II,[11] and both spoke for the common man. Their message, of course, was largely religious in content, and they claimed to speak on God's behalf rather than man's; but the physical plight of many ordinary Israelites is a recurring note in their prophecies and denunciations. In his introductory denunciation of Judah, Amos is concerned only with religious malpractice (Amos 2:4); but the very first charge he makes against Israel is that "they sell the innocent for silver and the destitute for a pair of shoes. They grind the heads of the poor into the earth" (2:6f.). If we put aside the religious teaching of the two prophets for later consideration,[12] we can legitimately extract the social content of their sermons, in order to illustrate the social conditions of the era. The basic fact was that the old tribal order, when a strong feeling of kinship and mutual responsibilities prevailed, had broken down, giving place to a "go-getting" society, with a very marked gulf between the living standards of rich and poor. The excavations at Tirzah, the capital of Israel before Samaria was built by Omri, have borne eloquent testimony to this stratification of society, as the archaeologists' spades have unearthed the well-to-do suburban mansions in one

10. Cf. *Scripta Hierosolymitana* 8 (1961), pp. 232-271.

11. Cf. Amos 1:1; Hosea 1:1. The ministry of Amos was probably of short duration (about 760 BC), but that of Hosea continued for some years after the fall of Jehu's dynasty. See H. L. Ellison, *The Prophets of Israel*, (Exeter, 1969), pp. 71, 95f.

12. See below, pp. 237-243.

quarter, and the slums elsewhere; two centuries earlier, by contrast, all the houses had been of the same size and structure.[13]

Israel could blame no Industrial Revolution for this unhappy development. Admittedly, the invading Syrian armies had caused a great deal of hardship during the earlier period of Jehu's dynasty; the devastation of small farms will have reduced their owners to penury, forcing others to sell their children and even themselves into slavery; their mortgaged farms went to swell the large estates of the rich. Even for Syrian misdeeds, however, the ineptness of earlier Israelite rule could ultimately be blamed, though Amos voiced the popular resentment against the Syrians without making any such charges against the Israelite kings. He was more interested to denounce the more direct iniquities of the upper classes. The destitute were sold into slavery in utter callousness (2:6); those who tried desperately to scratch a living from the soil were subjected to extortionate taxes (5:11). When the pauper went to buy food, he was robbed and cheated (8:5f.); and if he sought to obtain legal redress, he discovered that he was thrust out of court (5:12) by a society which turned justice upside down (5:7). Hosea's first thrust was directed at the Israelite royal court; "the line of Jehu", he asserted, would be punished "for the blood shed in Jezreel" (Hosea 1:4). The murderous deeds of Jehu at Jezreel have already been recounted, but the point in the prophet's words (or rather, in the oracle he received from the LORD) must surely have been that bloodshed had become normal practice for the royal line to achieve its own selfish ends. Naboth, who had died that Ahab's royal estate might be built up, may well have been the first in a long line of innocent victims. "One deed of blood after another" was Hosea's more explicit condemnation (4:2). He reinforces the charges brought by Amos; the extortion practised by the rich men of Samaria he describes thus: "They are thieves, they break into houses; they are robbers, they strip people in the street" (7:1). The crown was heedless of the common man, the judiciary blind to the injustices meted out to him, and as for the representatives of Israel's faith, who should have been more concerned about the situation than anyone, they are dismissed in a contemptuous sentence: "Priest? By day and night you blunder on, you and the prophet with you" (4:5).

When we turn from the genuine, deeply-felt resentments of Hosea and Amos back to the historical books of the Old Testament, we can readily understand why Israelite society fell apart as it did on the death of Jeroboam, and why any pretender to the throne could command a following. Israel was doomed; both Amos and Hosea knew that her downfall was inevitable — and well-deserved.

---

13. Cf. R. de Vaux, *Ancient Israel*[2] (London, 1965), p. 72f.

CHAPTER 10
The Fall of Samaria

THE death of the strong king of Judah, Uzziah, marked the end of an era for both kingdoms. The careful dating of the prophet Isaiah's call, "in the year of King Uzziah's death" (Isaiah 6:1), may well have significance beyond the chronological. Now both the long-lived and competent Hebrew kings were dead, and the Assyrians were once more on the march, led by one of their most able kings ever, Tiglath-pileser III. (See plate 3 facing p. 80.) The Syrian kingdoms had weakened themselves by a bitter struggle between themselves, Israel had fragmented, and Judah on its own was no match for the Assyrians. The old treaty friendship between Phoenicia and Israel had broken down, as is clear from the denunciation of Tyre by Amos (1:9), although such quarrels would no doubt have been patched up in face of a common enemy. But the general weakness of the Syrian and Palestinian states was such that the initiative lay wholly with the Assyrians. As it became evident that these invaders were now embarking on permanent conquest (a new policy on their part), the hapless Syro-Palestinian states must have cast around in their minds for potential allies, and naturally enough their thoughts turned to Egypt. An old enemy, Egypt, had not interfered in Palestinian affairs for many long years, so past hostilities could be conveniently forgotten. As for the Egyptians, they had no particular affection for their small northern neighbours, but they had no wish at all to see a powerful nation like Assyria establishing its position on Egypt's frontiers, and were accordingly ready to listen to pleas for help. Thus Egypt begins to come back into our story.

The Assyrian records relating to "Azriau of Yaudi" are broken and difficult to read, but there is no doubt that the anti-Assyrian coalition suffered a defeat, as a result of which tribute had to be paid to Tiglath-pileser III by no few local kings, including Uzziah himself, Menahem of Israel, and Rezin of Damascus.[1] The tribute which Menahem had to pay is detailed in 2 Kings 15:19f.;[2] it was a crippling sum, and one that did nothing to make Menahem a popular figure in Samaria, but at least it served to keep Assyrian troops out of Israelite territory, in itself no small gain.

For a short while the Assyrians left the Levant in peace, but the peace was not security, nor indeed was the interval uneventful. The king of Damascus, Rezin, retained his throne, but in Judah Uzziah's death was followed fairly soon afterwards by the death of his son Jotham, while in Israel similarly Menahem's son and successor Pekahiah had a very brief reign. Before long, accordingly, the three kings of these states were Rezin, Ahaz (Uzziah's grandson), and Pekah respectively. Pekah we have mentioned before; it seems quite probable that he had been virtually king in Transjordan since the death of Jeroboam II, and he made his bid for the whole kingdom once Menahem died. To raise the tribute for Assyria, Menahem had been obliged to levy a 50-shekel tax (roughly the price of a slave)[3] on all the land-owners of his realm, some 60,000 in all;[4] and 2 Kings 15:20 suggests that Menahem went so far as to enlist Assyrian support in order to retain his throne. Small wonder, then, that there was plenty of support for Pekah when he challenged Menahem's son and successor.

Thus Pekah usurped the throne in Samaria, and probably the throne-name of his predecessor too, for "Pekah" and "Pekahiah" are simply variant forms of the same name. We do not know what his personal name was. It is reasonable to assume that his "election manifesto", so to speak, included a pledge to take firm and effective action in the face of the Assyrian threat, and to renounce the sort of pro-Assyrian policy which Menahem had perforce embraced. Rezin of Damascus was more than willing to make alliance with him and to join him in making urgent military preparation for the inevitable conflict with Tiglath-pileser of Assyria. A strong coalition seemed to offer the only hope. Some smaller states were prepared to support them in the enterprise; but Judah declined to do so. King Ahaz lacked the courage and ability of his grandfather Uzziah, but in fact he was very prudent to stand aloof from such a project, foredoomed to failure as it was. At least, it is difficult to suppose that Tiglath-pileser with the full weight of the highly-trained Assyrian armies could have been successfully withstood by a confederation which included all the states of Syria and Palestine.

1. Cf. *DOTT*, p. 54.
2. In this passage, Tiglath-pileser is called "Pul", the name by which he was known in Babylon. See p. 191.
3. Cf. D. J. Wiseman, *Iraq* 15 (1953), p. 135.
4. Cf. J. A. Montgomery, *The Books of Kings (ICC:* Edinburgh, 1951), pp. 450f.

The ringleaders of the coalition, Pekah and Rezin, were dismayed at the refusal of Judah to be implicated; indeed, according to Isaiah, they were "burning with rage" (Isaiah 7:4). King Uzziah had made Judah a power to be reckoned with among its neighbours, and the confederates could not afford to have a neutral, potentially hostile, Judah in their rear when the time came to confront the Assyrians. Without hesitation, therefore, they now attacked Judah, hoping to frighten Ahaz into joining the confederacy, or to frighten his subjects into deposing him, or else, at the worst, to render his kingdom powerless to pose any threat to their enterprise.[5]

The Syro-Ephraimite war (as it is often called) succeeded to the extent that it frightened Ahaz. "King and people", Isaiah records, "were shaken like forest trees in the wind" (Isaiah 7:2) — a graphic simile reminiscent of the boasting language of Assyrian monuments and inscriptions.[6] Judah suddenly found itself ringed by enemies on all sides. The combined armies of Israel and Damascus swept resistance aside and besieged Jerusalem. The Syrian army also sent detachments to liberate Edom, Judah's vassal, according to the Hebrew text of 2 Kings 16:6. (Most recent translations and commentaries prefer to change the Hebrew text slightly, thus crediting Edom's liberation to its own endeavours.) The Edomites then swiftly captured Elath, Judah's Red Sea port, and began to raid southern Judah. Meanwhile, the Philistines were retrieving lost ground and taking over parts of Judaean territory on the west.[7] King Ahaz himself had an additional, personal cause for anxiety; his attackers had found a man they hoped would replace him as king of Judah, a certain "son of Tabeel" (Isaiah 7:6).[8] It is not revealed who he was, but the name is Aramaic, which suggests that Damascus rather than Israel meant to take over Judah.

Jerusalem was not easily captured, however, and Ahaz held on grimly. But not unnaturally, he cast about in his mind for any avenue of escape from the nation's predicament, and the only practical and effective solution that occurred to him was to appeal to Assyria for assistance. The only other course was to do nothing, in the hope that Tiglath-pileser would sooner or later invade Syria from the north, whether or not Ahaz invited him to do so. From our vantage point in history, it is clear to us that Tiglath-pileser would soon have relieved the pressure on Jerusalem in any case, without

5. Judah's quarrel with Israel and Damascus was in itself nothing new — see 2 Kings 15:37. Cf. B. Oded, *CBQ* 34 (1972), pp. 153-165.

6. For example, the Assyrian king Sennacherib was later to claim that Hezekiah of Judah was "shut up like a caged bird within Jerusalem, his royal city" (cf. *DOTT*, p. 67).

7. See maps in *MBA*, p. 92.

8. The spelling "Tabeal" (AV, NEB) accurately represents the Hebrew, but the Hebrew is no doubt a deliberately contemptuous mis-spelling to give the meaning "no good".

any intervention on the part of Judah; but it may be doubted if the royal information service could have given Ahaz assurance of that fact. For the time being, at any rate, he delayed, while taking what practical steps he could to promote the welfare of his citizens. One urgent task was to ensure an adequate water supply — always a problem for Jerusalem in time of siege. He ventured in person beyond the city walls to check on the situation at one of the few water conduits; and it while thus occupied that he received intelligence from a source not available to modern national leaders, a prophet of Yahweh. He was confronted by the prophet Isaiah, who predicted the downfall of both Samaria and Damascus, and advised him to keep calm and do nothing except to exercise faith in God.

It was the first time a prophet had intervened so directly in a context of national crisis and emergency, and Ahaz was probably taken aback. In Isaiah 7ff. we have a full record of what Isaiah said to the king, but apparently the latter had little to say in reply; he declined even to ask for a sign from heaven to reassure him.

It is clear that Ahaz did not have the firm faith which Isaiah recommended to him; but there was more to it than that. Isaiah's advice, though we know it was in fact politically realistic, was not based on political calculations, and Ahaz felt reluctant to ignore the well-reasoned arguments of his political experts. Perhaps he weighed the issues carefully first, but in the end he decided to turn a deaf ear to the prophet's words. Professor W. McKane has described very effectively the dilemma and the choice that confronted Ahaz:

> What Ahaz refused to do was just to abandon the well-charted routes of political negotiation and in this he would certainly have the backing of his professional advisers. Was he to scrap the ways of thinking and the attitudes which were universally current in diplomatic exchanges and political bargaining and to base the security of Judah on trust in Yahweh? We should not underestimate the revolutionary character of this demand nor wonder that the statesmen boggled at it and were moved to consternation and anger when it was formulated by a prophet of Yahweh.[9]

Discounting the prophet's advice, therefore, "Ahaz sent messengers to Tiglath-pileser, King of Assyria to say, 'I am your servant and your son, Come and save me from the King of Aram and from the King of Israel who are attacking me.' Ahaz took the silver and gold found in the house of the LORD and in the treasuries of the royal palace and sent them to the King of Assyria as a bribe" (2 Kings 16:7f.). These two verses indicate something of the humiliation and financial cost of Ahaz's appeal to Assyria. But one might be tempted to ask, was not that a small price to pay for

---

9. W. McKane, *Prophets and Wise Men (SBT,* 44: London, 1965), p. 115.

national security? And if Tiglath-pileser meant to attack Rezin and
Pekah in any case, did it make any serious difference to the situation
whether Ahaz made overtures to him or not? The answer is that
Ahaz's action had long-term effects which were anything but beneficial to Judah. First and foremost, Judah lost her right to
independent political policies; hitherto she could be hostile to
Assyria or neutral, as she pleased, but now she was to be firmly
under Assyrian direction, a mere puppet kingdom. A small, inland
state, she might have been relatively undisturbed by the Assyrians;
by her own choice, she had drawn Assyrian attention to herself. The
other long-term effect was religious. 2 Kings 16:10-18 is a passage
which is not altogether easy to interpret, but it is stated plainly in
verse 18 that the purpose of some at least of the innovations at the
Jerusalem temple was "to satisfy the King of Assyria". Foreign
idolatry had again come to Judah, and not this time at the hands of a
usurper like Athaliah. The royal acquiescence in idolatrous worship
was bound to have its effects on the religion of the nation;[10] and with
the religious decline went social injustices too, which had already
begun to affect Judah during Uzziah's prosperous reign. Isaiah and
Micah in Judah found nearly as much apostasy and social injustice
as Hosea and Amos had had cause to denounce in Israel a few years
earlier. A century and more later the prophet Ezekiel, in his outspoken allegory of the two fallen women (Ezekiel 23), maintained
that Jerusalem's degradation occurred later chronologically but
ultimately proved deeper and blacker than her sister Israel's.

But at least Ahaz reaped the short-term benefits he was seeking:
"The King of Assyria listened to him; he advanced on Damascus,
captured it, deported its inhabitants to Kir and put Rezin to death"
(2 Kings 16:9). Thus the spotlight turns from Judah back to the
northern confederates, Rezin of Damascus and Pekah of Samaria,
who could but withdraw their armies from Judaean soil and wait
and see what strategy Tiglath-pileser would adopt. The precise
sequence of events is uncertain, but it seems most probable that in
three successive years' campaigns (734-732 B.C.) the Assyrian
armies attacked and conquered the coastal plain, from Tyre down to
the Egyptian border, the northern and eastern parts of Israel, and
finally the kingdom of Damascus.[11] The first campaign served to
outflank the confederates, and to place Assyrian troops down on the
Egyptian frontiers, in order to forestall any Egyptian support for the
Palestinian states. The Philistine city of Gaza was taken, and its king
Hanunu fled to Egypt.[12]

10. Undoubtedly much of the idolatry in the reign of Ahaz was not specifically
Assyrian in origin, but was indigenous to Palestine and Phoenicia: see J. W.
McKay, *Religion in Judah under the Assyrians* (*SBT* ii, 26: London, 1973), *passim*.
    11. Cf. Y. Aharoni, *LB*, pp. 328-333. For alternative reconstruction of events, see
Noth, pp. 258-261; Hayes and Miller, pp. 427-432.
    12. Cf. *DOTT*, p. 55.

The fate of Damascus is briefly told on the Assyrian Nimrud Tablet:[13] "The widespread territory of Damascus in its whole extent I restored to the border of Assyria. My official I set over them as district-governor." In other words, not only was Rezin executed and some of his citizens deported (as 2 Kings records), but the kingdom became a mere Assyrian province, its political integrity a thing of the past.

But our chief interest lies in the kingdom of Israel, which seems to have felt the main thrust of Tiglath-pileser's second campaign of these three years. The capital, Samaria, and the central and southern part of the kingdom, Ephraim, emerged unscathed; but that must have been small comfort. The full weight of the Assyrian armies fell upon the north of the country, Galilee, and the great fortress city of Hazor fell; it was ruthlessly destroyed, and was never rebuilt. Further south, the no less important city of Megiddo suffered a similar fate; it was the Assyrians themselves who rebuilt it. Tiglath-pileser lists some of his captures in Galilee, and the evidence permits us to trace his three-pronged attack on Israel.[14] From Hazor some of his troops marched west, and mastered the coastal plain in the area of Acco and Dor; some marched south-west and destroyed Megiddo; and the third army marched south and east into Israelite Transjordan, making that territory their own.

The citizens of Samaria could not doubt that it would be their turn next, unless something were done swiftly to dissuade Tiglath-pileser from further attacks. The action they took is stated succinctly by both the Bible and the Nimrud Tablet, in slightly different but complementary terms. "Hoshea son of Elah", says 2 Kings 15:30, "formed a conspiracy against Pekah son of Remaliah, attacked him, killed him and usurped the throne." Tiglath-pileser records of the people of Israel that "Pekah their king they deposed and Hoshea I set as king over them."[15] In other words, Hoshea came to the throne as leader of a pro-Assyrian faction, and the Assyrian king was content to ratify his position (on receipt of tribute).

Thus Israel, like Judah, became a mere puppet kingdom of Assyria. Worse than that, she forfeited a great deal — at least two-thirds — of her territory, for the Assyrians did not return the conquered areas to the control of Samaria. Instead, Tiglath-pileser reorganized his conquests as Assyrian provinces, administered by Assyrian governors. Isaiah, who watched these events from the safety of Judah, alludes to Tiglath-pileser's invasion in 9:1, and may be referring to the three new provinces when he speaks of "the way of the sea" (i.e. the province of Dor, on the Mediterranean coast),

13. *Ibid.*
14. See *MBA*, map 147.
15. *DOTT*, p. 55.

"the land beyond the Jordan" (the province of Gilead), and "Galilee of the nations" (the province of Megiddo — the Assyrians rebuilt the city to serve as the administrative capital).[16] The old tribal areas of Zebulun and Naphtali, to which Isaiah also refers here, were among those lost to Israel, and many of their inhabitants were deported to far-off Assyria.[17] Deportation was no innovation in the ancient world, but this was the first time that either Hebrew kingdom was subjected to it.

What remained of the kingdom of Israel must have been both smaller and weaker than Judah, and the proud citizens of Samaria chafed at the humiliations to which Tiglath-pileser had subjected them, though for the moment there was little they could do about it. Hoshea dutifully paid his tribute to the Assyrian king, and ignored the unrest of his subjects. The death of Tiglath-pileser five years later (727 B.C.) no doubt seemed a propitious moment to the more rebellious spirits — there was always hope of internal weakness in any kingdom on the death of a king, and Tiglath-pileser had usurped the Assyrian throne. As it happened, however, Tiglath-pileser's son, Shalmaneser V, found no difficulty in succeeding to the throne, and any hopes of independence harboured by the citizens of Israel were foredoomed. We have no way of knowing what Hoshea's own personal view was; it may be that he, like Judah's last king, Zedekiah,[18] was forced into rebellion against his better judgement. His own advisers may well have counselled revolt, and nobody doubts that the Egyptians were urging him to defy the Assyrians; the tentacles of Assyrian power were by now much too near the borders of Egypt for the latter's comfort. At any rate, whether willingly or reluctantly, King Hoshea rebelled, and thereby signed the death-warrant of his kingdom: he himself faced arrest and imprisonment, his capital was to undergo a long siege with all that that implied, many of his citizens faced deportation, and his kingdom was fated to become just another Assyrian province.

Once again, the precise chronology and sequence of events is uncertain and disputed.[19] The biblical account of the fall of Samaria is rather concise, and not without some difficulties; and the Assyrian inscriptional records of the event raise their own problems. Two consecutive kings of Assyria undertook military campaigns against Israel, Shalmaneser V (who died in late 722 or early 721 B.C.) and his successor Sargon II (see plate 4 facing p. 81), and the basic problem is, which of them successfully concluded the siege of

16. Cf. Isaiah 9:1, RSV; but NEB translates the verse rather differently. There are several difficulties about this verse; cf. J. A. Emerton, *JSS* 14 (1969), pp. 151-175. See *MBA,* map 148, for Tiglath-pileser's provincial structure in Palestine and Syria.
17. Cf. 2 Kings 15:29; *DOTT, ibid.*
18. See below, p. 129.
19. See especially *DOTT,* pp. 58f.; *AOTS,* pp. 347f.; and J. Gray, *Kings,* pp. 60ff.

Samaria? The Babylonian Chronicle suggests that it was Shalmaneser; but Sargon, in one of the last inscriptions of his reign (though no earlier), claims the credit.[20] What does the Bible say? In 2 Kings 17:3 reference is made to Shalmaneser by name, but in the following verses the attacker is simply called "the King of Assyria" without further identification. In the following chapter there is equal ambiguity about the Hebrew text: "Shalmaneser King of Assyria came up against Samaria, and besieged it. And at the end of three years they took it" (2 Kings 18:9f. RV). Most modern English translations, however, prefer to translate "*he* took it", a reading which would explicitly identify Shalmaneser as the conqueror.[21] Thus on the one hand the biblical evidence is unclear, while on the other the claims of Sargon may have been exaggerated.[22]

What may be asserted confidently is that Shalmaneser besieged the city of Samaria, and that Sargon completed the subjugation of the Palestinian area.[23] The three-year siege may have ended as early as 723 B.C.,[24] though 722 is the most likely date. Later, Sargon was active in the west in several campaigns. The Philistines had not all taken warning from the fate of Damascus.and Samaria, and they provoked an Assyrian assault in the year 720. Hanunu king of Gaza, who had fled to Egypt in 734 when Tiglath-pileser's armies had invaded Philistia, returned with the aid of an Egyptian army, to make common cause with the king of Hamath and other Syro-Palestinian states against the invader. Sargon advanced to the vicinity of the Egyptian border to defeat and capture Hanunu and force back the Egyptian army, in a battle at Rapihu. Other Philistine cities followed the example of Gaza, and it was not until 712 that Sargon finally broke the resistance of the last would-be rebels. Sargon's own records list his conquests in and around Palestine.[25] In one inscription[26] he calls himself "subjugator of the land of Judah", but there is no record of his taking major military action in Judah.

This protracted period of unrest and opposition in Syria and

---

20. Cf. *DOTT*, p. 59.
21. This rendering (the difference in Hebrew is very slight) has the support of the ancient Versions.
22. Cf. J. Gray, *Kings*, p. 61.
23. On Sargon's campaigns, see H. Tadmor, *JCS* 12 (1958), pp. 22-40, 77-100.
24. First suggested by A. T. Olmstead, *AJSL* 21 (1906), pp. 179-182. Cf. E. R. Thiele, *MNHK*, pp. 141-154.
25. Cf. *DOTT*, pp. 59-62. The Egyptian commander-in-chief, "Sib'e" in *DOTT* and elsewhere, is now known to have borne the name "Re'eh". The puzzling name "So" in 2 Kings 17:4 cannot therefore be equated with a non-existent "Sib'e", and it probably indicates not the monarch's name but that of the important Egyptian city of Saïs (cf. J. Gray, *Kings*, p. 642). The Egyptian king at the time was Osorkon IV; see K. A. Kitchen, *The Third Intermediate Period in Egypt* (Warminster, 1973), §§333f. Kitchen's own view is that "So" is an abbreviation for "Osorkon".
26. Cf. *DOTT*, p. 62.

Palestine induced the Assyrian king to proceed further with the "pacification" of the conquered areas. His measures affected Israel in two respects. He made the newly-conquered remnant of the Northern Kingdom yet another Assyrian province, called after its capital city, Samaria, which he renovated. Thus the city itself, from a purely physical point of view, suffered little. It was otherwise with a large number of citizens; he records the capture and exile of no fewer than 27,280 people.[27] Large scale deportations like this served not only to wreak vengeance on those who dared oppose the Assyrians, but also to reduce effectively the likelihood of further rebellion, by removing from the scene the intelligentsia and the potential leaders.

Nearly 30,000 Israelites, accordingly, were transported, some of them as far away as Media, many miles to the east of Assyria. However one computes the population of Israel in its last days as a kingdom, this huge deportation must have formed a substantial percentage of the whole; Menahem had found 60,000 land-owners to tax, it will be recalled. But Sargon conquered enemies and subdued kingdoms elsewhere, and he applied the same deportation policy in the east as in the west, with the result that the gap created in the population of Israel was soon filled with people from Babylon and other areas.[28]

The Kingdom of Israel thus came to an end. It lost its royal house and its independence, and it lost many of its citizens in battle and by deportation (presumably the exiles gradually intermarried and so disappeared from history, in their various places of exile). It had already lost the purity of its worship of Yahweh many years before, but the religious picture was made worse, from the biblical point of view, by the settlement in this territory of many foreigners, who imported a multitude of idolatrous practices, and settled down to intermarry with the local population. One can well understand the view expressed by the writer of 2 Kings 17. Israel lost its name (becoming the Assyrian province of *Samerina*) and in the administrative reorganization lost every vestige of its old tribal structure; in these senses (and no other) were the ten tribes "lost". There was of course some measure of continuity between the citizens of Israel before 721 B.C. and the Samaritan community of later years; to this day there is a small Samaritan community which seeks to worship the one true God. Jesus, it may be recalled, said of such folk that they did not know what they worshipped (John 4:22); He made no accusation of idolatry.[29]

27. 27,290 is the figure in some of his records.
28. Cf. 2 Kings 17:24; Ezra 4:2, 10 shows that the process of repopulation continued for a generation or two. For an estimate of the population of Samaria, see R. de Vaux, *Ancient Israel: its Life and Institutions* (ET London,[2] 1965), pp. 65ff.
29. Cf. F. F. Bruce, *The Books and the Parchments*[3] (London, 1963), pp. 125ff.

CHAPTER 11

The Reign of Hezekiah

THE abrupt and disastrous end of the kingdom of Israel did not leave Judah unaffected. The downfall of her sister-kingdom must have dismayed prince and commoner alike in Judah, despite all the past rivalries between north and south, while the advance of the tentacles of Assyrian power to her own northern frontier must have been a constant anxiety to Judah. It may fairly be supposed that not a few northerners migrated to Judah during the troubled years preceding and immediately following the fall of Samaria, and their presence may well have affected Judaean attitudes. Judah had been spared a like fate by the submission of her king, Ahaz, to the Assyrians, and by a strict policy of loyalty to the oaths made to Assyria; but if some viewed this policy as only prudent, there were others who felt angry humiliation, and burned to resist the oppressor. By herself, it must have been obvious to all, Judah could scarcely hope to defeat the imperial power of Assyria, but had she not the God of battles to protect her? And on a more mundane level, she was by no means alone in wishing to thwart Assyria's plans. In the early years of her reign, Sargon of Assyria had several rebels and enemies to deal with, such as the Philistine Gaza. Another notable rebel city was Babylon, where a Chaldaean named Merodach-baladan seized and held the throne for fully twelve years (721-709 B.C.). Hamath in northern Syria also revolted, and evidently Samaria, not yet submissive to Assyria, joined the revolt, which was crushed by Sargon Of the citizens of Hamath deported by Sargon, many were placed in Samaria (cf. 2 Kings 17:24).

It appears that Judah made its first slight move towards resistance, together with its eastern neighbours Moab and Edom, at the instigation of the Philistine king of Ashdod, who rebelled, with

Egyptian support, in 713 B.C.[1] Sargon proceeded to crush Ashdod (and carved out a new Assyrian province called Ashdod), but took minimal action against Judah, Moab and Edom. His own inscription[2] testifies to the fact that he fully blamed Aziru king of Ashdod for their disaffection, and we may fairly assume that Judah and the other two small states "surrendered in the nick of time", as Y. Aharoni puts it. Judah's fortress of Azekah was captured by the Assyrian armies at about this time, but her nominal independence was not assailed.[3]

By now the king of Judah was Hezekiah, a very different man from his father Ahaz. The question of the precise dates of his reign is one of the most tantalizing problems of Old Testament chronology, but at the latest he came to the throne in 715 B.C.,[4] and he must therefore be held responsible for Judah's slight involvement with the revolt of Ashdod. Where Ahaz had panicked into making an appeal to Assyria for aid, Hezekiah always chafed at the Assyrian yoke, and sought every opportunity to regain independence. Hezekiah was a devout man and a religious reformer. In his dealings with Assyria he made mistakes, but the catastrophe in Samaria was too recent for him to ignore or overlook the dangers of revolt, and he exercised a certain caution in his bids for independence. He neither rushed into revolt without counting the cost, nor did he leave himself without some room for diplomatic manoeuvre. The result was that the Assyrians never captured him nor his capital city, and Judah retained its status as a kingdom, despite his revolts and despite the successes of the Assyrian armies. His kingdom did not get off scot-free by any means, however.

The abortive revolt in 713 B.C. was a flash in the pan, and Hezekiah made no further move so long as Sargon II was king of Assyria. His major attempt to break free came after 705, when Sargon died and was succeeded by his son Sennacherib. As usual, the death of an Assyrian monarch proved to be the signal for rebellion. Babylon again asserted its independence, once again under the Chaldaean Merodach-baladan. There is a brief but intriguing account in 2 Kings 20:12f. of Merodach-baladan's embassy to Hezekiah, at a time when the latter was recovering from a serious illness. In truly oriental fashion, the envoys laid much stress on the question of the Judaean king's health; but two details in the biblical record make it plain that the embassy was not really a courtesy visit. In the first place, the visitors took pains to investigate all Hezekiah's resources, financial and military; and secondly, the

1. Isaiah 20 should be read in this connexion.
2. Cf. *DOTT*, p. 61.
3. Cf. Y. Aharoni, *LB*, pp. 334f.
4. See Appendix. His reign (or co-regency with his father) may have begun as early as 729 B.C.

prophet Isaiah took it upon himself to give the king a plain warning not to associate himself with the Babylonians. A widespread conspiracy was afoot, despite the prophet's warnings.

If Hezekiah's diplomatic manoeuvrings were in the face of Isaiah's counsel, the prophet can have had no objection to the religious reforms which were in fact part of the rebellion. Both 2 Kings 18 and 2 Chronicles 29ff. have nothing but praise for these reforms, which were primarily intended to eradicate the idolatry fostered during the reign of Ahaz, though they did not stop there. Hezekiah had a praiseworthy ambition to eject everything which promoted idolatry, even the old brazen serpent Nehushtan, a purely Israelite symbol and relic. The Israelite hillshrines, which similarly had attracted idolatrous practices, were another victim of his reforming zeal. An interesting facet of his reforms is his attempt to attract the northern Israelites to worship at Jerusalem; the appeal was not very successful, however.

> So the couriers passed from city to city through the land of Ephraim and Manasseh and as far as Zebulun, but they were treated with scorn and ridicule. However, a few men of Asher, Manasseh and Zebulun submitted and came to Jerusalem.
>
> (2 Chronicles 30:10f.)

We need not doubt that Hezekiah's intentions were not wholly religious in character; he was seeking to unite the Palestinian states against Sennacherib, and it would have suited him well to have the ex-kingdom of Israel rally to his flag. Indeed he probably had hopes of becoming king of a united Israel, like David of old.

To Egypt Hezekiah sent envoys, and again provoked the prophet Isaiah to anger:

> Oh, rebel sons! says the LORD,
>   you make plans, but not of my devising,
>   you weave schemes, but not inspired by me,
>   piling sin upon sin;
> you hurry down to Egypt without consulting me,
>   to seek protection under Pharaoh's shelter
>   and take refuge under Egypt's wing.
> Pharaoh's protection will bring you disappointment
>   and refuge under Egypt's wing humiliation.
>
> (Isaiah 30:1-3)

Some Palestinian states prudently refused to support the rebellion, but Hezekiah persuaded the Philistine city-states of Ashkelon and Ekron to join it. The king of Ekron, by name Padi, was reluctant, but his citizens had no such inhibitions, and the luckless Padi found himself bound in iron fetters and placed in the custody of Hezekiah.[5]

5. Cf. *DOTT,* pp. 66f.

An eventual Assyrian onslaught was inevitable, and Hezekiah took what steps he could to meet it, though he must have been relying heavily (and unwisely) on Egyptian military support. His most famous operation in face of the Assyrian threat was the construction of the Siloam tunnel. The perennial problem of Jerusalem in times of danger and attack has always been its water supply — a specially acute problem in a country where the summer months are hot and dry. The city has always made good use of cisterns and pools, which have to depend on rain or aqueducts, but its only two actual sources of water, its only springs, lay well outside the city walls, on the east side. In time of siege, therefore, the citizens would be cut off from these springs, while the attacking army would have easy access to them. Hezekiah's own father, Ahaz, had been perturbed by this situation a generation earlier, when the attack on Jerusalem by the Syrian-Israelite alliance had been imminent, if we may judge from Isaiah 7:3. But where Ahaz had investigated but done nothing, Hezekiah took action and called in his engineers. They could do nothing about the lower and more southerly spring (En-rogel, now commonly known as Job's Well), so they concentrated their attention on the spring of Gihon (known now as the Virgin's Fountain) in the Kidron Valley. Hereabouts they "blocked up all the springs and the stream which flowed through the land" (2 Chronicles 32:4) and "blocked the upper outflow of the waters of Gihon" (2 Chronicles 32:30). As they pertinently asked, "Why . . . should Assyrian kings come here and find plenty of water?" (2 Chronicles 32:4).

The making of the tunnel is very briefly described in the Bible: "Hezekiah . . . made the pool and the conduit and brought water into the city" (2 Kings 20:20). The "conduit" was in fact no mean feat of hydraulic engineering; it was an underground tunnel to divert Gihon's waters to the upper pool of Siloam inside the city walls.[6] (See plate 5 facing p. 112.) The engineers excavated from both ends of their tunnel, which had to turn and twist in various directions;[7] we can only applaud their skill in ensuring that the two parties met in the middle, and that the level of the slope was correct.

The tunnel was long lost sight of, but it was rediscovered in 1880. On the tunnel wall was a Hebrew inscription (see plate 6 facing p. 113) placed there by the original engineers and it conveys something of their excitement and sense of achievement.

This is the story of the piercing through. While the stone-cutters were swinging their axes, each towards his fellow, and while there were yet

---

6. The pool lies outside the city walls as they are today.
7. See illustration in *NBD*, p. 1187; see also *MBA*, map 114.

three cubits to be pierced through, there was heard the voice of a man calling to his fellow, for there was a crevice on the right. And on the day of the piercing through, the stone-cutters struck through each to meet his fellow, axe against axe. Then ran the water from the Spring to the Pool for twelve hundred cubits, and a hundred cubits was the height of the rock above the head of the stone-cutters.[8]

The Siloam project was only one of the steps taken by Hezekiah to strengthen his defences. The prophet Isaiah gives some idea of the bustle and activity which took place:

On that day you looked to the weapons stored in the House of the Forest; you filled all the many pools in the City of David, collecting water from the Lower Pool. Then you surveyed the houses in Jerusalem, tearing some down to make the wall inaccessible, and between the two walls you made a cistern for the Waters of the Old Pool.

Isaiah's comment, however, was not complimentary: "But you did not look to the Maker of it all or consider him who fashioned it long ago" (Isaiah 22: 8-11).

From brief passages here and there in the Books of Kings and Chronicles[9] we can deduce that Hezekiah took great pains to organize Judah's defences, and to put pressure on Philistines and Edomites and others to join the anti-Assyrian forces. But all this activity was ultimately in vain; Hezekiah's schemes prospered, as the writer of Chronicles acknowledges, but only so long as the Assyrians stayed away.

Sennacherib had become king of Assyria in 705 B.C., but it was not until 701 that he was able to march into Palestine to confront Hezekiah and his allies. In the meantime he had dealt competently with revolts elsewhere; the Merodach-baladan who had recently defied Sargon for as long as twelve years was very speedily ousted from the throne of Babylon on this occasion, in 702 B.C. In his campaign to the west, Sennacherib first disposed of the Phoenician rebels. His own record puts it succinctly: "The awful splendour of my lordship overwhelmed Luli, King of Sidon, and he fled far off over the sea and died an infamous death."[10] He then marched down the coast into Philistine territory, and took effective action against the rebels there. An Egyptian army put in an appearance, but it was routed by the Assyrians at Eltekeh, halfway between Joppa and Ashdod. Before long the Assyrian king, having subjugated and secured the coastal plains, turned his attention to the hinterland — the little kingdom of Judah — and descended like a wolf on the fold.

8. *DOTT,* p. 210.
9. 2 Kings 18:8; 1 Chronicles 4:41ff.; 2 Chronicles 32:5f, 27ff.
10. *DOTT,* p. 66.

"As for Hezekiah, the Jew", Sennacherib records, "forty-six of his strong walled towns and innumerable smaller villages in their neighbourhood I besieged and conquered . . . I made to come out from them 200,150 people . . . and counted them as the spoils of war."[11] As for Hezekiah himself, he was "shut up like a caged bird within Jerusalem, his royal city."

One of the major cities which fell to Sennacherib was Lachish, nearly thirty miles south west of Jerusalem. Since they never captured Jerusalem, the Assyrians viewed the capture of Lachish as the climax of their campaign, and they commemorated their success by depicting the capture on several reliefs in the royal palace of Nineveh. (See plates 7 & 8 facing pp. 144, 145.) They made the city their base of operations, and it was from here that an armed embassy was dispatched to Jerusalem. From Lachish the king of Assyria sent the commander-in-chief, the chief eunuch, and the chief officer with a strong force to King Hezekiah at Jerusalem (2 Kings 18:17). The story which follows in 2 Kings 18 is a fascinating account. Some of the Assyrian chief officer's remarks were devastatingly true; for example, to those Judaeans who still hoped for an Egyptian army to appear and to defeat the Assyrians he declared, "Egypt is a splintered cane that will run into a man's hand and pierce it if he leans on it." Most of his speech, however, was a brilliant exercise in propaganda, in which even Hezekiah's recent religious reforms were turned to the Assyrian advantage. To make matters worse, he disdained to parley quietly with the Judaean envoys in the official tongue (Aramaic), preferring to shout out loud in Hebrew (presumably through an interpreter) all he had to say, so that ordinary citizens on the city walls might hear and draw their own conclusions.

Hezekiah submitted — he had no choice. Both Sennacherib's own record and 2 Kings 18:14 tell us the price he had to pay — thirty golden talents and also several hundred silver talents.[12] Sennacherib goes on to list other spoils of war, including precious stones, ivory couches, elephant tusks, and musicians, while 2 Kings 18 indicates that even the temple was despoiled of its treasures. Padi, the king of Ekron whom Hezekiah had taken prisoner, was restored to his throne, and he, along with other Philistine rulers who had remained faithful to Sennacherib, was given additional territory at Judah's expense. Judah was left as truncated a kingdom as Israel had been in the wake of Tiglath-pileser's invasion in 734; it is a matter of conjecture, however, how much territory was actually lost to Judah.

And there the matter rested — so far as the Assyrian records go.

---

11. *DOTT,* p. 67.
12. 300 according to 2 Kings, 800 according to Sennacherib.

But the biblical record offers us a good deal of information about what appear to have been subsequent events, and we cannot let the story rest there. Unfortunately, however, the whole chronology and order of events is very difficult to disentangle.[13] Some hold that the extra details, or most of them, are simply legendary, but this would seem too simple a solution. It is improbable that legend would have reported accurately the name of an Egyptian general (Tirhakah, 2 Kings 19:9); and it is even more unlikely that the story of an unexpected disaster suffered by the Assyrian army (2 Kings 19:35) should have been known among the Egyptians and Babylonians as well if it had never occurred.

It would seem, then, that in spite of the enormous indemnity Hezekiah had paid to him Sennacherib once again attacked Jerusalem, but on this occasion withdrew when word reached him of an advancing Egyptian army, and subsequently suffered a major catastrophe to his own army, in consequence of which he returned to Assyria and abandoned his military projects against Judah and Egypt. Georges Roux has summed it up thus: "Sennacherib planned to invade Egypt. He had already reached Pelusium (Tell el Farama, thirty miles east of the Suez canal) when his camp ws ravaged 'by the angel of the Lord, who went out at night and smote one hundred four-score and five thousand', says the Bible, 'by a legion of rats gnawing everything in the weapons that was made of rope or leather', says Herodotus (a fifth century Greek historian, on the basis of information gleaned in Egypt), or, as Berossus (a fourth to third century Babylonian writer) tells us, 'by a pestilential sickness' killing '185,000 men with their commanders and officers.' The Assyrian inscriptions are, as expected, silent on this inglorious episode."[14] A comparison of these ancient statements has often suggested to moderns that bubonic plague was the cause of the disaster.

As to when all this occurred, there are two widely-held views.[15] Either it was the immediate sequel to the previous events, and so occurred in 701 B.C., in which case we must assume that Sennacherib decided after all to depose Hezekiah and to make Judah an Assyrian province like Samaria; or else we must suppose that Hezekiah rebelled a second time late in his reign, thus provoking a second invasion, perhaps in 688 B.C.[16] The biblical record gives no

---

13. The most exhaustive discussion of recent years is that of B. S. Childs, in his *Isaiah and the Assyrian Crisis (SBT* ii, 3: London 1967). His conclusions are singularly negative, however. See also J. Gray, *Kings,* pp. 657-669; K. A. Kitchen, *The Third Intermediate Period in Egypt* (Warminster, 1973), §§128f.

14. Cf. G. Roux, *Ancient Iraq* (Pelican edition, London, 1966), pp. 289f.

15. For a convenient résumé of the two theories cf. B. Oded in Hayes and Miller, *Israelite and Judaean History,* pp. 450f.

16. Cf. J. Bright, *op. cit.* 283-6. Hezekiah died in 686 B.C. (probably), Sennacherib in 681. The last years of Sennacherib have left a minimum of records and annals to posterity, so it is difficult to guess at the course of events.

immediate impression that there were two separate campaigns by Sennacherib, but there may be hints for the modern historian in the mention of Tirhakah (who did not become king of Egypt till *c.*689 B.C., though admittedly he might have led Egyptian armies before that date) and in the suggestion that Sennacherib's assassination followed not too long after the events recorded (cf. 2 Kings 19: 36f.). Possibly, too, Isaiah 10:27-32 records the different route — an advance on Jerusalem from the north — taken by the invaders of 688.[17]

Whatever date be preferred, the significant feature of Sennacherib's invasion, in the eyes of Hezekiah's contemporaries, was that Jerusalem, miraculously, did not fall. Isaiah had prophesied that it would survive, and this was a promise that the men of Judah treasured and never forgot. Apparently they preferred to forget that Judah had lost so much else, and that the same prophet had declared that Jerusalem now resembled "a toolshed in an abandoned allotment", as F. F. Bruce has paraphrased Isaiah 1:8.[18] There is no doubt that the powerful preaching of Isaiah and other prophets was listened to, though not always heeded, and had its effects on the history of the ancient Hebrew people.

---

17. Alternatively, there may have been a pincer movement on Jerusalem in 701. But E. J. Young and others have argued that Isaiah is merely giving a vivid prediction of danger and not a literal description of actual events (cf. E. J. Young, *The Book of Isaiah* (*NICOT:* Grand Rapids, 1965-72), vol. 1, pp. 373ff.).
18. F. F. Bruce, *Israel and the Nations,* (Exeter, 1963), p. 71.

CHAPTER 12

Judah's Decline and Fall

HEZEKIAH was succeeded by his son, Manasseh, who was distinguished for two things. His was the longest reign in either kingdom; and in the eyes of the writer of Kings, he was also an outstandingly wicked king. Admittedly, 2 Chronicles 33 gives us reason to believe that his later years were more righteous ones, but apparently there was only a relative improvement.

We have very little information about the internal affairs of Judah during his long reign. He was twelve years old when he came to the throne (2 Kings 21:1), probably in *c.* 696 B.C. as co-regent with his father Hezekiah (who may have lived another ten years after this),[1] and his death did not occur before *c.* 632 B.C. We do know, at least, that he remained a vassal of Assyria throughout that long period, whether he submitted passively or only with reluctance. There was unrest in the western Assyrian empire more than once during Manasseh's reign, and several times powerful Assyrian armies marched into and through Palestine. It was the revolt of Sidon in 677 B.C. which first brought the armies of Esarhaddon (680-669), Sennacherib's son and successor, into the general vicinity of Judah. In 671 Esarhaddon returned to Phoenicia in force, Tyre now the target, and from there he promptly marched south into Egypt — by-passing Manasseh's kingdom en route. Egypt was still ruled by the Tirhakah who has already figured in the story of Hezekiah's attempts to shake off the Assyrian yoke. Tirhakah had never ceased

---

1. The speculation that if Hezekiah had not prayed for and been granted a miraculous recovery from illness, he would never have lived to beget the evil Manasseh, is intriguing; but in fact the probability of a ten years' co-regency suggests that Manasseh had been born *before* the illness Hezekiah experienced 15 years prior to his death.

to use every endeavour to bolster up anti-Assyrian movements in the Palestine area, and Esarhaddon had responded by a variety of efforts to woo the Arab tribes of the Syrian desert regions. In 671 Esarhaddon considered the moment propitious to invade Egypt. Intelligible though this project was, and in spite of its immediate success, the Assyrians were by now over-reaching themselves. Egypt could be conquered but not easily held, and a mere two years later Tirhakah was able to foment a rebellion against Assyria.

Esarhaddon died (669 B.C.), en route for Egypt, and it fell to the lot of his son Ashurbanipal[2] to reconquer Tirhakah's realm. This he achieved brilliantly, and Tirhakah was again forced into exile; but once more the Assyrian victories proved difficult to maintain, and Ashurbanipal was compelled to put his faith in the garrisons he set up and in the fidelity of local Egyptian princes who bound themselves to him by oaths of loyalty. The weakness of the Assyrian position can be gauged from the fact that when the Phoenician cities of Tyre and Arvad rebelled in 665, Ashurbanipal felt obliged, though he conquered both with all the usual Assyrian efficiency, to treat both rebels very gently, since he was fully committed in Egypt and desperately needed peaceful conditions on other fronts. About ten years later Egypt broke free, however, and once again an Egyptian became master of his own country; the man who achieved this was named Psamtik (or Psammetichus I). All these events must have deeply impressed Manasseh and the citizens of Judah in one way or another, as they stood on the sidelines, so to speak.

Events further afield must also have come to Manasseh's ears. Ashurbanipal had many other frontiers to defend and territories to hold down, and peace was by now something Assyria knew all too little of. One notable event in the east was the revolt of Babylon in 652 B.C. Here Ashurbanipal's own brother, by name Shamash-shum-ukin, was king, and he had been loyal to Ashurbanipal since their father's death in 669. He apparently now felt that he could take over the hegemony from Nineveh, and he mustered a formidable coalition against his brother. The confederates included Phoenicians and Egyptians and Philistines — and perhaps Judah too. However, Ashurbanipal was still able to maintain his stranglehold; ultimately all the rebels were brought to heel, and Shamash-shum-ukin perished in the flames of his own palace in 648. Even so, Assyrian power was by now gravely weakened.

If Ashurbanipal's demonstrations of power outside his own realm were in reality rather hollow, one cannot say that Manasseh's foreign contacts were demonstrations of anything but humiliation. Manasseh figures a few times in the Assyrian records of the reigns of

---

2. His name appears in the Old Testament in the more abbreviated form "Asnappar" (or "Osnappar").

both Esarhaddon and Ashurbanipal. He is listed with twenty-one other kings of the general Palestine area (called "Hatti-land" in Akkadian records) as having been commanded by Esarhaddon "to drag with pain and difficulty to Nineveh . . . supplies needed for my palace".[3] Needless to say, he obeyed. Ashurbanipal leaves us a similar list of kings whom he lists as "servants who belong to me",[4] from which it is clear that Manasseh was very careful to remain loyal to Assyria at the time of Ashurbanipal's campaigns in Egypt in the early years of his reign.

The tantalizingly brief note in 2 Chronicles 33:11 shows Manasseh in an even more humiliating situation — dragged in fetters to Babylon after an abortive revolt against "the King of Assyria". We are not told when or in what circumstances this occurred, nor even which king of Assyria was involved. The mention of Babylon rather than Nineveh, however, suggests that Manasseh must have given some support to the widespread revolt against Ashurbanipal organized by the king of Babylon in 652 B.C. The relative weakness of Assyria may be seen in the fact that Manasseh was restored to his throne, and permitted to strengthen the military defences of Judah (cf. 2 Chronicles 33:14), presumably in face of possible threats from Egypt.

The general biblical repudiation of Manasseh is based on two things, his religious laxity in permitting idolatry on a widespread scale, revoking all Hezekiah's reforms, and the fact that he "shed so much innocent blood" (2 Kings 21:16). According to 2 Kings 21 he fostered all sorts of foreign cults, and even submitted his own son to an abominable heathen rite. 2 Chronicles 33 allows that in his later years he had a change of heart and suppressed some of the idolatry; this partial change in affairs may have been due to a combination of pressures from his more devout subjects and of a partial relaxation of the tightness of Assyrian control, towards the end of his reign.[5]

The statement that he shed innocent blood is not further elaborated in the Bible, though later Jewish tradition seems to have viewed the prophets as the chief victims. Isaiah is said to have been sawn in two, and it is conceivable that Hebrews 11:37 is an allusion to his martyrdom.[6] This tradition is beyond proof, but it does seem to be true that the prophetic witness was virtually silenced during Manasseh's long reign. Equally speculative is the more modern suggestion that the Book of Deuteronomy was an "underground" production of his reign, which nobody dared to bring to light till the reign of his grandson Josiah.[7] But however the prophets may have

3. *DOTT*, p. 74.
4. *ANET*, p. 294.
5. It is improbable in the extreme that the Apocryphal *Prayer of Manasseh* is historical.
6. For references and details cf. F. F. Bruce, *Commentary on the Epistle to the Hebrews (NICNT*: London, 1964), pp. 340f.
7. See below, pp. 277ff.

fared, we may well believe that Manasseh's murderous acts extended to ordinary innocent folk as well. It is by no means impossible that he felt compelled to suppress anti-Assyrian movements at all costs, in order to preserve his throne.

Little need be said of the reign of his son Amon. It was a short reign (642-640),[8] though long enough to indicate that he was no religious reformer, nor a rebel against Assyria. But his son and successor Josiah was to prove a very different man.

Josiah's thirty-year reign was by no means uneventful inside Judah, while all around Palestine there was political turmoil. At the time of Josiah's accession the Assyrian king was still Ashurbanipal, under whom the Assyrian empire had reached its greatest territorial extent; when Josiah died in 609, that mighty empire had utterly collapsed. Egypt, not long before overrun by the Assyrian armies, had achieved independence before Manasseh's death, and was to play an increasingly active military role as Josiah's reign progressed. Babylon too was about to play a major part in world events, and as Josiah came to the throne the whole situation in the Near and Middle East was in a state of flux. Small states like Judah must have watched the development of events in relative bewilderment. Though they were only pawns in the game, they were obliged to make vital decisions, whether to support this or that major power, or when to make a fresh bid for independence. The overwhelming national sentiment in Judah was utter hatred of the oppressor. Let Nahum, a prophet of this era,[9] voice it for us: "Ah! Blood-stained city (i.e. Nineveh, the Assyrian capital), steeped in deceit, full of pillage, never empty of prey! . . . The dead are past counting, their bodies lie in heaps, corpses innumerable, men stumbling over corpses — all for a wanton's monstrous wantonness, fair-seeming, a mistress of sorcery, who beguiled nations and tribes by her wantonness and her sorceries" (Nahum 3: 1-4).

The Egyptians were shrewd enough to realize, in due course, that it might be a useful policy to give Assyria some support, in order to check the fast-growing power of Babylon; but Egypt had not suffered nearly so much at Assyrian hands as Judah had done, and to the citizens of Jerusalem the annihilation of Nineveh was but just retribution. Not that the prophets lacked realism; Habakkuk, whose prophecies date from the last years of Josiah's reign or shortly afterwards, was not blind to the menace Babylon presented. He described the Chaldaeans — now the ruling class of Babylon — as "that savage and impetuous nation, who cross the wide tracts of the earth to take possession of homes not theirs" (Habakkuk 1:6).

8. He died by assassination. See below, p. 126.
9. His ministry fell in the second half of the seventh century, but it is difficult to date it more precisely.

Probably the common people of Jerusalem, on the other hand, and even King Josiah too, failed to see in the Babylonians anything but the divinely-appointed scourge of Assyria.

Josiah was only eight years old when he became king, and naturally enough some years passed before he could formulate policies of his own. It was when he was about sixteen, according to 2 Chronicles 34:3, that he first showed his concern about the worship of "the God of his forefather David"; but four further years elapsed before Josiah felt secure enough to embark on a thorough-going policy of religious reform. It surely cannot be coincidence that his move came soon after the death of the Assyrian king, Ashurbanipal (668-627). By now the Assyrian grip on Palestine must have been very weak indeed. A year or two later the city of Babylon broke finally free from Assyrian control, under the kingship of a very able Chaldaean prince named Nabopolassar (626-605). Soon the Babylonians and their allies the Medes were exerting pressures on Assyria which she was too weak to resist. Her empire fell away, and her own cities began to fall. Asshur, the old capital, which had given its name to the country, was captured in 614, and Nineveh itself was conquered and laid waste in 612.

Josiah's religious reforms received their greatest impetus some nine years before the fall of Nineveh. In 621 B.C. a startling discovery was made in the Jerusalem temple — a literary discovery comparable with the finding of the Dead Sea Scrolls in our own century for the excitement it provoked! During repairs to the temple structure, occasioned no doubt by the reforms already in progress, a scroll came to light which the Bible names "the book of the law" and "the book of the covenant". The workmen of course handed over their find to the high priest Hilkiah, who was so impressed with it that he passed it on to the adjutant-general, Shaphan. He too read it, and in consequence brought it to the king and read it aloud to him.

The dramatic sequel is told in 2 Kings 22f. The scroll's contents were of such a character that Josiah, conscience-stricken, immediately tore his robes as a sign of distress and repentance, and then arranged to have the document publicly read at the temple, in the hearing of "the whole population, high and low". The people next pledged themselves to their God in solemn covenant, and the king proceeded to inaugurate yet more sweeping reforms. Every vestige of pagan religion was now outrooted from Judah; not only were specifically heathen shrines and cultic objects obliterated, but even sanctuaries dedicated to Yahweh, Israel's God, were systematically desecrated. The fact was that all too many of the country shrines had tolerated all sorts of syncretistic worship, the "official" worship having been adulterated by numerous popular superstitions. Josiah in his zeal for the purity of his faith now decreed that henceforth Jerusalem, and only Jerusalem, should be the place of worship. Ordinary people must have been startled at the great changes taking place; and town and village priests were instructed to move bag and baggage into the capital, to carry on their duties at the one sanctuary still functioning.[10] The climax of the reform seems to have been a joyous celebration in Jerusalem of the feast of the Passover, care being taken to observe it as the newly-found document prescribed. "No such Passover", the writer of 2 Kings 23:22 declares, "had been kept either when the judges were ruling Israel or during the times of the Kings of Israel and Judah".

But what exactly *was* this powerful document? The description of it as "the book of the law" (2 Kings 22:8) might suggest that it was the complete Pentateuch (i.e., Genesis-Deuteronomy inclusive); but the alternative title, "the book of the covenant", is a phrase which occurs in Exodus 24:7f., where it seems to designate no more than the preceding three or four chapters (specifically, Exodus 20: 22-23:33). The most widely-held view of the matter is that Josiah's document was either the Book of Deuteronomy or a substantial part of it. This view is very old, dating back to Chrysostom and Jerome, and is today widely, though not universally, advocated in circles both conservative and otherwise.[11] While the separate features of Josiah's reforms could undoubtedly have been based on biblical passages outside Deuteronomy, it is striking that in the compass of a few chapters Deuteronomy provides a basis for Josiah's entire programme. In chapter 12 we find an attack on pagan religion, and the command to establish a single sanctuary; in chapter 16 Passover regulations are given, and they specify that the feast should not be observed in every town and settlement; and chapter 18 refers to Levites coming to the one single sanctuary. Finally, the very strongly worded curses and warnings of chapter 27f. could readily explain the distress and alarm displayed by Josiah on his first acquaintance with the newly-discovered scroll.

Josiah's religious reforms were not without their political effects and overtones. The show of independence and the eradication from Judah of everything foreign would have been viewed with deep suspicion in Nineveh; but by the year 621 the Assyrians were much too concerned with events nearer home to pay any heed to such minor affairs in a minor subject state. Even so, the mention in 2 Kings 23:8 of Geba and Beer-sheba, which were probably the traditional northern and southern boundary cities of Judah, may well imply that Josiah now re-incorporated the territory which

10. In point of fact, this measure was one of the first of Josiah's reforms to be disregarded. It must have been a most unpopular decree — much as if all churches and chapels throughout Britain were to be closed down, and worship permitted only at Canterbury Cathedral, by act of Parliament.

11. The prohibitive size of any scroll containing much more than, say, Deuteronomy renders it unlikely that Josiah's "book of the law" comprised the whole Pentateuch.

Sennacherib had wrested from Judah in the time of Hezekiah. Be that as it may, Josiah showed even greater boldness and enterprise when he decided to implement his reforms in the old Northern Kingdom, long since an Assyrian province, as well as in Judah. Bethel, just north of the Judaean frontier, was his first target; meeting no opposition there, he proceeded to desecrate shrines and execute idolatrous priests all over the province of Samaria, even as far north as the old tribal territory of Naphtali (cf.2 Chronicles 34:6f.). It is evident that Josiah was free to act with impunity, and that he in fact reunited Judah and Israel under his kingship.[12]

The optimists — and Judah had plenty at this period — must have thought that a new golden age had dawned for the people of Israel, that Josiah was another David. But the realists knew otherwise; the prophetess Huldah had already given a grim warning of what future Judah could expect (2 Kings 22:14-20). The reality was that the steady collapse of the Assyrian empire was leaving a power vacuum. In David's era no major state had been powerful enough or ambitious enough to seek to control Palestine; but now both Babylon and Egypt were anxious to rule Syria and Palestine, and Judah was a match for neither of them.

The weakness of Judah was exposed a mere five years after Josiah's major reforms. The Egyptian king (still Psamtik I) had already realized the political necessity of bolstering up the Assyrian forces as a brake on the growing power of Babylon, and in 616 he sent an army to help the Assyrians, as we know from Babylonian records.[13] A glance at the map suffices to show that an Egyptian army could not have reached Mesopotamia without marching through Josiah's territory. The route followed was no doubt "the Way of the Sea", the road up the Philistine coast, through the pass of Megiddo into the Valley of Jezreel, and so across the Jordan, and away to Damascus and the north east. We have no way of knowing what action, if any, Josiah took; but at least it is certain that the Egyptian army was not stopped or turned back.

As far as Assyria was concerned, Egyptian assistance merely prolonged her death-throes. The climax came in 612, with the fall of Nineveh; but even yet the Assyrians fought back, moving their headquarters into Syria, where the last Assyrian monarch, Ashur-uballit II, set up court at Haran. Two years later the Babylonians and their allies drove him from there, across the Euphrates. In the following year came the end for Assyria; the Assyrians, again supported by an Egyptian army,[14] recrossed the Euphrates and

12   For details of the size of his realm, cf. *LB*, pp. 348-351.
13.   Cf. *ANET*, p. 304.
14.   Note that 2 Kings 23:29 must be translated as in modern translations, and not as in AV or RV; the Egyptians were supporting, not attacking, the Assyrians.

assaulted Haran, hoping to recapture it, but all in vain. The attempt failed miserably, and from now on all mention of the Assyrian regime drops out of the picture; the struggle was now a simple two-sided one, the Egyptians based on Carchemish on the west bank of the Euphrates, the Babylonians maintaining their position east of the river.

This was the situation which developed in 609, the year in which Psamtik was succeeded by his son Necho II as king of Egypt. Necho immediately set out with his armies for Carchemish, to join the fruitless Assyrian assault on Haran; but on this occasion Josiah chose to act, by blocking the pass of Megiddo against the passage of the Egyptian troops. The result is told in a laconic sentence in 2 Kings 23:29: "Josiah went to meet him; and when they met at Megiddo, Pharaoh Necho slew him." The wording almost suggests a parley, but the very name Megiddo, site of so many historic battles, implies more than that. 2 Chronicles 35:20-24 confirms that a battle did take place, and gives a few details of the affray; further confirmation has probably been provided by archaeologists: signs of damage to the walls of the city of Megiddo are visible,[15] and though one cannot date the destruction precisely, the events of 609 B.C. seem the most probable historical context for it.

So Josiah died in battle — not yet forty years of age, despite the length of his reign. In him died Judah's last king of any ability; and with him died any hope of Judah's remaining independent. If Necho declared before the battle of Megiddo that he had no quarrel with Judah, it was a different matter afterwards. His intention was to make Judah and the other small states in the area part of a new Egyptian empire; in the event, his empire was to be of very short duration, but for the next four years Judah was firmly controlled by him. In Jerusalem, Josiah's youngest son Jehoahaz[16] succeeded to the throne, but after a mere three months as king he was deposed by Judah's new overlord, Necho. It appears that Jehoahaz had to go to Necho's Asiatic headquarters, Riblah, to have his kingship confirmed (cf. 2 Kings 23:33); that would have been humiliation enough, but Necho demonstrated his power over Judah by deposing and deporting him and replacing him by his older brother Jehoiakim. It is not clear why popular opinion in Judah had preferred the younger brother as king, and it is equally uncertain why Necho's choice fell on the older man. Perhaps Jehoahaz had been expected to maintain an anti-Egyptian policy, whereas Jehoiakim may well have been taking a pro-Egyptian stand. Certainly Jehoiakim was an unscrupulous and self-serving man; on the other

15. Cf. W. F. Albright, *The Archaeology of Palestine* (Harmondsworth, 1960 edn.) p. 130.

16. His personal name was Shallum, cf. Jeremiah 22:11. Jehoahaz was his throne-name. He was the youngest of four brothers.

hand, the record indicates that he was consistently loyal to Egypt. He did not allow the fact that he was merely a puppet-king to deter him from putting on a show of royalty; in spite of the tribute his citizens had to pay to Egypt, he burdened them with taxes and worse to finance a brand new palace for himself, at Beth-hakkerem, just outside Jerusalem.[17] Such wanton luxury amounted to the oppression of his people, and the prophet Jeremiah was not slow to condemn it:

> Shame on the man who builds his house by unjust means
>   and completes its roof-chambers by fraud,
>   making his countrymen work without payment;
>   giving them no wage for their labour!
> Shame on the man who says, 'I will build a spacious house
>   with airy roof-chambers,
>   set windows in it, panel it with cedar
>   and paint it with vermilion'!
> If your cedar is more splendid,
>   does that prove you a king?

(Jeremiah 22:13ff.)

Necho's control of Judah lasted four years. During that time, the Babylonian armies never relaxed their struggle for supremacy over the Egyptians, and in 605 B.C. they gained the upper hand. A new and vigorous soldier came on the scene in that year, as commander-in-chief of the Babylonian forces. He was the crown prince of Babylon, son of the aging Nabopolassar. His name was Nebuchadrezzar.

As we have noted, Carchemish had been for some years the Egyptians' advance camp for operations in north Syria, while the Babylonians had remained poised on the eastern banks of the Euphrates. In 605 Nebuchadrezzar led his troops across the river, advanced on Carchemish and inflicted a heavy defeat on the forces of Necho (cf. Jeremiah 46:2). Routed there and again at Hamath, the surviving Egyptian soldiers fled homewards, hotly pursued by the victorious Babylonians, who set about annexing the territory to the south — including Philistia and Judah. The Babylonian army might have pressed on further than they did, but news arrived of the death of Nabopolassar, and Nebuchadrezzar immediately returned to Babylon for the important ceremony of accession to his father's throne.

Thus, without any choice in the matter, Judah exchanged Egyptian control for Babylonian control. "The King of Egypt did not leave his own land again, because the King of Babylon had stripped him of all his possessions, from the Torrent of Egypt to the

---

17. Modern Ramat Rachel. Cf. Y. Aharoni, *BA* 24 (1961), p. 118.

river Euphrates'' (2 Kings 24:7). It must be added, however, that the Egyptian rulers were not by any means reconciled to this situation, and Egyptian intrigues at the court of Jehoiakim and his successors were to pay no small part in the fate of Jerusalem.

Nebuchadrezzar took all necessary steps to ensure the internal security of his realm, paying special attention to the newly-acquired territories such as Judah. He records that in 604 and again in 603 he marched into "the Hatti-land" (the regular term used in Akkadian documents to embrace Syria and Palestine), and that "he took the heavy tribute of the Hatti-land back to Babylon".[18] The Babylonian Chronicle does not specify any of the states or kingdoms except Ashkelon, conquered in 603; but 2 Kings 24:1 notes explicitly that Jehoiakim became Nebuchadressar's vassal, perforce. If the first paragraph of the Book of Daniel refers to these events, we may conclude that Nebuchadrezzar's plunder was accompanied by hostages, of whom Daniel was one.[19]

Nebuchadrezzar's name is synonymous with the sort of arrogant pride which the Greeks called *hybris*. He had ample cause for satisfaction. In a few years the roles of Syria and Babylon were reversed, and Babylon had recovered the position, which she held a millennium before, of mistress of an empire. Babylonian armies had been everywhere successful; of her only two potential rivals, the one (Media) was friendly, the other (Egypt) humbled. Nebuchadrezzar had begun a long reign which would be for the most part peaceful and prosperous.

But it does not take much imagination to appreciate that Nebuchadrezzar's satisfaction was matched by a great deal of sullen resentment in Jerusalem. Assyria and Babylon's reversal of roles meant little to the Judaeans; both Assyrians and Babylonians came from "the Far East" as far as they were concerned, speaking (literally) the same language, and pursuing identical policies. There was no reason at all why Judaeans should prefer Babylonian rule to Assyrian domination; moreover the memory was green of some years of independence and success, under Josiah's leadership. Small wonder, then, that Jehoiakim and many of his subjects looked to Egypt for aid against their new Mesopotamian overlords. Jeremiah took an opposite view; he was shrewd enough to realize that Nebuchadrezzar's victory over Necho was no accident, and that the Babylonians were immeasurably more powerful than the Egyptians. His council was meek submission to Nebuchadrezzar (27:9ff.); but that advice was too bitter a pill for most of his fellow-countrymen, and consequently the prophet began to proclaim the inevitability of

18. Cf. *DOTT*, p. 79.
19. Cf. D. J. Wiseman in D. J. Wiseman and others. *Notes on some problems in the Book of Daniel* (London, 1965), pp. 16ff.

utter disaster for Judah. Here again we may see how in the prophets political realism, or to be more accurate a sure prescience of events, went hand in hand with a religious message: Jerusalem would fall, not because Nebuchadrezzar was all-powerful, but because Judah's sins invited divine retribution. Jeremiah, however, was not the only man wearing the prophet's mantle; other men gave opposite advice in the name of Yahweh, and we may well imagine that many Judaeans did not know whom to believe — until the very course of events proved that Jeremiah's opponents were the false prophets. It is particularly interesting to notice how Isaiah's proclamation that Jerusalem would not fall in Hezekiah's reign, almost a century earlier, had now become a sort of national dogma; the false prophets never tired of proclaiming that Jerusalem was impregnable to human armies. No doubt many were convinced by their arguments, since human nature is so prone to wishful thinking.

By the time of Jehoiakim's reign, Jeremiah had already been exercising a prophetic ministry for many years. Though not uncritical, he had had no open quarrel with Josiah; but at the very outset of Jehoiakim's reign the prophet took dramatic action which almost inevitably infuriated the new monarch. He entered the very temple court and proclaimed that the temple was destined to fall, exactly as the Shiloh sanctuary had done long before (Jeremiah 7:1-20). The temple personnel, priests and prophets alike, were enraged by this sermon, so very different from the false optimism of their own public utterances, and before long Jeremiah found himself on trial for blasphemy. His judges, however, had imbibed something of the spirit of Josiah's reform, and they gave him a fair trial and acquitted him. Jeremiah was fortunate to have some influential friends; another prophet of the day, Uriah by name, who preached precisely the same message as Jeremiah, was harried into exile, only to be dragged back to Judah and murdered — by royal command (chapter 26). Even Jeremiah did not escape a flogging and the indignity of a night spent in the stocks (Jeremiah 20:1f.).

In the year following the Babylonian victory at Carchemish Jeremiah decided to reinforce his message, by compiling a scroll of all his sermons to date, and having them read publicly at a major festival in the temple, when crowds of Judaeans were present. His secretary Baruch both wrote the scroll and gave the public reading of it. The temple authorities soon got to hear of it, and the scroll was seized and taken to the king. Friends rushed both Jeremiah and Baruch into hiding, while Jehoiakim had the scroll read aloud to him. Contemptuous of its contents, he chopped it to pieces with a penknife and burned it section by section. He made some endeavour to locate Jeremiah and Baruch, but otherwise proceeded, unmoved, to pursue his own policies (chapter 36). Jeremiah, equally unmoved by the royal threats, set about producing a second edition of his prophecies; it comprised the full contents of the first scroll, "and much else . . . to the same effect" (Jeremiah 36:32). The word of God was not easily stifled; his warnings might be ignored, but they could not be annulled or frustrated.

For three years, at any rate, Jehoiakim had no option but to pay tribute and remain subservient to Nebuchadrezzar (2 Kings 24:1); the grim fate of Ashkelon in 603 B.C., with its destruction and the deportation of many of its citizens, was incentive enough to be submissive. He then revolted, by the simple expedient of refusing or neglecting to pay the annual tribute. He judged the moment to be right because the Babylonian army had just (601) suffered a defeat or near-defeat on the Egyptian border; probably rumour had it that the Egyptians had won a handsome victory. The sequel clearly shows that both sides suffered heavy losses,[20] and needed some time to recoup and reorganize. Jehoiakim's revolt, therefore, was not immediately crushed; but it was only a matter of time. In the following year (600) "the King of Akkad (i.e. Nebuchadrezzar) stayed in his country. He organized his chariots and many horses".[21] In 599 Nebuchadrezzar moved into the Palestine area, but his first campaign was against the Arab tribes of the semi-desert regions. It was at the end of 598 that he finally assaulted Judah and besieged Jerusalem. In the meantime, however, Jehoiakim had been harassed by "raiding-parties of Chaldaeans, Aramaeans, Moabites and Ammonites" (2 Kings 24:2). Of these the Chaldaeans were such detachments of Babylonian troops as were in the area, while the remaining forces were drawn from the old enemies that were now under Nebuchadrezzar's domination.

There is some obscurity about the end of Jehoiakim's reign. We know that he ceased to be king at the very beginning of the siege of Jerusalem, since the siege lasted three months (December 598-March 597), and it coincided with the three month reign of Jehoiakim's son Jehoiachin.[22] 2 Chronicles 36:6 is ambiguous about the fate of Jehoiakim; according to the New English Bible and the Jerusalem Bible the verse states that he was taken in fetters to Babylon, but other English Versions (including the Authorized Version and the Revised Standard Version) are probably more correct to leave the matter an open question, and state merely that he was put in fetters preparatory to being taken to Babylon. It may be that he was assassinated, by his own people. It is intriguing that 2 Kings 24:6 records the mere fact of his death, but says nothing about the circumstances nor where he was buried (a detail which is supplied for most of the kings); however, we find in Jeremiah 22:19 the

20. Indeed, Babylonian records admit the fact: "they clashed in open battle and inflicted heavy losses on each other" (*ANET*, p. 564).
21. Cf. *ANET*, p. 564.
22. *Ibid.*; 2 Kings 24:8-12.

prediction that he would be "buried like a dead ass, dragged along and flung out beyond the gates of Jerusalem".

But if he was assassinated, who perpetrated the deed, and why? One plausible explanation is that he was murdered by the pro-Babylonian party in Jerusalem, in an effort to appease Nebuchadrezzar; if so, his son Jehoiachin sided with the pro-Egyptian party, and continued to resist.[23] Alternatively, it is not at all impossible that Jehoiakim decided to submit to Nebuchadrezzar — which would explain how he came to be captured before his capital fell — and was assassinated by the pro-Egyptian party, who then put pressure on Jehoiachin to resist Nebuchadrezzar. (This second possibility finds a measure of support in the history of Josephus.)[24]

One thing is certain, and that is the fact that by now the kings of Judah were puppets not only of the great powers controlling the area, but also of the various political parties and pressure groups within their own realm. Since the time of Hezekiah each king had represented one particular political viewpoint within Judah; Hezekiah and Josiah had been "nationalists" (and it must not be overlooked that their religious reforms were part of a nationalistic policy), while Manasseh and presumably Amon had been "collaborationists", pro-Assyrians. Jehoiakim was pro-Egyptian. But whereas the stronger kings no doubt imposed such policies on the state they ruled, by now the king was to a large extent governed by the strongest political party in Jerusalem. The death of Amon, Josiah's predecessor, as described in 2 Kings 21:23f., illustrates the point; some sort of palace revolution led to his overthrow and assassination, but a popular uprising occurred immediately, in which the conspirators were executed, and the youthful Josiah made king, obviously under the control of regents.

Jehoiachin,[25] then, was completely at the mercy of circumstances when he became king. One cannot but feel sympathy for a king who, at the age of eighteen, inherited as a kingdom a beleaguered city; and who three months later was taken into exile where he remained until his death, at least thirty-five years later.[26] Of his personal character we know little. 2 Kings 24:9 indicates that "he did what was wrong in the eyes of the LORD", which probably means that he did nothing to discourage idolatry; but on the whole the biblical writers treat him gently, and it may be significant that Ezekiel dated his prophecies by the year of Jehoiachin's exile, ignoring totally Jehoiachin's successor in Jerusalem, Zedekiah. Many Judaeans, evidently, long retained their allegiance to their king-in-exile.

23. Jehoiachin very swiftly decided to submit to Nebuchadrezzar, and it is not impossible that this was his intention from the outset.
24. *Ant.* x, 6, 3.
25. Biblical texts give two other forms of his name — Jeconiah and Coniah.
26. He lived longer than Nebuchadrezzar (605-562 B.C.), cf. Jeremiah 52:31-34.

Jerusalem opened its gates to Nebuchadrezzar in March 597 (see plate 9 facing p. 176); it could have held out much longer, as events a decade later were to prove, so we must assume that Jehoiachin or his counsellors now decided that submission was the prudent course of action. Such submission served to preserve the city from destruction and save many lives; moreover, it enabled Judah to retain its status as a kingdom. Nevertheless, having proved a disloyal vassal, Judah could not hope to escape scot-free. The Babylonian Chronicle sums up in a sentence the retribution that was exacted by Nebuchadrezzar: "He appointed therein (Jerusalem) a king of his own choice, received its heavy tribute and sent them to Babylon".[27] The new king was Jehoiachin's uncle Mattaniah (yet another son of Josiah), who took the throne, with the regnal name of Zedekiah (2 Kings 24:17). There is some evidence that his realm was reduced in size, and that the southern territories (the Negeb and Shephelah) were detached from it;[28] it is safe to assume that Judaean control of Samaria had ceased with Josiah's death.

Jehoiachin was deported, and many other men of substance with him; his family, leading officials, military commander and troops, and even skilled craftsmen were taken.[29] Ezekiel was exiled, but Jeremiah, who had proved himself so pro-Babylonian, was not. Thus Nebuchadrezzar hoped to decimate the pro-Egyptian and nationalist parties in Jerusalem, and to shore up the pro-Babylonian party under Zedekiah's leadership. It must be said, however, that the Babylonian measures were rather clumsy; Judaean hopes that Jehoiachin would return to the throne were kept alive by the fact that the Babylonians themselves seemed to acknowledge that he was the legitimate king of Judah. Texts discovered in Babylon explicitly refer to him as king of Judah,[30] while jar handles found in Palestine indicate that the crown property, in whole or part, still belonged to him.[31] It may be, of course, that if the pro-Babylonian party had gained the upper hand in Judah, and if Judah had shown signs of accepting Babylonian suzerainty, Nebuchadrezzar would have released and reinstated Jehoiachin. But Nebuchadrezzar underestimated both the extent of nationalistic feelings in Judah and the effectiveness of Egyptian propaganda, and in effect he undermined Zedekiah's authority, reducing his status virtually to that of regent. It appears that Zedekiah was no very strong character, but in any case, he had no opportunity to be strong.

27. *DOTT*, p. 80.
28. Cf. Y. Aharoni, *LB*, pp. 355f.
29. The exiles numbered 3,023, according to Jeremiah 52:28: the figures given in 2 Kings 24:14ff. would appear to be inclusive of later deportees. Possibly Jeremiah's figure excludes women and children, on the other hand.
30. Cf. *DOTT*, p. 86.
31. Cf. *DOTT*, p. 224.

The book of Jeremiah affords us many a glimpse of life in Judah and Jerusalem during the reign of Zedekiah. The prophet himself consistently supported pro-Babylonian policies, wisely enough, and the king was disposed to heed his arguments. But there were many in Jerusalem who denounced such policies as defeatist and unpatriotic, and sought only the opportunity to rebel against Nebuchadrezzar yet again. Such counsellors Jeremiah dismissed scornfully as "bad figs", asserting that all the "good figs" had been taken into exile (chapter 24); Jeremiah thus put his finger on one disadvantage of the Assyrian and Babylonian deportation policies — to remove the top men in an administration is tantamount to putting influence if not power in the hands of second-rate and upstart statesmen. One of Jeremiah's bitterest opponents was Hananiah; as a prophet, he too could claim that he spoke the oracles of God, and could allege that Jeremiah was the false prophet (chapter 28). Among the exiles, another prophet, Shemaiah by name, was contradicting Jeremiah's warnings and preaching an absurdly optimistic message; Jeremiah felt it appropriate to send a letter making the realities of the situation clear (chapter 29). Before long, however, one of the exiles, Ezekiel, received the call to be a prophet, and he was to preach among the exiles the same sort of message that Jeremiah was proclaiming in the homeland. Neither man saw the slightest basis for optimism.

The battle of words in Jerusalem was of course punctuated by events. One event of interest occurred in 594, when representatives of a number of small states in the area gathered in Jerusalem to discuss the possibility of concerted action against Babylon (Jeremiah 27:3); it is highly probable that Egypt was represented at the meeting, even if it had not engineered it. The background to this meeting was a revolt against Nebuchadrezzar in Babylonia itself (December 595-January 594); but Nebuchadrezzar soon restored order, and was to be found in Syria later in the year, receiving tribute from his western vassals. The would-be rebels among the latter decided therefore to bide their time.

A further four or five years elapsed, and then Zedekiah took the final and fatal step of rebelling. Records for the reign of Zedekiah are scanty, and we do not know the precise circumstances which led to the revolt. It was not completely spontaneous, for it seems that both Tyre and Ammon supported the suicidal enterprise,[32] and there can be no doubt that Egypt had promised strong military aid. It was certainly no sign of weakness on Nebuchadrezzar's part that occasioned the rebellion. Possibly the spark which set the revolt ablaze was the accession of Hophra to the throne of Egypt c. 589 B.C.; it

---

32. After the fall of Jerusalem, Nebuchadrezzar went on to besiege Tyre for 13 years. Ammon's involvement seems a natural inference from Ezekiel 21:18-22.

appears that he was rather more ambitious to recover lost ground in Asia than was his predecessor Psamtik II.[33] Whatever the external circumstances may have been, however, the real cause of Zedekiah's ill-fated revolt was internal pressures within Judah. The king's hand was forced by short-sighted noblemen and popular clamour, expressing the pent-up resentments at Babylonian oppression, coupled with burning nationalistic fervour and a coherent but specious theology (which maintained that Jerusalem could not fall). Such a combination of deep human emotions — hatred, pride, patriotism, and religious convictions — could not be permanently repressed.

Nebuchadrezzar's reaction was swift and sure. The Babylonian armies marched into Judah and proceeded to invest and reduce all the fortified towns and cities; Jerusalem itself found itself besieged towards the end of 589 B.C. (cf. 2 Kings 25:1). Before the end of the following year, only three cities were still holding out, Jerusalem itself, Lachish and Azekah (Jeremiah 34:6f.).

Lachish was a major city of ancient Judah, but it proved difficult to identify its site in modern times.[34] In the 1930s, however, an archaeological team excavated a mound called Tell el-Duweir, and some documents were found which seem to have settled the question. The documents are known as the Lachish Ostraca; most of them are letters written on potsherds, and they date from precisely the period we have now reached.[35] One letter addressed to the military governor of the city, Yaosh, testifies to the military liaison with Egypt. Another bears witness to the fact that not everyone in Jerusalem was whole-heartedly in favour of the rebellion. Of special interest is the fact that these letters, secular and military as they are, repeatedly name the sacred name of Yahweh; clearly the military officers were in no doubt that Zedekiah's revolt had God's blessing.

It appears from one letter that Azekah had just fallen, that its signal-beacons had been extinguished. Only Lachish and Jerusalem now remained; and Lachish did not last much longer. Its major buildings were deliberately burnt, its walls broken down. It was in the remains of the burned-out guardroom under the gate-tower of the city that most of the ostraca were found in 1935.

Jerusalem had one brief respite, when the Babylonian army raised the siege in order to confront an Egyptian army which was marching northwards to honour Pharaoh Hophra's promises to Zedekiah (Jeremiah 37:5). The citizens of the capital — Jeremiah excepted — were overjoyed, and convinced themselves that their problems were over. Even at this point of time, when the downfall of Jerusalem was

33. Cf. K. A. Kitchen in *NBD*, p. 346.
34. Cf. *AOTS*, pp. 296f.
35. Cf. *DOTT*, pp. 212-7; *ANET*, pp. 321f.

a matter of months away, they exhibited a materialistic and immoral self-interest which effectively demonstrates why the prophets had long been clamouring for social justice. Before the Babylonians had raised the siege, all slaves in the city had been set free by their owners; but as soon as Nebuchadrezzar's army moved off to confront Hophra's expeditionary force, the owners promptly re-enslaved them (Jeremiah 34:8-11). Jeremiah rebuked the immoral deed and also the blind faith in Egypt which engendered it, in no uncertain terms. He stated emphatically that the Babylonian troops would soon return and conquer the city (Jeremiah 37:9f.). He then prepared to leave the city, on a matter of private business; but his enemies interpreted his intended departure as a sign that he was going over to the enemy. He was arrested, flogged and imprisoned, in spite of his hot denials (Jeremiah 37:11-16). Even there his sane voice was not silenced, and his enemies took even more drastic measures, throwing him into a filthy dungeon, where he would have died of thirst and starvation but for the intervention of a palace official, who rescued the prophet at the king's instigation (chapter 38). But he remained in custody till the city fell.

The Egyptian army was soon repulsed, and the Babylonians resumed the siege. The end was not long delayed: "The siege lasted till the eleventh year of King Zedekiah. In the fourth month of that year, on the ninth day of the month, when famine was severe in the city and there was no food for the common people, the city was thrown open" (Jeremiah 52:5f.). Thus Jerusalem fell to the Babylonian armies in August 587 (or perhaps 586); a month later Nebuchadrezzar gave orders that the city should be systematically destroyed — city walls, houses, royal palace, and temple alike (Jeremiah 52:12ff.). The ancient sign of Yahweh's presence, the ark of the covenant, probably went up in flames with the temple which housed it — at least, it is never heard of again. Many other of Jerusalem's treasures were plundered.

As for the survivors, only "the weakest class of people" was left as vine-dressers and labourers (Jeremiah 52:16). Jeremiah records that 832 people were now deported to Babylonia (Jeremiah 52:29); this figure seems surprisingly low, and probably includes only adult males.[36] Some of the military commanders were put to death, together with the high priest and his deputy (Jeremiah 52:24-37). As for King Zedekiah and his entourage, they succeeded in escaping from Jerusalem, and went eastwards at top speed, hoping perhaps to get help and shelter with the Ammonites, Judah's ally in the revolt. But all in vain; the Babylonians overtook them in the vicinity of

---

36. The NEB emends Jeremiah 52:28 to mean that Nebuchadrezzar now took two batches of deportees, amounting to nearly 4,000 people, quite apart from the exiles removed to Babylonia a decade before.

Jericho, and Zedekiah was brought to Riblah, Neduchadrezzar's headquarters in Syria. Nebuchadrezzar pronounced sentence: Zedekiah's sons were killed in front of him, and then his eyes were put out. From Riblah the hapless ex-king went in chains to a prison in Babylon; and there he died, perhaps soon afterwards (Jeremiah 52:7-11).

Jeremiah, now at least sixty five years old, survived the holocaust, escaping his Judaean enemies' vindictiveness, death by starvation, and also Babylonian swords. Nebuchadrezzar had given special orders to show him favour and consideration, and the prophet was able to serve the new administration (Jeremiah 39:11-14). Nebuchadrezzar brought Judah into the Babylonian provincial system, and appointed as its governor Gedaliah, formerly a high palace official at Zedekiah's court. Gedaliah's administrative capital was Mizpah, some miles north of Jerusalem, which was of course too badly damaged to remain the capital. Jeremiah chapter 40 records that Judaeans who had taken refuge in neighbouring countries began to come back to Judah, when they learned of the new administration. Before long, however, nationalistic intrigues began once more, and the moderate Gedaliah (whose grandfather had been a leading supporter of Josiah's reforms, and whose father had befriended Jeremiah in Jehoiakim's reign) was assassinated. The conspiracy against him was led by a member of the royal family named Ishmael, and had the support of the Ammonites, who were still resisting the Babylonians. Some Babylonians were assassinated too, and Ishmael took good care to flee to Ammon, out of harm's way. It was natural to expect that Nebuchadrezzar would exact vengeance, and those Judaeans who had supported Gedaliah were apprehensive that the Babylonian king's anger might fall on them, innocent though they were. Accordingly, they fled to Egypt, taking with them the aged prophet, Jeremiah, who protested vehemently but in vain (chapters 40-43). Thus the whole Mizpah administration collapsed, and it was probably as a consequence of these events that Nebuchadrezzar, c. 582 B.C., exiled yet another group of Judaeans, 745 in number (Jeremiah 52:30). Jeremiah seems to have ended his days in Egypt.

Thus Judah was left in ruins, her population decimated.[37] Many of her people were in exile, whether perforce in Babylonia or voluntarily in Egypt and elsewhere, and many others must have died amid the horrors of warfare. Large parts of the country were depopulated, so much so that the Edomites (themselves under pressure from Arab tribes) had no difficulty in overrunning much of

---

37. The Negeb, in the far south of Judah, seems to have been the one area to escape serious Babylonian reprisals.

For an estimate of the population of Judah, and a perspective on the deportations, see R. de Vaux, *Ancient Israel: its Life and Institutions* (ET London,[2] 1965), pp. 65ff.

southern Judah and taking permanent hold there. The temple was destroyed, its long cultic ritual brought to an end. Above all, the throne had perished; David's family who had held that throne through all the vicissitudes of more than four hundred years, were now deprived of royal status. David and Zion were alike ruined.

The story of Judah did not of course terminate at this point. The exiles would return, Jerusalem and the temple would rise again, the Jewish faith would be purged and purified; and far in the future another scion of David's line would be born, King of a realm "not of this world". But that story must be left for others to tell.

We seem to be leaving the history of Israel and Judah on a note of almost unrelieved gloom. Yet it was precisely at this point of history that the ancient biblical author (or authors) of the Books of Kings broke off. We cannot imagine that it gave him any pleasure to recount the grim details of his country's downfall. What was his purpose in writing, then? A careful study of 1 and 2 Kings reveals that these books constitute an examination of the causes of the decline and fall of God's ancient people. If the future were to mean anything, the survivors of 587 B.C. must be able to ascertain and analyse those causes, for the lasting benefit of future generations. Besides, was there not one obvious lesson to be learned? The history of Israel and Judah had revolved around three personages — prophet, priest and king. In physical terms, all three had now been swept away, although it was true that all three might one day be restored. But in spiritual and moral terms, had not the prophet been vindicated? The king had been unable to save his kingdom; the priest had become a lackey of the royal court, voicing pious platitudes instead of the living oracles of God; but the very fall of Jerusalem itself had authenticated the true prophetic message, silenced the false prophets, and given every intelligent Judaean cause to go back and re-examine the recorded words of the prophets of many generations. Thus while we are familiar with the terms "Kings" as a title for two Old Testament books, we should not overlook the truer prospective of those ancient Jewish rabbis who recognised that the books of Joshua, Judges, Samuel and Kings belong collectively in the category "the Prophets".

We have now outlined the history of the Hebrew monarchy, concentrating attention on the figure of the king and on political events; it is now high time we sought a wider perspective, following the example of the Old Testament historians themselves.

Part Two
The Enemies

CHAPTER 13

The Philistines

WHAT was it that brought about the downfall of the dynasty of
David? The obvious answer is that it was the might of Babylon;
it was Nebuchadrezzar, Chaldaean king of Babylon, who exiled
Jehoiachin and imprisoned a blinded Zedekiah, far from the ruins of
their former capital on Mount Zion. It is beyond doubt, then, that
the Judaean monarchy died through the pressures of an external foe;
but it is equally true that the same monarchy was born of the
pressures of an external foe — for who can doubt that Saul's rise to
power in Israel was due to the menace posed by the Philistines? And
yet another enemy, Assyria, brought about the collapse of the
Northern Kingdom, a century and a half before Jerusalem
fell.

From the purely political aspect, then, the course of Israel's
history in these centuries was dictated as much by the activities and
demands of other nations as it was by the internal policies and
aspirations of the Hebrew kings. It is high time for us to pay more
detailed and systematic attention to these nations, whose
relationships with Israel and Judah had such far-reaching effects.

The first major enemy encountered by the Israelite nation were
the Philistines. The main wave of Philistines had found their
"promised land" only a short while after the Israelites had done so.
The Israelite exodus from Egypt is usually dated in the thirteenth
century B.C., perhaps as early as 1275, in the reign of the Egyptian
king Ramesses II. A little after 1200 B.C., Pharaoh Ramesses III
had to confront an invasion from the sea; the invaders, repulsed,
settled instead on the coast of Palestine, and made their own an area
which it is convenient to call "Philistia". For convenience, again,
we may call these people "Philistines" — for this we have good Old

Testament precedent — although the term "Sea Peoples" is more accurate. The total picture is somewhat blurred; there were several different ethnic groups involved, and some of them had arrived on the Levant coasts at least a century before 1200 B.C. They were to be found further north in Palestine, too. Where they originated from is a matter of uncertainty and debate,[1] but the general Aegean area seems likely enough. A small but perhaps significant link with the Aegean may be seen in the Philistine designation for their kings, *seranim* (the singular would be *seren*), which appears to be the equivalent of the Greek term *tyrannoi*, "tyrants". The dominant ethnic group, before long, was the Peleset, from which we derive, via Hebrew, the familiar word "Philistine". This group came from Caphtor, according to Jeremiah 47:4 and Amos 9:7; and Caphtor was the name for Crete. (The parallel term Kerethites (Cherethites) seems to link up more directly with our word "Crete"; cf. Ezekiel 25:16.)

At first these "Sea Peoples" mastered much of the Levant coast, and dominated the older population (the civilization familiar to us as the "Amorites" or "Canaanites" in the Old Testament books); but it was the strictly Philistine area, from Joppa southwards, where they settled most strongly and permanently, and which was most intimately concerned with the history of Israel. In this area there were five major cities, Ashdod, Ashkelon and Gaza on or very near the coast, and Ekron and Gath further inland. The rulers of these cities were independent of each other, but yet they co-operated well; we see in 1 Samuel 29:3-7 how the king of Gath was overruled by his fellow-rulers and was content to abide by their decision. There were other cities in Philistia (Joppa, for one), but evidently they were controlled by the pentapolis listed above.

In the two centuries prior to 1200 B.C., the whole of Palestine and Syria had been overrun by a variety of "outsiders", Aramaeans, Israelites, Ammonites, Moabites, and Edomites, in addition to the sea-invaders. The Canaanites, the earlier inhabitants, were by no means wiped out; they retained a considerable number of cities, and in the north west section of the land they were presently able to reassert their ascendancy, in the region we term Phoenicia (roughly equivalent to the modern Lebanon). The north east section became Aramaean territory; and the southern half of the country, west of the Jordan, was shared between Philistines, on the coastal plain, and the rather loosely-knit confederation of Israelite tribes inland. It was therefore almost inevitable that there should ultimately be a measure of conflict between the Philistines and the Israelites; but it took time for the hostilities to develop. Both peoples were fully occupied in consolidating their new territorial possessions, till 1100 B.C. at least.

1. See T. C. Mitchell in *AOTS*, pp. 410f., for details.

In the struggle with Israel, we see the Philistines endeavouring to expand eastwards, up into the hill country; but there can be no doubt that they sought expansion westwards too, in maritime trade.

An interesting tale relating to the early eleventh century comes from Egypt, but throws some light on the Philistines at this period. It is the story of Wen-Amun,[2] an Egyptian priest who was entrusted with the task of sailing to Byblos (the Old Testament Gebal) on the Phoenician coast to purchase timber. He put in first at Dor, a few miles south of the modern Haifa; Dor lay on a stretch of the coast which had been occupied by the Tjekker, a group of the Sea Peoples who had arrived in Palestine at the same time as the Philistines. While the ship was in harbour, a seaman absconded with Wen-Amun's money. Wen-Amun reported the theft to the king of Dor, expecting him to enforce law and order, and take steps to apprehend the thief; but the treatment he received was so casual and unconcerned that at last, in exasperation, he sailed further north and seized and looted a boat belonging to the Tjekker. In consequence, the Tjekker sent eleven ships to pursue him. Evidently Wen-Amun escaped, but the text breaks off, and we do not know the details.

This story confirms the extent of "Philistine" domination at this time, and shows how contemptuous they could be of other people's interests and rights. It also demonstrates something of their maritime prowess. Clearly the Philistines and their associates were unchallenged on the coastal plains; and the story of Saul reveals how easily they could move into the Plain of Jezreel, too. By now they were encircling much of Israel, for they had also expanded to the south east of Philistia, into the Negeb (as is clear from the Philistine pottery found abundantly in the Negeb).

Their monopoly of iron weapons and their thorough acquaintance with military techniques permitted them to make the attempt to conquer the hill-country, that is to say, the tribal areas of west Manasseh, Ephraim, Dan, Benjamin, Judah and Simeon. Dan was a major victim; the Samson narratives illustrate the pressures to which the Danites were subjected. West Judah also suffered from their inroads. After the disastrous battle of Aphek, the Israelites found themselves subject to the Philistines, who placed garrisons at strategic points in the hill-country. The Philistine successes were due to their advantages in the way of military weapons and skills, not to their numerical superiority. On the contrary, in their own area many of the indigenous Canaanite population had survived, though they were subservient to their rule. The fact that David and his men could serve as mercenaries for Achish of Gath in itself illustrates the relative lack of Philistine man-power.

2. Cf. *ANET*, pp. 25-29.

Saul's victories over the Philistines were partial and inconclusive, and his reign ended with the inglorious débâcle at Gilboa; nevertheless, Saul's achievements were sufficient to prove to the Israelites that, if united and given adequate generalship, they could defeat the Philistines. It was David who provided both; and in a generation the Philistines were crushed, never to prove a major power in the area again. According to 1 Chronicles 18:1 he even took the city of Gath; but if so,[3] he must soon have restored the city to the Philistines, since Achish was still king there early in Solomon's reign (cf. 1 Kings 2:39), though perhaps with merely vassal status. David respected the Philistines' fighting abilities sufficiently to take his personal bodyguard from their numbers; Gittites (i.e. men of Gath) are mentioned among his personal troops in 2 Samuel 15:18. David's success meant that the Philistines were from now on confined to Philistia proper; and even there they were tributary to him.

But in a sense, the Philistines were conquered by the Canaanites as much as by the soldiers of Israel. It may well be that the true Philistine element in Philistia was decimàted in the heavy military defeats they suffered, with the result that the Canaanites there once again rose to the surface. However, even before David's victories the process had begun. As early as Samson's time, the chief god worshipped by the Philistines in Gaza was Dagon (Judges 16:23); in Samuel's time, the same god was revered at Ashdod (1 Samuel 5:1f.); but Dagon is the name of an ancient Canaanite deity. True, the Philistines may have recognised that the indigenous Dagon had the same character and attributes as some deity of their own, and so equated the two deities, thus enabling their Canaanite subjects to worship at the same shrines as themselves. The fact remains, however, that we do not know the name of a single Philistine deity; Ashtoreth at Beth-shan (1 Samuel 31:10) and Baal-zebub of Ekron (2 Kings 1:2) were also Canaanite deities.

In other respects too, the Philistines adapted themselves rapidly to Canaanite ways. Their own language gave way to Canaanite;[4] their own distinctive culture and distinctive artifacts (such as pottery) gradually disappeared; and politically they fell into the independent city-state pattern so typical of the Canaanites. In future their five cities did not show the cohesion and common policies which had made the Philistines such a force to be reckoned with. It is not without good reason that in the Bible the distinctive term *seranim*

3. The parallel passage in 2 Samuel 8:1 does not mention Gath, a fact which raises textual and historical problems. See J. Mauchline, *1 and 2 Samuel (NCB.* London, 1971), *ad loc.* One possibility is that the reference is to a different Gath.
4. The statement in Nehemiah 13:23f. about "the language of Ashdod" as late as the fifth century must refer to a local Canaanite dialect, as would certainly be the case with Ammon and Moab.

("lords") gives way to the ordinary Canaanite word *melakim* ("kings").

The rest of Philistine history, therefore, can only be told in terms of the individual cities and their fluctuating fortunes, or of general political influences over the area. Israel's dominating influence began to ebb towards the end of Solomon's reign, to be replaced by Egyptian interest. The campaign of Shishak in Rehoboam's fifth year was able to use Gaza, the most southerly Philistine city, as its starting-point. But the Egyptians soon lost their interest in Palestine. Border fighting, sometimes on a fairly big scale, occupied Philistine and Israelite (i.e. the Northern Kingdom) troops for half a century (cf. 1 Kings 15:27; 16:15ff.). Jehoshaphat of Judah (873-848) was then able to reimpose Judaean suzerainty over the Philistines, and take tribute from them (2 Chronicles 17:11). In the reign of Jehoram of Judah, it was Judah's turn to suffer; but the most the Philistines could achieve consisted of plundering incursions (2 Chronicles 21:16f.). The major power in the Palestinian area at the end of this ninth century was the Aramaean kingdom of Damascus, which dominated the affairs of both Israel and Judah during this period; Philistia was at a greater distance from Damascus and suffered less, but at one point the Syrian king Hazael did seize the city of Gath (2 Kings 12:17).

By now, however, the Assyrians were poised for the control of Palestine, and before the ninth century ended Assyrian records were making their first mention of Philistia. Adad-nirari III relates that in his fifth year (c. 806) he "gave the word for the vast army of Assyria to march to the land of Philistia".[5] The great king was satisfied with tribute however.

In the first half of the eighth century, a quiescent Assyria allowed the twin Hebrew kingdoms to recover lost ground and to enjoy almost a second golden age. King Uzziah of Judah profited by this situation to attack Philistia yet again; the cities of Gath and Ashdod were among those he sacked (2 Chronicles 26:6). No doubt the Judaean settlements Uzziah planted in the neighbourhood of Ashdod did not long survive, once Judah's power declined again. A new Philistine town seems to have sprung up at Gath, but Gath was in fact doomed; at the end of the century the Assyrian king Sargon II attacked it again (715 B.C.). Even before that, the prophet Amos could ignore its very existence, when he pronounced doom on the other four leading cities of Philistia (Amos 1:6ff.).

These other four cities survived, but now that the day of the big empires' control of Palestine had arrived, they had no chance of independence. They fought against the inevitable, none the less, in common with other states round about. We can see how divided

---

5. *DOTT*, p. 51. In Akkadian, the name Philistia appears as "Palashtu".

among themselves the Philistines were by this date, in the complex of events culminating in Sennacherib's invasion in 701 B.C. Of their five major cities, Ashdod refused to act against Assyria — Sennacherib's predecessor, Sargon, had taken Ashdod by storm eleven years earlier (cf. Isaiah 20:1), and she had learned her lesson. The king of Ekron, who was called Padi, also remained loyal to Assyria, but his leading citizens had other ideas, and placing Padi in the custody of Judah's king Hezekiah, they committed their city to the revolt. Gaza, it seems, also declined to join the revolt, and suffered invasion by Hezekiah in consequence (2 Kings 18:8). But the fourth city, Ashkelon, under its king Sidqa, wholeheartedly supported Hezekiah's rebellion. The Assyrian king crushed the revolt, punished the rebels, and rewarded those who had remained loyal: Padi not only recovered the throne of Ekron, but a slice of Judaean territory as a bonus; Ashdod, too, had its territory enlarged at the expense of Judah.

As the seventh century proceeded, the Philistine cities meekly accepted Assyrian domination; they could do little else, in view of the powerful Assyrian presence, occasioned by the invasions of Egypt by Esarhaddon and Ashurbanipal. But as Assyrian power declined, other pressures exerted themselves on the area. One particular disaster of uncertain date (perhaps about 610 B.C.) suffered by Ashkelon is related by the Greek historian Herodotus.[6] One of the causes of the Assyrian decline was the inroads of nomad horsemen from the Russian steppes, notably the Scythians, who on occasion swept fiercely down the Palestine coast,only to be repulsed on the Egyptian frontier; as they returned northwards, they plundered the temple of Astarte in Ashkelon.[7]

For a few years, Egypt was the dominating force in Philistia, as her armies marched through it year after year to support Assyria in its death-throes and to defy Babylon. Gaza apparently tried to withstand Pharaoh Necho at about the same time that Josiah tried to do the same at Megiddo (609 B.C.); Jeremiah 47:1 mentions "Pharaoh's harrying of Gaza". Nevertheless, in the next few years the Philistine cities resisted the Babylonian armies to the best of their ability, aided and abetted by the Egyptians. A letter of the time (discovered in Egypt in 1942) from a Palestinian king, urgently requesting Egyptian military assistance against Babylon, is often thought to have come from Ashkelon.[8]

It was Nebuchadrezzar who virtually wiped out Philistia as a distinct political entity. For many years the Philistines had become

6. Herodotus i. 105.
7. It is not certain, however, how accurate Herodotus' information was. The Scythians appear in the Old Testament as "Ashkenaz" (e.g. Genesis 10:3; Jeremiah 51:27).
8. *DOTT*, pp. 251-255.

more and more indistinguishable from their Phoenician neighbours to the north, and Nebuchadrezzar's deportation policy, put into effect after his devastating conquest of Philistia in 604 B.C., put paid to the last vestiges of anything distinctively Philistine. The cities themselves remained, of course; Gaza and Azotus (= Ashdod) are mentioned in the New Testament, and some of the ancient names, especially Gaza, are still functioning today.

What legacy did these folk leave to posterity? Archaeologists have unearthed some of their material remains; but their distinctive pottery and their intriguing "anthropoid" coffins[9] (see plate 10 facing p. 177), they themselves abandoned after their heyday. A few Philistine words have survived, through the medium of the Hebrew Bible. Three Hebrew words are commonly credited to the Philistine language, namely *seren* ("lord" or "tyrant"), *kobha'* or *qobha'* ("helmet"), and *argaz* ("box"). All three survive in modern Hebrew, although the first two have changed meaning — *seren* now denotes an army captain, and today *kobha'* is the ordinary word for a hat.

Their most notable linguistic legacy is the name "Palestine", which is still a very convenient term, even though it no longer describes a political entity. The ancient Greeks in due course made the name *Palaistine*, i.e. "Philistine", do service for the whole country, in much the same way that in Britain we often call the Netherlands "Holland", a term which strictly should apply only to two coastal provinces of the country. The Greek term was given fresh currency by the Romans after the second Jewish revolt (A.D. 132-5), when they decided to abolish the term Judaea once and for all. The seventh century Muslim conquest later brought the term into ordinary Arabic usage.

Their most significant legacy, however, was their effect upon Israel. By the very fact of the challenge they threw out, they transformed the structure of Israel from a loose tribal federation to a unified kingdom. A less powerful enemy could have been dealt with by a single Israelite tribe, or possibly by a temporary alliance of two or three tribes, as happened often enough during the period of the Judges. On the other hand, a more powerful enemy, like the Assyrians two or three centuries later, would have steam-rollered over the Israelites, and a political unification of Israel could never have taken place.

The Philistine challenge, then, made Israel what it became under Saul, and more particularly under David, who may be said to have learned a great deal from the Philistines. They showed that there was a power vacuum in the area; it was David who proved the man

9. See illustration in *ANEP*, fig. 641.

to fill it, using military tactics learned from the Philistines. Thus in a sense they made David what he was, and thus they stand behind the Davidic dynasty, and the Messianic ideal, with all its consequences for Judaism and Christianity.[10]

10. For further information about the Philistines, see K. A. Kitchen in *POTT,* chapter 3.

CHAPTER 14

Transjordan and Amalek

A LTHOUGH it was undoubtedly Philistine pressure which brought about the unification of the Israelite tribes under Saul, the first military campaign of the monarchy, as recorded in 1 Samuel, was not after all with the major foe to the west but with the much smaller nation of Ammon, across the Jordan. During the monarchy, the northern part of what we can conveniently call Transjordan was peopled by Israelites; but south and south-east of the Israelite area (Gilead) lay the three small nations of Ammon, Moab and Edom.[1] Their relationship with the Israelites was one of friction when it was not outright hostility, even though all were closely related and appear to have spoken the same language, or rather, slightly varying dialects of the same language.[2]

The Book of Genesis sets the scene for this relationship. Genesis 19 depicts the origins of Moab and Ammon as distinctly sordid; and Genesis 36:1, which equates Edom with Esau, indicates that the tension between Jacob and Esau was symptomatic of the whole relationship between their respective progeny. Such passages in Genesis also acknowledge the fact that these three Transjordanian peoples were, unlike the Philistines, close relatives of the tribes of Israel, and of course each other. We may also glean from Genesis that the three groups were semi-nomadic at first.

By the thirteenth century B.C., Moab and Edom had established themselves strongly athwart the major trade route known as the

1. See the map in C. M. Jones, *Old Testament Illustrations* (Cambridge, 1971), p. 14.
2. Probably an Edomite would have understood an Israelite as readily as a Scotsman can understand a Yorkshireman today.

King's Highway;[3] Ammon took longer to abandon semi-nomadism, but all three kingdoms presented something of a barrier to the Israelite tribes as they sought to enter Transjordan via the King's Highway. Moses avoided causing them any offence by taking a circuitous route to avoid Edomite and Moabite territory, and then marching between the Moabite and Ammonite lands, en route defeating the king of Heshbon, Sihon by name (Numbers 20f.). Sihon was an Amorite, who had previously attacked Moab, so the Moabites must have welcomed the Israelites' action. It was the tribe of Reuben which came to occupy this region, and thus separated the Ammonites from the Moabites. The latter, however, who had earlier forfeited some of this territory to Sihon, lost no opportunities to infiltrate and overrun Reubenite lands; the Moabite boundary should have been the Arnon River (which runs west into the Dead Sea). This conflict came to a head when a Moabite king named Eglon was able to conquer Reuben, cross the Jordan, and make himself master of the Jericho area in Benjaminite territory; Ehud was the "judge" who drove the Moabites back across the Jordan (Judges 3:12-30). The Ammonites had supported the Moabites in this campaign, and in spite of Ehud's victories, the position of Reuben remained far from happy or secure, with hostile neighbours to the south and east. Later it was the Ammonites' turn to take the initiative against the Israelites in Transjordan; Jephthah was the Israelites' leader and deliverer on this occasion (Judges 11).

A period of peace followed, in which it was evidently safe and even advantageous for a Judaean family to migrate to Moab (Ruth 1:1); the consequence was that King David's great-grandmother was a Moabite woman. No doubt there was a good deal of friendliness between ordinary citizens of the Israelite tribes and Moab and Ammon; otherwise there would have been little temptation for Israelites to start worshipping Moabite and Ammonite deities (cf. Judges 10:6). It is difficult to be sure how to interpret the fact that during the conflict between Saul and David, the latter's family took refuge with the Moabite king (1 Samuel 22:3f.). It may be that David's family had always remained on good terms with the Moabites; alternatively, we may view the Moabite king's action as intended to be hostile to Israel, since David was a thorn in the side of Israel's king. It is not unlikely that the Ammonite king Nahash befriended David at the same time (cf. 2 Samuel 10:1f.), and in his case there was no reason why he should show favour to David except hostility to Saul.

There was every reason for Nahash to be hostile to Saul. Some time before David came on the scene, Nahash had endeavoured to

---

3. For a discussion of the uncertainties of the early history of Moab and Edom, and for further general information, see J. R. Bartlett in *POTT*, Chapter 10.

7. The Assyrians attack Lachish

make himself master of the Israelite territory to the north west, and had attacked and besieged the city of Jabesh-gilead. This Ammonite attack happened to coincide with Israel's half-hearted decision to adopt a monarchic constitution; and so it came about that the first enemy of the Israelite monarchy was Ammon. Saul, who had become king only a few weeks earlier, rose to the occasion nobly and inflicted a heavy defeat on Nahash's army. If we can credit Philistine pressures with leading Israel into a monarchy, we can in turn credit the Ammonites with supplying Saul with the opportunity to prove himself an effective king. His victory in Transjordan brought all Israel behind him (1 Samuel 11).

No details are given of his further campaigns against the Transjordanian kingdoms, but 1 Samuel 14:47 records that Saul inflicted defeats on Ammon, Moab and Edom alike. These campaigns were intended to secure Israel's frontiers, insofar as they were not defensive measures. Thus Edom, which had played little part in Israel's history during the period of the Judges, will have met Saul's armies in battle on the southern border of Judah, near the south west end of the Dead Sea; it is clear that Saul did not march right through Moabite territory in order to attack the Edomites.

It was David who turned defence into attack. What series of incidents precipitated his wars with Moab and Edom we have no way of knowing, but it seems clear that the Ammonites chose to pick a foolish quarrel with David.[4] No doubt both Moab and Ammon felt much less friendly towards David once he became king of a united and potentially powerful Israel. At any rate, the upshot was that in spite of such alliances as they could form, the three Transjordanian kingdoms were conquered by David, with a great deal of bloodshed. The Moabite ruler seems to have remained king, but as a mere tributary vassal of David. The Edomite royal house was all but exterminated; a lone survivor fled to Egypt. Edom had an Israelite governor appointed over it; but Ammon may well have had as its governor an Ammonite appointed by David. It is interesting to note that when David fled to Transjordan during Absalom's revolt one of his wealthy friends and benefactors there was Shobi, a brother of the defeated Ammonite king (2 Samuel 17:27). Quite conceivably Shobi was governor of Ammon.

The united monarchy of Israel had little difficulty in controlling Ammon and Moab, but Solomon evidently experienced some difficulty in maintaining his grip on Edom. The prince who had escaped to Egypt, Hadad by name, decided that he could safely return to Edom early in Solomon's reign, and he did so. "He maintained a strangle-hold on Israel and became king of Edom" (1 Kings 11:25). It seems likely, however, that his "rule" was purely

---

4. 2 Samuel 10:1-5. See above, p. 46.

nominal, and that a constant guerrilla compaign was all that he could achieve against Solomon. By contrast, Ammon probably endured Israelite suzerainty without too much concern, since her trading was healthy and rewarding. Solomon contracted diplomatic marriages with all three kingdoms, in an effort to keep the situation stable (1 Kings 11:1).

The situation changed dramatically on Solomon's death, when Israel broke into two halves. The Southern Kingdom, Judah, retained its hold on Edom, apparently, for more than half a century later a deputy of King Jehoshaphat ruled there. Ammon and Moab, on the other hand, which came now within the orbit of the Northern Kingdom, in due course took the opportunity to break free, apparently without any serious attempt by Jeroboam or his successors to hinder their defection. Omri was the king of Israel who imposed control over Moab once again. Ammon remained independent, and joined in the coalition headed by Israel and Damascus which confronted the Assyrian army at Qarqar, in 853 B.C. The king of Ammon, Ba'asa by name, sent a contingent of troops, Shalmaneser III records.[5]

Moab and Edom were not long in following Ammon's lead. The king of Moab who gained independence for his country was Mesha, whose rebellion is discussed in 2 Kings 3. This same Mesha left his own document recording the course of events — the so-called Moabite Stone,[6] discovered in 1868 in the ruins of the ancient Moabite city of Dibon. From this it appears that Israelites of the tribe of Gad had occupied the territory, formerly in Reuben's possession, which separated Moab from Ammon. Moab had always begrudged Israel's holdings in this region, and Mesha now determined not only to free his country from Israelite control but also to add to his realm this disputed territory; after a struggle he achieved both objectives. The strategy of the Israelite king Jehoram was clearly to surprise Mesha by attacking him where he least expected it — i.e. from the south, advancing via Judaean and Edomite country — but the ploy, though it came within an inch of success, failed to bring Mesha to heel. Moab's border was therefore now located considerably further north than had hitherto been the case.[7] The joint Moabite, Ammonite and Edomite attempt at reprisals against Judah was however unsuccessful.[8]

Edom's moves towards independence seem to have been more gradual. The Judaean governors of earlier days had before this campaign been replaced by an Edomite king, presumably a vassal of

5. Cf. *DOTT*, p. 47.
6. See *DOTT*, pp. 195-198 for translation, notes and a photograph of the inscription.
7. See *MBA*, map 131.
8. See above, p. 78.

Jehoshaphat (cf. 2 Kings 3:9); the next king of Judah was unable to maintain Judaean control, and the Edomite king became independent (2 Kings 8:16, 20).

In the first half of the eighth century, both Israel and Judah grew relatively strong again, after the collapse of the Aramaean kingdom of Damascus (which may well have been dominating Ammon and Moab as well as Israel).[9] The result was that all three Transjordanian kingdoms were brought to heel once again. Amaziah of Judah reconquered Edom, and his son Uzziah probably asserted control or partial control over the Ammonites and Moabites. By now Moab was in decline, partly due to Ammonite encroachment, it would appear. The power of Judah proved ephemeral, of course, and though immediately after Uzziah's death Ammon tried unsuccessfully to break free again (2 Chronicles 27:5), before long it was Assyria, not Judah, which was imposing its control upon Transjordan. Tiglath-pileser III (745-727) was the first king of Assyria to make the Transjordanian kings his vassals. They were unwilling vassals, naturally, and Assyrian records mention occasional revolts by them. Edom and Moab are explicitly mentioned along with Judah and Philistia as would-be rebels against Sargon II in 711 B.C.[10]

Of the three kingdoms, Ammon was the most prosperous under Assyrian rule; the Assyrians evidently permitted the Ammonites to make good use of their advantageous position on the trade-routes. But Ammon's decline was not long delayed; she proved as resolutely unwilling as Judah to permit the Babylonians to replace the Assyrians as the masters of the whole area, and showed the same folly in defying Nebuchadrezzar. At the same time as Jehoiakim's revolt, to be sure, Ammon remained loyal to Nebuchadrezzar, and sent detachments of troops to assist the Babylonians against Judah, as did also the Moabites (2 Kings 24:2). But at the "pan-Palestinian congress" of 594 B.C.,[11] Ammon, Moab and Edom were all represented, and from then on Ammon's hostility to Babylon became entrenched. After the destruction of Jerusalem in 587 B.C., many Judaeans fled to Transjordan, and one nobleman of Judah, Ishmael by name, conspired with the Ammonite king Baalis to assassinate the Judaean governor, Gedaliah, whom the Babylonians had appointed over Judah (Jeremiah 40:13-41:2).

Josephus[12] reports that the Babylonians in due course took punitive measures against Ammon, and archaeological investigation has revealed that the territories of the three Transjordanian

9. Cf. 2 Kings 10:32f. (The city of Aroer was by now in Moabite territory.)
10. Cf. *ANET*, p. 287.
11. See above, p. 128.
12. *Ant.* x, 9, 7.

kingdoms became significantly depopulated during the sixth century B.C., the vacuum being filled by wandering Arab tribes (who had in fact been putting considerable pressures on the settled population for some time past). One specific result of the Arab pressures was the displacement of the Edomites, who moved steadily westwards and northwards, occupying territory in the south of Judah. A comparison of a map of New Testament Palestine with a map of Old Testament Palestine will show how the Edomites had moved.[13]

It was no doubt an early assault on Moab by Arab tribesmen which led to the disasters depicted in Isaiah chapters 15 and 16. This passage is unusual among the prophetic oracles concerning foreign nations for its sympathetic tone: "My heart cries out for Moab", exclaimed the prophet (15:5). In general, the prophets felt that the misfortunes of the Transjordanian kingdoms were well deserved. Amos, for instance, attacked Ammon in these terms: "For crime after crime of the Ammonites I will grant them no reprieve, because in their greed for land they invaded the ploughlands of Gilead" (Amos 1:13). It is interesting that his denunciation of Moab, on the other hand, is based on Moabite injustices towards the king of its neighbour Edom (cf. 2:1), not on its dealings with Judah or Israel.

The Edomite encroachment upon south Judah was particularly resented; even if the Edomites were themselves under pressure, they showed unwarranted and unbrotherly harshness in their callous appropriation of Judaean lands at a time when Judah was reeling from the Babylonian onslaught. The exilic Psalm 137, recalling how "By the rivers of Babylon we sat down and wept", invokes the Lord to "remember . . . against the people of Edom the day of Jerusalem's fall, when they said, 'Down with it, down with it, down to its very foundations!' ". Similarly Ezekiel 35:5 accuses the Edomites thus: "You have maintained an immemorial feud and handed over Israelites to the sword in the hour of their doom, at the hour of their final punishment". And the whole of the little Book of Obadiah constitutes a vigorous denunciation of Edom.

We need not trace the history of these Transjordanian kingdoms further. The area became more and more Arab in character as time passed, though the ancient names of Ammon, Moab and Edom persisted into early Christian centuries. Indeed, the name Ammon still persists, in the form Amman, the capital of the Hashemite kingdom of Jordan. This city's full name in Old Testament times was Rabbath-beney-Ammon, i.e. "Rabbah of the Ammonites". Rabbah was the Ammonites' capital and only major town. David's men were able to capture it only after a siege which lasted a period of at least some months; it was during the siege of Rabbah that David

---

13. The New Testament Greek name for "Edom" is Idumaea; Herod the Great was an Idumaean.

committed adultery with Bathsheba, and her husband Uriah's death occurred outside the city walls (cf. 2 Samuel 11).

The Old Testament testifies to some of the chief pursuits and interests of the Transjordanian kingdoms. Moab, 2 Kings 3:4 indicates, gained its main wealth from sheep — the geography and climate still make sheep-farming very common in this region, which consists mainly of a high plateau (to the east), with a steep descent to the more fertile eastern shores of the Dead Sea. Its northern boundary was the gorge of the River Arnon, its southern boundary the Brook Zered. Its chief towns were Kir-hareseth (Kir-Moab) and Dibon, north of the Arnon, after Mesha's ninth century conquest of that district.

Moab's southern neighbour, Edom, was famed for its pursuit of wisdom, on which it prided itself. Wisdom was an international pursuit, and Edom's geographical position gave it ready contact with various countries — Egypt, North Arabia, Canaan, Syria and also Mesopotamia. It seems likely that Job's three "comforters" were wise men of Edom; Eliphaz, at least, came from Teman, one of the chief towns of Edom. The arrogant dogmatism of Job's friends seems to have typified Edomite wisdom, if we may judge by the challenge uttered by Jeremiah, as he predicted disaster for Edom: "The LORD of hosts has said: Is wisdom no longer to be found in Teman? Have her sages no skill in counsel? Has their wisdom decayed?" (Jeremiah 49:7). Obadiah referred to their "proud, insolent heart", as he prophesied the destruction of all their sages and their wisdom (Obadiah 3,8).

Edom's chief towns were Sela and Teman (both near Petra), and Bozrah further north. Her territory centred in the Arabah — the valley which lies between the Dead Sea and the Gulf of Aqaba — and it was here that the chief source of her wealth lay, in the copper that was mined and exported. At times both Edom and Ammon were richer than Judah, as can be judged from the relative size of tribute imposed on them by the Assyrians.

Religion of Edom and Moab

We are not well informed about the religion of ancient Edom; the Old Testament indicates that the chief deity of Ammon was named Milcom (cf. 1 Kings 11:5) and the state deity of Moab Chemosh (cf. 1 Kings 11:7), but there is no such information for Edom. Other sources, however, give the name Qaus as Edom's chief god. None of these three kingdoms was monotheistic, and the evidence is clear that all three worshipped a similar pantheon which included deities drawn from the North Arabian and also Canaanite cultic systems. The ubiquitous Canaanite Baal, for instance, was worshipped in

both Ammon and Moab; while the name of the lone survivor of the
Edomite royal family in David's time, Hadad, tells its own tale —
that Baal was worshipped in Edom too, but under his other name
Hadad. Some description of Canaanite religious belief and practice
is given elsewhere in this book;[14] but the further question arises
whether we can identify any of the Transjordanian state deities with
any deities worshipped elsewhere. Possibly the Edomite Qaus (if not
an Arabian deity) was yet another name for the storm-god Baal or
Hadad; and a good case can be made for thinking that the Ammonite Milcom was simply the Moabite Chemosh under another name,
and that both are to be equated with the Molech worshipped just
outside Jerusalem.[15] It is possible, on the other hand, that the
Moabite Chemosh, at least, was the same god as Baal once again.

Something of the Moabites' own conception of their faith can be
gauged from a study of the Mesha Stele — a document unique of its
kind. The Stele reveals both the degree of similarity and dis-
similarity between the faith of Moab and that of Israel and Judah.
The Moabite king who authorized the inscription believed that
Moab's political troubles had been due to his god's anger; in other
words, his philosophy of history was closely akin to that of the Old
Testament writers. On the other hand, the wrath of Chemosh,
unlike that of Yahweh in the Old Testament, has no moral or
religious quality about it".[16] The harsh Moabite god changed his
mind, King Mesha believed, because of the fact that the crown-
prince was put to death as a sacrifice, or so we may judge from 2
Kings 3:27. Such a practice and such a concept are far removed
from the biblical understanding of what would gratify Yahweh.

The Amalekites

Very close kin to the Edomites were the Amalekites (cf. Genesis
36:12, 16), who were a foe confronted by both Saul and David.
Unlike the Edomites, however, they were nomads, and the various
biblical references to them show how mobile they were. In the main
they roamed in the desert and semi-desert areas south and south-east
of Palestine, and it was here, therefore, that most of their recorded
clashes with Israel took place, from the time of Moses onwards (cf.
Exodus 17:8f.). They gained much of their livelihood from raiding
(in the immemorial nomadic fashion), and this feature made them
the inveterate and feared enemies of settled populations; thus in
Saul's reign the Philistines and the Judaeans were united in their

14. Cf. chapter 20.
15. See below, p. 205.
16. T. C. Vriezen, *The Religion of Ancient Israel* (ET London, 1967), pp. 62f.

hostility to the Amalekites, a situation from which David was able to profit (cf. 1 Samuel 27:7ff.).

No doubt the weak and disunited character of Israel during the later period of the Judges permitted and encouraged Amalek to prey systematically on the southern tribes of Israel; at any rate, they established a settled headquarters somewhere to the south of Judah, and they were sufficiently organized to have a king. They posed a sufficient threat to oblige Saul to embark on a full-scale and far-reaching campaign against them. It was a very successful campaign, too, and the Amalekite king Agag, was captured (1 Samuel 15).

David inflicted further defeats on them, after they had recovered sufficiently to start a fresh series of impudent raids on south Judah. It would seem that between them Saul and David decimated the Amalekites, and effectively prevented their raids on Israelite territory. We hear very little more of them; a mere five hundred Simeonites wiped out the last remnant of them in Hezekiah's reign, c. 700 B.C. (cf. 1 Chronicles 4:42f.).

CHAPTER 15

Syria

A NOTHER early and persistent enemy of the Israelite monarchy occupied the regions to the north east of Palestine, in other words the country we know as Syria, in Hebrew "Aram".[1] Modern Syria is a political unity, but in Old Testament times the Aramaeans were divided into a number of kingdoms; of these kingdoms the nearest neighbour to Israel at most periods was the kingdom of Damascus, and when the Old Testament refers to Syrians without further description, the inhabitants of this territory are usually intended.

The Israelites and the Aramaeans became masters of their respective areas at roughly the same time, though both peoples could lay claim to ancestors in these same regions in the preceding centuries. The name "Aramu" appears in Akkadian records as early as 2000 B.C.; no doubt Aramaeans gradually infiltrated the more fertile lands north of the Syrian desert (probably their original home) throughout the second millennium B.C., till by 1000 B.C. they were the dominant element in the population of Syria. In Genesis, the name Aram first appears as a son of Shem (10:22), and then as a descendant of Abraham's brother Nahor (22:21). Undoubtedly the patriarchs of Genesis were very close kin to the Aramaeans of their day; Jacob's wives were Aramaeans, and at a later date Israelites recognised that they could appropriately call their own forefathers Aramaeans (cf. Deuteronomy 26:5). In process

---

1. The names "Aram" and "Edom" are scarcely distinguishable in the Hebrew script, and as a result it is not always clear which people or territory is under discussion. In 2 Samuel 8:13, for instance, some Hebrew manuscripts have the one name, some manuscripts the other.

of time, however, a distinction in language grew up between the two peoples, the occupants of Syria speaking Aramaic, the Israelites Hebrew. The earliest witness to this difference is the narrative of Jacob's pact with his father-in-law Laban (Genesis 31). The cairn of witness bore the Aramaic name Jegar-sahadutha, and the Hebrew name Gal-ed (verse 47). Obviously these two names happen to be totally dissimilar, but in general the two languages were very alike,[2] as close as modern Spanish is to Italian, for example.

Friendly relations seem to have continued between Aramaeans and Israelites during the era of the Judges, while both peoples were settling down and establishing themselves. But Israel's very first king, Saul, clashed with at least one Aramaean king, according to 1 Samuel 14:47. The latter's territory was Zobah, to the north-west of Damascus; but we are not told where the battles were fought. Zobah was a rich kingdom and powerful at this time, and it is possible that its troops aided the Aramaean states south of it — Beth-rehob, Maacah and Geshur[3] — against Saul. But we can only conjecture.

Whether Geshur (which lay immediately east of the Sea of Galilee) was hostile to Saul or not, its king Talmai was quite prepared to befriend David. David married a royal princess of Geshur, who became the mother of Absalom (2 Samuel 3:3). Once David became king of a united Israel, we may judge from the silence of the records that Geshur, his nearest Aramaean neighbour, decided that discretion was the better part of valour. The other three kingdoms we have mentioned, however, plus the kingdom of Tob (east of Gilead) were drawn into conflict with David. Zobah no doubt took the lead, and sent troops to assist first the Moabites and then the Ammonites in their unavailing efforts to withstand Israelite pressure (cf. 1 Chronicles 19:7; 2 Samuel 10:6-19).

The king of Zobah, by name Hadadezer, though unsuccessful in extending his influence in Transjordan, had mastered the Aramaean states to the north of him, up as far as the Euphrates. One of his vassals, Toi of Hamath, organized a revolt against Hadadezer, who responded by setting out "to re-erect his monument of victory by the river Euphrates" (2 Samuel 8:3). Thus the major part of the Aramaean armies were directed northwards, away from Israel, and David chose this precise strategic moment to strike. Despite a hasty attempt by the Aramaeans of Damascus to cover Hadadezer's rear, David won a handsome series of victories, by which he smashed the power of Zobah, and himself became suzerain of the whole Aramaean region as far as the Euphrates. King Toi of Hamath sent David greetings and congratulations — but also tribute (2 Samuel 8:9f.). An Israelite garrison was stationed in Damascus (verses 5f.).

2. For instance, the Hebrew word *shekel* has *tekel* as its Aramaic equivalent, cf. Daniel 5:27.

3. See *MBA*, maps 101f.

So long as Israel remained united, the Aramaeans could not hope to retrieve their fortunes to any appreciable extent. Solomon held them as firmly under control as did David before him. One section of Aramaean territory sought to break away, but Solomon "went to Hamath-zobah and seized it", and felt secure enough to build store-cities in the neighbourhood (2 Chronicles 8:3f.). There was also a measure of trouble at Damascus. 1 Kings 11:23f. recounts briefly how a young Aramaean soldier of fortune, Rezon by name, deserted from the army of Hadadezer of Zobah and became captain of a guerrilla band based on Damascus. This adversary of Solomon ultimately became king of Damascus, and thus established a kingdom which was to give Israel a great deal of trouble in later days; but it is doubtful if Solomon considered Rezon a serious enemy.

When Solomon's kingdom fell apart, however, the Aramaeans found themselves independent, and Damascus soon achieved a power to rival Jeroboam's Israel (Zobah had now declined, and the only other Aramaean state to achieve power west of the Euphrates was Hamath). The first king of Damascus, after Rezon himself, to figure in Israel's history was Benhadad I, who came to the throne soon after 900 B.C. His father and predecessor Tabrimmon had made an alliance with Judah against Israel; but in Benhadad's reign some sort of pact was made between Damascus and Israel, until King Asa of Judah paid him to change sides and attack Israel. Benhadad willingly did so, and invested Dan and other Israelite cities on Israel's northern frontier (1 Kings 15:16-21). The sequel is not recorded, but presumably Benhadad withdrew once the main Israelite armies came to the rescue of their beleaguered cities. But by the middle of the ninth century we find a Benhadad — either the same king or (more probably) an identically-named successor[4] — firmly in control of the Israelite city of Ramoth-gilead, in north Transjordan (cf. 1 Kings 22.1ff.). The Syrian inroads into Israel had begun.

Meanwhile the Assyrian inroads into Aramaean territory had also begun. A century or two earlier the Aramaeans had put a great deal of pressure on Assyria itself, but the Assyrians had gradually resolved their difficulties and taken the offensive. In the early ninth century Ashurnasirpal II had sent armies through northern Syria, and now in 857 B.C. his successor Shalmaneser III defeated the major Aramaean state north of the Euphrates, Bit-Adini,[5] and went on to capture the city of Carchemish. The kingdoms to the south west took fright, as well they might, and a strong coalition was formed to stop the Assyrian advances. The kings of Damascus,

---

4. In Assyrian records he is called Adad-idri (cf. *DOTT*, p. 47), i.e. "Hadadezer" — unless Hadadezer was successor to Benhadad.
5. The Old Testament Beth-eden (cf. Amos 1:5).

Hamath and Israel (Ahab) were the leaders of this confederacy, which confronted the Assyrian armies at the battle of Qarqar in 853 B.C.[6] The Aramaean kings and their allies gained a temporary respite as a result of the battle.

In his more local struggles, Benhadad succeeded in deposing minor Aramaean kings and extending his own kingdom. Against Israel, he had some successes but more failures. He was able to lay siege to Israel's capital city, but was driven back and soundly defeated; an invasion south of the Sea of Galilee was also driven back (cf. 1 Kings 20); and it seems that he lost control of the city of Ramoth-gilead (cf. 1 Kings 22).

The king under whom the power of Damascus reached its zenith was Hazael, a usurper in whose accession both Elijah and Elisha took some interest. Early in his reign there was a fresh invasion by Shalmaneser III's armies, and twice over Damascus was assaulted (841 and 837 B.C.), but not captured. Otherwise Hazael was left free to pursue his own interests, until the closing years of his life. For the rest of the century Israel (ruled by first Jehu, then Jehoahaz) was almost helpless against him. He recaptured Ramoth-gilead, and proceeded to annex all Transjordan; he crippled the Israelite armies; he conquered parts of Philistia and threatened Judah, whose king hastily bought him off with a large bribe. By thus achieving control of Palestine and the Transjordanian trade-routes, he enriched his own kingdom at the expense of the other states in the vicinity, and bade fair to make Israel and Judah mere Aramaean vassals. But he failed to reckon with the Assyrians.

It was in the closing years of the century that Assyrian armies again took the field in the west, under Adad-nirari III. Numerous Palestinian states paid him tribute, possibly with the express intention of persuading him to take their part against Hazael. At all events, the Assyrian king tells us the sequel in his own words: "I marched to Aram and shut up Mari', king of Aram, in Damascus his capital city. The awful splendour of the god Ashur his lord overwhelmed him and he seized my feet, expressing submission. 2,300 talents of silver, 20 talents of gold, 300 talents of copper, 5,000 talents of iron, embroidered linen garments, an ivory bed, a couch embossed and inlaid with ivory, countless of his goods and possessions I received in his own palace at Damascus."[7] A further Assyrian attack on Damascus in 797 B.C. left this Aramaean kingdom yet weaker, and permitted the gradual resurgence of Israelite power.

The Israelite armies of Jehoash did not immediately profit from these disasters suffered by Damascus; Hazael's successor Benhadad

6. See above, p. 75.
7. *DOTT*, p. 51. Note that the record calls Hazael "Mari' ", which simply means "my lord".

III was at first successful against Israel (cf. 2 Kings 13:3). However, the kingdom of Damascus was drawn into a conflict with its northern Aramaean sister-kingdom, Hamath, now ruled by a king called Zakir. Zakir was originally king of a minor state called Lu'ash, but he succeeded in adding Hamath to his realm; that he achieved this success is rather surprising, and if looks as if he may have been a protégé of the Assyrians. At any rate, Benhadad of Damascus felt himself obliged to muster a coalition of considerable size against the usurper, and he led an assault on the city of Hadrach (or Hazrak). But he lost the battle.

For the story of the clash between Zakir and Benhadad, we are indebted to a monument in Aramaic which Zakir himself erected in commemoration of his victory.[8] It helps to explain why Damascus so rapidly lost its power; Jehoash of Israel inflicted several defeats on Benhadad, and then Jeroboam II was able to recoup for Israel all the territory which Jehu had lost to Hazael half a century earlier. Apparently Jeroboam was never able to make Damascus, and Hamath too, subservient to his wishes (cf. 2 Kings 14:28).

But in the middle of the eighth century a king came to the Assyrian throne who was to finish all hopes of Aramaean independence: Tiglath-pileser III. Hitherto Syria and Palestine had suffered occasional Assyrian forays and invasions; from now on they were to come under permanent Assyrian rule. The Syro-Palestinian states did not submit without a struggle, however; two major coalitions were formed against the invading armies, though both were doomed to failure. The first of these was led by ''Azriau of Yaudi'' — apparently Uzziah (= Azariah) of Judah,[9] although at a later date there was a north Syrian state with a name very like Yaudi,[10] a state possibly founded by Jews who migrated there at an unknown date. Azriau's efforts to thwart the Assyrian advance failed, while the second coalition fared even more disastrously. The second confederacy was headed by the kings of Damascus and Israel, Rezin and Pekah respectively. Ahaz of Judah, it will be recalled, refused to support the ill-advised venture, and was repaid by an attack on his own country and its capital by the confederates. It is of special interest that had Rezin and Pekah succeeded in capturing Jerusalem, an Aramaean would have been placed on the throne of Judah.[11]

---

8. Cf. *DOTT*, pp. 246f.
9. See above, p. 94.
10. The consonants of the Syrian state's name are Y'dy; the vowels can only be conjectured.
11. Cf. Isaiah 7:6 (and see above, p. 99).

It was now that the prediction of Amos came true:

> For crime after crime of Damascus
> I will grant them no reprieve,
> because they threshed Gilead under threshing-sledges spiked with iron.
> Therefore will I send fire upon the house of Hazael,
> fire that shall eat up Ben-hadad's palaces;
> I will crush the great men of Damascus
> and wipe out those who live in the Vale of Aven
> and the sceptred ruler of Beth-eden;
> the people of Aram shall be exiled to Kir.
> It is the word of the Lord.

(Amos 1:3ff.)

Israel lost three-quarters of its territory, and the annexed districts were reorganized into Assyrian provinces; similarly the former Aramaean states were all divided up and brought into the Assyrian provincial system. Damascus itself was captured and ravaged, and its monarchy brought to an end with the execution of Rezin (732 B.C.).

Thus ended all Aramaean independence. The Aramaean people, of course, was not exterminated, although many of them were uprooted and settled elsewhere by the Assyrian deportation policies.[12] Some of the citizens of Hamath were settled in Samaria after the fall of Israel's capital, a few years later.

After Assyria's fall, the Aramaean lands did not recover their lost independence, but came instead under the dominion of Babylon. After the Babylonians, the Persians became masters of the whole of Syria-Palestine, and on their heels came Alexander the Great. Soon after his death we find a kingdom in Syria again, but it was a Greek kingdom, ruled by the Seleucid Greeks. In the first century B.C. the Romans conquered Syria-Palestine. Damascus did become a Semitic king's capital once again in 85 B.C., when Aretas III made it the capital of the Nabataean Arabs' kingdom; but it is clear that Aretas ruled under the tutelage of Rome. It was Aretas IV, a century later, whose governor in Damascus tried to capture the apostle Paul (cf. 2 Corinthians 11:32f.); yet Damascus lay in the territory of the Roman province of Syria, and there can be no doubt who were the real rulers of the whole region.

In the early centuries A.D. Syria became a powerful centre of Christianity — Antioch was evangelized before Paul's conversion, and soon became the hub of a thriving missionary work. It was not until the eighth century Muslim conquests that the whole character of Syria changed.

12. See *IDB* i, p. 193 (s.v. "Aramaeans") for details.

Aramaean Religion

The names of several deities worshipped by the ancient Aramaeans are known to us. Most of the names are already familiar from other sources, but the most distinctive name, and the name most familiar to Old Testament readers, is that of Rimmon. Naaman, the Aramaean general healed by Elisha, apologized in advance for the fact that he was under obligation to join his master the king of Damascus in the worship of Rimmon (2 Kings 5:17f.). The implication of the passage is that Rimmon was the chief deity of Naaman's homeland.

Rimmon means "the Thunderer", and in fact the name signified the deity otherwise called Hadad,[13] the god of thunder. He was the chief god of the Aramaeans' pantheon, and his name is embodied in the names of such kings as Hadadezer and Benhadad. In the Zakir Stele, discussed above, several other deities are mentioned, but especially "Baal-shamen", or "the Baal of heaven". It would seem that this was the patron god of Zakir, and that there was a local cult in his honour somewhere in the state of·Zobah (Zakir's original home). However, Baal-shamen was probably just another designation of Hadad. The polytheists of the ancient Near East readily equated and identified gods originally distinct, and by the same token they seem to have localized deities who were strictly speaking cosmic.[14] Certainly, at any rate, both Hadad and Baal-shamen designated a god of the sky. At a much later date, Baal-shamen was given yet greater prominence in Syria, when under Greek rule Baal-shamen was equated with the chief Greek deity, Olympian Zeus. When Antiochus IV (Epiphanes) made his attack on Judaism in *c.* 167 B.C., it was an altar to this deity which was erected in the Jerusalem temple, to the horror of all devout Jews.[15] The name Baal-shamen would have had as its Hebrew equivalent "Baal-shamayim"; and this is the name parodied in the Book of Daniel by the term "the abomination of desolation", or rather "the abominable thing that causes desolation" (Daniel 11:31, 12:11), in Hebrew a pair of words of which the first replaces "Baal" and the second (*shomem* or *meshomem*) caricatures the word *shamayim*, "heaven".

Another Baal was worshipped by King Benhadad I of Damascus, who set up a brief inscription in honour of the god Melqart.[16] The name means "King of the city" (i.e. of the underworld). The

13. The two names are bracketed together in Zechariah 12:11.
14. Thus it was possible to speak of Baals (or Baalim) and other deities in the plural. The word *Ba'al* meant "lord" or "possessor" and can have been made the title of various deities, moreover.
15. Cf. 2 Maccabees 6:2.
16. Cf. *DOTT*, p. 239.

worship of this deity was particularly favoured by the Phoenicians, of whose city, Tyre, Melqart was the patron deity.

Other divine names in Aramaean religion were Elyon and Yahu. The former is the same name as that found in Genesis 14:18ff., and usually translated "Most High". The latter can be none other than "Yahweh", the name of Israel's God; it is thought that this worship must have commenced in Hamath in consequence of David's victories, which bought Hamath under Israel's jurisdiction for the time being.[17]

Aramaic Language

On the whole it seems that the Aramaeans were borrowers rather than creators where religion was concerned. But in another cultural aspect they were the benefactors of much of the ancient Near East; both their language and their script came to have very wide currency. The script was a simple alphabetic one, and it was very much more convenient than the cumbersome cuneiform syllabary used by the Assyrians and Babylonians, for example. It had its predecessors — it was a development of the Canaanite alphabet — but it in turn fathered a great many other alphabets, including the Greek, Roman (and so our own), Arabic, and a variety of Indian scripts. Even Hebrew came to adopt the Aramaic script in preference to its own earlier alphabet; the familiar "square" Hebrew letters, as in printed Hebrew, came from the Aramaeans.

The Aramaic language was of a relatively simple structure, and it had been taken into Mesopotamia by Aramaean migrants, so that it was not unknown there. Syria itself was something of a cross-roads in the ancient world, moreover, so that the language of Syria was well placed to carry its influence in all directions of the compass. Before the Assyrian empire collapsed, therefore, Aramaic had come to function as the diplomatic language of that empire, and indeed was widely spoken in Mesopotamia itself. The Babylonian empire, and after it the Persian, continued to use Aramaic as the diplomatic language. Moreover, the deportation policies of the Assyrians and Babylonians had given it prominence as the *lingua franca*. The result was that before New Testament times Aramaic had come to be the vernacular of many areas all round Syria, even though by now Greek too had wide currency in the Levant. One of the languages which suffered because of the advance of Aramaic was Hebrew itself.

17. Fo further details of Aramaean religion, cf. T. C. Vriezen, *The Religion of Ancient Irael* (ET London, 1967), pp. 56-59.

A small part of the Old Testament is in Aramaic — principally a few chapters in Ezra and Daniel. But by New Testament times Aramaic was so widespread in Palestine that even in Jerusalem itself Aramaic place-names abounded, such as Gethsemane, Gabbatha and Golgotha. Without doubt our Lord could read the Hebrew Scriptures (cf. Luke 4:16-20), and it is possible that he could speak Greek; but beyond a shadow of a doubt Aramaic was his everyday tongue. "Abba" and "Talitha cumi" are Aramaic words from his lips; and to them the early church added "Maranatha", "Come, O Lord!".

If today the Aramaic tongue has almost died out (the effect of the Muslim conquests, again), its imprint in the substratum of the New Testament can never be eradicated.[18]

18. For further information on the Aramaic language, cf. F. F. Bruce. *The Books and the Parchments*[3] (London, 1963), chapter 4. For further details about the Aramaeans see A. Malamat in *POTT*. chapter 6.

CHAPTER 16

Phoenicia

THE last of the Semitic neighbours of ancient Israel to deserve discussion are the Phoenicians. It may be disputed, however, whether they should really be included with Israel's "enemies", since there was little political hostility between the Phoenicians and the Israelites. At most there was occasional friction; and to this we may add that there was certainly some religious tension from time to time.

"Phoenicia" is not a word we meet in the Old Testament (though it occurs once or twice in the New). Its inhabitants called themselves "Canaanites" in Old Testament times, but it is convenient to have a different name for them, to avoid confusion with the normal use of the term Canaan to denote the whole of pre-Israelite Palestine with its occupants. The term Phoenicia was coined by the Greeks, and is conceivably a translation of the word Canaan, both names deriving from the purple dye for which the area was noted in ancient commerce.[1]

Ethnically, the Phoenicians were Canaanites; their homeland was the one area of the ancient Levant where the Canaanites were not permanently overrun by some other nation. Like the Canaanites before them, their land was not normally a political unit, but was split up into small independent city-states. Their most notable cities were Tyre, Sidon and Byblos (the Old Testament Gebal), all of them Mediterranean ports; the Phoenicians were great maritime traders, and expanded westwards across the Mediterranean, thus avoiding to a great extent territorial conflicts with their neighbours.

1. For further information on the Phoenicians see D. R. Ap-Thomas in *POTT*, chapter 11; he discusses the meaning of the names "Phoenicians" and "Canaanites" on page 263.

The mountains of Lebanon, in any case, formed a natural geographical frontier and defence on the east side of Phoenicia. Their
southern border, with Israel, shifted from time to time, and it is
possible that it was the subject of more hostilities than the Bible and
other ancient documents record.

Phoenician history goes far back into antiquity, though it is not
well documented. In the second millennium B.C. the Phoenician
cities suffered attacks from various major powers, particularly the
Egyptians, who laid claim to the whole Levant coast. Then came an
invasion from the sea, c. 1200 B.C., by the Philistines and associated
peoples, and Ugarit and Byblos were among the cities which were
destroyed at that time; at this date Sidon was the most influential
Phoenician city (and in consequence the Old Testament uses the
term "Sidonian" for the Phoenicians in general), but by 1,000 B.C.
Tyre was the most powerful, and its King Hiram I,[2] who established
good terms with his contemporaries David and Solomon, dominated
Phoenicia as a whole. In general, however, the city-states acted
independently of each other.

In the ninth century Phoenician power began to wane, as the
Assyrians began their incursions to the west. If Hiram's treaty with
David had been primarily a commercial arrangement, the ninth
century treaty between Eth-baal[3] of Tyre and Omri of Israel was no
doubt to cement a defensive alliance. The Syro-Palestinian confederacy which fought with the Assyrian armies at Qarqar in 853
B.C. included a contingent from the most northerly of the Phoenician cities, Arvad. Several times during this century the Phoenician
cities had to pay tribute to Assyria. Shalmaneser III records that in
841 B.C. he "marched as far as the mountains of Ba'ali-ra'si, a
headland by the sea, and put up on it a representation" of his royal
person.[4] Hereabouts (at the mouth of the Dog River) some of Shalmaneser's inscriptions, cut in the rock face, have survived to this day.

A century later the kings of Tyre ruled Sidon as well, but their
greater realm gave them no greater strength with which to confront
the Assyrians. Tiglath-pileser III and his successors put strong
pressures on the Phoenician capital and though Tyre — one of the
most impregnable cities of the ancient world, due to its island loca-
tion — did not fall, its king Luli was forced to flee to Cyprus in 701
B.C. (the year when Sennacherib besieged Hezekiah's Jerusalem).
It was Esarhaddon, Sennacherib's successor, who brought
Phoenicia into the Assyrian provincial system, after sacking Sidon
and besieging Tyre. Phoenicia looked to Egypt for help throughout
the seventh century, but as vainly as Judah did, until at last

---

2. A shortened form of "Ahi-ram".
3. Or Itto-baal.
4. Cf. DOTT, p. 48.

Assyria's rapid decline set in. Phoenicia's independence was regained then, but it was the last flicker before the Babylonians crushed the flame of independence for ever. Tyre suffered a thirteen-year siege before finally submitting in 572 B.C. to Nebuchadrezzar.

Sidon was later to revolt against Persia, and soon afterwards Tyre tried to oppose the advance of Alexander the Great; the result was that both cities were laid in ruins during the second half of the fourth century, and the old distinctive Phoenician culture broke up and was overlaid by the Hellenistic ways imported by Alexander. The old Phoenician language, too, like Hebrew a dialect of Canaanite, gave way before Aramaic. In terms of language, culture and political units the New Testament use of the term "Syro-Phoenician" is wholly appropriate for later centuries.

Outside their homeland, however, there were Phoenicians who held on to power and independence for a much longer period. As the early Phoenicians had developed their maritime commerce, they had established trading-postings here and there across the Mediterranean, and in course of time some of these posts became independent Phoenician colonies. In their heyday such colonies were to be found right across the Mediterranean from Cyprus to Spain, though nowhere so strongly as in North Africa, in what is today Tunisia. The most powerful Phoenician city in North Africa was Carthage, which proved such a formidable rival to Rome from the fourth century on, until finally the Romans sacked it in 146 B.C. In the colonies the Phoenician language survived longer than in the homeland. The Malta on which St. Paul was ship-wrecked in the first century A.D. was still Phoenician-speaking, to judge by Luke's term *barbaroi* (Acts 28:2), i.e. people who did not speak Latin or Greek. The name "Carthage" meant "new city" (like "Neapolis" in Greek, which survives in the names Naples and Nablus) in Phoenician;[5] its famous sons such as Hannibal and Hasdrubal bore Phoenician names.

The cultural accomplishments of the Phoenicians were considerable. Unfortunately few of their literary achievements have survived, but there is no doubt that the Phoenicians mediated much of the learning of the east to the Greeks. Their alphabet was one of the earliest to be invented. The city of Byblos ("papyrus") was so named by the Greeks because they saw papyrus scrolls in full use here; the name Byblos is a distant relative of our word "Bible". The Phoenicians' abilities as sea-farers were second to none, and it is clear that Solomon and his successors knew where to turn when the Israelites wished to embark upon maritime trade. Again, as architects and builders they were highly skilled; it was to Hiram of Tyre that Solomon was obliged to turn for both building materials and

5. The original spelling of the name Carthage will have been *qart chadasht*.

skilled craftsmen. The temple of Yahweh in Jerusalem owed much for its beauty to the cedars of Lebanon and the architects of Tyre. Perhaps we may say that this temple was the Phoenicians' major legacy to Israel.

Phoenician Religion

Nevertheless, the Phoenicians are not always described in neutral or complimentary terms in the Old Testament. One reason for this, we may be sure, is that the Phoenicians maintained, on the very borders of Israel, the ancient Canaanite religion to which the Israelite prophets were so vehemently opposed. Canaanites existed within Israel too, and were not without influence there, but the religious dangers they posed were more subtle and insidious; in Phoenicia, the full-orbed Canaanite religion continued unchecked by the Israelites and the Israelite faith.

The Canaanite religion is given some description elsewhere in this book, but we may here specify one element of the Phoenician faith, namely the veneration accorded to the god Melqart. This deity was worshipped in Carthage too, and his name is to be seen in the Carthaginian personal name Hamilcar,[6] i.e. "servant of Melqart". He was worshipped in Aramaean circles as well, as we have seen, but to the Phoenicians he was the patron deity of Tyre, the "Baal of Tyre" (just as Ekron had its own Baal, Baal-zebul, cf. 2 Kings 1:2). It seems highly probable that the Baal worship fostered in Israel by Jezebel, a Tyrian princess, and in Judah by her daughter Athaliah, was specifically Melqart worship; and that the Baal challenged by Elijah on Mt. Carmel was again Melqart.[7] (See plate 11 facing p. 208).

Prophetic Denunciation of Tyre and Sidon

It seems, however, that religious tensions do not fully account for the prophetic denunciations of Tyre and Sidon. Amos castigated the Tyrians thus:

> For crime after crime of Tyre
> I will grant them no reprieve,
> because, forgetting the ties of kinship,
> they delivered a whole band of exiles to Edom.
> Therefore will I send fire upon the walls of Tyre,
> fire that shall consume its palaces.

(Amos 1:9f.)

6. I.e. 'Abd Milqart.
7. But cf. D. R. Ap-Thomas in *PEQ* 92 (1960), pp. 146-155.

This brief passage is intriguing; we are not even told the nationality of the "whole band of exiles". Perhaps their nationality is irrelevant; H. L. Ellison finds here an allusion to slave trading, about which he writes: "It was the Phoenician, more and more enslaved by the conscienceless commerce that had become his life, who had made it a reality in the western Fertile Crescent, until in the craze for gain solemn treaties . . . were swept away."[8] Ezekiel (two centuries later than Amos) would certainly have agreed with the phrase "conscienceless commerce"; he pronounced doom on a Tyre characterized by its "wicked trading" (28:18).

But is is equally possible that Amos was thinking in specific terms of some Phoenician breach of treaty obligations towards Israel. Jehu's violent overthrow of Omri's dynasty in Samaria, with the assassination of the queen-mother Jezebel, must have caused considerable ill-feeling against Israel in Phoenicia, and it may be that Amos knew of some unrecorded reprisals taken by the Tyrians. The slave-trade he denounced may have consisted primarily of the sale of Israelite prisoners of war.[9]

Once the commercial greed of Tyre set her upon such a course, she did not look back. In the early sixth century, Ezekiel's disgust with Tyre had reached epic proportions; his denunciations occupy almost three chapters (26:1-28:19). His opening words depict vividly the callous selfishness which characterized Tyre, which could gloat thus over Jerusalem: "I grow rich, she lies in ruins" (26:2). As Gottwald comments, "Tyre thinks only of her own trade advantage when other peoples are destroyed".[10]

Finally, there is some reason to think that there were social aspects to the prophet's feelings about Tyre. When Ahab, though king of Israel, met a rude rebuff from Naboth, who exercised his ancestral rights in refusing to sell his vineyard, Jezebel expressed her scorn in these words, "Are you or are you not king in Israel?" (1 Kings 21:7). Clearly her conception of kingship and its privileges differed from Ahab's, and we may well attribute the difference to the fact that she was the daughter of a king of Tyre. For a sweeping and devastating invective against kingship as exercised in Tyre there is nothing to equal Ezekiel 28. It has long been recognized that the portrait of the Tyrian monarch in that chapter is larger than life, but it is quite unnecessary to look beyond Tyre for an explanation of the fact (as has sometimes been done). The portrait may be said to represent Tyre as a whole, but more particularly all its monarchs and their concept of royal rule. The king is set against the background of Eden, which at once recalls Genesis 2f., but it is an Eden

8. H. L. Ellison, *The Prophets of Israel* (Exeter, 1969), p. 73.
9. Cf. N. K. Gottwald, *All the Kingdoms of the Earth* (New York, 1964), pp. 104-109.
10. *Ibid,* p. 315.

with one or two differences, in particular the holy mountain for which one looks in vain in the Genesis account. It is difficult to resist the conclusion that the prophet is drawing upon a Phoenician version of the story of Eden, and that the royal ideology of Tyre was founded upon the story as they knew it. Thus the king of Tyre claimed to be the living embodiment of Adam, created god-like and perfect in every respect, but especially in wisdom. The claim to deity or at least semi-divine status was characteristic of most monarchies in the Near East of B.C. times; but in the case of Tyre, Ezekiel observed that the proud boasts were coupled with an unfeeling arrogance, a total disregard of the needs and conditions of peoples outside Phoenicia. N. K. Gottwald sees Ezekiel's denunciation as an attack on an egocentric commercialism. To worship at the shrine of Commerce leads, Professor Gottwald would say, to "inordinate pride, to violence of hand and hardness of heart".[11] Ezekiel 28 is also an attack on a certain type of kingship, and it is of special interest that this denunciation was made precisely when in Judah the dynasty of Davidic kings had come to its inglorious end, thereby writing its own sermon on the fallibility and failings of human monarchies. The experience of both Tyre and of Jerusalem pointed the desperate human need for a government of a different order entirely.

To Ezekiel, it is evident, the major enemies of Judah were Tyre and Egypt, not Babylon as one might have predicted. The prophet was convinced that the Babylonians were God's instrument to punish Judah for its sins; but the ever-optimistic Judaeans, even in exile, were pinning their hopes on the anti-Babylonian nations to defeat Babylon (and so free the exiles and liberate Jerusalem). And of all the nations, Tyre and Egypt were at the time the most doggedly hostile to Babylon. Ezekiel therefore denounced them both vigorously, and prophesied disaster and destruction for them both. Not all the vaunted wisdom of the kings of Tyre would avert calamity from the Phoenicians — nor rescue Judah and its people from the pit they had dug for themselves.

11. *Ibid*, p. 316.

CHAPTER 17

Egypt

W ITH Egypt, we come to the first of the major powers which con-
flicted with ancient Israel. An internally strong and determined
Egypt was always more than a match for its much smaller
neighbours in Palestine. If anything, it is surprising that Egypt
played such a small part in the history of the monarchies of Israel
and Judah; for Egypt was geographically much closer to the Hebrew
states than were Assyria and Babylon, and by long tradition considered Palestine as rightfully part of Egyptian domains.

An Egyptian priest Manetho in the third century B.C. wrote a
history of his country in which he provided a useful framework, still
utilized today, of a list of the royal dynasties. The dynasties, down to
the conquest of Alexander the Great, numbered thirty-one, and can
be traced in considerable detail back to the king of upper Egypt,
Narmer by name, who in c. 2850 B.C. conquered the Delta region,
thus uniting Egypt, and established its first dynasty. The period of
the Old Kingdom (Dynasties III-VI, c. 2650-2200 B.C.) was the
pyramid age, when the culture and civilization of Egypt reached a
peak of attainment — and this before ever Abraham took his
journey by stages from Mesopotamia to the Promised Land.

The third millennium ended with a period of internal disorder for
Egypt, brought about by a measure of economic discontent among
the lower classes and by the desire for power on the part of the
aristocracy. Egypt's internal weakness permitted numerous
Asiatics, semi-nomads and others, to infiltrate the Delta region. The
land-bridge from the Delta into Palestine, though passing through
an arid region, was a permanent weak spot in Egypt's defences, and
at different times throughout their history the Egyptian kings built
protective walls or embarked on military expeditions which had a
defensive purpose.

At last two Theban families (Dynasties XI and XII) succeeded in bringing order out of chaos, reuniting the country, and inaugurating the Middle Kingdom, which lasted from the twenty-first to the eighteenth centuries B.C. This was another period of prosperity and great cultural attainment, at a time when in Palestine the patriarchs of Israel were roaming with their flocks and herds. The more settled Canaanite population of Palestine, on the other hand, was considerably influenced by the impressive culture of Egypt, and probably to some extent politically dominated by the Egyptian kings.

The Execration Texts[1] of the nineteenth and eighteenth centuries give us an interesting picture of Egyptian political fears. The kings, for all their competence and achievements, saw reason to fear potential enemies on every side — local rulers in Canaan, Nubia and Lybia, as well as ambitious noblemen in Egypt itself. Accordingly, they took religious steps to ward off the dangers; set in magical formulae, the names of such foes were inscribed on bowls and figurines which were then ritually smashed, in order to bring confusion and calamity to these enemies. One such text is content to name hostile forces in general: "Every evil word, every evil speech, every evil slander, every evil thought, every evil plot, every evil fight, every evil quarrel, every evil plan, every evil thing, all evil dreams, and all evil slumber". Many other texts, however, are much more specific; and among the names from Canaan which were thus execrated there appears one of the first references in history to the name of Jerusalem. Its rulers Yaqar-'Ammu and Setj-'Anu were both consigned to oblivion in the fashion we have described.

That the fears were by no means groundless is clear from the sequel; internal disorders broke out afresh, permitting a fresh wave of Asiatic migration into Lower Egypt, and the upshot was that northern Egypt found itself ruled by foreigners from *c.* 1720 till *c.* 1570 B.C. (They permitted a puppet kingdom at Thebes; their own capital was in the Delta region.) These Asiatics have long been known as the "Hyksos" kings, a name which derives from an Egyptian phrase meaning "rulers of foreign countries" (none too explicit a designation!). Whatever their precise origins, it is of interest that one of their kings was called "Simeon", another "Jacob-har", and it can only be concluded that they bore some sort of relationship, not necessarily very close, to the ancestors of Israel. It is widely supposed that it was one of the Hyksos kings whose minister Joseph became; certainly they looked with favour upon Semites like themselves, whereas the Egyptians had no love for Asiatics, and once the Hyksos were driven out tried to eradicate every vestige of their period of rule.

---

1. Cf. *ANET*, pp. 328ff.

The New Kingdom (Dynasties XVIII-XX) began for Egypt when a native Theban king named Ka-mose decided that the time had come to expel the foreigners, and he and his successor Ah-mose I in a succession of campaigns drove the Asiatics back into Palestine. The experience of subjection to foreign domination had turned the Egyptians into nationalists and imperialists, and once their own realm was consolidated, the Eighteenth Dynasty kings embarked on the conquest of Palestine and south Syria. The victory which gave Egypt the control it sought was achieved by the very able Tuth-mose III in a battle at Megiddo in 1468 B.C.; against him were ranged no fewer than 330 local kings, a figure which testifies to the degree of political fragmentation of Syria-Palestine at the time.

Thus the New Kingdom is the period also known as the Egyptian Empire. Syria-Palestine was organized as an Egyptian dominion, its petty kings becoming mere vassals of Tuth-mose and his successors. Egyptian military bases were set up at strategic points, and an active trade was fostered, which brought as much Asiatic influence into Egypt as it did Egyptian influence into western Asia. Many Semitic words and Canaanite deities (i.e. Baal and Anat) found their way into Egypt.

In the fourteenth century the residents of Syria-Palestine grew restive, though they expended their energies in local conflicts rather than in attacking the Egyptians. The Amarna Letters[2] give an interesting picture of the situation. These documents have survived from the Egyptian record office of the first half of the fourteenth century, and consist of letters written (in Akkadian) to the Egyptian king by various petty kings in Syria-Palestine, together with copies of some of his rescripts. Once again, the name of Jerusalem occurs; its king (by name 'Abdu-Kheba) was one of the Palestinian rulers who begged for Egyptian aid against his local enemies. But this help was not forth-coming; for one reason or another the Egyptian king declined to despatch troops to the trouble-spots. The king in question was Amen-hotep IV, a man who sought to bring about a social and political revolution in Egypt. Royal power was being challenged from several directions, notably the army, the civil service and the powerful Amun priesthood, and in his endeavours to remedy this situation Amen-hotep moved his capital from Thebes (where the Amun priesthood was well entrenched) to a new city, which he called Akhet-aton in honour of Aton, the deity whose worship he sought to make supreme in Egypt. At the same time and for the same reason he changed his own name to Akh-en-aton. It was in the ruins of this city (abandoned soon after his reign ended), near a place now called el-Amarna, that the Amarna tablets were discovered. It is clear that Akh-en-aton was no weakling, but

2. *ANET,* pp. 482-490; *AOTS,* pp. 3-15.

nevertheless his revolution was ill-fated and in his efforts to sustain its impetus in Egypt he allowed events in Syria-Palestine to get out of hand. (He, rather than any Hyksos king, may have been the Pharaoh in whose reign Joseph came to Egypt and rose to prominence.)

The Eighteenth Dynasty declined after Akh-en-aton's death, and ended in weakness and confusion in *c.* 1303 B.C. The next dynasty was at first a powerful one, with able soldiers as kings. They transferred the centre of power and administration from Thebes in the south to the Delta region, where they built a capital, and from where they launched campaigns in order to bring Syria-Palestine into full subjection once more. For most of the thirteenth century the two kings Seti I (1302-1290 B.C.) and Ramesses II (1290-1224 B.C.) held their own in Syria-Palestine though they confronted a powerful enemy in the Hittite Empire, which was seeking to impose its domination on the northern part of the region. A decisive battle was fought at Kadesh on the Orontes in 1286 B.C.; the Egyptian army won, but by a narrow margin, and both the major powers thereafter accepted Kadesh as the boundary between their spheres of influence. The treaty left Ramesses in full control of Palestine and south Syria.

Seti and Ramesses II are of special interest, since they are in all probability the two Pharaohs who oppressed the Israelites in Egypt, according to Exodus 1f.[3] The Israelites were put to building work in the Delta region, helping to erect the new capital and centre of government. One of the cities built by Israelite labour was named after Ramesses — the Pi-Ramesse of Egyptian texts, called more simply Rameses (or Raamses) in Exodus 1:11. It was at some time during his long reign, then, that the Israelites escaped into the Sinai wilderness; the whole impression given by the early chapters of Exodus is that the Pharaoh whom Moses and the Israelites thwarted was a powerful monarch, and that it required a miracle to save the Israelites. Ramesses was certainly such a king, till, perhaps, the final years of his long reign. When Joshua and the Israelites were making Palestine their home, however, there was apparently no Egyptian interference, or at least none worth mentioning.

The process of Israelite settlement was evidently taking place during the reign of Merneptah (1224-1214 B.C.). It was now that the Sea Peoples, i.e. people related to the Philistines,[4] began to put pressures on Egypt, and in 1220 B.C. Merneptah had to fight a defensive operation on his western frontiers, to prevent a combined invasion by Libyans and Sea Peoples. To commemorate his victory,

---

3. This at least is the widespread view; but the recent study of J. J. Bimson, *Relating the Exodus and Conquest (JSOT Supplement 5:* Sheffield, 1978) places the exodus two centuries earlier, thus supporting the traditional dating.
4. See above, p. 136.

Merneptah set up a monument in a temple in Thebes; the monument is commonly called the "Israel Stele", since it is the earliest document outside the Bible, and indeed the only Egyptian document, to mention Israel by name.[5] After discussing the battle in the west, the text of the inscription proceeds to turn its attention to Palestine:

Canaan is plundered with every evil;
Ashkelon is taken; Gezer is captured;
Yanoam is made non-existent;
Israel lies desolate; its seed is no more.

It is not clear to what extent these words recount a genuine campaign in Palestine; Egyptian kings were prone to make proud boasts which were not based on fact. At any rate, Merneptah can have done little harm to the Israelites, in view of the fact that the Old Testament does not deign to mention him.[6] From now on Israelites and Philistines were to fight each other for the mastery of Palestine; Egypt's days of empire were over. The Philistines settled strongly on the Palestinian coast after an attempted sea invasion of Egypt had been driven off by Ramesses III in the early twelfth century. Such outside pressures weakened Egypt considerably, but she was beginning to crumble internally, too, for a variety of reasons. Her holdings in Canaan were not lost to her overnight, but they gradually fell away, so that when in the mid-eleventh century Saul came to the throne of Israel, the least of his problems was Egypt. By this time even the mines in Sinai had been abandoned by the Egyptians.

From Dynasty XXI onwards (c. 1090 B.C.) Egypt went into a gradual decline, and never again achieved more than the occasional foray into Palestine. It was rarely united; it constantly broke up into two states (Upper and Lower Egypt respectively) or even more. Lower Egypt, with its capital at Tanis, was the mercantile centre, and Egypt's contacts with Solomon were probably of a commercial nature. Solomon married the daughter of one of the kings, doubtless to secure a favourable commercial treaty.

Shortly after the Israelite kingdom had broken into two, one king of northern Egypt found the ability and energy to make a foray into Palestine. His name was Shoshenq (the biblical Shishak), a man of Libyan origins who rose to power and founded the Twenty-second Dynasty in 940 B.C. His plundering campaign caused considerable damage and loss to both Rehoboam of Judah and also Jeroboam I of

5. Cf. *DOTT,* pp. 137-141.
6. It is possible that the phrase "the waters of Nephtoah" (in the Hebrew *mey neptoach)* of Joshua 15:9 commemorates the name of this Egyptian king. For the conjectured route of his campaign, see *MBA,* map 36.

Israel.[7] But it was a mere flash in the pan; for two centuries thereafter Egypt was weak and uninfluential.

A little before 700 B.C., a Cushite or Ethiopian family achieved the control of Egypt. The founder of Cushite power was a man called Pi-ankhi, whose successors constituted Dynasty XXV. They at first showed more ability than their predecessors, and perforce they showed more interest in Palestine, not because they wished to conquer it, but because the Assyrians were by now dominating it and threatening Egypt too. As early as 725 an Egyptian prince (it is not clear who he was) had persuaded Hoshea, the last king of Israel, to defy Assyria — with disastrous consequences for Israel (cf. 2 Kings 17:4). The early Ethiopian rulers of Egypt conspired in similar fashion with Hezekiah of Judah, and were prepared to send an army into Palestine but Sennacherib's forces defeated it at Eltekeh in 700 B.C.

It was Esarhaddon of Assyria who carried the struggle on to Egyptian soil; he invaded in 671 B.C. and drove the king of Egypt, Taharqa (the biblical Tirhakah), back to his native Cush. Esarhaddon's successor Ashurbanipal at first maintained the Assyrian grip on northern Egypt. Many local Egyptian chiefs were by no means averse to the defeat of the Ethiopian dynasty, and the Assyrians responded by recognizing several of them as local princes, loyal to Assyria. The prince of the city of Sais in the Delta region was one man thus honoured; Psamtik (in Greek form, Psammetichus) by name, he gradually enlarged his realm within Egypt, and as the Assyrian power rapidly waned, he became independent, and king of all Egypt. His Saite dynasty (663-525 B.C.) — Dynasty XXVI — proved to be Egypt's last ruling family with any claim to power. Its early rulers endeavoured to recover some of Egypt's past glories; but they had to depend on Greek mercenaries to wage their wars.

Psamtik I invaded Palestine, if Herodotus is to be believed, and his successor, Necho (609-594 B.C.), right at the outset of his reign, sent an army as far as the Euphrates; Necho's chief purpose was to maintain the balance of power in western Asia by supporting the Assyrians against the Babylonians, but he had no objection to adding Palestine and southern Syria to his own domains. It was he who defeated Josiah of Judah in battle at Megiddo (609 B.C.); and who installed Jehoiakim on the throne in Jerusalem as an Egyptian vassal. However, Babylon's new king, Nebuchadrezzar, speedily put an end to Egypt's hopes of another empire in Asia. Necho's armies suffered two major defeats in 605 B.C., and had to be withdrawn from Palestinian soil.

Necho's successors, Psamtik II and Hophra (the Greek Apries), continued his anti-Babylonian policies, and put a great deal of

7. See above, p. 69.

pressure on Judah's last king, Zedekiah, to rebel against Nebuchadrezzar. When Zedekiah at last yielded to Egyptian wishes, an army was sent to his aid, which did for a brief spell break Nebuchadrezzar's stranglehold on Jerusalem. But Egypt's help was worthless, though she provided a refuge for many Judaeans who fled from their native land (Jeremiah among them).

From then on Egypt declined rapidly. So serious were the internal disorders that when in 525 B.C. the Persian king Cambyses conquered the country, many Egyptians welcomed his arrival and collaborated willingly with him. After that puppet kings in Egypt once or twice tried to reassert Egyptian independence, but the Persians, followed by Alexander and the Greeks, and after them the Romans, held Egypt in a firm grip for many centuries.

Egyptian Language

Genesis 10:6 recognizes Egypt[8] as one of the chief descendants of Ham — that is to say, as cousins rather than brothers of the Israelites. This relationship rather aptly describes the affinities between the ancient Egyptian language and the Semitic languages such as Hebrew. Egyptian perhaps stood halfway between the Semitic and the Hamitic language families; it stood close enough to Canaanite dialects such as Hebrew to permit ready borrowing in either direction, though in fact the Egyptians seem to have done more of the borrowing than the speakers of Hebrew. The most obvious Egyptian loan-word in Hebrew is the name "Pharaoh", which derives from a pair of words denoting "Great House", originally applied to the Egyptian palace and court, and only later to the person of the king. The word for Noah's "ark", in Hebrew *tebah,* is another example of a loan-word from Egyptian.

The Egyptian language can be traced back to 3000 B.C. or a little later, when a writing system was devised and soon put to extensive use. The script, traditionally described as "hieroglyphic", was deciphered early last century, in consequence of the discovery of the Rosetta Stone (by Napoleon's expedition of 1798). It began as a pictographic script, that is to say that words or parts of words were drawn as representational pictures; human figures, birds and other objects can easily be observed in Egyptian hieroglyphic documents. At an early date the signs came to represent short syllables, and even simple sounds, but the Egyptians never used the potential alphabet they had in their hands, except to write down foreign words.

The invention of writing was early put to good use, and the Egyptian literature that has survived is abundant, written on stone,

8. The "Mizraim" of AV and RV represents the Hebrew word for Egypt, *Mitsrayim.*

potsherds and papyrus (which lasts much longer in the dry climate of Egypt than in neighbouring countries like Palestine). Proverbial and "wisdom" literature from Egypt dates back to the third millennium, and bears eloquent witness to the intellectual powers of the ancient Egyptians, as also to their literary interests and abilities. Some parts of the Old Testament have been compared with this or that item of Egyptian literature; it is interesting to note than in nearly every case the Egyptian material is the older — indeed, little original literature appears to have been written in Egypt after 1000 B.C. Akh-en-aton's "Hymn to Aton" (fourteenth century)[9] has sometimes been thought to have inspired Psalm 104; and it is widely held that the "Teaching of Amenemope" (eleventh century or later)[10] lies behind Proverbs 22: 17-24:22, in view of close verbal parallels.

These parallels, whether or not they imply borrowing on the part of the Israelites, at least illustrate the point that when David and Solomon created a new Israel, transforming it from a loose tribal society into a well-organized kingdom where all the arts of civilization might flourish, they could turn to Egypt for advice, precedent, and literature. The lists of officials in the administrations of David and Solomon show that something of a bureaucracy was built up, quite possibly on Egyptian models, and perhaps even with one or two Egyptian personnel.[11]

Egyptian Religion

On the other hand, Israel stands in marked contrast to Egypt where religious belief and practice is concerned. If all too many Israelites were drawn to Canaanite gods, few appear to have seen any attraction in the Egyptian pantheon. This fact is probably related to the fact that geographically Palestine and Egypt were so different, and we must not forget that ancient man's religious concepts were based on his experience of and understanding of nature. Palestine has few rivers, a very varied, sometimes mountainous terrain, for the most part a temperate climate, and a regular cycle of the seasons, with the life-giving rains falling in the winter months. Egypt, on the other hand, has a remarkably unvaried geography and climate. It is low-lying, consisting of a long valley through which the Nile flows, with the broad Delta to the north; wherever the Nile waters do not reach, there is desert, for rainfall is minimal. Hence all ancient Egypt's major cities — Thebes, Hermopolis, Heliopolis (the biblical On), Memphis, Sais, Tanis (from south to north) lay on or near the great river and its mouths. The sun's heat is powerful all the year round.

9. Cf. *DOTT*, pp. 142-150.
10. Cf. *DOTT*, pp. 172-186.
11. Cf. R. de Vaux, *Ancient Israel*[2] (London, 1965) pp. 127-132.

Thus where the people of Canaan felt it an urgent matter to please and placate the god of storm and thunder, it was the sun which dominated the religion of Egypt — though worshipped in different ways and under different names, notably Re (or Ra) and Aton. More local deities included Amun at Thebes, Thoth at Hermopolis and Ptah at Memphis; much depended on the king and his seat of government as to which deity received most prominence. (We have already noted how Amen-hotep IV changed his name, to Akh-en-aton, when he changed his capital and when he sought to break the power of the Amun priesthood.) The king was also held to be a god in ancient Egypt; he was revered as the embodiment of Horus son of Osiris, whose cult came closest to being the national cult. Osiris was at once god of vegetation and of the underworld (two concepts which often went together in the ancient world). The well-being of their divine king was vital to the Egyptians, as ensuring their own well-being, in freedom from famine and in the preservation of law and order.

The cult of Osiris developed alongside a highly complex belief in the afterlife. The Egyptian faced death cheerfully and optimistically, prepared for it thoroughly, and ensured that all he would need in the next world should be entombed with his corpse. The tombs of the rich, especially the kings, were very elaborate; and of course the practice of mummification was a characteristic of the funerary rites.

All this made little impression on the ordinary Israelite, and the prophets of Israel and Judah saw little need to denounce the gods of Egypt. Amos in the early eighth century saw no need to denounce Egypt at all. But once Egypt began once more to play a political role in Palestine, the prophets spoke out; it is true, after all, that up to a point Egypt can be blamed for the fall of both Israel and Judah, since she intrigued in both capitals and persuaded both kingdoms to rebel, against Assyria in the one case and against Babylon in the other. In her intrigues Egypt made promises of military support which she was unable to fulfil; we have already observed how weak and divided Egypt became before ever the Hebrew monarchies started, and her final show of power in the time of Nebuchadrezzar was based on foreign mercenaries.

Isaiah, Jeremiah and Ezekiel were the prophets who had most to say against Egypt. The burden of their arguments was the emptiness of Egyptian boasts and the intrinsic weakness of Egyptian shows of military strength. We may single out a statement of biting scorn from each of these three prophetic books. "Vain and worthless is the help of Egypt; therefore have I given her this name, Rahab Quelled" (Isaiah 30:7); thus Isaiah depicted the proud and ancient kingdom as the very embodiment of a powerful monster of primeval chaos (Rahab) — powerless and sitting idle (as other versions have it). Jeremiah's comment needs no commentary: "Give Pharaoh of

Egypt the title King Bombast'', said he, ''the man who missed his moment'' (46:17). Finally Ezekiel summed up Egyptian promises of help thus: ''The support that you gave the Israelites was no better than a reed, which splintered in the hand when they grasped you, and tore their armpits; when they leaned on you, you snapped and their limbs gave way'' (29:6f.).

9. Babylonian Chronicle tablet recording the capture of Jerusalem

10. Anthropoid coffin from Beth-Shan

CHAPTER 18

Assyria

THE name Assyria comes to us via Latin from the Greeks, who used it to denote the country and empire which grew up around the city of Asshur; in their own (Akkadian) language the Assyrians used the word Asshur (or more accurately, Ashshur) alike for their patron city, and for the kingdom.

Asshur on the northern Tigris was one of the oldest cities in ancient Mesopotamia,[1] emerging from pre-history before the middle of the third millennium B.C. It is not known who its earliest citizens were, but culturally it was no different from contemporary cities in Sumer, much further south. The whole civilization can therefore be called Sumerian. There appear to have been at least three distinct racial elements in the Mesopotamia of the period, distinguished by language, but culturally the whole area was unified. One of the languages was Sumerian, a tongue with no known relatives, the second was Akkadian, one of the Semitic language family, and the third still remains to be identified. In the course of time it was Akkadian which came to predominate, and the other two died out. It is widely conjectured that the people who first brought the Akkadian language into Mesopotamia were originally semi-nomads from the Syro-Arabian desert, who probably infiltrated Mesopotamia during the fourth millennium.

The early Mesopotamian cities were self-contained city-states, each having its satellite villages around it, and these independent units were separated by the uncultivated steppe-land. Each city-state had its temples and deities, one of whom was viewed as the owner of the state. Asshur's patron deity bore the same name as the city. One man had the rule in each city-state, and was styled either governor or king. It was only gradually that the kingship came into

1. A convenient term coined by the Greeks. It is applied to the area dominated by the two great rivers Tigris and Euphrates, and to roughly the area today called Iraq.

the control of one family, or dynasty. Then the city states began to try to influence and dominate each other; though Asshur was too far north to be affected by the local quarrels in Sumer.

The first man to impose his will on the whole region was Sargon the Great, an Akkadian who began his career as the royal cup-bearer in the city of Kish and ended it by carving out an empire which extended the full length of the Tigris and Euphrates and beyond. He reigned *c.* 2371-2316 B.C., founded a long-lived dynasty, and left behind a goal for many another Mesopotamian with ambition. The citizens of Asshur were among those who cherished the dream of empire, though after losing their independence to Sargon they did not regain it for some centuries.

Sargon's empire slowly fell apart, both from internal pressures and also by attacks from outsiders; the Mesopotamian civilization could not be isolated from the other peoples east, west, and north, who at different periods of history infiltrated or invaded. Towards the end of the millennium it was Dynasty III of the city of Ur which re-constituted the empire; but that empire again fell to pieces. It was the Elamites to the east who supplied the *coup de grâce* in 2006 B.C.; but the people who had seriously weakened Ur were the Amorites — a fresh wave of Semites presumably from the same Syro-Arabian desert fringes as the Akkadians a thousand years earlier. The Amorites readily accepted the Sumerian culture they found in Mesopotamia, but it was the Akkadian language, closely related to their own, which they adopted.

The early second millennium saw a Mesopotamia composed not of city-states but of distinct, centralized kingdoms, one of which was centred on Asshur; the term Assyria therefore now becomes appropriate, though at first it covered no very great area. Steadily expanding under able kings, whose purposes in war and conquest were largely commercial, Assyria soon embraced other cities such as Nineveh (in Akkadian, "Ninua"), which was to figure as the last and most famous capital of the kingdom.

The first Assyrian empire was created by Shamshi-Adad I (himself apparently a foreigner who conquered Assyria) in the early eighteenth century. The great city of Mari on the central Euphrates was annexed, and diplomatic relations were established with states further afield, such as Carchemish in Syria. But the empire was very short-lived, because a more able man than even Shamshi-Adad occupied the throne of Babylon, an Amorite named Hammurabi (1792-1750 B.C.), who gave Babylon her first empire. He conquered the other parts of Mesopotamia first, but by 1755 Assyria too had been conquered, although it was permitted to retain its dynasty. The rivalry of the two great Mesopotamian kingdoms had begun.

After Hammurabi's death Assyria soon broke free of Babylonian suzerainty, but her power was strictly limited. The middle of the second millennium was a period when Mesopotamia was over-shadowed, and at times dominated, by various peoples from beyond the mountain ranges to the north and east, particularly the Kassites and the Hurrians (the Old Testament "Horites"). Few documents from this period have survived, but it appears that Assyria, though infiltrated by outsiders, held on to a precarious independence, though some of her kings had to pay tribute to the Hurrian kingdom of Mitanni to the west of Assyria. In the fourteenth century, however, Mitanni suddenly collapsed under pressures from the west, and this event at one stroke gave Assyria full independence and also an enlarged realm. Ashur-uballit I was the Assyrian king who profited by Mitanni's fall, and he wasted no time in embarking on a career of greater conquest; he and his successor Adad-nirari I waged war on several fronts. Assyria, a highland region, was circled on the north and north-east by mountain ranges, and her primary need here was defensive — to secure the frontiers, and drive back the mountain tribes and those beyond the mountains who might have threatened to invade. In other directions Assyria looked abroad with greedy eyes. The great trade-routes in and through Syria she saw and coveted, and from now on her chief ambitions for expansion and conquest were westward, towards the Mediterranean. Southward, too, there were rich pickings, and ancient rivalries as well; Babylon was an early victim of the Assyrian aggression of this period. One of the greatest warriors was Shalmaneser I, in the mid-twelfth century; and his son Tukulti-ninurta I went on to reach the Mediterranean coast with his armies. Thus at a time when Israel was marching into Palestine from the south, the Assyrian armies were already dangerously near the Promised Land; but the time for the two peoples to come into conflict had not yet arrived.

This same thirteenth century ushered in an era of general unrest and migration in the Near East; it has often been called a time of confusion. Assyria had its internal weaknesses, and the king who reached the Mediterranean coast died ignominiously, besieged in his own palace by a revolt of the Assyrian nobles. The Hittite empire crashed at the end of the century, and a power vacuum in Syria resulted which Assyria was not yet ready to fill. The vacuum was instead filled by the Aramaeans, who seem to have chosen their moment well to swarm from the desert fringes and make Syria their own. Nor were they content with their conquest there; they made their appearance in all sectors of the Fertile Crescent, and infiltrated Assyria and Babylonia, putting fresh pressures upon these king-doms. For more than three centuries the Assyrians were fully occupied in resisting the pressures, holding their own, and finally gaining the ascendancy. The greatest Assyrian king of the period was Tiglath-pileser I (1115-1077 B.C.), but his victories were initially defensive ones, in the face of Aramaeans and others besides;

once again, however, Assyrian armies reached the Mediterranean, and Sidon, not so far from Israelite territory, paid tribute to the victorious Assyrian king. These successes were ephemeral, in point of fact; the Aramaean tide flowed yet more strongly, and Assyria was nearly crushed by the Aramaean network of kingdoms during the tenth century. So while David gave Israel an empire by mastering the western Aramaeans, the eastern Aramaeans were almost choking the kingdom of Assyria out of existence. But not quite; her survival proved her inner strength, determination, and fighting qualities. (See plates 13 and 14 facing pp. 240, 241)

Adad-nirari II (911-891 B.C.) was the Assyrian king who turned the tide, and began to retrieve the territory lost to the Aramaeans; and with him begins the Assyrian Empire, although the early achievements were primarily defensive measures, once again. A pattern of annual campaigns soon built up, the king leading his army forth to attack and subdue one tribe after another. Submission and tribute were demanded, to promote both the defence and the economic well-being of Assyria. As the territory held by the Assyrians increased in area, the victims of their aggression became states instead of petty princedoms; but the kings of Assyria never knew when to cry halt.

Ashurnasirpal II (884-859) perhaps typifies the Assyrian monarchy. Thoroughly warlike in every respect, he was characterized by the virtues and the vices of the soldier — courage and energy coupled with cruelty and ruthless ambition. His first campaigns were to the north and the south of Assyria proper, but he soon turned his attention westward, and invaded the important Aramaean kingdom of Bit-adini (the Old Testament Beth-eden). His 877 B.C. campaign brought his army to the Mediterranean. He records that his troops ceremonially washed their weapons in the sea and made offering to the gods; and then they set about collecting the rich tribute of the Levant coast as far south as Tyre. But all this was not empire-building; it was merely a predatory raid. Nor was it only men's treasure chests which were affected; Ashurnasirpal was one of the most cruel conquerors in the whole of history, an exceptionally cruel king in an exceptionally cruel race. If any people dared oppose him or rebel against him, "unarmed prisoners, innocent civilians, men, women and children alike, were tortured with sadistic refinements".[2]

It was Ashurnasirpal who changed the capital city of Assyria, rebuilding Kalhu (the Old Testament Calah) and erecting a palace there which has been excavated in a remarkably good state of repair. The original opening ceremony took place in 879 B.C.; the disinterment began in A.D. 1949.

2. G. Roux, *Ancient Iraq* (Penguin edition, Harmondsworth, 1964), p. 263.

Shalmaneser III (848-824), Ashurnasirpal's son, was the first king to come into contact with Israel. It was now that the Assyrians began to clash with bigger ethnic groupings than hitherto, and Shalmaneser's successes were less brilliant achievements than his records claim. In the east, he fought the Medes and Persians, but an Assyrian victory or two did not stop them consolidating their position in Iran, from where the Medes were later to help crush Assyria. In the north-east, he fought with a new kingdom, Urartu (the Old Testament Ararat), again gaining successes; but Urartu nevertheless continued to grow in strength, and was later a powerful rival. He had more success in the west, where no single state was powerful enough to thrust back the Assyrian armies. Nevertheless, here too he had difficulties and setbacks. Time and again western states, neo-Hittites, Aramaeans and Israelites, banded together to resist him, most notably at the battle of Qarqar in 853 B.C. The eastern Aramaean state of Bit-adini was crushed, but Damascus he never did succeed in capturing, and he finally gave up his attempts on it. For the first time, however, Israel (under Jehu) paid tribute, in 841 B.C. As for Babylonia, it had its internal problems at this time, and Shalmaneser involved himself in its affairs and emerged as its benefactor and nominal overlord. But after that Assyria itself was torn by a civil war which continued after Shalmaneser's death; the high-handed arrogance of the ruling classes was and remained a cause of discontent to the Assyrians themselves. As soon as the civil war began, reluctant vassals such as Babylon withheld tribute and asserted their independence, as one might have predicted. For half a century, therefore, Assyria's wars were aimed at reasserting her authority and regaining lost ground.

Mention should be made of Assyria's ruler from 810 to 805 B.C., since her fame is legendary. She was the queen-mother Sammuramat, better known to posterity as Semiramis. In its literary form, the legend goes back to the fourth century Greek historian Herodotus; eventually the tale came to credit her with the conquest of Egypt and India, among other things. In fact the legend seems to be totally without foundation; probably her outstanding beauty, lustfulness and cruelty are as unhistorical as her conquests. She may have been a Babylonian who took a leading part in the propagation of Babylonian culture in Assyria, a process that is clearly discernible in Assyria's history at that period; but even that achievement is a matter of conjecture.

Her son Adad-nirari III (810-783 B.C.), once he came to manhood, took over the reins of office from his mother and proved to be another capable soldier. In 804 he marched west, and this time Damascus fell, swiftly. Israel again proffered tribute, and states still further south too, though not Judah as yet. His victories in Iran and Chaldaea were equally brilliant; but there was again no systematic attempt at conquest, and his successors proved weak and ineffective. With Assyria quiescent, others could and did prosper. Israel and Judah enjoyed a second golden age, while to the northwest of Assyria Urartu grew and expanded rapidly.

Assyrian fortunes were restored by the accession in 745 B.C. of one of her greatest kings, Tiglath-pileser III, perhaps a usurper. He thoroughly reorganized every aspect of Assyrian administration, at home and abroad, and at last made the empire a reality. From now on victories would mean conquests, not mere occasions for plunder and booty. Much of the defeated territory would be turned into provinces, under direct Assyrian rule, and the will to resist would be broken by massive deportations. Tribute would be paid regularly. He also strengthened the army by beginning a policy of conscription from conquered populations.

An early campaign brought him into conflict with a coalition in North Syria led by "Azriau of Yaudi".[3] His victories gave him territory, control and tribute from the Aramaean states, Phoenicia and Israel; but it has to be recognized that his primary objective was to lessen the threat Urartu posed to Assyria; for the Aramaean states had been the vassals and allies of Sardur III of Urartu. His successes were impressive; before his death (727 B.C.) a chain of Assyrian provinces stretched as far south as the northern part of Israel, the kingdom of Israel surviving as a very truncated realm. He was the first Assyrian king to whom Judah became tributary.

On most other fronts he was equally successful. He led Assyrian armies further east across Iran than they had ventured before, and annexed territory there, beyond the Zagros range. He also brought Babylonia more firmly into the empire, by taking the throne of Babylon himself in 729 B.C.; his campaigns in Babylonia, however, were not directed against Babylon itself but against the very troublesome Aramaeans and Chaldaeans who had overrun southern Babylonia, and he was more of a benefactor than an aggressor to the capital city and nobility. At some stage in his reign he invaded Urartu itself, but was unable to capture the capital city, Tushpa.

Shalmaneser V had a short reign (726-722 B.C.), the chief event being the revolt of Samaria. Shalmaneser's army invested the city, which may not have fallen until after the accession of Sargon II (722-705 B.C.). Sargon's reign was fully occupied with campaigns against rebels and enemies on every hand. Tiglath-pileser's conquests had frightened Egypt on the west and Elam on the east, and both responded by fomenting all the trouble they could for Assyria. Babylon was lost to him fully twelve years, when a Chaldaean named Merodach-baladan captured the throne there. Sargon had his hands full in the west, to begin with, until he had twice defeated

3. See above, p. 94.

Egyptian armies; then he had to force back into Asia Minor King Midas of the Muski; thirdly, urgent campaigns against Urartu were necessary. Sargon emerged victorious from all these campaigns; Urartu suffered a crushing defeat when he conquered its sacred city of Musasir. Then at last he could turn his attention to Babylon. Driving out Merodach-baladan, Sargon himself took the throne of Babylon as his two predecessors had done. Undoubtedly he was an able soldier, and he celebrated at home by building a new capital bearing his own name, "Fortress of Sargon" (*Dur-Sharrukin*), near Khorsabad.

He was killed while campaigning in Asia Minor once again, and was succeeded by Sennacherib (705-681 B.C.), whose campaigns in the west have been recounted above.[4] His major problems were with Babylon, where Merodach-baladan engineered all the difficulties he could for the Assyrian king, retreating into friendly Elamite territory when necessary. Sennacherib was induced into a major war with Elam, in which he suffered several defeats and setbacks. Eventually he captured Babylon in 689, and vented his anger on the city by destroying it systematically. No previous Assyrian monarch had treated the proud city so contemptuously; from now on Babylon was to be relentlessly hostile to her old rival.

At home, Sennacherib abandoned the newly-built capital Dur-Sharrukin and set about building up Nineveh to serve as the capital. Some sort of discontent with his regime must have broken out, for he was ultimately assassinated. Two of his sons were implicated, according to 2 Kings 19:37, but they gained nothing thereby, the throne going to the crown-prince Esarhaddon.[5] Once he had consolidated his position, the new king attempted to atone for his father's treatment of Babylon by rebuilding the city in as magnificent a fashion as possible, a major task which occupied most of his reign (681-669 B.C.). For the time being the Babylonians were placated. In the west the king of Sidon was the only rebel, and he was efficiently defeated and executed in 677 B.C., with the subsequent deportation of many Sidonians.

It was to the north that Esarhaddon looked most anxiously. The power of Urartu had been broken by his predecessors, and with it the ability of Urartu to resist the inroads of barbarian nomads from further north. The Cimmerians (the Old Testament Gomer) had been active in this quarter for a generation or two, and they were now reinforced by the Scythians (the Old Testament Ashkenaz). By dint of a victorious campaign and diplomatic manoeuvres, Esarhaddon was able to divert them westwards into Asia Minor. On his

---

4. See pp. 110ff.
5. For Assyrian and Babylonian references to Sennacherib's death, cf. *DOTT*, pp. 70-73.

north-east frontiers he had some successes against the Medes; and
south-east he was able to secure an alliance with Elam.

With all his frontiers thus secured, Esarhaddon at last embarked
on fresh conquest. He had first made overtures to the various Arab
tribes who might otherwise have molested his lines of communication; and now he marched through Syria and down the Palestinian
coast, and invaded Egypt. The battles were, on Esarhaddon's own
account, "very bloody", but the victory was his. The Egyptian
king, Taharqa (the Old Testament Tirhakah), fled to his native
Ethiopia, leaving Esarhaddon to appoint local rulers, impose
tribute, and do what he could to consolidate his new conquest. But
however brilliant the victory, Egypt was not so easily held. Once the
Assyrian army withdrew, that of Taharqa returned to the fray, and
only two years later Esarhaddon felt obliged to invade Egypt once
again — but fell ill and died en route. He left his kingdom divided
between two sons, Ashurbanipal as king in Nineveh and Shamash-
shum-ukin as king of Babylon (independent, but subordinate to his
brother). This arrangement was designed both to honour and pacify
Babylon and also to promote the unity and stability of Mesopotamia
as a whole, and at first it promised to achieve its ends.

At the beginning of his reign, therefore, Ashurbanipal (668-627
B.C.) (see plate 12 facing p. 209) was free to continue his father's campaign in Egypt. Taharqa was once again driven south, and the conqueror marched proudly into the capital, Thebes. But it was quite impossible for Assyria to hold Egypt, however many battles might be
won. There were insufficient Assyrian troops to garrison the land
effectively, and revolt followed revolt. To maintain the pressure on
Egypt Ashurbanipal was compelled to neglect other fronts; and this
proved fatal in the long run. Psamtik I of Egypt drove out the last
Assyrian soldiers in 655 B.C., and Egypt was free again.

By now Ashurbanipal was fully occupied in a fresh war with
Elam, where a hostile king had taken the throne. No sooner had the
Elamites been crushed than Babylon revolted, under Ashurbanipal's
own brother, in 651 B.C. The latter had taken steps to create a wide-
ranging confederacy against Assyria; even Judah was implicated.
Ashurbanipal attacked in the nick of time, and even so it took him
three hard years of fighting before he won the victory. Shamash-
shum-ukin died in the flames of his own palace in Babylon, and
Ashurbanipal had no further troubles in that quarter. The Arab
tribes who had joined the coalition were next on his agenda; he was
no less successful against them, but again the victories were by no
means easy. Finally Elam, once again, defied him, and another
major war proved necessary. Elam was finally crushed (639 B.C.),
and its capital Susa (the Old Testament Shushan) sacked.

Scarcely anything is known of the last decade of Ashurbanipal's
reign. Perhaps little of consequence took place; but in fact Assyria

was now doomed, despite all the victories achieved by Ashur-banipal. He had over-reached himself, especially in Egypt, and already the frontiers of the empire had begun to retract; he had exhausted the Assyrian army with constant hard fighting; and he had won no real friends in any quarter. Babylon, in particular, felt a burning resentment, while beyond the eastern mountains the Medes made little secret of their hostility. And in Assyria itself civil strife broke out, probably even before Ashurbanipal's death in 627 B.C.

Assyria's last governor in Babylon, a Chaldaean named Nabopolassar, revolted as soon as he heard of Ashurbanipal's death, and in 626 B.C. made himself king of Babylon. The kings of Assyria, Ashur-etil-ilani (627-623 B.C.) and then Sin-shar-ishkun (623-612 B.C.), fought Nabopolassar as strongly as they could, but he gradually proved the stronger. The old capital, Asshur, was briefly besieged in 616 B.C.; and Assyria in desperation now sought help from Egypt, so recently her victim. Egypt responded, but not soon enough to be of any assistance; on the other hand, Babylon's armies were suddenly reinforced by the Medes, whose King Cyaxares invaded Assyria without warning in 615 B.C. Cyaxares captured Asshur in the following year, and then the two allied armies joined forces for the final assault on Nineveh, which fell in 612 B.C. On the death of Sin-shar-ishkun, an army officer made himself king under the name Ashur-uballit, and set up court in Harran in Syria, with Egyptian support. Two years later that last stronghold fell to the Medes, who repulsed a counter-attack in 609 B.C.; and there Assyrian history ended. The whole of Assyria lay in ruins, and the population was decimated. Assyria disappeared so totally that to the Greeks, for instance, she was a mere memory, and the source of legends such as that of Semiramis. We know far more than the Greeks ever did, thanks to the literacy of the Assyrians and to the rich finds in ruined Assyrian palaces made by the archaeologists of the last 150 years.

Assyrian Religion

The names of several deities worshipped by the Assyrians can be extracted from the names of their kings. The god Asshur, who gave his name to the capital city, is to be seen in many royal names, for instance Ashurnasirpal and Ashurbanipal. Another god was Ninurta, as in Tukulti-ninurta.[6] These two appear to have been the most prominent deities worshipped in Assyria; other names include Shulman (as in Shalmaneser), Sin (as in Sennacherib) and Adad (as

---

6. The "Nisroch" of 2 Kings 19:37 may be Ninurta, but more probably another deity, Nusku.

in Adad-nirari). The last named is the "Hadad" worshipped in Syria as the god of thunder.

Though some of these names are characteristic of Assyrian worship, the religion practised in ancient Assyria cannot be divorced from the older, Sumerian religion which was adopted by the Semitic peoples who came into Mesopotamia later — the Akkadians and the Amorites. If the Egyptian religion was dominated by their natural environment — the Nile and the perennial sunshine — Sumerian worship was no less influenced by the great rivers Tigris and Euphrates, and the violent annual storms which produced widespread flooding. Where the sun took prominence in Egyptian thought, the gods of heaven (Anu) and of wind (Enlil) held pride of place in the early Sumerian pantheon, along with a third male deity (Enki or Ea — symbolising the earth) and a mother-goddess, Ninhursag. These were the gods who created order in the universe by defeating the monster-deities of the primeval waters.

A second triad of cosmic male deities may have been imported by the Akkadians; they were the gods of the moon (Sin — in Sumerian, Nannar), the sun (Shamash — in Sumerian, Utu) and of storm (Adad). Their associated goddess was Ishtar — the Ashtoreth of the Old Testament — who became the most prominent goddess in Mesopotamia, as goddess of war and love.

At the other end of the scale, there were deities to be found in the most ordinary everyday articles and objects, even things like salt. The whole of life, everything that confronted man, was religious in the eyes of the Assyrians and Babylonians. The total list of deities is enormous, and it is impossible to identify many of the names. Some deities became associated with special cities, and if one of those cities rose to prominence, so did its tutelary god or goddess. This is precisely what happened in the case of Asshur. The symbolism of this deity escapes us (some would connect the name with the Egyptian Osiris), but as the city of Asshur rose to power, so did the deity, and in due course the god Asshur became the national patron deity of Assyria, and second to none. Hence the ancient myths were amended to make him the chief god where Anu's name had previously stood. Asshur owned Assyria, and the king was his high priest.

Ninurta and Shulman seem to have been the same deity by different names; the god of war, he was a very appropriate deity for the Assyrians to revere! One other Mesopotamian deity deserves mention here, since he is specifically mentioned in Ezekiel 8:14: Tammuz, for whom the Jerusalemite women were ritually wailing, as the prophet saw in his vision. This god (who gave his name to a month of the Babylonian and hence the Jewish year), originally Sumerian (Dumuzi), had a widespread cult in the ancient Near East, and probably reached the people of Judah via the Phoenicians. The "wailing" Ezekiel describes was because of the god's descent to the underworld, where he was ritually married to the goddess Ishtar, who followed him thither. Their union was doubtless thought to promote the growth of vegetation. The Adonis cult of the Greeks was very similar.[7]

The Assyrian kings, in their inscriptions and records, regularly credit the god Asshur with their victories, but it does not seem to have been their custom to impose the worship of Assyrian deities upon the nations they conquered.[8] However, 2 Kings 16: 10-18 recounts how King Ahaz of Judah introduced innovations in the very temple of Jerusalem in consequence of paying a visit to his new overlord, Tiglath-pileser III, at Damascus. The altar Ahaz saw at Damascus may well have been Syrian rather than Assyrian, but his installation of a similar altar in Jerusalem suggests Assyrian pressures, to say the least. First Hezekiah, and later Josiah, sought to eradicate such foreign pagan trappings from the temple. The latter king got rid of various cultic personnel and their paraphernalia, we read in 2 Kings 23: 4f.; the cults listed included sun, moon, planets (or signs of the zodiac), and "all the host of heaven", some if not all of which were ultimately of Mesopotamian origin.

There is evidence of such astral cults in the Northern Kingdom, too, in the words of Amos 5: 26. The verse presents difficulties, and if the New English Bible rendering is right, the nature of the idolatry is not specified; but the Revised Standard Version (for instance) mentions explicitly "Sakkuth your king, and Kaiwan your star-god". These two names are known to have been applied to the planet Saturn in Babylonian worship.[9] Amos therefore seems to be telling his contemporaries in the Northern Kingdom that they would soon be in a position to take such idols back home to Mesopotamia — for Israel faced "exile beyond Damascus" (verse 27).

The attitude of the eighth century prophets to Assyria was that God — Yahweh of Israel, not the vaunted Asshur to whom the Assyrians credited their victories! — had ordained that this mighty nation should punish Israel for her idolatries. Hosea, for instance, poured scorn on "the calf-god of Beth-aven" (by which he meant Bethel), and predicted that the idol would be "carried to Assyria as tribute to the Great King" (Hosea 10:5f.). At the end of the century, Isaiah succinctly explained God's purposes for Assyria: "The Assyrian! He is the rod that I wield in my anger, and the staff of my

7. For some further details of the religion, see H. Ringgren, *Religions of the Ancient Near East* (London, 1973), pp. 64ff.

8. Cf. J. W. McKay, *Religion in Judah under the Assyrians (SBT,* ii. 26: London, 1973), *passim.* Until recently it was widely supposed that the Assyrians did impose a degree of Assyrian worship upon their subject peoples.

9. Stephen quoted from the Greek translation of this passage in Acts 7:43, on which cf. F. F. Bruce, *The Acts of the Apostles*[2] (London, 1952), p. 174.

wrath is in his hand. I send him against a godless nation, I bid him march against a people who rouse my wrath" (Isaiah 10:5f.). Assyria, however, went far beyond her writ; the Assyrian's "purpose is lawless", the prophet complained, "His thought is only to destroy and to wipe out nation after nation" (10:7). So this same prophet foretold doom in turn for Assyria — "I will break the Assyrian in my own land and trample him underfoot upon my mountains" was the divine promise (14:25).

This last oracle found partial fulfilment in the disaster to Sennacherib's army described in 2 Kings 19:35, but nearly a century more passed before the final destruction of Assyria. The prophets of that era could not mourn for Assyria. Nahum openly rejoiced over the fall of the "blood-stained city (Nineveh) . . . full of pillage, never empty of prey!" (3:1). The very last word of his prophecy was this, addressed to the now broken empire: "Are there any whom your ceaseless cruelty has not borne down?"

CHAPTER 19

Babylon

BABYLON'S history was closely intertwined with that of Assyria. Both Asshur and Babylon are known to us from the middle of the third millennium B.C., when both were among the cities of the Sumero-Akkadadian civilization which then embraced the whole of Mesopotamia. At that early stage, Asshur was already an important city, in its rather isolated position on the upper Tigris. Babylon, however, located on a branch of the Euphrates, was an insignificant town until the second millennium, over-shadowed as it was by more powerful and perhaps more ancient cities all around. Its position was fairly central in the heart-land of Mesopotamia. Under the Third Dynasty of Ur it came to serve as a provincial capital, in the twenty-second and twenty-first centuries B.C.

When the Amorite wave of migration took place, about 2000 B.C., Babylon was one of the towns occupied by the newcomers; and an Amorite chieftain in 1894 B.C. proclaimed himself king of the city, thus creating its first dynasty in history. His name was Sumu-abum. He and his successors immediately set about making Babylon the capital of a powerful kingdom, and by a combination of skill, chance and force they succeeded dramatically. Almost exactly one hundred years after the first king had taken the throne, the great Hammurabi[1] ascended it. His achievements are legendary, although it has to be acknowledged that his empire was not so large as used to be supposed; a contemporary of the same name was king of Aleppo in Syria, and his achievements were not inconsiderable in that area — achievements which were formerly mistakenly credited to Babylon's Hammurabi.

Hammurabi reigned from 1792 till 1750 B.C. He inherited a kingdom smaller and less powerful that its four neighbours — to the

---

1. The spelling "Hammurapi" is probably more accurate.

south, Larsa, and to the north, Mari, Eshnunna, and further north
still, Asshur. To conquer these kingdoms required cunning and patience as well as able generalship; Hammurabi had all the requisite
abilities, creating and discarding alliances as the needs of the
moment dictated. The king of Mari was the obvious ally — the two
kings between them dominated many miles of the Euphrates and the
trade-route which followed its course. In due course the other cities
made common cause and twice attacked Hammurabi, but he
defeated these coalitions and went on to master the whole of central
and southern Mesopotamia. He then turned against his ally Mari,
and that great city was sacked in 1759, never to be rebuilt. Finally he
defeated the kingdom of Asshur and made its king his vassal. What
further triumphs he achieved are not clear, but at any rate he felt it
appropriate to add to his regnal titles the phrase "King of the four
quarters of the world". Babylon's rulers were never noted for their
humility. At home his achievements were again far from negligible.
His law-code is famous, and though it had its antecedents, it showed
originality in its attempts to promote justice for all his subjects. The
punishments it specified appear barbarous and the class distinctions
it embodies unpalatable by modern standards, but we can still
admire the efforts made to promote the well-being of every member
of society, including women and children.

The kingdoms conquered by Hammurabi had their own proud
heritage, however, and it is not surprising that his successors found
it impossible to hold his empire together. It gradually dwindled in
size, as rebels broke free and invaders marched in. Finally in 1595
B.C. a powerful invader, King Mursilis I of the Hittites, who had
fought successful campaigns in Syria, suddenly marched down the
Euphrates, captured and plundered Babylon, and put an end to its
First Dynasty, which lasted exactly 300 years.

South Mesopotamia, or Babylonia as we may now call it (since
Babylon was from now on its recognized capital), came under the
rule of invaders from the east, the Kassites. The Hittites retired as
suddenly as they had come, and the Kassites filled the gap they left
behind. These people from Iran, hitherto peacefully inclined, had
recently come under the control of Indo-European leadership, and
they now showed themselves thoroughly efficient in the arts of war
and peace. It would seem that they were benefactors to Babylonia,
which they unified politically and to which they gave a long era
(poorly documented) of peace and reasonable prosperity. The
Kassite kings of Babylon respected the existing Mesopotamian
religion and culture, and in due course themselves bore Akkadian
names, so that they *were* Babylonians in all but origin.

Towards the end of the fourteenth century, when the Mitanni
kingdom fell, Babylon's days of peace ended, due to the resurgence
of Assyrian power; and in the following century the accession of a

powerful and energetic dynasty in Elam, Babylonia's eastern neighbour, left Babylon incapable of fighting off the inroads of two strong kingdoms. Thus Tukulti-ninurta I of Assyria (1244-1208 B.C.) was able to conquer Babylonia, though that proved a relatively short-lived humiliation for the southerners. After that it was the Elamites who proved the more troublesome; their final victory in 1162 B.C. brought to an end the Kassite dynasty. Soon, however, native Babylonian kings retrieved the throne from the Elamites, and one of them, who bore the famous name of Nebuchadrezzar (I, 1124-1103 B.C.), achieved notable victories on Elamite soil. No sooner had he died, however, than Assyria's Tiglath-pileser I attacked and captured Babylon, which he plundered and partially sacked.

By now the Aramaean wave of migration, which threatened to engulf the Assyrian kingdom, had struck Babylonia hard. Aramaeans settled in all parts, but especially strongly in the eastern part of the kingdom, while a similar migrant group, the Chaldaeans (*Kaldu,* in Akkadian records), made the south of Babylonia their own. These newcomers came to adopt Babylonian ways in nearly every respect, except that they preserved a distinct social order (with their own kings), and in time became a naturalized part of the Babylonian kingdom, but at first they severely weakened their unwilling hosts, whose three dynasties between 1050 and 1000 B.C. were none of them native, it appears. Four centuries were to elapse before Babylon once again achieved real power.

During the period of the Assyrian ascendancy, which began at the end of the tenth century, Babylon found herself dominated by her powerful neighbour to the north, but on the whole treated with respect and consideration. Some of the Assyrian kings were her benefactors, in fact, driving back enemies such as the Elamites and subduing the Aramaeans in the south. The first Assyrian king to aid Babylon in this fashion was Shalmaneser III, who in 851 B.C. upheld the Babylonian king Marduk-zakir-shumi against an Aramaean-backed conspiracy headed by his own brother. In consequence Babylon became the vassal of Assyria, but it cost her little. Nevertheless she threw off the Assyrian yoke once Shalmaneser died, and thereby provoked an attack by his successor Shamshi-adad V. These events set the pattern for the following century or two; Babylon broke free when she could, but otherwise submitted to a relatively light Assyrian yoke. A united and stable Mesopotamia was vital to Assyrian interests, and it paid her, therefore, to treat the Babylonians as generously as possible.

A new departure in Assyro-Babylonian relations took place when Tiglath-pileser III of Assyria took the throne of Babylon in 729 B.C., taking the regnal name of Pulu; in effect, he made himself king of a twin kingdom. In similar fashion his son Shalmaneser V reigned in Babylon as Ululai. Some native Babylonians may have been well content with this arrangement, which did no dishonour to their venerable capital; but the Chaldaean elements in Babylonia were more unremittingly rebellious. In the unrest which followed the accession of Sargon II in 722 B.C., a Chaldaean prince named Marduk-apal-iddina (the Old Testament Merodach-baladan), whose proper realm was the small state of Bit-Yakin on the Persian Gulf, seized the throne of Babylon, and held it for twelve years, with the support of the Elamites. It was to Elam that he retreated when eventually Sargon managed to force him out of Babylon, and from there he continued to foment trouble for the Assyrians. As soon as Sargon died, he reappeared in Babylon, and held it for three years this time. It was now that he conspired with Hezekiah of Judah. Sennacherib in 702 B.C. drove him out yet again, and Babylonia was now subjected to the Assyrian deportation policy, while the throne of Babylon was occupied by an Assyrian called Bel-ibni, Sennacherib's own appointment. Further troubles ensued, and in 689 B.C. the Babylonians with Elamite help all but defeated Senna-cherib; it was now that the infuriated Assyrian king took his revenge on Babylon, destroying much of it, inundating it by diverting the waters of the Euphrates, and leaving it kingless for the remainder of his reign.

This humiliation at Assyrian hands was quite unprecedented, and Esarhaddon of Assyria spent his reign (681-669 B.C.) trying to undo the damage. The city was rebuilt, and treated with great respect once again. When he died, one of his sons, Shamash-shum-ukin, became king of Babylon, and Assyrian though he was, his subjects proved loyal to him. He, however, did not prove loyal to Assyria. We may suppose that he had personal ambitions to rule Assyria as well as Babylon, and also that he was subjected to strong pro-Babylonian pressures in his own kingdom. He organized a confederacy of many peoples, most of them Assyria's vassals; and if Judah was one of the rebels, it would explain the statement of 2 Chronicles 33:11 that King Manasseh was carried off in fetters to Babylon, presumably after the fall of that city in 648 B.C.

Ashurbanipal, the victorious Assyrian king, appointed a Chaldaean as the new viceroy of Babylon. At the end of Ashur-banipal's long reign (627 B.C.) another Chaldaean, Nabopolassar, held that position, and he now broke free, and began the last great dynasty of Babylon in 626 B.C. We have already traced the course of events by which he conquered Assyria, in alliance with Cyaxares king of Media, an alliance cemented by the marriage of Babylon's crown-prince Nebuchadrezzar with the Median princess Amytis.

The collapse of Assyria permitted Babylon to become the new rulers of most of the Near East; the Medes might have contested it, but they remained loyal to their treaty. The Egyptians tried to salvage something for themselves, but the attempt failed miserably. It is unnecessary to trace again the stages by which Nebuchadrezzar II, who succeeded to the throne in 605 B.C., conquered the Levantine seaboard, put down revolts in Judah and Tyre, and inflicted serious defeats on Egypt. In every respect Nebuchadrezzar showed himself the equal of the greatest Assyrian kings, whose techniques and policies he adopted wholeheartedly. He even shared their building propensities, and Babylon was greatly enhanced and strongly fortified by his efforts — so much so that it became, with its famed hanging gardens, one of the wonders of the ancient world.

The last years of Nebuchadrezzar are unchronicled and obscure, and probably the swift decline of the Neo-Babylonian empire started before his death in 562 B.C. Three successors came and went very rapidly, and then Nabonidus (556-539 B.C.) was elected to the throne. He proved more and more unpopular with his subjects; and he chanced to be the contemporary of a man who turned out to be one of the greatest kings and conquerors in history, the Persian Cyrus II. Cyrus inherited the throne of Persia and Anshan, two small states on the Persian Gulf, in 559 B.C.; in 550 B.C. he fought victoriously against the major power to the north, Media, and created Medo-Persia; and then he proceeded step by step to make the Babylonian empire his own property. When at last he came to conquer Babylonia itself, neither Nabonidus nor his crown-prince Belshazzar had much support from their own people. Belshazzar was killed in battle at Opir on the Tigris, but "the troops of Cyrus entered Babylon without battle".[2] The year was 539 B.C.

The Babylonian empire was thus a much briefer affair than its Assyrian predecessor, but at least it had less time in which to create enemies, and escaped the devastation Assyria had suffered. Cyrus showed Babylon every mark of respect, and it survived for some centuries. Nevertheless its days of glory were a thing of the past, and its proud inhabitants never knew independence again. In due course the Greeks replaced the Persians as its masters. The Greeks built a new city, Seleucia, not far away, and gradually the population moved away from Babylon itself. Its population had shrunk to village dimensions by the beginning of the Christian era.

Babylonian Religion and Culture

The name Babylon is the Greek form of the Hebrew *babel*, the Akkadian *bab-ili*, "the gate of the god". One is reminded of Jacob's description of Bethel, "the house of God" and "the gate of heaven" (Genesis 28:17). It was no single deity who was revered at Babylon,

2. *DOTT*, p. 82.

however — "Babel" truly denoted a "confusion" of deities, many of whom had their temples in the great city on the Euphrates. The pantheon for Babylonia was in general the same as for Assyria, drawn from the Sumerian beliefs, modified over the years by the addition of Semitic gods and by local developments. Thus while the general fabric of the religion was identical, the most prominent deities were different in the two kingdoms. From the names of the Assyrian kings we extracted the names of the deities Asshur, Ninurta and Shulman; from the Babylonian king lists we can extract three other divine names occurring and recurring: Marduk (in Hebrew "Merodach", as in Merodach-baladan), Bel (as in Belshazzar) and Nabu (as in Nebuchadrezzar or Nabonidus). Nabu (Hebrew "Nebo") was the principal deity at the important city of Borsippa, seven miles south of Babylon, though he was worshipped throughout Mesopotamia as the god of literature. In the pantheon he was held to be the son of Bel, originally a title of Enlil, one of the most prominent of the Sumerian gods. In Babylon itself, however, the title Bel[3] was transferred to another deity, Marduk, who was the patron deity of the city.

Babylon, as we have seen, was an obscure and unimportant city till the end of the third millennium B.C.; the same can be said for its patron deity, who began life, so to speak, as the mere "bullock of the sun-god" — the apparent meaning of the Sumerian form of his name. But as the city rose to power and prominence, so did its god, till finally he was the chief god of the whole of Babylonia and then of the Babylonian empire. The Babylonians accordingly transferred to him many of the attributes of other deities, notably those of Enlil.

The Babylonian Creation Epic, which first came to light in the 1870s, has often been compared (or contrasted) with Genesis 1, since both describe the creation of the world and of man in much the same sequence. Here, however, we may consider it as a most interesting piece of politico-religious propaganda. The narrative opens with a primeval scene of watery chaos, symbolized by three deities of whom the most noteworthy was Tiamat; then a second generation of gods was born, which included Anu (the chief Sumerian deity), and before long discord broke out in heaven. War was declared, and at first Tiamat and her allies looked like winning; it was found that Anu was not strong enough to overcome her. At this point "a god then engendered the strongest, the 'Sage of the Gods' " — Marduk, no other, who had "twofold divinity imparted to him".[4] It was obvious that he was the ideal champion, and the gods speedily met together to appoint him their king, by democratic election, notwithstanding his lack of seniority.

3. "Bel" is linguistically the equivalent of the Canaanite word "Baal", and meant "lord".

4. *DOTT*, p. 8.

Battle royal followed, and needless to say Marduk emerged victorious. Using the winds as weapons, he slew Tiamat. The corpse he divided up and he "created" the universe from it, beginning with the heavenly bodies, signs of the zodiac, and the like, and proceeding to fashion the earth — the Euphrates and Tigris, for instance, were to flow through Tiamat's eyes. Next a city had to be planned in which the gods would live; it would have to be an incomparable city, with majestic homes for all the gods. It would of course bear the name "Babylon". But all cities require menial labourers, and Marduk went on to create man as the lowly slave of the gods. Finally the gods set to and built Babylon according to the blueprint, one of the most sumptuous edifices being a home for Marduk (the temple Esagila), and proceeded to install Marduk as their king for all time, Anu himself seating Marduk on the throne.

This narrative acknowledges the junior position that Marduk once held among the gods of Mesopotamia, but justifies his rise to power and his kingship; at the same time it glorifies the city of Babylon. He is king of the gods because the other gods acclaimed him such, and also because he had brought order out of chaos; that is to say, he is credited with the power to subdue the annual rains and flood-waters. It is beyond doubt that the story had originally honoured another god, the Sumerian Enlil, but it was adopted and adapted to honour Marduk — and Babylon. (An Assyrian copy of the Epic in turn replaced Marduk by Asshur!)

If the Epic gives us some insight into the religious concepts of the citizens of ancient Babylon, it may also serve as an introduction to their cultic practices. One of the great occasions of the Babylonian year was the long-drawn-out (eleven days) new year festival in the month Nisan, each spring. Each day of the festival had its fixed rituals, including prayers, sacrifices and processions from one temple to another. Esagila, Marduk's own temple, played a big role, and so did a special edifice called the Akitu temple just outside the city. On the fifth day the king of Babylon went into Esagila and yielded up his royal insignia to the god. The king was ritually humiliated, being struck in the face by a priest, and he then retrieved his insignia — to reign for another year. On the following day the idol of Nabu arrived in procession from Borsippa; and in due course Marduk himself was taken to the Akitu temple, the king in person leading the idol by the hand. There is uncertainty about the remaining rituals, but they included a sacred marriage ceremony of some sort, and perhaps also a ritual combat between Marduk and Tiamat. The liturgy included the Epic of Creation, recited on the fourth day of the festival.

Such ceremonies were very important to the Babylonians (and similar rituals were practised at all the Mesopotamian sacred cities), for their well-being depended on the faithful observance of prescribed ritual, they were convinced. The neglect of the New Year festival by the last king of Babylon, Nabonidus, caused his subjects no little distress. The harsh geographical and climatic environment in which the Mesopotamians found themselves led to a pessimistic strain in their thought which stood in marked contrast to the Egyptian outlook. It is clear that they sought desperately to look into and to manipulate the future, by means of astrology, hepatoscopy, and kindred superstitious measures, on which Isaiah 47:12-15 gives a sarcastic commentary. Addressing the Babylonians the prophet challenged them thus: "Persist in your spells and your monstrous sorceries, maybe you will get help from them . . . but no! in spite of your many wiles you are powerless. Let your astrologers, your star-gazers who foretell your future month by month, persist and save you!"

In general, the cultural attainments of the Mesopotamians were no whit inferior to those of Egypt. The literature which has survived, written in the cuneiform script invented by the Sumerians, is by itself proof of that fact. But the Old Testament writers were little interested in intellectual attainment *per se:* in the case of Babylon, they saw that such attainment only served to puff up the ego of an already pretentiously vain city and nation. The day would come when the vaunted deities, Bel-Marduk and Nebo, would stoop low, their images nothing more thana wearisome burden for pack-animals (cf. Isaiah 46:1).

The overweening pride of Babylon was traced back by the Hebrew writer to its very earliest days, when the building of the city was not yet complete — though to be sure, the story of the tower of Babel may well have been intended as a denunciation of the Sumero-Akkadian culture and faith as a whole. Towers such as that described in Genesis 11 were to be found throughout Mesopotamia; they are known as ziggurats, and many ruined examples can still be seen.[5] Babylon's ziggurat must have been very impressive in its heyday. It was situated near the temple to Marduk, and bore the name Etemenanki — "House of the foundation of heaven and earth". Like all ziggurats, it was a temple set on a stepped pyramid. The purpose of these huge edifices has yet to be fully explained, but it was doubtless in some fashion to establish contact between heaven and earth, between god and man. The repair of such buildings remained important throughout the great days of Assyria and Babylon. Nebuchadrezzar was careful to restore Etemenanki, and the very last king of Babylon, Nabonidus, did the same for the great ziggurat of Ur, the famous city where Abraham was born, of which the tutelary deity was the moon god.

5. For illustrations and photographs, cf. C. M. Jones, *Old Testament Illustrations* (Cambridge, 1971), pp. 30f.

Prophetic Attitudes to Babylon

The prophets' treatment of Babylon in general resembles that of Assyria. Just as Isaiah had described Assyria as the rod of God's wrath against Israel and Judah, so we find in Jeremiah 51:20 Babylon depicted as Yahweh's battle-axe, to punish Judah and other nations. Babylon, Jeremiah was sure, was raised up by God to be the new master of the whole Fertile Crescent, Judah included. But neither he nor other prophets had any illusions about the Babylonians' character. Habakkuk asked God, very pertinently, "Why keep silent when they devour men more righteous than they?" (1:13). Perhaps they were less cruel and rapacious than the Assyrians had been, but it was only a matter of degree; and for arrogant self-confidence, it would seem, they were worse than their predecessors, and had learned nothing from the fate of Assyria. Through his prophetic spokesman Yahweh addressed Babylon thus: "Never again shall men call you queen of many kingdoms. When I was angry with my people, I dishonoured my own possession and gave them into your power. You showed them no mercy, you made your yoke weigh heavy on the aged. You said then, 'I shall be a queen for ever' " (Isaiah 47:5ff.).

Finally, we may note the "song of derision" levelled at the king of Babylon in Isaiah 14: "How you are fallen from heaven, bright morning star! . . . You thought in your own mind, I will scale the heavens; I will set my throne high above the stars of God, I will sit on the mountain where the gods meet . . . Yet you shall be brought down to Sheol, to the depths of the abyss." It must have been on the basis of this passage in particular that in the New Testament the name "Babylon" was used to typify not only Rome but the totalitarian, godless, arrogant state of any and every era of human history.

CHAPTER 20

The Enemy Within: The Canaanites

BY THE time that Saul came to the throne, the Canaanites no longer posed any sort of political threat to the Israelites. They still retained independent control of a number of individual cities and enclaves within Israel's frontiers, but a generation later David captured these cities and incorporated them fully into his realm. The result was that the non-Israelite element in Palestine mingled with their conquerors, intermarried with them, and in course of time lost their separate identity. From a political point of view, therefore, the Canaanites were never a foe to Israel during the period of the monarchy. On the other hand, the Old Testament makes it clear that the prophets and the prophetic movement in Israel were convinced that the Canaanites posed a very serious and abiding threat to the true religion of Israel. From a religious point of view they were the enemy within the gates.

The Canaanite civilization was established in Palestine long before the exodus took place; indeed, it was flourishing as early as the days of Abraham. We should not think of the Canaanites as a single, uncomplicated ethnic unit; the term "Canaanite" implies residence in Canaan rather than close ties of kinship.[1] Their origins were to some extent diverse; but at least their society and culture seem to have been homogeneous. The origins of that culture go back well before 2000 B.C., when migrant peoples known to the occupants of Mesopotamia as *Amurru* ("westerners") moved into Syria and Palestine and settled there in strength. The word *Amurru* has "Amorite" as its biblical equivalent; and in the Bible the terms Canaanite and Amorite are to some extent interchangeable.[2]

1. Strictly speaking, by etymology and early usage, the word Canaanite is thought to have denoted a merchant who traded in purple.
2. For precise details of biblical usage, a Bible dictionary should be consulted.

The table of nations in Genesis 10 associates Canaan with Ham's descent, thus recognizing the close relationship that existed between Egypt and Canaan throughout the second millennium B.C. The Canaanites' language, however, though distantly related to the ancient Egyptian language, belonged to the Semitic linguistic family. The Hebrew language can be classified as a dialect of Canaanitic; in other words, there was no language barrier between Israelites and Canaanites. The eighth century Israelite prophet Isaiah recognized that his native tongue was "the lip of Canaan" (Isaiah 19:18).

Though their language and culture united them, the Canaanites sought no political cohesion, but were content to live in small independent city-states, each ruled by its own king. They were thus not adequately organized to resist a strong foe, and Egypt (whenever it was strong and united) was able to dominate Canaan throughout the millennium. Egyptian documents as early as the nineteenth century and as late as the fourteenth century testify to both the political fragmentation of Canaan and also to the measure of Egyptian control. Such documents offer us, for instance, the names of several kings who ruled over Jerusalem during this long era, to add to the names of Melchizedek and Adoni-zedek to whom the biblical writers introduce us.

The Canaanite population was unevenly spread, and the mountainous hinterland, lying between the coastal plains and the Jordan rift valley, was thinly populated, otherwise Abraham and the other patriarchs could not have roamed there freely with their flocks and herds. If Genesis 14 records a friendly relationship between Abraham and the king of Jerusalem, Genesis 34 indicates that a rather different situation sprang up in the Shechem area some time later. Both Shechem and Jerusalem lay in the hill-country, and some contact between their citizens and the patriarchs was perhaps inevitable; but for the most part it seems that the patriarchs endeavoured to keep away from the more populous Canaanite areas.

From 1400 B.C. onwards the Canaanite civilization was subject to new outside pressures from several quarters, including the Israelite invaders. The Amarna letters of the fourteenth century give some idea of the political upheavals in Canaan. These documents come from the Egyptian record office of the day, and consist of letters and copies of letters exchanged by the Egyptian crown and some of the Palestinian rulers;[3] it is clear from them that the settled population of Canaan was being harassed continuously by raiders called "the Khabiru". It is an impossible task — and a controversial one — to unravel the whole chain of events which transformed Canaan within the next two centuries; but the sequel was that what had been a

3. See above, p. 169.

homogeneous Canaanite country was broken up into four diverse political regions. In the south-west, the Philistines and related peoples arrived and took control. Further north too they at first mastered the Canaanite cities, but in course of time the Canaanites reasserted themselves, and by the time of the Hebrew monarchy the area was again thoroughly Canaanite (though it is convenient to refer to this region as Phoenicia, and its inhabitants as Phoenicians). In the north-east the invaders were the Aramaean tribes, who were to remain distinct from the other peoples of Syria-Palestine by the fact of their language; Aramaic was closely related to Hebrew and other Canaanite dialects, but was nevertheless a distinct language, even if the evidence suggests that Hebrew and Aramaic had common ancestry. In the south and south-east the new masters were the tribes of Israel, Edom, Moab and Ammon.

In none of the four regions, however, were the Canaanites wiped out, and in certain respects the conquered became the conquerors, as so often happens. The Canaanites had developed many of the arts of civilization, and from a cultural point of view semi-nomadic tribes-men like the Israelites were distinctly more primitive. Where archi-tecture is concerned, for instance, it is noticeable that Canaanite cities destroyed by the Israelites were at first replaced by very inferior buildings — this fact the archaeologist's spade has often revealed. Needless to say, it did not take the Israelites long to realize how much they could learn from Canaanite craftsmen of all kinds; and in practical terms they came to owe a great debt to the previous occupants of the land.

No doubt the relative sophistication of the Canaanites made its appeal to the Israelites, and the latter fell readily into Canaanite ways of thought and behaviour. Some there were who reacted strongly against Canaanite culture; a notable example of such a group was the Rechabites, who as late as the time of Jeremiah were still clinging on to a rustic, indeed semi-nomadic, way of life.[4] Not only were they strict teetotallers, but they went so far as to refuse to build houses and even to sow crops. But without doubt the Rech-abites were the exception that proved the rule, and most of the Israelites felt few such inhibitions. The ascetic life rarely makes a wide appeal.

Probably the Israelites fell into Canaanite ways without a great deal of conscious thought, and they will often have adopted the Canaanites' religious modes and manners along with everything else; in any case, ancient man made less distinction between sacred and secular than we are prone to do. Before many generations had passed, the popular religion of Israel had become an amalgam of Israelite and Canaanite belief and practice; and to some extent at

4. See especially Jeremiah 35.

least the same is true of the official religion of Israel, for it was the prophets, not the priests, who eventually cried, "Hold!"

It must be recognized, in any case, that there were individual aspects of Canaanite religious beliefs and cultic practice which not even the prophets had any wish to contradict or battle against. Even before the Israelite conquest of Canaan, one could undoubtedly have found numerous points of contact and similarity between the two faiths. How much the Israelites actually "borrowed" from the Canaanites is open to dispute, but we may instance, at the very least, a certain amount of religious *language*. If the Canaanites proclaimed their chief god as creator and lord, could Israel call their God, Yahweh, anything less? It is of course not only possible but very likely that some such descriptions of deity arose quite independently, and it is as a rule safe to speak in terms of a common outlook rather than of specific borrowings. However, there can be little doubt that some religious language was adopted from the Canaanites. Isaiah 27:1, for instance, describes the God of Israel as about to punish "Leviathan that twisting (or primaeval) sea-serpent, that writhing serpent Leviathan". But who or what is "Leviathan"? The Old Testament nowhere offers any explanation of the term. The word itself properly belongs, as we now know, to Canaanite myths about the god Baal, for an ancient Canaanite poem found at Ras Shamra praises the Baal in the following terms: "Thou didst slay Lotan (i.e. Leviathan) the Primaeval Serpent, didst make an end of the Crooked Serpent".[5] In Canaanite mythology, Baal had to do battle royal to assert his control over hostile deities who symbolized the forces of nature. Such a view is foreign to the Old Testament concept of Yahweh, but some of the biblical writers were willing to use the language of Baal myths to emphasize Yahweh's control over historical forces, such as Egypt and Assyria.

Even the name Baal itself could appropriately be used as a title for Yahweh. In Canaanite religion too it was strictly a title, meaning "lord" or "master", the usual designation of the storm-god Hadad, though it came to be virtually a name in its own right. Was not Yahweh "lord" of his people? Saul was not worshipping Canaanite gods when he named one of his sons "Eshbaal" (1 Chronicles 8:33). It was not until the time of Hosea that it became apparent that there were dangers in adopting identical religious language for the Israelite faith (cf. Hosea 2:15 ff.); "Baal" was by now a "dirty word", and one to be avoided.

Nor were there marked, self-evident contrasts between Israelite and Canaanite worship where sacred buildings were concerned. When Solomon came to erect the temple in Jerusalem, he found himself obliged to call in Phoenician craftsmen as well as materials;

5. *DOTT*, p. 132.

and the sanctuary they put up resembles not only the blueprint of the tabernacle outlined in the Book of Exodus (explicitly stated to be God-given), but also, in varying degree, the pattern of various pagan temples as revealed by archaeological excavations. The Canaanite temple at Hazor, destroyed by Joshua and his armies (Joshua 11:10f.), is particularly similar to the Jerusalem temple in its ground-plan and structure.[6]

Other Israelite sanctuaries were in any case simply taken over from the Canaanites and used for the worship of Yahweh — a practice which King Josiah finally tried to put an end to. It must be remembered that the patriarchs had been associated with various sanctuary-towns of Palestine, such as Bethel and Beer-sheba, and it was inevitable that the patriarchs' descendants should revere the sanctuaries in question.

As regards the ritual practices which were performed at the shrines, we are much better informed about Israelite worship than about any thing comparable in the ancient world. Sacrifice itself, of course, was commonplace, but the Old Testament tells us of many different types of sacrifices and offerings. For all we know, it may be that the Canaanite sacrifical system was very different; but one suspects that there were again close similarities, in view of the fact that a number of the Old Testament technical terms have exact parallels in the Ras Shamra ritual texts. In annual feasts and fasts we can see other general points of similarity.

One can appreciate, therefore, that many an ordinary Israelite could see little harm in Canaanite religious practices, and perhaps little essential difference in them. When he did observe distinctions, moreover, he may have been tempted to think that the Canaanites had the better of it, since they were such gifted and civilized people. Was Yahweh perhaps the god of the deserts outside Palestine, with little power or influence in Canaan?

The most glaring contrasts between the two faiths lay not so much in their material fabric, as in the theology and the whole ethos of the two. We are immediately struck by the contrast between Israel's monotheism and Canaan's polytheism. For the Israelites, there was Yahweh, and Yahweh alone; whereas the Canaanites revered not only Baal but a whole pantheon. The Old Testament provides us with several names of Canaanite deities, but the Ras Shamra texts have given us much fuller information about them. The senior deity for the Canaanites was not in fact Baal, but El, who was viewed as the creator-god. Baal was the most prominent god in their thinking and ritual, however; he was pre-eminently the storm-god, the god of thunder and rain (so vital to Palestine's agricultural economy). (See plate 15 facing p. 272.) Baal's father in the pantheon was Dagan

6. Cf. Y. Yadin, *Hazor: excavation of a biblical city* (London, 1958), pp. 13-16, and fig. 20.

(Old Testament "Dagon"), the god of corn and vegetation. Other male deities included Horon, whose name survived in the place-name Bethhoron. Goddesses also figured in the pantheon; of these the Old Testament mentions Ashtoreth (the Canaanite Athtarat, the Mesopotamian Ishtar, the Greek Astarte) and Asherah (Athirat in the Ras Shamra documents), while a third, Anat, is again to be found in a place-name, Anathoth, Jeremiah's birthplace. All three were goddesses of fertility; Asherah was El's consort, Anat was Baal's. A male deity, Athtar, seems to have represented the planet Venus; and the sun and moon were not forgotten, but worshipped by name (as Shepesh and Yerach respectively). A minor deity called Shalem, possibly another sky-god, also deserves mention, since his name survives to this day in the place name Jerusalem.

In our modern world, where the choice seems to be between monotheism and atheism, it is very difficult for us to understand, let alone feel any sympathy for, polytheistic religions like that of Canaan. All too readily we condemn them in quite the wrong terms. One still hears sometimes debates as to whether Muslims and Christians (or even Catholics and Protestants!) worship the same God; the linguistic philosophers would tell us, and rightly so, that such arguments are not only pointless but, worse, meaningless. If one looks behind the divine names and the crude myths (as they appear to us) of their faith, we can perceive that the Canaanites were looking at the same reality as the Israelites, but observing it through different eyes. They had no conception of the unity of function and purpose in the godhead which is recognized by Jews, Christians and Muslims alike. Thus they cast the attributes of deity in all-too-human terms of conflict and caprice. It will not do to say that the gods they worshipped were non-existent, for those deities were symbols of genuine reality — storms, vegetation, etc. St. Paul showed a better understanding of the nature of polytheistic worship when he told the Athenians, not that their "unknown god" was a figment of their imagination, but on the contrary, One who could be declared unto them (Acts 17:23). Nor did our Lord deny the existence and reality of Baal: the Beelzebub of the New Testament is none other than the Baal of Ekron which figures in 2 Kings 1.[7]

When Israelites turned to Canaanite worship, therefore, as did King Ahaziah, they were losing the sense of God's unique majesty and of his systematic, orderly, purposeful intentions for his people. Canaanite thinking was above all dominated by their concern for fruitful harvests — and in these days of relative affluence, we should feel sympathy for that concern. The plight of peasant-farmers when

7. Cf. Mark 3:22-27. The name probably meant originally "lord of the high place" (strictly, baal-zebul), but was slightly changed in Jewish tradition to the derogatory baal-zebub, "lord of flies". Other explanations of the name are also current.

Palestine was afflicted by drought and disease of crops was indeed desperate. Small wonder, then, that they isolated "corn" as one deity, "fertility" as another. In seeking to worship Dagon and the fertility goddesses, they were in effect trying to understand the forces of nature, and secondly trying to control those forces. To harness them, they felt, one must first of all get on good terms with the appropriate deities, by sacrifices, offerings and rituals, and then proceed to co-operate with those deities. The latter purpose could be achieved — as they thought — by the practice of what we now call "sympathetic" or "imitative" magic. Knowing nothing scientific about the reproduction and growth of plants, they envisaged these processes in terms of human sexual relations (as did many ancient peoples). To secure the fertility of the ground, therefore, Baal and his consort Anat were depicted as having sexual intercourse; and it is certain that in Canaanite rites the worshippers emulated the gods, believing that such conduct would promote the good harvests they so much desired. Accordingly, each Canaanite shrine had its cult-prostitutes, both male and female.

The Canaanite faith, then, can be characterized as a fertility religion. We may say that it was in its outworkings both amoral and materialistic, even though Canaanite literature here and there does betray some consciousness of sin and some interest in righteousness. By contrast, Israel's faith can be characterized as a covenant religion; Israel's religious teachers emphasized that while God did, of course, give fertility to the soil, his most important attribute was his lordship of history, in which he had acted over and over again in blessing for Israel, who had committed themselves irrevocably to him in the bonds of the covenant of Sinai. To "control" their environment, Israel's first need was to make sure that they were fulfilling the terms of that covenant, both in relation to Yahweh and to each other. For Israelites to turn to the fertility cult, therefore, was not merely to renounce morality and ethics, but to reject the covenant and all that it implied.

Hence the bitter invective of the prophets against Canaanite practices. The cultic prostitution was condemned vigorously, and was exposed as the immorality it was, while the special trappings of the fertility cult were also singled out for denunciation. Its special symbols were sacred wooden poles associated with the goddess Asherah,[8] and stone pillars (Hebrew *matstsebot*), examples of which have been unearthed in Palestine.[9]

The fertility cult devalued and debased human beings, and its

8. These sacred poles explain the use of the Old Testament phrase "to cut down the Asherah" (e.g. Judges 6:25), which in turn led to the mistranslation of "Asherah" as "(sacred) grove" in the Septuagint and hence the AV.
9. See *BA* 35 (1972), pp. 34-63 for illustrations of *matstsebot*.

pervasive influence throughout Palestine was of special concern to the Old Testament prophets. When they accused fellow-Israelites of "playing the harlot" with foreign deities the metaphor was extremely well-chosen — more literal than metaphorical, in fact. Another, fortunately rarer, feature of Canaanite religion was one which put even less value on the individual human being's life and dignity; this was human sacrifice, a practice which the prophets repudiated with horror, as well they might. It is not certain how widespread this practice was, but the two centres with which it was associated in the Old Testament records were Moab, in Trans-jordan, and the environs of Jerusalem itself. The deity in whose honour the rite of child sacrifice was carried out seems to have borne several names or titles, including Chemosh, Athtar, Shalem, and Milcom or Melek[10] ("the king").[11]

The Jerusalem shrine (no doubt an open air one, like most of the "high places" as opposed to temples) to this deity lay in the valley of Hinnom, just east of the city, at a place called Topheth. Here even royal children were at times sacrificed as burnt offerings (cf. 2 Chronicles 28:3, 33:6). King Josiah, during his religious reform programme, desecrated Topheth (2 Kings 23:10), and the prophet Jeremiah predicted that the idolatrous Jerusalem would lose so many people in the disasters soon to fall upon her, that Topheth would perforce be turned into a cemetery (Jeremiah 7:31ff.). The very name of Jerusalem commemorates this Canaanite deity, for it means "Founded by Shalem"; at few times in its history was the "holy city" a city of peace ruled by a king of righteousness, as God intended it to be (cf. Hebrews 7:1f.). Even Solomon gave sanction to this unpleasant cult, in order to please his pagan wives, according to 1 Kings 11:7.

The social pattern of the Canaanites cannot be entirely divorced from their religious beliefs. The king was not only the absolute monarch of his people, but also considered to be the channel of divine blessing to them. The Ras Shamra literature includes legends about two ancient kings named Keret and Danel which help us to understand the Canaanite conception of kingship. The Canaanites did not deify their kings, but they called them "sons" of the supreme god El, and Danel is specifically described as "the dispenser of fertility"; it was even believed that royal illness must result in bad harvests. The king was also the channel of divine revelation. His person, therefore, must have been sacrosanct. Below him stood a whole feudal system; on the bottom rung of the social ladder stood the serfs, completely at the mercy of their rulers. At the top, the king

10. In the Hebrew Bible the spelling is "molek",, a hybrid form which invited the pious Jewish reader to pronounce the word as "boshet" ("shame") instead of "melek" ("king").

11. See J. Gray, *The Legacy of Canaan*[2] (*VTS* 5: Leiden, 1965), pp. 169-174.

had absolute rights over property, taxes, commerce, and direction of labour.

It is true that there was something of a social conscience among the Canaanites, and also that by time-honoured convention the king was largely bound to observe duties of justice and charity.[12] But the general truth stands that absolute power tends to corrupt absolutely; and when one observes that Solomon's unpopularity, and the subsequent division of the Hebrew kingdom, arose precisely because he exercised the Canaanite king's privileges regarding taxes and direction of labour, one can appreciate why the prophets felt an increasing dislike of Canaanite ways. It was perhaps inevitable that the simple tribal society of early Israel, in which each man was keenly aware of his duties towards (and equality with) his fellow, should break down as time passed, and all the more rapidly once non-Israelites were incorporated into the polity of Israel; but human nature being what it is, we can be sure that many of the richer and more influential members of Israelite society will have seen the advantages for their own pockets of a feudal system.

Insidiously, therefore, Israel and Judah came more and more under the influence of Canaanite thought, practices and religion. As the period of the Hebrew monarchy ended in disaster, the prophet Ezekiel in a chapter of mordant reproach taunted Jerusalem thus: "Canaan is the land of your ancestry . . .; an Amorite was your father and a Hittite your mother" (Ezekiel 16:3). It remained for the exiles in Babylon and later Jewish generations to root out from their midst the legacy of Canaan.

12. Cf. J. Gray, *The Canaanites* (London, 1964), p. 118.

CHAPTER 21

The Enemy Within: False Religion

THE influences upon ancient Israel were many and various, and
we cannot fairly blame the Canaanites for all the facets of
Israelite life which attracted the rebukes of the prophets. It is a
remarkable fact that some of the bitterest enemies who ever
confronted the Old Testament prophets were not priests and
worshippers of Baal but other prophets of Yahweh. The Israelite
faith was by no means monolithic in character; there was "official"
religion, to be found among the priests, "prophetic" religion as
evidenced in the prophetic books of the Old Testament, and no
doubt a great deal of "popular" religion as well. While recognizing
the differences, we must not on the other hand draw too sweeping
contrasts between them. It is notoriously difficult to find appropriate
terminology to distinguish the Old Testament prophets from their
prophetic opponents. The latter no doubt came from the ranks of
cult-prophets, that is to say the prophets who were closely associated
with the sanctuaries, and who therefore depended on the "official"
religion for their livelihood. The "writing prophets" of the Old
Testament, on the other hand, seem to have been altogether more
independent, although it has been conjectured that some of them too
may have been attached to sanctuaries. One thing that seems to
have marked them out is their "vocation", their personal experience
of a call from Yahweh to the prophetic office.

The Old Testament prophets who received the most significant
attention from "false prophets" were Micaiah, Micah and
Jeremiah. The issue was simple enough in the first case: Micaiah's
fellow prophets were assuring King Ahab that he would achieve unqualified military success in his campaign at Ramoth-gilead,
whereas Micaiah himself was convinced that Ahab was going to his
death (1 Kings 22). Events swiftly proved Micaiah in the right of it.

His opponents were proven false by the mere fact that their predictions were not fulfilled; this is the test of false prophecy offered by Deuteronomy 18:21f. They were not telling deliberate lies, however; they spoke out of conviction, and were most indignant at Micaiah's allegation that their oracles were false. Micaiah's own description of the scene in the heavenly court in itself implies that the other prophets did not know they were being deceived. No doubt they were convinced of the righteousness of Ahab's cause — did not Ramoth-gilead legitimately belong to Israel?

When we turn to the Book of Micah, we find that the false prophets of Judah a century after Micaiah's time were equally sincere in their convictions, and indeed held to a coherent theology. To be sure, Micah accused them of promising prosperity "in return for a morsel of food" (3:5); but a careful study of the text of the Book of Micah reveals that whatever their motives they based their comforting predictions on solid religious beliefs. This fact has recently been clarified by a penetrating exegesis of relevant sections of the book by Professor A. S. van der Woude of Groningen.[1] Passages which had previously puzzled readers because of their rapid alternation between promises and threats can now be seen as disputes between Micah and the false prophets: the warnings are his, the specious optimism theirs. We must therefore place quotation marks against certain verses in Micah; similarly St. Paul in Colossians 2:21 was not counselling a policy of "Do not handle this, do not taste that, do not touch the other", but quoting his opponents' advice — in order to refute it.

In Micah 3:11 there is not the slightest doubt that the false prophets are the speakers. " 'Is not the LORD among us?' they say; 'then no disaster can befall us'." The ground of their optimism was their certainty of Yahweh's presence in their midst; was not the temple at Jerusalem his throne?

In Micah 2:7 we hear their voice again — "ranting", Micah tells us in the preceding verse. " 'Is the LORD's patience truly at an end? Are these his deeds? Does not good come of the LORD's words? He is the upright man's best friend'." Micah had been solemnly warning his fellow-citizens that the Assyrian army's approach heralded utter disaster for Judah, a fact which should have been obvious to any realist. The false prophets' reply was to the effect that God could not possibly lose patience with his own "upright" people, and since God controlled history, the Assyrian menace was negligible. Therefore they could accuse Micah of heartless cruelty, deliberately causing distress of mind to good folk who had nothing really to worry about. His gloomy prognostications, they claimed, amounted to stripping "the cloak from him that was

1. Cf. A. S. van der Woude, "Micah in dispute with the pseudo-prophets", *VT* 19 (1969), pp. 244-260.

1920

safe'', and taking away ''the confidence of returning warriors''
(verse 8).

But in point of fact Sennacherib's army caused havoc to the cities
of Judah, and went on to invest Jerusalem. Would not these grim
realities silence the optimists once and for all? Not a bit of it! They
had their answer ready, probably even beforehand:

> I will assemble you, the whole house of Jacob:
> I will gather together those that are left in Israel.
> I will herd them like sheep in a fold,
> like a grazing flock which stampedes at the sight of a man.
> So their leader breaks out before them,
> and they all break through the gate and escape,
> and their king goes before them,
> and their king goes before them,
> and the LORD leads the way.   (Micah 2:12f.)

Nor was it merely orderly escape they predicted; their ideas, as
enunciated in the next chapter, were even more grandiose:

> Now many nations are massed against you;
> they say, ''Let her suffer outrage,
> let us gloat over Zion.''
> But they do not know the LORD's thoughts
> nor understand his purpose;
> for he has gathered them like sheaves to the threshing-floor.
>
> Start your threshing, daughter of Zion;
> for I will make your horns of iron,
> your hooves will I make of bronze,
> and you shall crush many peoples.
> You shall devote their ill-gotten gain to the Lord,
> their wealth to the Lord of all the earth.
>   (Micah 4:11ff.)

These hopeful prophets, then, in terms reminiscent of Micaiah's
rivals' false promises to Ahab, maintained that the people of
Jerusalem would sally forth from their beleaguered city and utterly
crush the foe. In point of fact, the siege was lifted, and Jerusalem did
escape Sennacherib's wrath; but Judah gained no military glory
whatever in the process.[2]

These men's promises were hollow, as events soon proved; but a
little reflection will show that their confidence in God, and their convictions as to what he would do, could be paralleled more than once
in canonical Scripture. Ezekiel 38f., for instance, portrays the utter
defeat in Palestine of the heathen nations, led by Gog; but of course

2. See above, pp. 110ff.

those chapters were written long after Micah's day. Where did the false prophets and their followers find the promises they abrogated to themselves? The answer seems to be, above all, in the liturgy of the temple. That liturgy, so far as we are acquainted with it at all, is embedded in the Book of Psalms, much of which seems to have formed part of "the hymn-book of the first temple" (just as much as of the second, postexilic temple).

In Christian circles we are familiar with the fact that a considerable number of Psalms are not only prophetic in character, but find their fulfilment very adequately in the work of Christ; indeed, the New Testament supports such an interpretation. Psalm 2, for example, has often been called a "Messianic psalm"; and it is associated plainly with our Lord in several places in the New Testament.[3] Psalm 110, again, which links God's king with that ancient king of Jerusalem, Melchizedek, is thoroughly discussed in the Epistle to the Hebrews, and invariably in terms of the person of Christ. But we should not suppose that such Psalms were intended as a sort of pen-portrait, in order that contemporaries of Jesus of Nazareth should be able to recognize in him their Messiah; rather, they set out the pattern of what the ideal king in Jerusalem ought to be like — and when Jesus at last came, the first Christians realized that he, and only he, lived up to the pattern. If, however, we study the individual statements in such Psalms, we can see that many of them could have been true of the kings of Judah; indeed, most of them are fair descriptions of the founder of the dynasty: David himself. God did undeniably enthrone David as his king on Zion (cf. Psalm 2:6), where he did in a sense take up the succession of Melchizedek (cf. Psalm 110:4); David was undoubtedly enabled to break his foes with a rod of iron, shattering them like a clay pot (cf. Psalm 2:9), and to take over foreign nations as his inheritance (cf. Psalm 2:8). There are dimensions, to be sure, greater than those applicable (in a literal fashion, at any rate) to David; Jesus was Son of God in a way that David never was. It is undeniable that the Davidic king was styled the son of God, however, for 2 Samuel 7:12ff. predicates precisely that title of Solomon. Psalm 2, then, we may well suppose, formed part of the coronation liturgy for each successor on David's throne, if the sentence "This day I become your father" (verse 7) offers any clue.[4]

Nathan's prophecy to David, recorded in 2 Samuel 7, indicates that from the very beginning of the dynasty God made wonderful promises to the king, promises which linked together the future of the Jerusalem sanctuary and of the line of David. A single sentence (in verse 14) warned that if a Davidic king did wrong, God would

3. Acts 4:25f., 13:33; Hebrews 1:5, 5:5; 2 Peter 1:17; Revelation 2:26f.
4. Cf. J. H. Eaton, *Psalms: introduction and commentary (TBC:* London, 1967), pp. 31-34.

punish him; the promises, accordingly, though they never failed to point ahead, were conditional to the extent that they might be reversed in any particular generation. The promises were the stipulations of one Party in a covenant the existence of which is evidenced in 2 Samuel 23:5; for his part, the Davidic king must have taken upon himself strict obligations both to obey God's decrees and to serve the interests of God's people. We may make a shrewd guess that the covenant obligations of the king included the duty of maintaining the laws laid down at Sinai, and that thus the Davidic covenant was in some way firmly attached to the Sinai covenant.

The beginning of each reign, therefore, will have seemed a time of high promise, to king and people alike: the option was open to the new king to fulfil his side of the covenant, and then God would surely fulfil his covenanted obligations. Perhaps — or so it is widely conjectured — there was an annual ceremony in which the divine promises were rehearsed in liturgical fashion and claimed afresh. We can understand how it happened that in the process of time the divine promises became more and more emphasized, but the royal obligations more and more muted. Very few men in public life even in our own enlightened times are prepared to admit openly even to errors and mistakes, let alone to total failure to fulfil specific obligations; we have all become somewhat cynical regarding election promises. What king of ancient Judah, then, was going to admit that he had departed from his covenant obligations? And what courtier or priest was going to have the courage to tell the king the truth? All too few, evidently. The great prophets had the perspicacity to see through the facade; but the great majority of the cult-prophets, that is to say those who depended for their livelihood on the whole royally-patronized machinery of temple and sanctuary, conveniently shut their eyes to breaches of the ancient covenant traditions and laws, and pinned their faith on the divine promises they saw written large in the temple liturgies.

The temple rites thus had the effect of bolstering up a partial truth which amounted to a lie.[5] If we today read Psalm 2, for example, as the Word of God, with Christ in our mind's eye, our faith in Christ is stimulated; but if an ancient Judaean priest, prophet or worshipper recited it, equally convinced that it was the Word of God, but applying it automatically to the monarch of his own day, his faith was stimulated in quite the wrong direction, and he became dogmatically convinced that God would grant miraculous victory to Judah in the immediate future. He certainly became blind to political realities, and indeed historical realities too.

5. Did the ritual, as it developed under the monarchy, gradually play down the king's responsibilities? Psalm 89, at least, would suggest otherwise — note verses 30ff. in particular. This psalm was probably composed in consequence of some national disaster, however.

The temple cult, therefore, in some sense became the target of attack for several of the Old Testament prophets. Its foundation was sound, and its liturgy was sacred; but in practice it was proving a hindrance to true religion, despite the ethical instruction it undoubtedly incorporated. They saw too that since Nathan's prophecy had linked the continuance of the temple with the continuance of the royal line and also of the nation, there was a widespread popular conviction that so long as the prescribed sacrifices and rites continued, all was automatically well with the nation and its rulers. Ritual had taken over the place of religion. Hence the outspoken words of several prophets in criticism or condemnation of the ritual; of course, their words became doubly vehement when that ritual was visibly contaminated by Canaanite practices into the bargain, as was particularly the case in the Northern Kingdom. Thus Hosea 2:11ff. reads: "I (the LORD) will put a stop to her merrymaking, her pilgrimages and new moons, her sabbaths and festivals . . . I will punish her for the holy days when she burnt sacrifices to the Baalim." Isaiah said no word about Baal-worship in this context, but the tone is the same:

> Your countless sacrifices, what are they to me?
>   says the LORD.
> I am sated with whole-offerings of rams,
>   and the fat of buffaloes;
> I have no desire for the blood of bulls,
>   of sheep and of he-goats.
> Whenever you come to enter my presence —
> who asked you for this?
> No more shall you trample my courts.
>   The offer of your gifts is useless,
> the reek of sacrifice is abhorrent to me.
> New moons and sabbaths and assemblies,
> sacred seasons and ceremonies, I cannot endure.
> I cannot tolerate your new moons and your festivals;
> they have become a burden to me,
>   and I can put up with them no longer.
> When you lift your hands outspread in prayer,
> I will hide my eyes from you.
> Though you offer countless prayers,
>   I will not listen.

(Isaiah 1:11ff.)

Several other prophetic passages deplore the elaboration of cultic practices which had gradually taken place, and recall with nostalgia the simplicity of worship which had characterized the era of Moses.[6]

---

6. Cf. Jeremiah 7:21ff.; Amos 5:21-25. On the vexed question of the interpretation of such passages, see especially D. E. Cowan, "Prophets, Deuteronomy and the syncretistic cult in Israel" in J. C. Rylaarsdam (ed.), *Transitions in Biblical Scholarship* (Chicago, 1968), pp. 93-112.

After the division of Solomon's kingdom, the Northern Kingdom did not of course look to David's line for salvation, but nevertheless a very similar theology of hope developed there. The monarchy was no very stable institution in the North, but there too sanctuary and king were firmly bound together, as we can see from the interesting altercation between the prophet Amos and the priest Amaziah at Bethel, recorded in Amos 7. Amos predicted doom for sanctuary and king alike; and in angry reply, Amaziah told him, "Be off, you seer! Off with you to Judah! . . . But never prophesy again at Bethel, for this is the king's sanctuary."

That the same theologically motivated political optimism was to be found in the Northern Kingdom is evidenced by Amos, again. Evidently there existed a popular expectation of "the day of the LORD" (cf. Amos 5:18). Such an expectation runs through the Old Testament and on into the New; but what did it signify for the eighth century citizen of Israel? Whatever precisely he expected, there is no doubt that it was an optimistic anticipation, in view of Amos's warning that the day of Yahweh would in fact mean darkness and gloom. The origins and content of this item of Israelite belief have been much discussed and debated, but it seems not improbable that the background to it was provided by ancient days of battle, when Yahweh had given his people victory over their enemies, especially perhaps under the heroes of the Book of Judges.[7] If this be so, then once again we can see how political optimism grew out of faith in Yahweh; what he had done for Israel long before, through the leadership of a Deborah or a Gideon, he would surely do again through the medium of the present king in Samaria. If some realists pointed out that Israel's armies were puny compared with the mighty Assyrian war machine, the ready reply — so convincingly theological! — was that Gideon had won the day against Midian with a mere 300 men in the face of a colossal army.

By the year 721 B.C., the Day of the Lord had indeed dawned for the Northern Kingdom — and it had proved to be utter darkness and unrelieved gloom for Israel, as Amos had predicted. The Assyrians swept away the monarchy, and any Israelite false hopes attached to the person of the king were for ever crushed. Twenty years later Judah almost suffered the same fate, but not quite. Jerusalem, almost alone of the cities of Judah, escaped the ravages of the Assyrian soldiery, and King Hezekiah managed to retain his throne. From our standpoint in history, we can see that both Micah and Isaiah were vindicated, ultimately; the latter had prophesied that Jerusalem would not fall, since the temple still symbolized the reality of Yahweh's presence in it, whereas Micah had prophesied that Jerusalem's days were numbered, and that its wickedness inevitably

7. On the Day of Yahweh, see especially G. von Rad, *Old Testament Theology* (ET Edinburgh and London, 1962-5), vol. ii, p. 119-125.

presaged its fall. Isaiah's prophecy was fulfilled in 701 B.C.; Micah's had to wait a full century more for its fulfilment. "The mills of God grind slowly." But all too many citizens of Judah in 700 B.C. and the century that followed refused to believe that Micah had been a true prophet;[8] on the contrary, they turned Isaiah's prediction into a dogma that would hold true for all time and in all circumstances. God, they were convinced, would *never* let Jerusalem fall into enemy hands; the enemy would always be defeated, if only at the very gates. Jerusalem had never once fallen since David had captured it some 300 years before, and the very passage of time increased their convictions. But Isaiah's words of moral condemnation were conveniently forgotten.

Not even Nebuchadrezzar's capture of Jerusalem in 597 B.C. provided a challenge to such dogmas; the Babylonian conqueror left the city and the temple standing, and did not even put an end to the Davidic dynasty, although he did deport King Jehoiachin. It would even seem that this event, political disaster though it was, was hailed as yet another triumph for the dogma! It is undoubtedly true that Jeremiah, both before and after 597 B.C., was confronted by arrogant false prophets to an unprecedented extent.[9] He, more than any of his predecessors, felt the menace of false religion, the threat of "falsehood" (Hebrew *sheqer*), as a recent book, more literally, describes it.[10]

Jeremiah's response to this situation enables us to discern the general tenor of his opponents' teaching; and we sometimes read their statements *expressis verbis*. One of their catchwords was evidently "This place is the temple of the LORD, the temple of the LORD, the temple of the LORD."[11] Another favourite phrase, as they stood in the fancied security of the temple courts, was "We are safe", or (more literally) "We are delivered" (Jeremiah 7:10). Jeremiah's bitter commentary on this dictum was that (for the moment!) they *were* "safe" — safe to proceed with all the immoral and unethical behaviour to which they were addicted, which he represents as oppression of the poor, repeated breaches of the covenant laws, and of course idolatrous practices into the bargain.

Secure in unshakeable dogma and the stout temple walls, one prophet, Hananiah by name, only a few months after the débâcle of 597, confidently predicted that within two years all would be well — the exile over, King Jehoiachin home again, and the yoke of Babylon broken. History records that Hananiah died two months later —

8. See below, pp. 243ff.
9. See below, p. 256.
10. T. W. Overholt, *The threat of falsehood: a study in the theology of the Book of Jeremiah* (*SBT* ii, 16: London, 1970).
11. Jeremiah 7:4. One is inevitably reminded of our Lord's words about "vain repetition" (Matthew 6:7).

an event which in itself vindicated Jeremiah's more sombre prophecies — but also that it was not until the much more crushing national disaster of 587 B.C. that the voice of false prophecy was finally stilled.[12]

One significant insight of Jeremiah's into the nature and character of this false religion is recorded in Jeremiah 7:8ff. Shrines like the Jerusalem temple had long been the places to which those guilty of homicide might flee for refuge; if their deed had been accidental manslaughter, the sanctuary proved to be a sanctuary indeed, but if murder were proven, then the slayer must be taken from the altar and handed over to the avenger of blood. Jeremiah claimed that the complacent Jerusalem populace was in effect gaining unlawful asylum from the penalty of their deliberately evil deeds by resorting to the Jerusalem temple. The temple, therefore, had become "a robbers' cave".[13] The logic of his position was of course that the guilty must be, and would inevitably be, dragged from the sanctuary to which they had resorted. The temple of Yahweh gave shelter only to those who deserved asylum.

We may allow the prophets to draw our attention to another area of ancient Israel's life and thought which sometimes tends to be forgotten. In a critique of false religion, Isaiah 29:13f. enunciates Yahweh's view of Judah thus:

> Because this people approach me with their mouths
>> and honour me with their lips
>> while their hearts are far from me,
> and their religion is but a precept of men, learnt by rote,
> therefore I will yet again shock this people,
> adding shock to shock:
> and the wisdom of their wise men shall vanish
> and the discernment of the discerning shall be lost.

Jeremiah also had a word for the wise (Jeremiah 8:9f.):

> The wise are put to shame, they are dismayed and have lost their wits. They have spurned the word of the LORD, and what sort of wisdom is theirs? . . . Prophets and priests are frauds, every one of them.

These passages show that the Old Testament prophets had their criticisms of a professional group who stood outside the more religious and cultic circles of priests and prophets. The term "wise" and "wise men" (Hebrew *chakham, chakhamim*) do not always in the Old Testament designate a profession, but very often they refer

---

12. Jeremiah 28 describes the events outlined in this paragraph.
13. Cf. T. W. Overholt, *op. cit.,* pp. 17f.

specifically to what we may call the administrative class in the kingdom — the circles which provided the king with his advisers and
ministers of state. These circles also had some educational functions,
though we are ill informed as to the exact nature of the educational
system. Perhaps the nearest equivalent in English to the Hebrew
chakhamim is the word "intelligentsia", which suggests not only
people occupying intellectually demanding positions in society but
also those who take a certain pride in the fact. Without doubt book
learning was much prized in the ancient world, and the "wise" were
the men who both studied books and produced them. In Judah (as
often elsewhere) the king was their patron. The Book of Proverbs
testifies to the patronage of both Solomon and Hezekiah, and also to
the involvement of the professional "wise men" in the collection and
publication of proverbial material.[14] It is interesting, moreover, that
Proverbs 30f. offers material which is associated with non-Israelites.
In fact, the wisdom movement in Judah and Israel was simply part
of a much more widespread phenomenon of the ancient world. We
may observe that the fullest biblical description of the equipment of
the professional wise man occurs in the context of a foreign court
(although the wise men happened to be Jewish). Daniel and his com-
panions at the Babylonian court are described as "at home in all
branches of knowledge, well-informed, intelligent, and fit for the
service in the royal court"; they were to be instructed "in the
literature and language of the Chaldaeans", and "their training was
to last for three years" (Daniel 1:4f.).

The international character of wisdom circles is fairly obvious
simply from a perusal of the Book of Proverbs. Many individual
proverbs could be shared with virtually any nation of any period of
history — they frequently offer advice of a timeless and universal
character. Much of the material is purely secular in character,
although a verse at the beginning of the book indicates that the
essential basis of wisdom and wise conduct is true religion: "The
fear of the LORD is the beginning of knowledge" (1:7). Apart from a
certain amount of material which mentions Yahweh by name,
much of Proverbs could be paralleled from a variety of ancient
wisdom documents from Mesopotamia and Egypt.[15] But we must
not suppose that a fair quantity of "secular" content and of
"pagan" affinities renders such literature of little or no religious
value — Proverbs is in the canon of Holy Scripture, and rightly so.
The prophets certainly did not attack the practice of wisdom as such;
on the contrary, they made use of its methods on occasions, and very
effectively: see for instance Isaiah 28:23-29 and Jeremiah 17:5-11,

14. Cf. Proverbs 1:1, 22:17, 24:23, 25:1.
15. See E. Jones, *Proverbs and Ecclesiastes: introduction and commentary (TBC:* London,
1961), pp. 32-41, for a list of examples of kindred material.

passages which would be equally at home in the Book of Proverbs. Amos's condemnation of the nations begins with a phraseology borrowed from proverbial material: "For three transgressions . . . and for four . . ." (Amos 1:3, 6, 9 etc.).[16] Psalm 1 can well be described as a "wisdom psalm"; which fact shows that wisdom concepts and techniques found their way (by whatever route) into the temple liturgy too. We may next instance the Book of Judges as a whole, which is the product of a wise man, that is to say a man who studied the facts of his country's earlier history, observed that there was a recurring pattern in it, and accordingly offered a philosophy of that history; the Book of Judges is an expanded proverb. Finally, even the Old Testament law-code explicitly speaks of wisdom, thus:

> You must observe (God's statues and laws) carefully, and thereby you will display your wisdom and understanding to other peoples. When they hear about these statutes, they will say, 'What a wise and understanding people this great nation is!'
>
> (Deuteronomy 4:6)

There can be no denying that human wisdom, that is to say the careful, deliberate use of the rational powers of observation and deduction which God has given men, is viewed throughout the Bible as one important medium of divine revelation.

Why then, did an Isaiah and a Jeremiah choose to criticize the professional wise men of their day? The prophets did not attack the office in itself, any more than they attacked the priestly and prophetic offices as such. They recognized that the ordinary citizen could not do without the guidance of the priests, the oracles of the prophets, and the advice of the wise men (cf. Jeremiah 18:18). The wise man's special commodity, this verse shows, was "advice" (Hebrew *etsah*); thus, no less than priests and prophets, he took the future into account, presuming to tell his clients what was likely to happen and how they might best cope with the situation in which they found themselves. We can appreciate, therefore, that the Old Testament prophets observed that too often the wise men were just as guilty as the cultic prophets and the priests of uttering complacent reassurances instead of urgent warnings, and predicting a rosy and unrealistic future.

The potential conflict between the prophetic word from God and the wise man's "advice" can be illustrated from Isaiah's career. When the armies of Israel and Damascus descended upon Judah and besieged Jerusalem, King Ahaz in fright sought advice from his professional counsellors and also from Isaiah. "Do nothing — except trust in God" was the gist of the prophet's advice (Isaiah 7).

---

16. The NEB rendering obscures the numerical phraseology, for which cf. Proverbs 30:15-31.

But the political savants of the day saw salvation in an appeal to
Assyria for help; they knew on rational grounds that this policy
would work, and indeed it did, though at no little cost for Judah.
They provided reasoning where Isaiah offered signs; and Ahaz
preferred the former. The fact is that no man can absolutely predict
the future on the basis of reason; there is always the unpredictable
element, the incalculable factor. The prophets objected, therefore,
to any suggested policy which did not take God into account.
Human reasoning was in itself good and necessary; but it must not
be divorced from submission to the will and purposes of God, or it
would inevitably fail.

In other words, the prophets found a certain arrogance in contemporary wisdom — always a characteristic of the intelligentsia in
society, the more so when they have official, in this case royal,
patronage. The prophets could be particularly scathing about the
wise men of other nations. Edom was renowned for sagacity; but
Jeremiah could say of it: "Is wisdom no longer to be found in
Teman? Have her sages no skill in counsel? Has their wisdom
decayed?" (49:7). The diplomats and politicians of Edom were in
fact helpless in the face of imminent disaster; Jeremiah described the
fate in store for them, and added, "Listen to the LORD's whole purpose against Edom and all his plans against the people of Teman"
(verse 20). The policies which count in history, said Jeremiah, are
those of God, not man.

The arrogance of some of Judah's wise men is rebuked in Isaiah
5:21: "Shame on you! You who are wise in your own eyes and
prudent in your own esteem." At the personal level, we can see in
the Book of Job how cruel and immoral an arrogant wisdom can be.
One wonders how many a good man's reputation has been permanently injured by the mechanical application of proverbs like
"There's no smoke without fire".

Reverting to the case of Ahaz and Isaiah, we observe that the
policy of Ahaz was permitted to be put into effect, even though it
was a foolish and ill-advised stratagem. Much earlier, in David's
reign, there is an interesting story of a piece of brilliant strategy
which was overruled by sheer folly. Absalom needed advice how to
achieve full victory and to secure his newly-won throne, and he
turned to a man whose wisdom was comparable with the oracles of
Yahweh themselves (2 Samuel 16:23). Ahithophel as usual proffered
sound strategy; but Absalom, not content, sought further counsel,
this time from his father's loyal adviser, and heard a different story.
As we study Hushai's words (17:7ff.), we find a skilful mixture of
emotive language, exaggeration and flattery — and it found a ready
ear. Why? "It was the LORD's purpose to frustrate Ahithophel's
good advice and so bring disaster upon Absalom" (17:14).

King Rehoboam was another man who could not tell good advice from bad, and it cost him more than half his kingdom (1 Kings 12:1-17); again the historian tells us "the LORD had given this turn to the affair" (verse 15). Israel and Judah might have learned several lessons from such episodes. First, that since Yahweh controlled their history, his revealed word — through his prophets, those who were prophets by vocation rather than profession — was the only sure pointer to the future. Secondly, the wise men could only extrapolate from past and present, and therefore their predictions should always be presented with due modesty and heeded with caution. Thirdly, the very patrons of wisdom — and even Solomon himself — were capable of the most egregious follies. The first king of Israel once confesed, "I have been a fool, I have been sadly in the wrong" (1 Samuel 26:21). Even David, whose shrewdness was second to none, was once told to his face, "Your majesty is as wise as the angel of God" — by a women who had just made a complete fool of him (2 Samuel 14:20).

The presumptuous wordly-wise politician was therefore not only the target for the strictures of Isaiah and Jeremiah, but also the living proof of the folly of kings (and few were as weak and/or foolish as the last three kings of Judah). No wonder the prophets sighed for a king who should be victorious in battle, a model of equitable precept and practice, but first and foremost, "in purpose wonderful", a "wonderful counsellor", a "Wonder-Counsellor" (as various modern versions render a familiar phrase from Isaiah 9:6).

We are now in a position to offer some analysis of the false religion which was the chief enemy of the Hebrew monarchy. Basically it consisted in breach of promise, coupled with an untroubled conscience. All the great pre-exilic prophets were deeply conscious of the extent to which their contemporaries in Israel and Judah alike were guilty of breaking their covenanted vows to God. Yet the people's consciences were being dulled by the scrupulous exercise of religious practices. Evil deeds were being hidden under a veneer of piety, and indeed sheltered and thus encouraged by the official religion of the day.

That the people censured by the prophets had "faith" is undeniable; but it was a misplaced faith. To begin with, it represented faith in buildings and rituals rather than in the God whom such buildings and rituals were designed to honour. It was thus a faith in externals; ritual confessions of sin, and the sacrifices prescribed for sin, took the place of sincere self-examination and repentance. Secondly, it consisted of a faith in certain parts of Holy Writ (as it came to be) to the detriment of others; Psalm 2 with all its promise was proudly claimed and appropriated, whereas the Ten Commandments were recited (no doubt) but quietly set aside; Isaiah's prophecies about the temple were on every lip, but his description of his people as a "sinful nation"; a "people loaded with iniquity'' whose sins were ''scarlet'' (Isaiah 1:4, 18) was treated lightly, ignored if not forgotten. All too many people made the false assumption that to possess the Law of God was automatically to honour and obey it (cf. Jeremiah 8:8f.).

The false religion also comprised an uncritical acceptance of dogma. Those who believed that Jerusalem and the temple would never fall could find ancient and genuine prophecies to support their viewpoint; but — as Jeremiah pointed out — the dogma failed the acid test of history, since Shiloh, formerly just as central and sacred to Israel as Jerusalem had now become, lay in ruins for anyone to see (Jeremiah 7:11f.). Even the very Word of God can become false if it is treated as a collection of slogans (political or otherwise) to be employed like magical charms. Jeremiah himself showed a better way; when Hananiah in the name of Yahweh contradicted Jeremiah's predictions and proffered his own instead, the startled Jeremiah did *not* immediately resort to clichés and dogmatic utterances, but on the contrary went away to think the matter over, and did not come back until he had a fresh message from God (Jeremiah 28).

Perhaps most important of all, the type of religion which the prophets repudiated was centred on a false theology, a wrong view of God, a view which probably owed more than was imagined to Canaanite ways of thinking. The Canaanites' concept of deity was cyclic, governed by the seasons of the year but not by the passage of history; thus in a sense it was static, almost timeless. The Old Testament writers insist repeatedly, however, that the God of Israel is the Lord of history and of the whole historical process. This outlook is nowhere more startlingly expressed than in Isaiah 43:16ff., where the prophet first makes reference to the Exodus, that unforgettable event way back in Israel's history, still lovingly and proudly remembered in every Jewish Passover celebration to this day, and having called it to mind, dismisses it thus: ''Cease to dwell on days gone by and to brood over past history. Here and now I will do a new thing''. The challenge follows — ''Can you not perceive it?'' It was this dynamic view of God which characterized the Old Testament prophets; hence they can unblushingly talk of God's ''changing his mind'' or ''repenting''. If God wished to spare the Jerusalem of Isaiah's day, he was not in consequence bound to do the same in Jeremiah's era. ''God is not slavishly bound by his own decisions,'' writes H. W. Hertzberg, ''but is almighty to such an extent that he is Lord even of them. Just as he takes the action of men into consideration in his decisions, so that omnipotence never means that man is deprived of his responsibility, so, too, the election of the king (Saul) is not irrevocable.''[17]

17. H. W. Hertzberg, *I and II Samuel: a commentary (OTL:* London, 1964), p. 126.

But the election of Jerusalem and of the house of David *was* irrevocable, was it not? The Old Testament prophet did not challenge the abiding truth of such divine promises; but he insisted that God could certainly set them aside for so long as he chose to do so, or even transmute them along new channels. So one prophet could predict an exile from the Promised Land of fully seventy years (Jeremiah 29:10), while another could speak of the transfer of the royal covenant promises from David's line to the nation as a whole (Isaiah 55:3ff.).[18] (From the Christian standpoint, we should wish to add that this transfer was again only a temporary measure in God's plans.)

Finally, we can probably deduce from the fact that the Old Testament prophets bracketed "the wise" with priests and false prophets that they were aware of a secularized religion, which operated too much on slogans and mechanical formulae, and which made expediency its god. Anything which took to itself the name of Yahweh but which patently breached the ethic taught in his covenant laws became the target of prophetic denunciation.

The Old Testament prophetic literature is our primary sourcebook for information on the false religion which we have described as the worst enemy of Israel and Judah during the period of the monarchy. Priestly intercession, prophetic forecasts, and the skilfully devised policies of trained diplomats alike failed to divert God's chosen people from the collision course on which they were set. The true prophets did what they could to expose the false religion for what it was, and hence have left on record for posterity an adequate description of it. But in investigating this topic we have, necessarily, looked at the prophets' words in a purely negative way, seeking to find out what they denied, not what they affirmed. They deserve more than that; and we must now make some endeavour to study these unique individuals in their own right, against the background of the history of their times.

---

18. This seems to be the most natural interpretation of the passage. Cf. C. R. North, *The Second Isaiah* (Oxford, 1964), pp. 257f.

Part Three

The Prophets

CHAPTER 22

The Early Period

UP TO this point, we have considered the history of Israel and
Judah largely in terms of kings and their subjects — the rulers
and the ruled. This is a natural enough approach; if there are few
kings in our twentieth century world, we are familiar with the
presidents and prime ministers who exercise similar political
leadership, power and influence. Moreover, it is the approach of our
basic literary sources for the period, the Books of Samuel, Kings and
Chronicles; and much of the extra-biblical material was written in
the name of some ancient king, to celebrate his power and
achievements. But even if we have given pride of place to the kings
of old, and concentrated on the political and the secular, we have
already found it impossible to ignore the prophets entirely. Such
remarkable figures were never easy to ignore! It is now high time we
gave them their rightful place in the narrative. It is surely no
accident, no mere historical coincidence, that the era of the Hebrew
monarchy coincided with the hey-day of the prophets. The compilers
of the Hebrew Bible showed a true insight when they bracketed the
Books of Joshua, Judges, Samuel and Kings with the prophetical
books, and labelled the whole collection "the Prophets". The deeds
of the kings and the words of the prophets can be seen to
interconnect and interplay, from the time of Samuel and Saul until
that of Jeremiah and Zedekiah.[1]

We may readily grant their importance; but who *were* these
individuals? The very word "prophet" is one that today requires
some explanation; and it is very difficult to think of any modern
analogy to the place such men held in ancient Israelite society. We

---

1. Prophecy did not, of course, come to the same abrupt end as did the
monarchy; but the story of the exilic and postexilic prophets does not come within
the scope of this book.

may be sure, however, that unique as they were as individuals, their office was a natural enough one in their own milieu.

The Old Testament itself acknowledges the fact that other deities had their own prophets; Elijah threw out his famous challenge not to the priests of Baal, as we might have expected, but to the Baal prophets. Within the stream of the worship of Yahweh, moreover, there were false prophets as well as true. After the period of Old Testament prophecy had long since expired, we meet Christian prophets in the New Testament; centuries later still there were prophets in Arabia, culminating in the person of Muhammad of Mecca; and J. Lindblom also hails St. Bridget of fourteenth century Sweden as a similar figure. Long before the "classical" prophets of the Old Testament, too, comparable figures were to be found in the ancient Near East. An interesting Egyptian tale about a traveller called Wen-Amun (*c.* 1100 B.C.) relates that at the court of the prince of the Phoenician city of Byblos, not so far from Palestine, a young man was suddenly possessed by the god Amun, and uttered an oracle giving instructions to the prince.[2] Earlier still, and further east, we find a similar situation pertaining in the great city of Mari on the Euphrates, during the eighteenth century B.C.; here too there were individuals who uttered divine oracles at the royal court.[3]

Professor Lindblom describes all such prophetic figures thus: "There are *homines religiosi* to whom religious experiences as such are the essence of their religious life. Personal communion with God, prayer, devotion, moral submission to the divine will are the principal traits in their religious attitude. That which distinguishes a prophet from other *homines religiosi* is that he never keeps his experiences to himself; he always feels compelled to announce to others what he has seen and heard. The prophet is a man of the public word. He is a speaker and a preacher. The prophet is an inspired man . . . The prophet is compelled by the spirit".[4]

Such a general description fits the Old Testament prophets very aptly. But let us turn specifically to the period of the monarchy, and to the prophets of Israel and Judah. The first individual figure that confronts us is that of Samuel. He was certainly a prophet, but apparently also a priest and a "judge", and it is an impossible task for the historian to distinguish between the various roles that he played. In any case, he lived at a unique point in Israel's history. But contemporary with him, there were also bands of prophets in Israel, one of which is described for us in 1 Samuel 10:5: "a company of prophets   led by lute, harp, fife, and drum, and filled

---

2. Cf. *ANET*, pp. 25-29.
3. Cf. A. Lods in H. H. Rowley (ed.), *Studies in Old Testament Prophecy* (Edinburgh, 1950), pp. 103-110.
4. Cf. J. Lindblom, *Prophecy in Ancient Israel* (Oxford, 1962), pp. 1f.

with prophetic rapture''. These folk were by no means unique; they play a very minor rôle in the story, and the implication of the chapter is that the biblical writer did not wholly approve of them. We do not know anything about their leadership or organization (if they had any). The spotlight rests on the unique individual, Samuel.

When Saul was made king, Samuel lost his rôle as political leader, but retained his religious rôle, that of prophet-priest. He did not, however, choose to "opt out" of the political arena altogether. At the very beginning of Saul's reign, he executed a document which in some sense was intended to hinder any despotic behaviour on the part of the king. The New English Bible rendering of the relevant verse (1 Samuel 10:25) tells us that "Samuel then explained to the people the nature of a king, and made a written record of it on a scroll which he deposited before the LORD". This might be taken to refer to some such warning about the despotic tendencies of kings, as is set out in 1 Samuel 8: 11-18. The Revised Standard Version, however, speaks of "the rights and duties of the kingship". The verse, says J. Mauchline, "is concerned with the rights and duties of an anointed king united with Yahweh and his people in covenantal obligation"; and Professor Mauchline suggests that whenever the king afterwards worshipped at that shrine (Mizpah), and set eyes on the document, he was reminded of the charge laid upon him by Samuel in Yahweh's name.[5] One is reminded of the passage in Deuteronomy 17:14-20. The Hebrew monarchy was from the start a "constitutional" monarchy. The king was bound by covenant, and the man who ensured that this should be so was Samuel, who may well, by practice and maybe precept too, have laid the foundation for the distinctive rôle of the prophets who followed him. The prophet was to be not only the man who uttered oracles at court (as at Byblos and Mari) but also the man who constituted himself the people's watchdog, the Ombudsman of Israel and Judah. He would keep a keen eye on any breach of the laws of Yahweh — by king or people.

Before long, there was a bitter quarrel between Samuel and Saul, resulting from two incidents which have been represented as the new king's attempt to make himself master of both priests and prophets.[6] Be that as it may, two aspects of this quarrel are of particular interest. The first is that both incidents occurred in the context of foreign wars, one with the Philistines, the other with the Amalekites. The second important feature is the result of the quarrel — the fact that Samuel proceeded to anoint another man, David, as king of Israel. In other words, Samuel set two further precedents for future

---

5. J. Mauchline, *1 and 2 Samuel (NCB:* London, 1971), pp. 102f.
6. See H. L. Ellison, *The Prophets of Israel* (Exeter, 1969), p. 26. The incidents are recounted in 1 Samuel 13:8-14 and 15:1-33.

prophets; he established their right both to pronounce God's word about international affairs, and to take revolutionary action, if need be, in their own political context. One can well understand why both kings and their secular advisers came to view prophets with suspicion.

The in-built tensions between prophet and king were muted during the reign of David; there might well have been conflict between David and Nathan, in view of the latter's strictures over the Bathsheba affair, but since David proved willing to humble himself (having after all pronounced judgement upon himself), no quarrel ensued. This particular episode concerned private morality, we might be tempted to think; but adultery and murder were specifically forbidden by Israel's covenant laws, and Nathan was a true prophet, a true guardian of the covenant, when he challenged David's behaviour.

Nathan also figured prominently in another matter. 2 Samuel 7 reports that when David proposed to built a temple, Nathan intervened and dissuaded him; at the same time, he informed the king that God had chosen him to found a dynasty. Thus David was signally favoured, where Saul had been rejected. W. Zimmerli has written: "when we set this promise in the wider context of the promise of God to Israel, we can see that it expresses a new, and hitherto unknown, demonstration of the gracious attitude of God to his people and their king. This history of Yahweh's saving action towards Israel was thereby continued".[7]

In the sequel, Nathan himself took a leading part in the accession of David's son Solomon, fulfilling (in part) the prediction made to David, but also indicating God's choice in the matter, that is to say which son of David was to succeed him.

In all these various interventions on the part of Samuel and Nathan, we observe another hallmark of the prophet: his message from Yahweh very frequently embraced a future as well as a present dimension. Samuel had predicted Saul's loss of the throne; Nathan predicted both the death of David's first son by Bathsheba, and the fact of the dynasty which would presently succeed to David's throne. Prophecy always included a measure of prescience; if second sight tends to be largely discredited by our materialistic contemporaries, the fact remains that some such ability has been widely attested for seers and soothsayers of many epochs, and not merely for the biblical prophets. Whatever approach we may adopt to Scripture, men like the prophets are not to be judged by normal standards.

Our information about Nathan is severely limited, and we know

7. W. Zimmerli, *The Law and the Prophets* (ET Oxford, 1965), p. 63. Zimmerli's approach contrasts with that of a number of scholars who have rejected the historicity of much of 2 Samuel 7. Cf. Lindblom, *op. cit.*, pp. 76f. See also A. Weiser, *ZAW* 77 (1965), pp. 153-168.

even less about the functions and activities of his contemporary, Gad. He is referred to as "David's seer", in addition to the title "prophet" (cf. 2 Samuel 24:11), and it seems probable that he was a sort of private chaplain to the king; he first appears at David's side in the days of the latter's fugitive existence in southern Judah (1 Samuel 22:5), long before he gained the throne. In the narrative recounted in 2 Samuel 24, Joab chose to approach the king via the good offices of Gad, which again suggests that there was a close personal relationship between David and Gad. Gad left one permanent legacy to the whole nation, however; it was he who instructed David to set up an altar on the threshing-floor of Araunah the Jebusite (2 Samuel 24:18), thus making sacred the spot where the temple of Solomon would be erected.

No doubt there were prophets during Solomon's reign, and no doubt they disapproved of some of Solomon's actions; but there is no record of any prophet's having confronted him with his misdeeds. Possibly the divine warning contained in 1 Kings 11:11ff. was delivered to Solomon through the agency of some prophet, but the text does not say so; it is equally possible that the passage is the historian's comment on Solomon's conduct, but we may confidently deduce from the sequel that this was a prophetic viewpoint held at the time.

Before Solomon died and was succeeded by Rehoboam, a prophet from Shiloh called Ahijah had already taken steps to divide the kingdom. He it was who not only predicted that division, but conveyed the word of Yahweh to Jeroboam that he was to be king of the northern tribes. He tore a new cloak into twelve pieces, and handed ten of them to Jeroboam as a symbol and pledge of what Yahweh purposed for Jeroboam and for Israel (1 Kings 11:26-39). Such symbolic action is another characteristic of the Old Testament prophets. The torn robe signified that there could be no escaping the word of God; what God willed, must be. Thus Ahijah pronounced the irrevocable fate of the united Hebrew kingdom. Political realists of the time might have foreseen that the tensions within the kingdom must inevitably lead to division; but the prophets did not operate on the ground of political analysis and assessment. For Ahijah, the imminent disruption of the monarchy was not a political inevitability, but God's plan and decision in the light of Solomon's idolatry. Solomon, in other words, had breached the solemn covenant with Yahweh; he had in some measure failed to observe the First Commandment, and to some degree oppressed the covenant people.

Ahijah was a northern prophet — Shiloh lay in the tribal territory of Ephraim — but there is a brief indication that his view of the matter was shared by his Judaean counterpart, Shemaiah. When Rehoboam mustered his troops to do battle with the upstart,

Jeroboam, the prophet Shemaiah dissuaded him from major hostilities with a brief but pungent oracle from Yahweh: "You shall not go up to make war on your kinsmen the Israelites. Return to your homes" (1 Kings 12:24).

Thus from the earliest years of the Hebrew monarchy, we find prophets making kings and deposing them, dividing a kingdom and stopping a war. Such men were far from being preachers of pious platitudes, eloquent in the pulpit and ineffective outside it. They were men whom kings and statesmen had to reckon with. Jeroboam might have supposed that Ahijah had allowed him *carte blanche* in Israel; if so, he soon discovered his error. He endeavoured to make the shrines of Dan and Bethel attractive rivals to the Jerusalem temple, and in doing so appears to have catered to all the idolatrous and syncretistic tastes of his citizenry. The priesthood became his lackeys, and raised no objections; but prophets such as Ahijah were scandalized, and voiced their objections in no uncertain manner (see 1 Kings 13:1-14:18). Jeroboam might have been known to posterity as the man who created the kingdom of Israel; instead he is "the man who made Israel to sin". He might have founded a long-lived dynasty to rival David's in Judah; instead, his son Nadab could hold the throne for only a couple of years before falling by conspiracy and assassination. There was to be tension, if not downright hostility, between king and prophet throughout the history of the northern kingdom. Jeroboam sought to place one prophet under arrest (1 Kings 13:4); Ahab went so far as to imprison another (1 Kings 22:26f.); even the great Elijah had to flee from a royal threat to his life (1 Kings 19:1ff.), while Amos was served with a deportation order (Amos 7:12). Equally, prophets might at times take strong action against a king, as when Elisha organized the *coup d'état* which overthrew the dynasty of Omri. The fact that prophets were not eliminated altogether in itself testifies to the fact that none of their contemporaries could deny that God spoke through them. They were to a large extent shielded by the power seen to reside in them, and also by popular esteem — even when the people paid little heed to what they were saying. The alternative policy was to establish other prophets who could contradict them, even ridicule them; in part the kings of Israel (and Judah too, in due course) may have created the phenomenon of false prophets. At all events, they certainly fostered the phenomenon by their patronage.

We have already considered a number of examples of the predictive powers of the prophets. Sometimes they merely indicated what would happen; sometimes their very words created the event they predicted, as when Ahijah in effect offered the northern kingdom to Jeroboam. The fact that such predictions were made cannot be doubted by any serious investigator. But 1 Kings 13:2 contains a particularly remarkable prognostication. An unnamed prophet from

Judah, we are told, confronted Jeroboam at the altar of the Bethel shrine and cried out as follows: "O altar, altar! This is the word of the Lord: 'Listen! A child shall be borne to the house of David, named Josiah. He will sacrifice upon you the priests of the hill-shrines who make offerings upon you, and he will burn human bones upon you'." Jeroboam lived before 900 B.C.; the Josiah who fulfilled the prophecy lived fully 300 years later, long after the down-fall of the kingdom of Israel. What are we to make of a passage like this? Did the prophets really make predictions at such long range and in such remarkable detail as this?

Perhaps they did, on occasions. There might be parallels in history — there were those, for example, who (on theological grounds) predicted the creation of the modern State of Israel many years before it came into being, or even loomed on the horizon. Moreover, we must at all costs resist the temptation to reduce the prophets to twentieth century political commentators. However, the reference to Josiah is not the only surprise in the chapter, and a paragraph from H. L. Ellison's book *The Prophets of Israel* is worth quoting. He writes (pp. 22f.):

> The story in 1 Kings 13 has obviously been edited, probably by the compiler of the book, for the mention of Samaria (verse 32), which was not founded until the time of Omri (1 Kings 16:24), must be an adaptation of the prophet's words to later terminology, a practice we find more often in the Old Testament than is normally suspected. Since the men of Bethel recognized the fulfilment of the prophecy (2 Kings 23:17) but showed no recognition of the name, it seems likely that 'Josiah by name' (verse 2) is also an editorial addition pointing forward to the fulfilment.

Certainly in the case of the historical books of the Old Testament, and very probably in the case of the prophetic literature, we have to reckon with editorial activity, undertaken not to destroy or overlay the original wording of earlier documents or of prophetic oracles, but rather to bring home to the readers the importance and rele-vance of their message. (In the same way, Old Testament quotations are sometimes modified and adapted in the New, for a new genera-tion of readers.) It is therefore perfectly legitimate, and sometimes indeed essential, for the modern critical historian to assess what is "original" and what "secondary" — such a decision need not be, and should not be, a value judgement at all — in Old Testament records. Nevertheless, it is to a large extent a subjective exercise, yielding uncertain and debatable results.

Half a century after Ahijah's time, we meet the formidable char-acter of Elijah, who confronts the reader of 1 Kings with the same startling impact with which he confronted King Ahab, son of Omri, who founded the third dynasty of the kings of Israel. With the nar-

ratives about Elijah and Elisha, the modern critical historian meets
not only a literary, but an historical question of some moment.
Prediction is a relatively rare phenomenon, but is at least well
authenticated as such; but what is the historian to make, for
instance, of the resuscitation of dead children, or the destruction of
whole bands of troops by fire from heaven? As a Christian man,
convinced of the plenary inspiration of the Scriptures, he may accept
the factual accuracy of such narratives on faith; but as a scientific
historian, he is compelled to admit that such events stand outside
normal human experience, and would be rejected as legendary if
they appeared outside the Canon of Holy Writ. Needless to say, the
critical historian who is *not* convinced of the plenary inspiration of
Scripture is almost bound to view such stories as legends. Much
depends, then, on one's theological viewpoint and presuppositions.

Some of the narratives are patient of "natural" explanations, it
must be admitted. Professor Gray, for instance, has observed that
the actual wording of the story recounted in 1 Kings 17:17-24 permits us to suppose that the son of the widow of Zarephath, though at
death's door, never actually died.[8] A careful study of the Hebrew
statements confirms that this is so. If modern medical science has its
difficulties about defining the precise moment of death, it must be
allowed that the ancients will not have been able, and perhaps will
not have wished, to draw too precise a dividing line between a mori-
bund and a dead condition. For the biblical writer, 1 Kings 17 in
any case depicts a miracle, and whether it was a miracle of healing or
a miracle of resurrection was for him of little consequence.

The crucial narrative involving a miracle in the chapters about
Elijah is to be found in 1 Kings 18, where the contest on Mount Carmel is described. The chapter has been very widely discussed and
debated.[9] There is little agreement among scholars as to what
elements are "original" and which are "secondary", nor what is
historical and what legendary, nor even what the purpose and the
function of the narrative was. But here is a narrative where the
critical historian *qua* historian is in no position to shrug his shoulders
and say that it all depends on one's attitude to the Bible whether one
believes the story or rejects it. Let us assume that we choose to reject
the story: fire did *not* fall from heaven and consume Elijah's
sacrifice. Very well; then it follows that Elijah did not win his contest
with the Baal prophets — for the whole scene demands that something remarkable happened to convince the populace that Elijah was
in the right, and to persuade them to slaughter the Baal prophets. If
nothing remarkable happened, the only logical conclusion,

8. Cf. J. Gray, *Kings,* pp. 382f.
9. See for instance D. R. Ap-Thomas, *PEQ* 92 (1960), pp. 146-155; H. H.
Rowley, *Men of God* (London, 1963), pp. 37-65.

ultimately, is that the contest itself never happened . . . and before long one has emptied the whole story of Elijah of all its content, and reduced the great prophet to negligible proportions. With all great figures of history, in the Bible or outside it, one is forced to find some basis for the reputation for greatness. Many legends came to surround Alexander the Great, but no historian could deny his greatness — it was the greatness which attracted the legends. But if we deny the events of 1 Kings 18 *in toto,* we have nothing adequate left to support the greatness of Elijah.

The late Professor Rowley has left us an excellent common-sense summary. His approach to the Bible is not doctrinaire, and he is quite willing to consider the possibility of legend, but against those who "have thought to dissolve the story into pure fabrication" he maintains that "what precisely happened it is impossible for us now to say; but that something remarkable happened is overwhelmingly sure". He goes on to show the insuperable difficulties in historical reconstruction for those who deny it, and finally asserts: "Hence it seems impossible to escape the certainty that *something* remarkable happened on Mount Carmel, something which not alone in Elijah's eyes vindicated his faith, but which vindicated it in the eyes of the people also, something so remarkable that the prophets of Baal were discredited and slain."[10]

We may cite Rowley once more to good effect. "Without Moses," he wrote, "the religion of Yahwism as it figured in the Old Testament would never have been born. Without Elijah it would have died."[11] This is a strongly-worded statement, but not too strong, surely, when we consider the historical background of the Carmel incident. Ahab's queen, Jezebel, not content with the amount of idolatrous activity that was already in vogue at shrines like Dan and Bethel, was bent on making the worship of Yahweh, the God of Israel, subordinate to the worship of her own native deity, Melqart of Tyre.[12] We may be sure that the final result of her policy, if it had succeeded, would have been the slow disappearance of the religion of Yahweh — in Israel, at least, if not in Judah. The faith was in jeopardy; so a prophet arose to meet the crisis, a man who was utterly devoted to the covenant with Yahweh, whose First Commandment stated unambiguously: "You shall have no other god to set against me" (Exodus 20:3). So great was the prophet's sense of peril that he ruthlessly exterminated the prophets of the hated foreign deity. We have already seen how Elijah's single-

10. H. H. Rowley, *op. cit.,* pp. 59ff. It should perhaps be added that there is some little objective evidence for the historicity of the chapter, in that the great drought was also reported by the historian Menander of Ephesus, as is reported by Josephus (*Ant.* viii, 13, 2).

11. *Ibid.,* pp. 64f.

12. See above, p. 80.

minded devotion to the covenant led to a prophetic feud with the ruling dynasty which resulted in the overthrow of the latter some years later, in the time of Elisha's ministry.

The First Commandment was not the only one to interest Elijah, however; the same covenant law-code prohibited murder and the giving of false evidence, and Elijah was just as concerned to ensure that the royal court should observe this aspect of the covenant too. Naboth, the Jezreel land-owner, was not murdered in the normal sense of the term, to be sure; he was executed quite legally, although an innocent man. But the legal indictment was procured by deliberate, malicious, false evidence, at the instigation of the queen, Jezebel. 1 Kings 21 says nothing of the fate of the two rogues whose voices actually gave the false testimony; the word of God commissioned Elijah to pin the blame where it really belonged — on Jezebel, and on King Ahab who had turned a blind eye to her deliberate breach of the covenant with Yahweh.

Elijah was no "private chaplain" to the king, at Ahab's beck and call. Ahab saw that it was politic not to replace the slaughtered Baal prophets, so he took care to organize a body of men who would prophesy in the name of Yahweh. We need not doubt that they were sincere men; their leader, Zedekiah by name, showed a genuine anger when another man threw doubt on the accuracy of his predictions (1 Kings 22:24). Nevertheless, the fact remains that their message to the king was what he wanted to hear — a prophecy of victory in battle. How could it be otherwise when their bread and butter depended on his goodwill? One of their number, Micaiah, had already earned the king's displeasure by showing some independence of thought, as Ahab's naïve remark to Jehoshaphat of Judah makes plain: "He prophesies no good for me; never anything but evil" (1 Kings 22:8). We are not told how Ahab had responded previously to gloomy prophecies from Micaiah, but we may guess that his response was designed to serve as a warning, both to him and to any other prophets of an independent turn of mind. His last prediction to Ahab, at any rate, earned him a spell in prison, on a "prison diet of bread and water" (verse 27).

1 Kings 22 is a fascinating chapter in several respects. How, for instance, did Jehoshaphat come to suspect that Ahab's 400 prophets were not all that they seemed? Like any other prophet, they did the right things, enacting a parable to symbolize Ahab's predicted victory. How was it that when Micaiah arrived and gave exactly the same prophecy as the other had done, Ahab accused him of telling lies?[13] Why, when he did tell the truth, did Jehoshaphat and Ahab alike proceed into battle without further consideration? It should

13. H. L. Ellison, *op. cit.*, pp. 40ff. should be consulted for plausible suggestions and useful discussion.

have been clear by now that the true prophets of Yahweh character-istically spoke in terms of judgement and warning, and only rarely in terms of blessing and promise. Ahab, it seems, was given to wishful thinking, and in his enthusiasm he carried Jehoshaphat along with him. Ahab did take the precaution of disguise, of course, but in spite of it, the ensuing battle saw him killed by a stray arrow, fired at random, which "just happened" to find a weak point in the king's armour. We are left to guess what happened to Ahab's prophets; Ahab's successors — with good reason — seem to have distrusted them, to judge by 2 Kings 3:13, and they fade into the background. Ahab's son and successor Ahaziah sought to get divine advice from outside Israel altogether (cf. 2 Kings 1), but the four kings who followed him were all willing to consult Elisha.

Many of Elisha's activities are similar in character to those of earlier prophets, and we need not study the narratives of 2 Kings in detail. We may observe one point of special interest, however; the man who organized what turned out to be a bloody *coup d'état* gained a reputation for his willingness to help simple folk in simple situa-tions, as several stories about him bear witness. Was this a case of Jekyll and Hyde? Not at all; it was the national covenant with Yahweh which governed his thinking and behaviour, as it did all the true prophets of the Old Testament. This had now become the touch-stone; those who kept that covenant deserved covenant kind-ness, but those who, like Ahab and his court, had spurned it could expect no covenant mercy, but only fearful judgement. The prophet divided the nation — in accordance with the word of God received by his master Elijah (1 Kings 19:17f.).

The Books of Kings are silent about prophecy in Judah during this period. It is always dangerous to argue from silence, but it seems a natural assumption that there were no prominent prophets in Judah between Nathan and Isaiah. 2 Chronicles indicates that they certainly existed, and seeks to give the gist of their message from time to time; but the very fact that the author of Chronicles recounts a story of a letter from Elijah to a king of Judah tells its own tale — that Judah had no prophet of Elijah's stature.

CHAPTER 23

The Eighth Century

B EFORE the eighth century dawned, then, prophecy in Judah and more particularly in Israel had already had a long and impressive history. But had prophecy died out with Elisha, we should be very much the poorer, and so would the Old Testament, because a large portion of it bears the names, and offers us the teachings, of the so-called "writing" prophets, none of whom appeared before the eighth century B.C. Four of them are very frequently bracketed together as "the eighth-century prophets" — Amos and Hosea, in the North, Isaiah and Micah in Judah. (This listing of the four names may serve to make the point that the prophetic books of the Old Testament are not altogether in chronological order, as we have them.)

As it happens, however, there was a fifth eighth-century prophet, earlier in point of time than any of the others: Jonah ben Amittai. The Book of Jonah and the story of Jonah, however, are both so unique that one would not readily bracket man or book with the other four men and books. The Book of Jonah gives not the slightest indication as to the date of the prophet, except that his ministry was prior to the fall of Nineveh (612 B.C), but a brief reference to him in 2 Kings 14:25 dates him securely in the reign of Jeroboam II (782-753). Even if the book of Jonah be taken as a historical document (and in fact very few scholars do so take it),[1] we know singularly little of the prophet's ministry to his contemporaries; according to 2 Kings 14:25 he predicted some Israelite victories, and according to Jonah 3:4 he prophesied disaster for the Assyrians, and

---

1. For a discussion of the meaning and interpretation of the book of Jonah, cf. R. K. Harrison, *Introduction to the Old Testament* (London, 1970), pp. 904-918; H. L. Ellison, *The Prophets of Israel* (Exeter, 1969) chapter 8; G. A. F. Knight, *Ruth and Jonah*[2] (*TBC*: London, 1966), pp. 49-58; L. C. Allen, *The Books of Joel, Obadiah, Jonah and Micah* (*NICOT*: Grand Rapids, 1976), pp. 175-194.

that is the sum total of our knowledge of his message. Both elements in it were the sort of things his countrymen would have enjoyed hearing (the second element was not uttered in their hearing, of course).

These twin aspects of Jonah's message serve as an excellent introduction to the more detailed prophecies of Amos, a little later in the same reign.[2] "In forty days Nineveh shall be overthrown!" is the wording of the one and only prophetic oracle in the Book of Jonah; Amos began his preaching in a not dissimilar vein — "For crime after crime of Damascus I will grant them no reprieve" (Amos 1:3). No Israelite, with bitter memories of the days of Syrian supremacy, would have disapproved of that oracle. "For crime after crime of Gaza I will grant them no reprieve", the prophet continued (1:6), turning his attention to the Philistines, and his denunciations, all spoken in the name of Yahweh, went on to embrace Tyrians, Edomites, Ammonites and Moabites, thus including virtually every neighbour (and erstwhile enemy) of Israel. He gave examples of their "crimes" which must have been familiar to his audience, and predicted defeat, exile and destruction for one nation after the other. Such oracles of judgement against foreign enemies were the very stuff of prophecy, and one can readily imagine the nods of approval and the murmurs of assent from his hearers, even though none of these neighbours posed any threat to Israel at this date. Amos did not specify the source of the military disasters he predicted, but since his first denunciation prophesied for the Damascenes exile to Kir, in far-off Mesopotamia, nobody could doubt that the Assyrians must be, in the prophet's mind, the agents of the forthcoming disasters for the Syrian kingdoms. As Amos's list of denunciations proceeded to embrace nations lying to the south of Israel, the most thoughtful of his listeners might have begun to wonder how Israel was going to fare while the Assyrian armies were rampaging through neighbouring regions.

Even the least intelligent of his audience will have been startled by his seventh denunciation: "For crime after crime of Judah I will grant them no reprieve" (2:4). Possibly some listeners welcomed even that statement, for not so many years earlier Judah, under King Amaziah, had provoked an entirely unnecessary war with Israel;[3] but it is highly unlikely that many Israelites would have harboured seriously hostile feelings towards Judah. Besides, Amos himself came from Judah — from Tekoa, some 10 miles south of Jerusalem — and no doubt his regional accent betrayed him as clearly as Simon Peter's Galilean one did, centuries later.[4] What was

2. By general consent, between 763 and 750 B.C. Cf. H. L. Ellison, *op. cit.*, pp. 62, 71.
3. See above, p. 92.
4. Cf. Matthew 26:73.

this Judaean doing, cursing his own homeland? The initial pleasurable impact of the prophet's words must have given place to surprise and wonderment; certainly none of the audience was bored! To our twentieth century generation, the prophetic books often make difficult and dull reading; but recent research has emphasized the brilliance and skill with which the prophets addressed their own contemporaries.[5] They knew how to hold an audience spell-bound, chiefly by taking a stereotyped and traditional form of language and filling it with new, startling and sometimes very incongruous content — much as if, sitting back in our comfortable church pew, we were to hear the vicar parody our favourite hymn. Perhaps the clearest example for modern readers is to be found in Isaiah 5. The prophet began to intone a charming love-poem:

> I will sing for my beloved
>   my love-song about his vineyard;
> My beloved had a vineyard
>   high up on a fertile hill-side.
>   He trenched it and cleared it of stones
>   and planted it with red vines;
> he built a watch-tower in the middle
> and then hewed out a winepress in it.
> He looked for it to yield grapes . . .

All very idyllic; the beauty of the language would lull the ear, and no doubt Isaiah's original audience will have expected him to continue in terms of rich harvests and joyful merrymaking, like the "mellow fruitfulness" and "maturing sun" of John Keats. But the prophet continued, " . . . but it yielded wild grapes", and the poem proceeds, getting more blunt and pointed and hard-hitting as verse succeeds verse. Of course, our modern poets too have used incongruity and anticlimax for effect; one thinks of T. S. Eliot's *The Hollow Men* and its startling conclusion: *"This is the way the world ends/ This is the way the world ends/ This is the way the world ends/ Not with a bang but a whimper." But literary men of our modern era, if they often* succeed in making thoughtful men think, rarely convey a note of authoritative truth to the ordinary man in the street. Israel's ancient prophets' thunderous "Thus saith the LORD!" was a different matter; nobody, however simple or illiterate, could fail to understand their message, or to be affected by it.

But to return to Amos: his sudden denunciation of his own native Judah will have caused his listeners to ask themselves why, Amos

---

5. The familiar sonorous cadences and archaic vocabulary of the AV will often have the effect of reducing for present-day readers the original impact of the prophets' words. Who but a prophet would have dared to describe God as "a festering sore" and as "dry-rot" (Hosea 5:12, NEB and J. B. Phillips)?

had listed various anti-social "crimes" of Damascus and the other nations, to explain the reason for their impending punishment; what similar international misdeeds had Judah perpetrated? The prophet broke in on their thoughts — "because they have spurned the law of the LORD and have not observed his decrees, and have been led astray by the false gods that their fathers followed" (2:4). In short, their crimes were not international but religious; they had flouted the covenant, notably by their idolatry. Amos's primary concern, like that of so many of his predecessors, was with the covenant of Yahweh, established at Sinai long ago.

Bethel, where Amos was preaching (cf. 7:12f.), was no great distance from the borders of Judah, and conceivably some of his listeners had seen for themselves signs of idol-worship in Judah; others will have accepted that if a Judaean said so, it was so. But again the more thoughtful people in his audience will have started to ask themselves whether Israel's observance of the Sinai covenant had been any more punctilious than Judah's; or whether there was any less idolatry in Israel than in Judah. Why, it was well known that a goddess was worshipped in the capital, Samaria, itself — as Amos was aware (cf. 8:14) (he had probably visited the city). If Amos was right to pronounce doom on Judah, he was logically bound to do the same for Israel.[6]

"For crime after crime of Israel I will grant them no reprieve" (2:6). So the pronouncement of the divine verdict upon Israel was uttered; and those who has eagerly listened to the prophet's initial words, so like Jonah's in tone and character, were now hearing a very different story, which must have brought dismay to every man of them. Even now Amos had a surprise to spring on them; presumably they all expected him to launch into an immediate diatribe against the idolatries of the Northern Kingdom, but on that score he chose to say very little! Nor did he immediately explain what the divine punishment in store for Israel was to be, as he had done in each of his previous denunciations; Amos well knew how to build up suspense, and hold an audience.

The prophet's first diatribe against Israel shows us, if we read between the lines, that he was addressing a well-ordered, religious society, where "proper" legal and religious ceremonies were dutifully observed. It was a prosperous society and a complacent society — or rather, the upper classes were; but Amos had eyes to see the great rift between rich and poor, between upper classes and

6. This discussion of the oracle against Judah assumes that it was an original part of Amos's first sermon, rather than a later editorial addition, as many scholars have held. J. L. Mays in his commentary on Amos outlines the arguments for viewing this oracle as secondary, but they are far from being conclusive. Cf. J. L. Mays, *Amos (OTL*: London, 1969), pp. 40ff.

lower classes, and the fact that the function of due legal process was all too often to aid the rich and defraud the poor. Israel was riddled with legalized immorality — and with prostituted religion. Under the veneer of law and equity, everything conspired against the poor man. If his case were good, the judge could easily be bribed to declare against him (''They sell the innocent for silver'', 2:6); he could be fined and have his property seized; and finally he would have no option but to sell himself into slavery, when his debts became too heavy.

This was the immediate indictment Amos brought against Israel; later on he was even more explicit about the courts: ''You that turn justice upside down and bring righteousness to the ground, you that hate a man who brings the wrong-doer to court, and loathe him who speaks the whole truth . . . you levy taxes on the poor and extort a tribute of grain from them . . . you . . . persecute the guiltless, hold men to ransom and thrust the destitute out of court'' (5:7-12). The poverty of Israel had been very much aggravated by the depredations of the Syrian armies at the end of the ninth century; but clearly in the more prosperous days of the early eighth century, nothing was done to ensure an even distribution of the prosperity; on the contrary, the poor seemed to be worse off, not better.

The prosperity of the upper classes is outlined equally vividly in Amos 6:4ff.:

> You who loll on beds inlaid with ivory
>   and sprawl over your couches,
> feasting on lambs from the flock
>   and fatted calves,
>   you who pluck the strings of the lute
> and invent musical instruments like David,
>   you who drink wine by the bowlful
>   and lard yourselves with the richest of oils.

In a famous phrase, the prophet contemptuously dismissed the society women of the capital as ''you cows of Bashan who live on the hill of Samaria'' (4:1). Amos was not attacking wealth as such, but wealth based on social injustices; for him, the society of Israel was deeply guilty of wholesale breaches of the covenant laws, and as such warranted punishment on a national level. There is evidence that although the law of the day was (at least outwardly) adhered to, some ancient laws protecting the rights of ordinary citizens had been allowed to lapse; one example is the law of the pledged garment, as a comparison of Exodus 22:26f. with Amos 2:8 will show.

The new element in the preaching of Amos was the denunciation of a whole society. Elijah had indicted the royal court of his day, and had prophesied its downfall; Amos now pronounced a whole

13. Assyrian cavalrymen

14. Assyrian infantry

guilty of breach of the covenant with Yahweh, and pronounced doom accordingly. The book of Amos time and time again returns to the theme of national disaster to come — death and destruction and "exile beyond Damascus" (5:27).

Thus the book of Amos gives us a picture of Israel in the eighth century of which the historical books of the Old Testament give little hint. The old tribal ideal, cemented in the covenant laws, of a closely knit community caring for all its members, had by now broken down; now the nation consisted of two classes, one of which had every reason to be resentful of its lot. We cannot be surprised that the well-to-do, represented by the priest Amaziah at Bethel, hastily drove Amos out of the kingdom, back to his native Judah. Quite apart from the general alarm and despondency his threats might engender, there will have been fears that his denunciation of social oppression might lead to seditious feelings and actions among the under-privileged.

Amos was more concerned with hypocritical worship at shrines to Israel's God than he was with idolatry as such. He made just one or two brief references to such false worship (cf. 5:26, 8:14); and if we had had only Amos as a guide to the Northern Kingdom, we might well have jumped to the conclusion that idolatry was no great problem there. Hosea, however, makes it clear how false such a conclusion would have been.

Hosea's ministry seems to have covered a period of about a quarter of a century, from shortly after 750 B.C. until the eve of the fall of Samaria (c. 722 B.C.). His first recorded prediction was that the dynasty of Jehu would fall (1:4), a prophecy fulfilled in 752 B.C. By now the Assyrian threat was looming large, and the Israelite prosperity which Amos had observed was fast ebbing away. Hosea says nothing of the luxuries enjoyed by the society women, for instance.

Hosea, victim of a bitterly unhappy marriage,[7] was particularly interested in the question of the relationship of Israel to God. He saw Israel as the unfaithful spouse of a loving and tender God. He recalled the very start of their covenant relationship: "I have been the LORD your God since your days in Egypt, when you knew no other saviour than me, no god but me. I cared for you in the wilderness, in a land of burning heat, as if you were in pasture." But in response the Israelites "were filled, and being filled, grew proud; and so they forgot me" (13:4ff.). In Hosea's own day, they were demonstrating their abandonment of their God by turning to idolatry. God had so recently granted them new prosperity, in "corn, new wine, and oil"; but the "silver and gold" he lavished upon

---

7. See especially H. L. Ellison, *op. cit.* chapter 11; H. H. Rowley, *Men of God* (London, 1963) chapter 3.

them, "they spent on the Baal" (2:8). At other times the prophet inveighed against "the calf-gods" of Samaria and Bethel (8:5; 10:5). For this state of affairs, which distressed him greatly, Hosea could only blame the religious leaders, in bitter invective: "Priest? By day and night you blunder on, you and the prophet with you" (4:5). And he warned them in God's name that "people and priest shall be treated alike. I will punish them for their conduct and repay them for their deeds" (4:9). Hosea, like Amos, recognized that physically the altars and shrines of Yahweh had not been neglected. He saw the crowds of worshippers with their sacrifices of sheep and cattle on their way "to seek the LORD" (5:6); but he also saw only too clearly that two vital aspects of a true relationship with God had long since been forgotten: "Faithful love" and "personal knowledge of God". These two concepts are none too easy to translate into English, but they dominate Hosea's thought; 6:6 is the key verse — "It is true love that I have wanted, not sacrifice; the knowledge of God rather than burnt-offerings" (J. B. Phillips).[8] The first concept, embodied in the Hebrew word *chesed*, denotes the requisite fidelity to the marriage bond and all that springs from it; the other has been summed up thus: "To know God is to respond to him in faithful love and to have the whole of life determined by the understanding of oneself and one's fellow men that becomes possible in this relation".[9]

So Hosea could but prophesy divine punishment, even while he appealed to his fellow-countrymen to "return to the LORD" (6:1). He could look beyond to a brighter future, but meanwhile he depicts in brief remarks the anarchy and the hopelessness of Israel's last years as a kingdom. "King after king falls from power, but not one of them calls upon me" (7:7). "Ephraim is a silly senseless pigeon, now calling upon Egypt, now turning to Assyria for help" (7:11). "There is nothing but talk, imposing of oaths and making of treaties, all to no purpose; and litigation spreads like a poisonous weed along the furrows of the fields" (10:4). The end of it all was the day when, as Hosea predicted, "Samaria and her king are swept away like flotsam on the water; the hill-shrines of Aven (i.e. Bethel) are wiped out, the shrines where Israel sinned; thorns and thistles grow over her altars" (10:7f.).

One of the most traumatic events for Hosea occurred *c.* 735 B.C., when the kingdom of Israel, in league with Damascus, tried to force Judah into an anti-Assyrian alliance. Ahaz of Judah wisely refused, and in consequence found his kingdom attacked and his capital besieged. But when the confederate forces beat a hasty retreat, in face of the Assyrian threat from the north, it appears that Ahaz

8. J. B. Phillips, *Four Prophets* (London, 1963).
9. J. D. Smart, *IDB* ii. p. 652.

seized the opportunity to appropriate some Israelite territory. Such internecine strife, as stupid as it was unjust, elicited Hosea's swift rebuke:

> On the tribes of Israel I have proclaimed this unalterable doom:
> on the day of punishment Ephraim shall be laid waste.
> The rulers of Judah act like men who move their neighbour's boundary;
> on them will I pour out my wrath like a flood.
>   Ephraim is an oppressor trampling on justice,
>   doggedly pursuing what is worthless.
>
> (5:9ff.)

Judah ought not to have taken revenge, despite the provocation, but it was Ephraim who had been the real aggressor, and for her Hosea predicted the more severe punishment.

And what of Judah? Both Amos and Hosea threw out asides about Judah, but it was left to two other prophets to state more directly and more thoroughly Yahweh's indictment of the Southern Kingdom. They were Micah and Isaiah, both of whom were contemporaries of Hosea, though both survived the northern prophet by a number of years. They lived to see the momentous events which destroyed the Northern Kingdom, and which nearly overwhelmed Judah too twenty years later, when Sennacherib ravaged Hezekiah's kingdom and all but captured Jerusalem. Such was the political background to their ministry; but both of them viewed these events as Yahweh's hand in history, punishing his people for their many breaches of the covenant faith.

Micah's home was in the Shephelah, the lowland area separating the hills of Judah from the coastal plain occupied by the Philistines. His hometown, Moresheth-gath, was not so far from the Philistine city of Gath; and it lay equally close to the Judaean fortress city of Lachish. It was precisely in this region that the spear-head of the Assyrian invasion of 701 B.C. was launched against Judah and her allies; and the first chapter of Micah's prophecy lists some of the towns and cities, both Philistine and Judaean, which suffered the full force of Sennacherib's assault. His own town was among them.[10] The enemy's troops went on to besiege Jerusalem, and Micah summed up the situation thus: "disaster has come down from the LORD to the very gate of Jerusalem" (1:12).

As a countryman, Micah could see good reason why the God of Israel should bring such disaster on His people. To him, Jerusalem represented not so much the centre of Israel's faith, the abode on earth of Yahweh himself, as the centre of oppression and the abode of rich property-grabbers. The big land-owners, in their fine homes in the capital, were exploiting the country farmers in exactly the

10. See map 154 in *MBA*.

same way that the wealthy classes of Samaria had been oppressing the poor of Israel. Micah addressed them thus:

> Shame on those who lie in bed planning evil and wicked deeds
> and rise at daybreak to do them,
>   knowing that they have the power!
> They covet land and take it by force;
>   if they want a house they seize it;
> they rob a man of his home
>   and steal every man's inheritance.

(2:1f.)

The traders were no better than the landowners; God's challenge to the dishonest traders is thus stated in Micah 6:10ff.:

> Hark, the LORD, the fear of whose name brings success,
>   the LORD calls to the city.
> Listen, O tribe of Judah and citizens in assembly,
> can I overlook the infamous false measure,
>   the accursed short bushel?
> Can I connive at false scales or a bag of light weights?
>   Your rich men are steeped in violence,
>   your townsmen are all liars,
>   and their tongues frame deceit.

Nor could members of other professions in the capital be exonerated: "Her (Jerusalem's) rulers sell justice, her priests give direction in return for a bribe, her prophets take money for their divination" (3:11). Micah was particularly angered by the arrogant and immoral attitudes of the false prophets, whom he describes as leading God's people astray, "who promise prosperity in return for a morsel of food, who proclaim a holy war against them if they put nothing in their mouths" (3:5). Such was the Jerusalem Micah saw, and he could see no hope for it; God's righteous anger was such that inevitably "Zion shall become a ploughed field, Jerusalem a heap of ruins, and the temple hill rough heath" (3:12). In fact, of course, Jerusalem survived the Assyrian onslaught, as Isaiah predicted it would; are we then to say that Micah was the false prophet?

We find a most interesting historical commentary on this prediction of Micah's recorded in another prophetical book — in Jeremiah 26:17ff. Far from being forgotten, Micah's unfulfilled prophecy was recalled word for word a century later, by some of the elders of Judah, who went on to ask:

> Did King Hezekiah and all Judah put him to death? Did not the king
> show reverence for the LORD and seek to placate him? Then the LORD
> relented and revoked the disaster with which he had threatened them.

(26:19)

In other words, the fulfilment of the prophecy depended on the response it evoked from the people to whom it was directed. It is clear that there were those in Judah who had fully appreciated the conditional nature of prophetic promises and threats and warnings.

A more recent commentator may also be quoted with profit: "The city of Jerusalem was miraculously delivered, and the Assyrians returned speedily to their own land. This unexpected turn of events may have discredited the ministry of Micah in the eyes of his contemporaries. He had predicted the destruction of the city 'built with wrong' — and Jerusalem had survived intact. 'The mills of God grind slowly.' If to his contemporaries of short sight he appeared mistaken, nevertheless the words of Micah were treasured by his disciples, and in the long run were vindicated by history, when Jerusalem was destroyed by the Babylonians in 587 B.C.''[11]

Meanwhile in Jerusalem itself, in the very city whose ruling classes Micah could vividly describe as butchers (3:2f.), lived the prophet Isaiah. Called to exercise a prophetic ministry in 742 B.C., the year that Uzziah's long, peaceful and prosperous reign ended, he advised the kings of Judah and warned their subjects through the vicissitudes of the rest of the century, down to Jerusalem's darkest hour in 701 B.C. It is clear that he had access to the royal court; that fact, and the interest he exhibited in political affairs, have often resulted in his being called a "statesman-prophet". The description is not inapt, but it should be borne in mind that many of the prophets, from Nathan to Jeremiah, were in a position to discuss political issues with the king, and did so.

It has been remarked that all the important aspects of Isaiah's teachings can be found in germ in chapter 6, the account of his call. His vision of God impressed on him deeply the divine lordship of history, and the "awful purity" which is God's nature as well as his requirement in his people. The other side of the coin was the sinful and obstinate condition of the people of Judah, to whom Isaiah was called to preach — in an exasperating ministry to deaf ears — so long as any people remained in the land. These things he learned at the very start of his ministry, and like St. Paul long centuries later, he was not disobedient to the heavenly vision.

Isaiah's awareness of the gulf between his God's purity and his fellow-citizens' immoralities is shown in his denunciations of Judah in the early chapters of the book: "O sinful nation, people loaded with iniquity, race of evildoers, wanton destructive children who have deserted the LORD, spurned the Holy One of Israel and turned your backs on him" (1:4). Like his contemporary prophets, he insisted that moral behaviour and religious observances could not be divorced; God, he declared, was "sated with whole-offerings of

11. S. F. Winward, *A guide to the Prophets* (London, 1968), p. 65.

rams and the fat of buffaloes'', could not endure the feasts and festivals, and would listen no longer to countless prayers. God's requirement was thus: "Cease to do evil and learn to do right, pursue justice and champion the oppressed; give the orphan his rights, plead the widow's cause'' (1:11-17). Isaiah saw the social evils of Jerusalem just as clearly as did Micah; and just as Amos had drawn attention to the ill-gotten luxuries enjoyed in Samaria, so Isaiah poured contempt upon the fineries of the ladies of Jerusalem, in a passage which gives us a great deal of detail about the fashions of the day:

> In that day the Lord will take away all finery: anklets, discs, crescents, pendants, bangles, coronets, head-bands, armlets, necklaces, lockets, charms, signets, nose-rings, fine dresses, mantles, cloaks, flounced skirts, scarves of gauze, kerchiefs of linen, turbans, and flowing veils.
> (3:18-23)

As the political scene steadily darkened in the forty years or so that he prophesied, Isaiah put out plea after plea for his people to listen — or reap the bitter consequences.

Isaiah's interest in, and attempts to influence, international diplomacy, have been touched on earlier in this book.[12] In this sphere too, he believed firmly that it was quite wrong to divorce one's religious faith from ordinary day-to-day concerns and conduct. He stood out against foreign alliances of any sort, since he was convinced that God was sufficient to look after Israel's needs as a nation. In this respect too, we see how the prophet was motivated by his concern for the covenant. If Yahweh had declared that Israel was his people, his own nation, then he would be true to his covenant bond. Nor had Isaiah the slightest doubt that Yahweh was able to keep his bond; weaker souls might fear that other nations had more powerful deities, but not Isaiah. His conviction was summarized in one sentence he addressed to King Ahaz: "Have firm faith, or you will not stand firm'' (7:9).

After King Ahaz had declined to accept Isaiah's wise advice, and had concluded an alliance with Assyria, the prophet seems to have withdrawn from public life for a number of years, during which time he probably banded round him a number of disciples (cf. 8:16ff.). Once Hezekiah came to the throne, however, he resumed his ministry at the royal court. Since Isaiah had previously counselled against the alliance with Assyria, Hezekiah might have expected the prophet to welcome a renunciation of that alliance; but on the contrary, Isaiah opposed any such move, especially since its success depended on yet more foreign alliances. The king gave indifferent

12. See above, p. 99.

heed to the prophet's advice, so Isaiah resorted to the startling device of walking about the streets naked and barefoot, for three full years, as a symbol of the destitution which Egypt — Hezekiah's strongest ally against Assyria — would suffer at the hands of the Assyrians (chapter 20).

Micah, we have been, could predict nothing good for a corrupt city like Jerusalem; and Isaiah agreed with his strictures. However, Isaiah's vision took in a far wider compass; almost the whole of chapters 13-23 consists of his oracles about foreign nations, and a perusal of his words makes it clear that he had no illusions about them. He castigated one after the other "for their offences against the moral law and against neighbourly obligations as they knew them".[13] In particular, he recognized that Assyria, though raised up by God as the rod of his anger (10:5), was arrogant, cruel and rapacious. He therefore prophesied:

> When the Lord has finished all that he means to do
> on Mount Zion and in Jerusalem,
> he will punish the king of Assyria
> for this fruit of his pride and for his arrogance
> and vainglory, because he said:
> By my own might I have acted
> and in my wisdom I have laid my schemes;
> I have removed the frontiers of nations
>   and plundered their treasures,
> like a bull I have trampled on their inhabitants.
> My hand has found its way to the wealth of nations,
>   and, as a man takes the eggs from a deserted nest,
>   so have I taken every land;
>   not a wing fluttered,
>   not a beak gaped, no chirp was heard.

(10:12ff.)

This is the background to Isaiah's conviction that Jerusalem would finally be spared and the Assyrians discomfited. Jerusalem had this one virtue, that though full of idols (10:10f.), she also housed the temple, which bore the divine oracle, "I will shield this city to deliver it, for my own sake" (37:35). The deliverance would also be "for the sake of my servant David"; we may see this as a sign that Hezekiah, for all his faults and mistakes, sincerely worshipped God and turned to his prophet for guidance, or else we may think that the phrase related to the future. Isaiah certainly anticipated a much greater son of David than Hezekiah proved to be, a king who should be called "in purpose wonderful, in battle God-like, Father for all

---

13. J. Mauchline, *Isaiah 1-39 (TBC:* London, 1962), p. 35.

time, Prince of peace'' (9:6). But this is a theme to which we must return.

The man who succeeded Hezekiah was not remotely like the king depicted in Isaiah 9:6; he was Manasseh, one of the most wicked of all Judah's monarchs, and during his long reign it appears that the voice of prophecy was silenced. But Isaiah, like Amos, had predicted the survival of a ''remnant''; indeed, he had named one of his sons Shear-jashub, ''a remnant will return''. The name had once served as a warning, to indicate that *only* a remnant would escape Judah's well-deserved punishment; but during Manasseh's reign the word adequately describes those who, like Elijah's remnant, did not in any sense bow the knee to Baal (cf. 1 Kings 19:18). The fact that Isaiah's teachings were preserved, no doubt by his disciples, and Micah's sermons remembered, in itself shows that the Judah of Manasseh's reign was not wholly given over to false religion.

CHAPTER 24

Jeremiah and his Contemporaries

IN the half-century or so that elapsed between the death of Manasseh (642 B.C.) and the destruction of Jerusalem (587) a number of prophets came on the scene. Apart from the towering figure of Jeremiah, there were Zephaniah, Nahum and Habakkuk, to say nothing of Daniel and Ezekiel (whose ministry was not, however, exercised in pre-exilic Judah).

The first of this group of prophets seems to have been Zephaniah, who was called to the prophetic ministry in 625 or a little earlier, during the early period of the reign of Josiah (to whom Zephaniah was related). The international scene was by now one of both confusion and hope; the Assyrian power was visibly waning, Babylon and Egypt were about to spring into fresh prominence, and for the moment Judah appeared to be on the verge of independence. King Josiah had probably already taken the first tentative steps towards autonomy. The internal religious scene was one of long-entrenched idolatry, fostered without overt opposition during Manasseh's long reign. It looks as if Assyrian cultic practices, in particular, had a fascination for many Judaeans.

It may have been the Scythian raid down the Palestinian coast[1] which spurred Zephaniah to prophesy; he does not mention them by name, but this picture of widespread desolation, engulfing lands as far apart as Assyria and Egypt, may well have been drawn from the havoc and fear such barbarian horsemen had recently caused. The Scythian raid had bypassed Judah, and all the old complacency of well-to-do Judaeans continued undisturbed. Time had healed the wounds caused by Sennacherib's depredations three quarters of a century earlier, and the Assyrian rule had been relatively well-disposed in recent years, so there were again plenty of wealthy

1. See above, p. 140.

citizens in Jerusalem. Zephaniah depicts them as guzzling wine and opining in drunken dogmatism, "The LORD will do nothing, good or bad" (1:12). The prophet offered no reproaches against the young king, who could scarcely be blamed for the existing situation, but the court and regents he declared would be punished:

> I will punish the royal house and its chief officers
> and all who ape outlandish fashions.
>   On that day
> I will punish all who dance on the temple terrace,
> who fill their master's house with crimes of violence and fraud.
>
> (1:8f.)

The foreign worship, he declared, would be swept away:

> I will wipe out from this place the last remnant of Baal
>   and the very name of the heathen priests,
>   those who bow down upon the house-tops
>   to worship the host of heaven
>   and who swear by Milcom,
> those who have turned their backs on the LORD,
> who have not sought the LORD or consulted him.
>
> (1:4ff.)

As for those who should have given the people of Judah God's authoritative word, the prophets had been "braggarts" and "impostors", while the priests were profaning the holy things and doing violence to the law (3:4, J. B. Phillips). Viewed as a whole, the Jerusalem which was just regaining a precarious political independence could only be described as "the tyrant city, filthy and foul" (3:1), and the prophet offers us a vivid glimpse of God Himself searching with a lantern the dark city streets for those whom He must punish on the Day of his judgement. That Day was at hand!

We have no historical record of how Zephaniah's words were received, but there were those who felt the urgent need for religious reform, King Josiah among them. His reform programme and its effects may explain why a decade or so later, the prophet Nahum felt no call to pronounce doom on Judah, nor even to rebuke it; Jeremiah, too, seems to have adopted a "let's wait and see" policy about these reforms. Nahum's whole concern was with Assyria and its capital, Nineveh, which Zephaniah had described as "the city that exulted in fancied security" (2:15). It is disputed whether Nahum was similarly predicting its fall, or whether he was exulting over the fact that it had fallen; in either case, his prophecy may be dated c. 612 B.C., the year of the destruction of Nineveh. He depicts the battering-ram mounted against Nineveh's bastions, the siege closing in (2:1); he contrasts the triumphant soldiery (of the Medes and Babylonians) with the terrified citizens being led away as slaves (2:3-8). We can readily hear in Nahum's words the pent-up feelings of hatred and revenge; but we must not overlook the reasons he gives for Nineveh's fall. Nineveh was a "blood-stained city, steeped in deceit, full of pillage, never empty of prey" (3:1), and therefore merited divine punishment. The vengeance and the anger were those of God himself, not of Judah and its citizens (1:2). The fall of Nineveh was simple justice.

Nineveh's fall meant permanent release from Assyrian bondage for both Israel and Judah (1:12-15). Thus far Nahum's words were true; but a mere three years later, Judah was already coming under foreign sway yet again, first that of Egypt and then Babylon. It was left to another prophet, Habakkuk, to address this new situation. He seems to have prophesied a few years later than Nahum, not earlier than 609 B.C. By now the Babylonians, under their Chaldaean king Nebuchadrezzar, were on their way to becoming masters of the whole of Palestine, whether Judah liked it or not; and in Jerusalem the well-intentioned, pious Josiah had been replaced by the selfish and despotic Jehoiakim, while Josiah's reforms had died with him. Habakkuk did not relish any aspect of these new conditions, and where most other prophets uttered oracles and sermons from God to the people, his book is notable for its two complaints, addressed to God. "Why" he challenged the Almighty, "Why dost thou let me see such misery, why countenance wrongdoing?" (1:3). He observed that in Jerusalem, where only twenty years before king and populace had hailed the new-found book of the law of God,[2] the law was now losing its hold, and justice was visibly distorted (1:4, J. B. Phillips). Why was God permitting the wicked to outwit the righteous in his holy city?

The answer he received to his first complaint was to the effect that the invincible Babylonians were coming, and they would impose their own "justice and judgement" upon the recalcitrant Judaeans (1:7). The awe-inspiring progress of the Babylonians armies is told in impressive language (1:8-11). Habakkuk could not doubt that all this was true, nor did he doubt that God himself was appointing them to execute judgement (1:12); but the very description of the Babylonians as "that savage and impetuous nation" (1:6) raised fresh doubts in his mind, and sparked off his second complaint. God, he recognised, was too pure to overlook the many evils to be found in Jerusalem; but by the same token, how could he tolerate the wickedness of the Babylonians, who after all had less to commend them than the Judaeans? "Why", he demanded of God, "why keep silent when they (the Babylonians) devour men more

---

2. See above, pp. 118f.

righteous than they?[3] . . . Are they then to unsheath the sword every day, to slaughter the nations without pity?'' (1:13, 17).

Habakkuk did not receive an immediate reply, and he portrays himself as climbing a watch-tower to look out for the answer that must surely come (2:1); a striking metaphor this, in a land and at a time when all too soon the invading armies would be descried approaching. The answer did come, in a famous but cryptic divine oracle (all the more cryptic for us, because of problems of text and translation): ''The reckless will be unsure of himself, while the righteous man will live by being faithful'' (2:4). The strictures in the rest of Habakkuk 2 indicate the sort of people whose position was so precarious — the traitor, the money-grabber, and the oppressor at home and abroad: ''Woe betide you!'' was the prophet's refrain. But the future of ''the righteous man'' was not further elaborated; nevertheless the promise stood, that he would live, as he both exhibited faith and kept faith. It was a statement that did not lose its force with passing centuries; the men of Qumran appropriated it,[4] the apostle Paul treasured it, and Martin Luther rediscovered and proclaimed it.

The last chapter of Habakkuk seems to have a separate history from the rest of the little book, and many scholars have sought different authorship for it. But if it circulated separately, its authorship may have been the same;[5] it is at all events satisfying to think that the man who poured out such heart-felt complaints and received such a thought-provoking response, should have gone on to experience full confidence in his God's power and control of history, so that he could conclude thus:

> Although the fig-tree
>   does not burgeon,
> the vines bear no fruit,
>   the olive-crop fails,
> the orchards yield no food,
> the fold is bereft of its flock
>   and there are no cattle in the stalls,
> yet I will exult in the LORD
>   and rejoice in the God of my deliverance.
> The LORD God is my strength,
> who makes my feet nimble as a hind's
>   and sets me to range the heights.

(3:17-19)

---

3. It is possible that Habakkuk had in mind King Jehoiakim's oppressive deeds as well as those of the Babylonians.

4. Cf. G. Vermes, *The Dead Sea Scrolls in English* (Harmondsworth, 1962), p. 237.

5. Cf. W. F. Albright, in H. H. Rowley (ed.), *Studies in Old Testament Prophecy* (Edinburgh, 1950), pp. 1-18.

Habakkuk was not the only biblical character to challenge God for a reply; Abraham did so and Job did so; but nobody showed quite the same audacity in addressing the Almighty as did Jeremiah, Habakkuk's greater contemporary. He began his prophetic ministry about the same time as Zephaniah, and he survived Zephaniah, Nahum and Habakkuk in turn, continuing to proclaim God's message in Judah till and after the fall of Jerusalem. For fully forty years, therefore, he had the wretched experience of not only witnessing the death-throes of the kingdom of Judah, but also being obliged to diagnose the nation's sickness and repeatedly state the true prognosis to a patient of blind and irremediable optimism. The task brought him no joy, and at times he demanded to know why God had called him to the prophetic office. His most bitter outburst came when he pronounced a curse on the day he was born, and asked "Why did I come forth from the womb to know only sorrow and toil, to end my days in shame?" (20:14-18). He was deeply affected by the ostracism and persecution his preaching aroused, and he felt the nation's suffering as keenly as his own; but he was under the tremendous compulsion of the word of Yahweh, and that gave him the strength and courage to pursue his ministry without faltering or breaking down.

The book of Jeremiah presents many problems, not least among them the difficulty of dating much of the material; in particular, it is not at all easy to decide which of his oracles and sermons antedate the death of Josiah in 609 B.C. One would have expected that the prophet would have shown deep interest in Josiah's reforms; yet one searches the book in vain for a clear and unambiguous exposition of his viewpoint about them. It could be argued from 11:6 that Jeremiah was a "peripatetic evangelist" for the reform programme; but it could be argued from 8:8f. that on the contrary he denounced the newly-discovered "book of the law" as a hoax and a fraud! In fact, neither possibility is at all likely to be the truth; but the mere fact that such diverse interpretations are possible serves to illustrate something of the difficulties inherent in any attempt to reconstruct the course of the ministry of Jeremiah. Nevertheless, the attempt must be made.[6]

Called to be a prophet in the thirteenth year of Josiah, c. 627 B.C., Jeremiah may well have shared the concerns of his contemporary Zephaniah during his early ministry; his vision (1:13f.) of a burning cauldron tilted away from the north, threatening disaster from the north for Judah, is reminiscent of Zephaniah's words, and his challenge to Judah regarding "her adulterous worship of stone

---

6. The following outline owes much to the reconstruction of Jeremiah's life and ministry offered by J. Bright, *Jeremiah (AB:* Garden City, 1965), pp.LXXXVI-CXVIII.

and wood'' (3:9) again recalls Zephaniah's condemnation of the wide-spread idolatries Manasseh's recent reign has fostered.

Then came Josiah's reforms, implemented mainly in 621 B.C. and the years following; as has been indicated, Jeremiah's reaction to them is a matter of debate and dispute. Since it must be admitted that he said very little in plain language about them, it seems probable that he realized that they had their pros and cons, and could not be either strongly supported nor condemned out of hand. He gave unqualified praise to their instigator, Josiah (22:15f.); and without question he must have rejoiced to see the removal of so many of the trappings of idolatry. But the reform programme changed little except externals, and Jeremiah's summing up was as follows: ''Judah has not come back to me (i.e. to God) in good faith, but only in pretence'' (3:10). Even before the death of the reforming king in 609 B.C., a fresh paganism, if on a lesser scale than before, was setting in: ''You burn sacrifices to Baal, you run after other gods'' (7:9), the prophet declared in his famous temple sermon a few months after Josiah's death. Worse, perhaps, was the false sense of security the reforms had engendered — few are so prone to arrogant spiritual pride as those who declare that they are ''reformed''. Jeremiah had this to say of such self-righteous practitioners of the faith: ''Prophets and priests are frauds, every one of them; they dress my people's wound, but skin-deep only, with their saying, 'All is well'. All well? Nothing is well!'' (6:13f.).

Josiah's death in battle and the Egyptian take-over which brought Jehoiakim to the throne should have given such self-righteous optimists cause to think. Why had the God in whose name they spoke so boldly allowed such a tragedy? Probably few of them troubled to ask themselves such an awkward question; but for those who had ears to hear, Jeremiah supplied the answer: ''Men of Noph and Tahpanhes (i.e. Egyptians) will break your heads. Is it not your desertion of the LORD your God that brings all this upon you?'' (2:16f.).

Jehoiakim was no reformer, and there is not the least ambiguity about Jeremiah's attitude to him and his deeds. What raised Jeremiah's deepest anger and most biting invective was Jehoiakim's decision to build a new palace and to utilize forced, unpaid labourers to do it. ''If your cedar is more splendid, does that prove you are a king?'' he enquired scornfully — and proceeded to pronounce personal sentence on the petty tyrant (22:13-19). Such a deed was totally inconsistent with the old covenant morality, which the Davidic king was pledged to uphold; and for that reason the prophet took the courageous step of threatening that the long and proud dynasty of David would be removed, by God himself. ''These are the words of the LORD'', he announced, ''Deal justly and fairly . . . do not shed innocent blood, . . . If you obey, and only if you obey, kings who sit on David's throne shall yet come riding through these gates in chariots and on horses, with their retinue of courtiers and people'' (22:3f). The fate of Jehoahaz could be taken as a symbol of the reality of this threat; he had become king on Josiah's death, only to be deposed and exiled by the Egyptian's a few months later. Said Jeremiah, ''These are the words of the LORD concerning Shallum[7] son of Josiah, king of Judah, who succeeded his father on the throne and has gone away: He shall never return; he shall die in the place of his exile and never see this land again'' (22:11f.). The royal house was closely linked with the temple, which in the popular thought and theology of the day was even more secure and imperishable than the Davidic dynasty; so Jeremiah was sent under divine compulsion to proclaim, in the temple itself, that a shrine which deserved the description of a robbers' cave would be destroyed by God himself. Again, the prophet could offer a token proof of his words; he advised his audience to go and inspect the ruins of Shiloh, the ancient sanctuary of Israel which had been destroyed many years before (7:1-15).

The audacity of Jeremiah nearly cost him his life (chapter 26). Influential friends saved him, but throughout Jehoiakim's reign the prophet was confronted by deep resentment and violent opposition on every hand. Even in his native village of Anathoth his neighbours and even some of his relatives threatened his life (12:1-6). Deeply hurt and distressed though he was, he refused in any way to mute or modify the word of God. Where he might have been wholly taken up with his personal concerns, his eyes were on the wider horizons of history. From 609 to 605, King Jehoiakim was the puppet of Egypt, and was apparently happy enough to co-operate with the Egyptians; but by now Jeremiah's convictions about the foe from the North had both hardened and crystallized — Babylon was the power raised up by Yahweh to be master of the Near East, and of Palestine in particular. The royal court proved deaf to his arguments, and so the prophet determined on one more dramatic bid to bring Judah to its senses. The story is told in Jeremiah 36; the prophet had his secretary Baruch write down on a scroll the full record of his sermons and oracles about Judah and its neighbours, and then sent him to read the scroll publicly in the temple, amid the crowds of a fast day. (Since his own temple address about three years earlier, he had been barred from the temple.) Baruch complied, and there were those who were deeply impressed; but not the king nor his intimate courtiers. The scroll was contemptuously destroyed in the king's personal brazier. Jeremiah's response was to prepare a fresh scroll, and to pronounce final doom on the house of David.

Judah was by no means the only nation to receive stern warning

7. Shallum was the personal name, Jehoahaz the throne name, of Josiah's successor.

from Jeremiah about the folly of seeking to oppose Nebuchadrezzar; Philistines, Phoenicians, Arabs and Elamites were all addressed by the prophet in terms of rebukes and threats. Jeremiah's viewpoint was not deterministic, however; though convinced that the Babylonians were God's chosen instrument in history (he could even call Nebuchadrezzar the "servant" of Yahweh, 27:6), he nevertheless applied moral judgements where appropriate. Thus the Ammonites, who in 601 fought a campaign on behalf of the Babylonians, far from being praised by the prophet, were attacked by him for their wilful renunciation of neighbourly standards of behaviour (49:1-6).

The facts of history themselves conspired to condemn Jehoiakim and to justify Jeremiah. Well might the prophet have lapsed into an "I told you so" attitude; instead, he showed a compassion and sorrow for his fellow-citizens, and not least the unlucky King Jehoiachin, when Nebuchadrezzar's forces marched into Judah and deported the young king and many exiles with him 597 B.C. "How can I bear my sorrow? I am sick at heart. Hark, the cry of my people from a distant land" (8:18f.). Thus Jeremiah referred to the exiles; and he went on to ask sadly whether the exiled king was not "a mere puppet, contemptible and broken, only a thing unwanted" (22:28).

The Babylonians placed Zedekiah on the throne of Judah, hoping to have broken the spirit of revolt. Jeremiah, having been proved right by the recent disasters, did not now find himself in quite such direct conflict with the royal court as in Jehoiakim's reign. The king himself and some of his leading men recognised him as a true prophet who had to be reckoned with. But the honeymoon period, if such it can be called, was of short duration, largely because of the incredible optimism and lack of realism which soon rose to the surface in Jerusalem circles. The exiles would soon return, it was said, and Babylon's grip would soon be relaxed, or rather permanently broken. We can attribute this folly partly to the efficiency of Egyptian propaganda, no doubt, but much more to the unshakeable religious dogmas of the Judaeans themselves, voiced now by such prophets as Hananiah in Jerusalem and Shemaiah far off among the exiles (chapter 28f.). False prophets they were, and false they were soon proved to be; but they nonetheless spear-headed a very powerful counter-attack against Jeremiah and his sane advice. One comforting idea which circulated in Jerusalem was that the exiles had been the guilty party, and that God would now bless and prosper a Judah purged of their presence; Jeremiah retorted scathingly that the "refined" Judah consisted of nothing but spurious silver (6:30). Changing his metaphor, he further described the exiles as good figs, the remaining Judaeans as bad figs, unfit to eat (chapter 24).

At the same time, true and honest prophet that he was, he made no pretence that Babylon was perfect nor that its power was per-

manent. Where Habakkuk had questioned the moral stance of
Babylon, Jeremiah went further, and pronounced doom on it
(51:60-64) — but not in the immediate future. He also predicted
that the exiles would return — but not until seventy years had
elapsed (29:10).[8] Such hope deferred for seventy years must have
been small comfort to the Judaeans of Jeremiah's lifetime.

The climax of Palestinian pretentious folly was the council of war
held in Jerusalem in 594/3 B.C., when representatives of various
local states solemnly discussed plans for revolt against Nebuchadrezzar.[9] Jeremiah could not let that event pass in silence, and his un-
compromising words of warning told the envoys that Babylon's rule
was too strong to resist, and that any prophet or diviner in any
country who claimed otherwise was a liar; to resist Babylon meant
exile and destruction (27:1-11). Moab may have been the leader of
the would-be revolt, if we may judge by the sustained violence of
Jeremiah's oracle against the Moabites (chapter 48).

Whether or not Jeremiah's warning helped to postpone the revolt
against Nebuchadrezzar, he could not prevent it, and the irrevocable step was taken in 589. Nebuchadrezzar's armies soon took the
field, and Jerusalem's final agony began. Even now, Jeremiah had
practical advice to offer, urging the king to surrender, and when that
suggestion went unheeded, the citizens to desert the doomed city. It
is small wonder that many Jerusalemites viewed Jeremiah's
behaviour as that of a traitor, and had him thrown into prison; and
that on his capture of the city the Babylonian king offered the
prophet preferential treatment, even an honoured place in Babylon
itself, though in fact Jeremiah chose to stay and seek to help a
crippled Judah to reorganize, under the administration of Gedaliah
(40:1-6).

Taken against his will to Egypt, Jeremiah's last recorded oracles
(apart from those we are unable to date) were in warning to the
Egyptians that they too would be overwhelmed by the Babylonians,
and in final expostulation to the many Judaeans who had taken
refuge in Egypt that they should learn the lessons past history would
teach them, and above all turn from idolatry (43:8-44:30). To the
last, his prophecies fell on deaf ears.

*   *   *   *   *   *

We have now outlined the history of the two Hebrew monarchies
from two different angles. We have seen that the stature of the
prophets seemed to increase as that of the kings diminished; yet not

8. On the authenticity of this prediction cf. N. K. Gottwald, *All the Kingdoms of the
Earth* (New York, 1964), pp. 265f.
9. See above, p. 128.

even a Jeremiah was able to convince his contemporaries of the truth of his words, in spite of the accurate fulfilment of prophecy after prophecy. Must we then view the prophets as a glorious failure? We may admire their zeal and courage, their moral stature and their spiritual perception; but must we add the rider that they were sadly out of touch with the mood of their times, and doomed to failure as unrealistic dreamers? Superficially, such a criticism might seem fair, but if it were so, how could one explain the fact that the Jewish people, survivors of the Babylonian holocaust, went on to collect, edit, treasure, study and canonize the words of these same prophets? As we view them now in historical perspective, we can see that their message was not only for their own contemporaries, but even more, perhaps, for later generations. But what did they say that was so relevant for posterity? Many abiding general truths, to be sure; but beyond that, they uttered many hopes and expectations and convictions which could only find fulfilment and illumination in later epochs. It now becomes apparent that in seeking to see Israel's history through the prophets' eyes, and the prophets through the eyes of history, we have neglected a vital part of their over-all message. It is to the faith that inspired them and the faith that they in turn inspired that we must now devote our attention.

Part Four

The Faith

CHAPTER 25

The God Who Speaks

A New Testament writer, looking back to the era of the prophets, observed, "When in former times God spoke to our forefathers, he spoke in fragmentary and varied fashion through the prophets" (Hebrews 1:1). A devout Israelite of the era in question would have agreed wholeheartedly that God did indeed speak to him and his contemporaries, and not only through the prophets but by other channels as well. The New Testament writer probably singled out the prophets because of the future perspective of their words, if indeed he was not using the term to include all the Old Testament writers.

When today the phrase "the word of God" is used, very frequently the Bible, God's written revelation, is meant; but the ancient Israelite would have thought more readily of the *spoken* word. Parts of the Old Testament were already in written form before the monarchy began, to be sure, and other parts were written during the monarchic period (though the precise dating of much of the Old Testament is a very complex and controversial question); but it seems hardly likely that the ordinary Israelite had direct access to the sacred writings. We must remind ourselves, to begin with, that publication as we know it today was impossible before the invention of printing. Even when the Old Testament was finally complete, only the rich few could have afforded personal copies; it was the synagogue (and later the church) which brought the Scriptures to the common man, and the synagogue cannot have come into being before the Babylonian exile. If proof be required that during the period of history we are considering no part of the Old Testament in written form was in any sense "published", then the total loss of

Deuteronomy till its discovery in Josiah's reign should be evidence enough.[1]

Nevertheless, the Israelite had access to the *spoken* word of God in various ways. There were different modes of divine revelation, and different mediators of the divine word. The prophet, the king, the sage, and the priest each had his special part to play in providing the community and the individual with the message of God. From the prophet came the oracle and the vision; from the king came judgement, above all; from the wise man, divine counsel; and from the priest, divine instruction. To a limited extent these rôles overlapped, but as late as the exilic period the prophet Ezekiel could diagnose his nation's malaise thus: "Disaster comes upon disaster, rumour follows rumour; they seek a vision from the prophet, but the law perishes from the priest, and counsel from the leaders. The king mourns, the prince is wrapped in despair" (Ezekiel 7:26f., RSV).

A familiar illustration of the king's exercise of judgement is the story of Solomon's handling of the dispute between the two harlots over the child of one of them (1 Kings 3:16-28). The narrative ends with the note that "when Israel heard the judgement which the king had given, they all stood in awe of him; for they saw that he had the wisdom of God within him to administer justice". Solomon's legal decisions, in other words, were the voice of God to the citizen of Israel.

The priest's rôle was to supply *torah,* divine instruction. In due course this Hebrew word came to denote the divine law as a whole, and the Jews still call the Pentateuch the Torah; but the term at first denoted an individual instruction, and the plural *torot* is sometimes used in the Old Testament.[2] Sometimes, we know, the priests' "instructions" were sought on cultic matters, such as ritual cleanliness (cf. Haggai 2:11ff.) and fasting (Zechariah 7:3); but we may be sure that their competence extended to wider matters of religious practice and ethical behaviour, and that the Levites (at any rate) went out from the sanctuary on a teaching mission to the community. The sons of Levi, says Deuteronomy 33:10, "teach thy precepts to Jacob, thy law to Israel". The priestly oracle will have been drawn from the ancient, prescribed laws which were in the priests' care; we may be sure that just as the two stone tablets containing the Ten Commandments had been deposited with the ark of the covenant (Exodus 25:16, 21), so every sanctuary in monarchic Israel housed copies of the written law. Other decisions from God could be obtained by recourse to the ephod or the Urim and Thum-

---

1. This is true, at least, if it be granted that the document then discovered was indeed Deuteronomy (in whole or part).
2. E.g., Nehemiah 9:13; Isaiah 24:5; Ezekiel 44:24.

mim — at least, in the early days of the monarchy. By whatever mode, God gave his living word through the priesthood.

The prophet had recourse neither to mechanical means like the Urim and Thummin, nor to ancient written laws; to him God spoke directly, and that is why he was called "the man of God" par excellence. Each true prophet experienced a divine call to office, and though he might at times reason or argue, his oracles were normally introduced by an unambiguous "thus saith the LORD". The people — though they did not always obey, to be sure — undoubtedly believed that God did speak to and through the prophet. As a non-Israelite woman summed it up (addressing Elijah), "Now I know for certain that you are a man of God and that the word of the LORD on your lips is truth" (1 Kings 17:24). This type of oracle differed from the priestly one in that it was a particular message for specific circumstances. Should King Ahab go to war with the Syrians at Ramoth-gilead or not? He turned to the prophets for the divine word. How and where could a young private citizen find some lost donkeys? Saul knew that the local prophet or seer was the man to seek out. Denied access to the prophets in later life, Saul still sought one out — though a dead one, and the king had to resort to necromancy — and still heard the living word of God.

The members of the priesthood, we have noted, might leave the sanctuary to teach the community God's instructions, whether the people sought them out or not. The prophet, to an even more marked degree, took God's message to the people, who would rather not have listened to it. "This people's wits are dulled, their ears are deafened," God warned Isaiah (6:10); and when Elijah confronted Ahab on one occasion, the discomfited king responded in patent sincerity, "Have you found me, my enemy?" (1 Kings 21:20). Ahab's successor took deliberate steps to avoid hearing the prophetic word when he desperately needed an oracle, and sent instead to a foreign and idolatrous sanctuary (2 Kings 1:2); but it was the oracle of Yahweh through Elijah that pronounced his doom, nevertheless. Other prophets — Amos and Jeremiah — seized the opportunities presented by large crowds attending temple ceremonies. God's people could not escape his living voice.

The wise men's prerogative was "counsel". A purely human source of instruction, the product solely of human and fallible intelligence? One may occasionally hear such a view of the matter propounded in some Christian circles today, but it is certainly not the view presented in the Old Testament. It is only fools who scorn wisdom (Proverbs 1:7), for they are despising one of God's valuable gifts to man. Nowhere is the value of wisdom made clearer than in 1 Kings 3:12, where God bestows wisdom and discernment upon Solomon. No king could have ruled Israel properly without divine "counsel", whether it resided in himself or in his advisors and statesmen, the highest rank of wise men in ancient Israel. Ahithophel, Absalom's adviser, stands as the exemplar of such a wise man: "In those days a man would seek counsel of Ahithophel as readily as he might make an inquiry of the word of God" (2 Samuel 16:23).

Not only in matters of the greatest political moment did Israel require wisdom; the Book of Proverbs deals with some of the most mundane areas of life — and offers divine wisdom, mediated through wise men of the day. It is self-evident that many of their findings were indeed products of human intelligence and reasoning and observation; it requires no voice from heaven to tell one that "A soft answer turns away anger, but a sharp word makes tempers hot" (Proverbs 15:1), or that "Endless dripping on a rainy day — that is what a nagging wife is like" (Proverbs 27:15)! But human reasoning is one mode of divine revelation, the Old Testament would assure us — or else the Book of Proverbs should not stand in the Canon of Scripture. The wise men were fallible, true; but priests and prophets are sometimes condemned in the Old Testament too (cf. Micah 3:11).

The wise man, then, also offered Israel the word of God; and as with priest and prophet, we may well believe that he too undertook a deliberate teaching rôle, and did not merely make himself available for consultation. The promulgation of the Book of Proverbs itself was part of the teaching rôle of Israel's sages.

In every area of life, then, God-appointed mediators and messengers were to be found, and the word of God heard. But we must give closer attention to one specific area of life vital to the devout Israelite of old: his worship in the sanctuary. Here, to be sure, the worshipper's voice was also heard; but we must not think that the liturgy was in one direction only, from man to God. The Psalter provides us with rich examples and illustrations of the liturgy familiar to Israel during the period of the monarchy; and in it we hear God's voice as well as the worshipper's. The worshipper offered God prayer, supplication, praise and confession; God responded in tones of promise, assurance, forgiveness, blessing, and occasionally warning.

No doubt a rich ceremonial ritual accompanied the liturgy we find preserved in the Psalter; but let us note some of the passages which make God's speech explicit. Such an emphasis we find in Psalm 50, which begins with the words, "God, the LORD God, has spoken" and continues, "Our God is coming and will not keep silence" (verse 3). The words of God commence in verse 5 ("Gather to me my loyal servants"), and in verse 7 he addresses Israel: "Listen, my people, and I will speak." The bulk of the psalm is God's challenge to his people — *verbatim*.

Psalm 15 addresses a question to God in the first verse; the rest of the psalm is God's reply. Psalm 24 is similar, though the questions are here interspersed with the responses: "Who may go up the mountain of the LORD?" (verse 3); "Who is the King of glory?" (verse 8).

Without doubt the priest functioned in the sanctuary as the mouthpiece of God, pronouncing blessing and giving assurance. On such special occasions, it may be, the king too played a rôle in the ceremonial and the liturgy. It is clear that the words of Psalm 2, for instance, can have been appropriate only on the lips of a king of Judah; it is a psalm in which the king speaks and in which God speaks to him. Psalm 45 is addressed to the king — "in a king's honour", says its author, "I utter the song I have made". The king was a symbol of the well-being of the community; their well-being was bound up with his, and it was therefore fitting that he should play a special rôle in the sanctuary. When God spoke to the king in blessing, the people knew themselves to be equally blessed.[3]

In these many and varied ways, then, the ancient citizen of Israel and Judah was aware of the voice of God. It was always accessible to him, and at times it was thrust at him when he least expected or wanted to hear it. Perhaps we should ask the further question, however, what sort of a God was it whose voice he heard? This question will be partially answered in the next two chapters, for the Israelites knew that their God was especially a God who had done great things and who promised to do great things in the future. At this juncture we may content ourselves with seeking some indication as to how the Israelites envisaged his character and being, as opposed to his works and words.

His name was Yahweh, a truly distinctive name. There is no evidence that it was borrowed from any other people in the way that the gods of Mesopotamia or Canaan tended to move from one country to another. The meaning of the name, unfortunately, is not at all certain; even Exodus 3:14 conceals as much as it reveals, whether deliberately or otherwise.[4] In a world of many deities, in any case, the Israelite needed more than a name to make it clear what sort of God he worshipped, important though that name was. (Indeed, names were considered far more important in those days than in our modern western society.) Hence the Old Testament writings describe God in a variety of ways, and with a variety of epithets.

The name Yahweh itself, in any case, was used by Israel long before the period of the monarchy. While we cannot isolate the

---

3. For the rich ideal of the king's value to his people, see J. H. Eaton, *Kingship and the Psalms (SBT* ii, 32: London, 1976), pp. 135-197.

4. The NEB translations in text and margin give some idea of the range of possible understandings. Nor is it clear whether the verse is interpreting the etymology or merely the function of the name.

monarchic era from what went before and what came after, the endeavour must be made to set Israel's faith against a monarchic background; in other words, to see what aspects of that faith were either new or else received new and particular emphasis during that era. One point of interest is a description of God, which far from receiving new emphasis seems to have been used sparingly and selectively by the preachers and writers of the day: the phrase "Yahweh (God) of hosts". The word "hosts" (Hebrew *tsebaot*)[5] means "armies", and although it is disputed whether angelic armies or the Israelite troops were originally meant, it is clear that this description of God was appropriately used against a background of military activity. Yahweh was the God who gave his people military defence and victory as they needed it. In the period of the Judges, he had raised up men of his choice to act as deliverers by putting his spirit upon them. The term "Lord of hosts" seems to have been specially associated with the Shiloh sanctuary, or perhaps one should rather say with the ark of the covenant, to judge by the occurrences of the title in the early chapters of 1 Samuel.

After David's time, however, when Israel's wars were altogether more professional and profane, and when the ark was never moved from its shrine in Jerusalem, we may conclude that to Yahweh's spokesmen it was no longer so clear that Israel's wars were his wars; and the prophets had no wish to bolster up national pride by a false theology, or rather a misplaced faith in Yahweh. But at a time of a desperate military emergency for Judah, when Sennacherib's armies were on the point of snuffing God's people out of existence, then once more a prophet offered hope and courage in the name of "Yahweh of hosts". The prophet was Isaiah, who heard the phrase uttered by the seraphim at his call to prophesy (Isaiah 6:3), and who was never afraid to repeat it in appropriate circumstances; it was "the zeal of the LORD of hosts" (Isaiah 37:32) which would bring discomfiture to the proud Assyrian king. Against the background of the imminent fall of Jerusalem, the prophet Jeremiah was again not afraid to use this divine title. But in most of the pre-exilic prophets one finds the familiar phrase used very sparingly if not avoided altogether. The wars of God's people are not all holy wars.

The title "Yahweh of hosts", therefore, serves to illustrate how we may isolate some of the special emphases of the monarchic period; its use also shows that we must beware of viewing descriptive divine epithets as purely conventional; each one had its special function.

The use of the term *ba'al* for Yahweh has already been mentioned.[6] It was a term which not only fell out of use but was in

---

5. Cf. "Sabaoth" in Romans 9:29 (AV).
6. See above, p. 201.

fact firmly rejected before the monarchy ended. During the Judges period and early monarchy it was freely used to describe Yahweh, as can be seen from personal names in Saul's family such as Merib-baal and Esh-baal. As a title its meaning was unexceptionable, for it meant "lord" or "owner"; but its all-too-familiar use in Canaanite worship for the chief Canaanite deity made it ultimately unacceptable in Israel. There were other synonymous Hebrew words which had no such unfortunate overtones, as Hosea recognized (Hosea 2:16f.) Eventually so great was the antipathy of devout Jews to the name *ba'al* that they eliminated it even from the personal names which were then written with the word *boshet,* "shame". Hence the Mephibosheth and Ish-bosheth.

The use and disuse of the name *ba'al* in Yahweh worship reminds us that the major battle with Canaanite religion was fought during the monarchic era, and hence the descriptions given of Yahweh in the writings of the period often have some bearing on this conflict. Sometimes it was important to stress that Yahweh was quite different from Baal; at other times it was necessary to emphasize that Yahweh did no less for his worshippers than Baal did for his, and then descriptions similar to those used in Canaanite worship were considered appropriate. It has been observed that especially in the Psalter there are descriptions of Yahweh strikingly comparable with the language used of Baal in the Ras Shamra texts. In Psalm 68:4, for instance, the God of Israel is depicted as the One "who rides upon the clouds";[7] an almost identical phrase occurs in the Ras Shamra literature, but is there applied to Baal. Baal was especially associated with the skies; very well, then Israel must be reminded that Yahweh, not Baal, ruled the weather. The Canaanites believed that Baal by giving rain brought fertility to the ground; another Psalm therefore addressed Yahweh in worship thus:

Thou dost visit the earth and give it abundance,
    as often as thou dost enrich it
with the waters of heaven, brimming in their channels,
    providing rain for men.

(Psalm 65:9)

Every ancient pantheon had its creator god; Israel's God was no less, as is made clear from early Genesis to the incomparable passage in Isaiah 40:12-31, and in many a Psalm. Many pantheons named one deity as "King"; we have already seen how the god Marduk became king in the Babylonian pantheon,[8] while nearer Israel there were deities worshipped under the name "king" — Milcom, Molech, Melqart. In Israel, then, worshippers were reminded in the

---

7. RSV, cf. JB. The Hebrew could also mean "deserts", cf. NEB.
8. See above, pp. 194f.

liturgy that "The LORD is King; he is clothed in majesty" (Psalm 93:1). King over whom? Over his people, to be sure; but lest anyone should suppose that anyone could rival his lordship in heaven, Psalm 95:3 declares, "The LORD is a great God, a great King over all gods". This is not the language of a systematic monotheism, clearly; it is the language of religious polemic.

Thus one can see how rôle after rôle attributed outside Israel to a variety of gods and goddesses were all brought together and seen as fitting designations and descriptions of Yahweh. There was not unnaturally a certain polarity in some of the descriptions; the Song of Hannah, for example, recognizes that

> The LORD kills and he gives life,
> he sends down to Sheol, he can bring the dead up again.
> The LORD makes a man poor, he makes him rich,
> he brings down and he raises up.
>
> (1 Samuel 2:6f.)

A well-known feature of this polarity is the characterization of God as both love and wrath. So often this contrast has been postulated as distinguishing the Old Testament from the New; but in fact the same polarity can be seen in both Testaments. There is scarcely a more common noun in the Old Testament than the Hebrew *chesed,* a word difficult to translate precisely ("lovingkindness", or "kindness" or "mercy" in the Authorized Version as a rule), but indicative time and time again of God's abiding and faithful love for his people and mercy towards them. His wrath, on the other hand, far from being a whimsical exercise of irrational irritability, is particularly associated with his "zeal". Here again, English has no exact equivalent of the Hebrew terms, which at one and the same time denote both "zeal" and "jealousy". God's zeal on behalf of his people was inseparable from his claim to exclusive lordship over them. Baal shared his worshippers with Dagon and Ashtoreth and the rest; Yahweh shared his people with no other deity, not even a consort. The mercy and wrath of Yahweh were established for Israel long before the monarchy began, of course; but the prophets stressed both facets of the divine character more than other Old Testament writers. Among the prophets, Hosea's picture of the stern yet aching heart of Yahweh for his people is unique.

A striking epithet for Yahweh is the thrice-repeated adjective we encounter in Isaiah 6:3: "Holy, holy, holy is the LORD of hosts". The Hebrew adjective (*qadosh*) and its equivalents in other ancient Semitic languages had been in use for many centuries before Isaiah's time, to designate deities and objects or personnel devoted to cultic use and service. Whatever the word's original significance, it had come to mean "sacred" or "religious" in most contexts; even prostitutes of the Canaanite sanctuaries were "holy" (*qadesh*, feminine *qedeshah*) in this sense. Some such prostitutes were even attached to Yahweh sanctuaries during the monarchy, except when eradicated by reforming kings like Hezekiah and Josiah. The prophets of the eighth century, however, recognized that God's own holiness was of such a character as to be incompatible with "holy" prostitution. Isaiah's immediate reaction to the revelation of Yahweh's holiness was to confess the uncleanness of himself and his fellow-citizens. The holiness of God was a frightening thing to all Israelites, something to be shunned and feared; had not Uzzah died, in David's time, for venturing to set profane hands on the sacred ark (2 Samuel 6)? A Phoenician woman expressed a similar thought when she blamed Elijah's very presence in her home for bringing her son to death's door (1 Kings 17:17f.). But Isaiah put his finger on what constituted the holiness of God: "By *righteousness* the holy God shows himself holy" (Isaiah 5:16).

"Righteousness" (Hebrew *tsedeq* or *tsedaqah*) primarily denotes correspondence to a standard or norm, and such a description of Yahweh serves to differentiate him from the capricious deities that were in truth the religious norm of the ancient Near East. It must have required a real faith to enable the prophets to see God working to norms; the ambiguity of events and the apparent shapelessness of history and of life more readily lend themselves to the outlook of the ancient polytheists, who saw a medley of gods of differing and conflicting attributes and wishes and actions. With their total disregard for other gods, the prophets were compelled to see in Yahweh the author of *all* the varied and conflicting phenomena of the universe. This they did unhesitatingly; but they still maintained that Yahweh followed undeviating standards of moral perfection, and hence required equal standards from his people, whom he had constituted "holy".

God's holiness and righteousness, therefore, could only be seen revealed in history; and of all ancient peoples Israel seems to have the clearest awareness of the march of history. The Hebrew language had no word for "history", or we may be sure that the Old Testament would frequently have designated Yahweh "the lord of history". The nearest equivalents we find are "the everlasting God" and "the living God'. The former is a reminder that Yahweh had created the world and set human history afoot, and continued unchanged and unchanging in his control of both. This is a timeless, possibly static, description; but the other term, "the living God", is a dynamic one, stressing the power of Yahweh and his intervention in human affairs. We may note how Elijah predicted the three-year drought by taking an oath on the "life of Yahweh" (1 Kings 17:1). Elijah's mockery of the Baal prophets is instructive, too; they could utter a triumphant cultic acclamation to their god,

"Victorious Baal lives!",[9] in which Baal's annual victory over the god Mot ("death") seems to have been recalled. The signs of spring do show themselves annually, even when adversely affected by drought conditions; but Baal could at times absent himself, deep in thought, engaged, journeying, or even asleep, said Elijah (1 Kings 18:27). But the God of Israel answered by fire — for he neither slumbers nor sleeps.

The more one studies the character of Yahweh depicted in the Old Testament, the more one comes to appreciate that it is bound up with human history; "pure", abstract theology is strikingly absent from the Old Testament. We cannot content ourselves, therefore, with a consideration of the God "who is" or the God "who speaks"; above all, the Old Testament presents us with a God who acts.

---

9. A phrase found in the Ras Shamra texts. The selection of texts about Baal in *DOTT* (pp. 129 ff.) offers many parallels to Old Testament language about Yahweh.

CHAPTER 26

The God Who Acts

A T the start of the monarchy, Israel could already look back to a
rich body of traditions and national memories, the material
transmitted to us in the Books of Genesis, Exodus, Joshua and
Judges in particular. In all their history they could see God had been
at work. He had created the universe and man upon it; he had
brought Abraham out of Mesopotamia, led him to Canaan and
covenanted with him to give his offspring the Promised Land; he
had raised up Moses, led the Israelites out of Egypt, and constituted
them a nation at Sinai; he had led them into Canaan and given them
victory in Joshua's day; he had repeatedly given them deliverers
during the exigencies of the era of the Judges. All this and more
besides was common knowledge among the Israelites of Samuel's
day; their history was already clearly *Heilsgeschichte*, "salvation-
history". The recognition of God as "saviour" long antedated the
New Testament pages.

But Israel's history did not end with the Judges, of course, and by
the same token neither did God's activity in history, for those with
eyes to see it. There were many events of the period of the monarchy
which proved to be full of theological significance. An obvious
example is the history of Jerusalem, which is today for three faiths
"the Holy City"; in Samuel's lifetime it was still just one Canaanite
city, neither more or less (in spite of Abraham's visit to it long centuries before). It was David's capture of the city, and his subsequent
re-creation of it as capital, royal city, and central sanctuary, which
transformed all its future history, and gave it all its theological significance for Jew, Muslim and Christian alike.

We must go back earlier than the capture of Jerusalem, however,
for the first significant event of our period of history; the creation of
a monarchy was in itself of primary importance, both historically

and theologically. The day that Saul became king inaugurated a new
and formative era for Israel. A strong, centralized government was a
political necessity, in view of the Philistine aggression; but what sort
of government was it to be, and what sort of rôle would the king
fulfil? In our day, such questions would be purely political; but in
ancient Israel, such questions were just as much religious ones.
Israel's polity was already a theocratic one; Yahweh was the King of
Israel, and the existing political institutions and laws were divinely
ordained. How would a human monarch fit into this pattern? It is
clear that the new institution was capable of breaching the old; 1
Samuel 8:7 reports that Yahweh told Samuel, "Listen to the people
and all that they are saying; they have not rejected you, it is I whom
they have rejected, I whom they will not have to be their king."
Nevertheless, Yahweh through the prophet did put Saul on the
throne, while David had the full and unambiguous blessing of God
in becoming king.

Monarchs may gain their authority from a variety of sources.
Many have usurped a throne by military conquest; others hold it
constitutionally and by the right of hereditary succession; some have
been elected to the throne; others again, in the ancient world,
became king by some religious right or guarantee. In Egypt, the
reigning king was indeed held to be a god; while in Babylon the
kings had a semi-divine status, to which they were thought to be
appointed by the gods in order to maintain the rule of the gods in
Babylonia. What of Israel? Saul was popularly acclaimed king, and
David fought for his throne; but neither dared become king without
having his reign guaranteed by Yahweh. The wording of the royal
psalms sometimes suggests that the Davidic king had a sort of semi-
divine status conferred on him; the king was the "son" of Yahweh
(Psalm 2:7), and it is not impossible that the king could be actually
addressed as "God". Such, at any rate, is the most natural interpretation of Psalm 45:6, "Your throne, O God, stands for ever and
ever" (NAB).[1]

The lofty position of Israel's king was however one of subser-
vience where Yahweh was concerned. Firstly, the divine choice was
necessary; Samuel, guided by Yahweh, chose Saul to be king; in the
Northern Kingdom we find prophets choosing Jeroboam and Jehu;
and in David's case, exceptionally, it stands recorded that Yahweh
chose not only the man but his family to succeed him (2 Samuel
7:8-16). (Jeroboam's successors in the north tried to establish the
dynastic principle, when they did not capture the throne by a
military coup, but history testifies to their large degree of failure.) In
the case of Saul and David, Yahweh's spirit visibly marked out the

---

1. The NEB and RSV, however, offer a different translation which transfers the
divinity from the king to his throne.

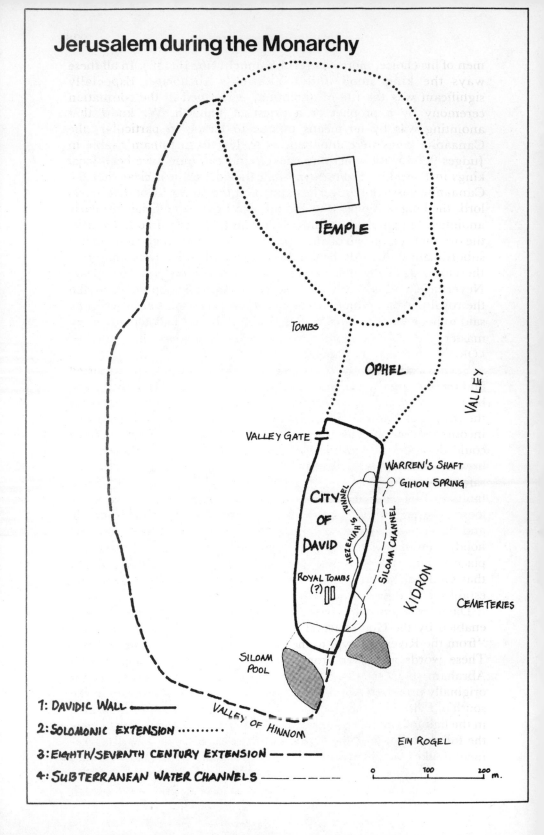

Jerusalem during the Monarchy

TEMPLE

TOMBS

OPHEL

VALLEY

VALLEY GATE

WARREN'S SHAFT

GIHON SPRING

CITY OF DAVID

HEZEKIAH'S TUNNEL

SILOAM CHANNEL

ROYAL TOMBS (?)

KIDRON

CEMETERIES

SILOAM POOL

VALLEY OF HINNOM

EIN ROGEL

1: DAVIDIC WALL ————
2: SOLOMONIC EXTENSION ··········
3: EIGHTH/SEVENTH CENTURY EXTENSION — — —
4: SUBTERRANEAN WATER CHANNELS ————

0   100   200 m.

men of his choice, moreover (cf. 1 Samuel 11:6; 16:13f.). In all these ways the king stood under Yahweh's authority. Especially significant was the rite of anointing, performed at the coronation ceremony by a prophet or a priest of Yahweh. We know that anointing was by no means unique to Israel; in particular, the Canaanite kings were anointed, as is clear from Jotham's fable in Judges 9:7-15, for which the background can only have been local kings in Palestine. From extra-biblical evidence, it is clear that the Canaanite vassal kings were anointed on the authority of their over-lord, the king of Egypt, who had his own Egyptian officials similarly anointed, but who did not himself submit to the rite. In other words, the original symbolism of anointing was to confer a high-ranking but subordinate status. All the kings of Israel and Judah were anointed, therefore, as Yahweh's vassals, his "local-rulers", so to speak. Nevertheless his authority was thereby conferred upon them, so that the royal person became sacrosanct. David recognized this when he said to his men regarding Saul, "God forbid that I should harm my master, the LORD's anointed, or lift a finger against him; he is the LORD's anointed" (1 Samuel 24:6).

Such was the Davidic covenant, whereby Yahweh both permitted and blessed the Davidic king. He was to be the channel of the divine blessing to others, the protector and upholder of the divine laws for the people of Yahweh. Even after a succession of weak, wicked and incompetent monarchs, the writer of the Book of Lamentations could describe the Davidic king thus: "The LORD's anointed, the breath of life to us . . . we had thought to live among the nations, safe under his protection" (Lamentations 4:20). Indeed, for all the faults and follies of the Hebrew kings, they did at least transform a loose grouping of tribes into a nation (or must we say two nations?); and that people was never to lose its identity and sense of brother-hood, even in days of exile and dispersion. The kings had their vital place in Israel's history; and the Israelites of the day did not doubt that God had acted in history when he first provided a king and established a dynasty for them.

David was not only given royal status by divine decree, he was enabled by the God of Israel to master an empire which extended "from the River of Egypt to the Great River, the river Euphrates". These words are taken from the record of God's covenant with Abraham (Genesis 15:18). It has been argued that this covenant originally promised Abraham no more than a limited territory in the south of Palestine, and that the words of the promise were expanded in the light of David's conquests.[2] Other writers would prefer to view the full description of the Promised Land as original. The disagreement makes no difference to the theological motif; Yahweh had

2. Cf. R. E. Clements, *Abraham and David* (SBT ii, 5: London, 1967), pp. 21f.

made startling, even incredible, promises to Abraham, which were fulfilled to some degree in Joshua's time, but which in David's time came to even greater and more wonderful fulfilment. The erstwhile slaves of Egypt, the erstwhile vassals of Philistia, were now unchallenged rulers of their own land, and exercised lordship over several other nations.

In Solomon's day the frontiers began to retract, and after his reign the empire collapsed; but God had once acted, and his people never forgot. God had given them wide horizons. Jerusalem, so recently acquired by David, could now be viewed as the capital of an international realm. Against this Davidic king and that, "the kings of the earth stood ready, the rulers conspired together, and determined to break the Israelite fetters, to throw off their chains" — thus we may adapt Psalm 2:2f. But they had no chance of success against Yahweh, the God of all the earth, so long as it was his will to make these peoples subject to a king in Jerusalem. The psalm continues, with Yahweh addressing his anointed:

> . . . I have enthroned my king
>   on Zion my holy mountain . . .
> I will give you nations as your inheritance,
> the ends of the earth as your possession.

We may now revert to Jerusalem, the capture of which falls here into its correct chronological setting. It was one of David's conquests, and he made it the religious centre of his kingdom; his son went on to build a magnificent temple there. Other sanctuaries continued to exist till Josiah's time, but none captured the imagination as did Jerusalem. As N. W. Porteous has written, "No city has stirred emotion at a deeper level than the strange, enigmatic city of Jerusalem. There was something of the beauty of Athens about it; for did not a psalmist once describe it as God's 'holy mountain, beautiful in elevation, the joy of all the earth'? There was something of Rome about it too; for a prophet made the prediction that 'out of Zion shall go forth the law' and that the city on the Judaean hills would be the centre of a peaceful world."[3]

Jerusalem's proud theological position was bound up with the twin fact that it functioned as the capital of the king God has chosen, and that it was the final home of the ark, the symbol of God's presence. Psalm 132 recalls Yahweh's oath to David: "A prince of your own line will I set upon your throne" (verse 11); and goes on to add "For the LORD has chosen Zion and desired it for his home: 'This is my resting-place for ever, here will I make my home, for such is my desire' " (verses 13f.). Jerusalem, that is to say, was as

---

3. N. W. Porteous, *Living the mystery: collected essays* (Oxford, 1967), p. 93. The Old Testament references are to Psalm 48:3, Isaiah 2:3f. and Micah 4:2f.

clearly "elected" by Yahweh as were David and his dynasty. It was "the city of the Great King" as well as "the city of David". From that conception grew the Judaean conviction of the inviolability of Jerusalem; God, Yahweh himself, dwelt in Jerusalem, and he could not permit any human agent to molest it, certainly not the "uncircumcised" and the "unclean" invader. We have already observed something of the part played by this view-point in the arguments of the prophets true and false.

One interesting feature of the Old Testament references to Jerusalem is its description as a mountain. Isaiah 31:4, for example, speaks of "Mount Zion and her high summit". The altitude of the city is considerable, and its hilly contours gave it reasonable natural defences on three sides; but the biblical language clearly suggests something more than merely a defensible city in a mountainous area. Or should we put it down to mere poetic adornment? Psalm 48:2 offers a better clue, even though the verse is puzzling at first sight. Jerusalem is extolled as the city of God: "His holy mountain, beautiful in elevation, is the joy of all the earth, Mount Zion, in the far north, the city of the Great King" (RSV). We might put down the phrase "the joy of all the earth" as poetic exaggeration, but from what possible standpoint is Jerusalem to be described as "in the far north"? Once again we may turn to the Ras Shamra texts for elucidation; near the ancient city of Ugarit (Ras Shamra is the present day name of the site) was a mountain bearing the name Zaphon, the same word as the Hebrew "north",[4] and in the Canaanite mythology it functioned in the same way as the Mount Olympus of the Greeks, the traditional abode of the gods. Thus it seems that the Psalmist was in effect calling Jerusalem "Mount Olympus" — the true home of the true God. Nothing therefore could compare with it for beauty, elevation and holiness. At a more prosaic level, everything possible was done in Solomon's Jerusalem to make the city beautiful to the beholder.

God had acted in giving his people David and Jerusalem and all that they stood for; but still the march of history continued, and soon the high promise gave way to a shabby and shoddy new reality. Israel and Judah separated and lost their power, while new nations rose to power and inflicted crushing blows upon the people of Yahweh. How was this unhappy development to be explained? Ultimately the answer was to be given its definitive canonical form in the Books of Kings; but before then Yahweh acted once more, in raising up the great prophets of Israel. To them fell the task of explaining to their contemporaries that Israel and Judah's lowly position was as much in the control of Yahweh the Lord of history as

4. Cf. NEB margin.

their earlier days of glory had been. The newly-found recognition that God elected David and his dynasty had been allowed to overshadow the fact that the older covenant at Sinai had never been abrogated by God. Clearly the covenant laws were being ignored by kings and neglected by their officers of state, with disastrous results for the poorer classes. Greed and rapacity, to say nothing of idolatry, had become the order of the day; and the prophets denounced these ugly national characteristics, and pronounced not only that the present political weakness was Yahweh's will, but also that he purposed even greater disasters for the future. Moreover, against the wider political horizons which David's career had opened, the prophets came to recognize more clearly than earlier generations that Yahweh controlled other nations just as much as he did Israel and Judah. He was not only "the God of Israel", true in a special way though that was, but the God of the nations. And so we find that foreign oracles became a natural part of the teachings of the prophets.

The prophetic ministry laid a sound basis for Judah to come to terms with the collapse of her sister kingdom. Israel's fall vindicated the prophetic analysis and the prophetic warnings, and it is no doubt precisely because of this vindication that the prophetic word was carefully preserved in writing, later to be brought into the Canon of Scripture. Judah went her own way towards a similar (but not identical) fate, but the prophetic ministry regarding Samaria's fall exercised a continuing influence during the dark days of Manasseh and his ilk. The "remnant" spoken of by Elijah and Isaiah had already come into being, and on it were the prophetic hopes for the future based.

Josiah's reform was encouraged by Yahweh, or so it seemed; yet twelve years later God allowed that godly king to fall in battle, after which Judah lost again its new-found independence. These events gave fresh pause for thought; indeed, some scholars have suggested that Josiah's unexpected death at Megiddo in 609 B.C. is greeted in the Old Testament by a "resounding silence". Good, reforming kings ought not to perish in this way; however, Jeremiah at least had never seen a panacea for all ills in the reform programme, and he for one was enabled to develop a strongly spiritual sense of religion, divorced from externals. It was the same sense which inspired the Psalmist to write, "Sacrifice and offering thou dost not desire . . . Burnt offering and sin offering thou hast not required" (Psalm 40:6, RSV). It was no new insight in Jeremiah's day, certainly; Samuel had told Israel's first king that "obedience is better than sacrifice, and to listen to him than the fat of rams. Defiance of him is sinful as witchcraft, yielding to men as evil as idolatry", as 1 Samuel 15:22f. records. It was however a desperately needed new emphasis at a time when Judah faced the imminent loss of all it had treasured most dearly — Jerusalem and its temple, the ark of the covenant, and the line of David.

The prophets, then, first and last, saw God active in the events of political history, and sought to instil this belief into their contemporaries. But one of the last acts of God in the monarchic period was of a different, indeed a unique character. In the year 621 B.C. a lost document was accidentally found by workmen engaged in the repair of the temple; but neither the high priest Hilkiah nor the king, Josiah, had the slightest doubt that this discovery was ordained by God. The scroll played an important role in the short-lived reform Josiah instituted; and it was to play an even more important role in the future, if indeed it was an edition of the book we know as Deuteronomy.[5]

Standing under the authority of Moses, and promulgated by the king himself, Deuteronomy had a great deal to say to those with ears to hear. In the first place it reminded the people that all the benefits they had enjoyed so long were God's gifts to them — their land, their leaders, their Law, and their claim on God himself. All these things they treasured were unmerited favours, and betokened God's love for his people. All too long, however, Israel and Judah had taken these things for granted, accepting the gifts without accepting the responsibilities, which were to love and obey God, and to act justly and kindly towards their fellows. These responsibilities are all stressed in Deuteronomy. Their importance is obvious when we consider that within a generation or so of Josiah's reform the disasters that befell Judah were of such a kind that she could easily have lost her faith in Yahweh along with her temple, and her sense of brotherhood along with her nationhood (which in a real sense was taken from them by exile and by the fall of the royal house).

Far from decrying cultic ritual, Deuteronomy insists that it must be properly executed, and in fact rules out every sanctuary but one for it (cf. Deuteronomy 12:5f.). This centralization of the cult had never been practised (since pre-Conquest days, at any rate), and Josiah found himself unable to enforce it. Nevertheless the emphasis in Deuteronomy on a single sanctuary highlighted the degree of false and idolatrous worship to be found outside Jerusalem, and gave an impetus for the Jews to codify their faith, to purify and protect it. Moreover, the fall of the Jerusalem temple so soon after the promulgation of Deuteronomy had the effect of spiritualizing that faith, and making it less dependent on externals. It is to the Book of Deuteronomy that we owe that most inward and demanding of commandments, which our Lord himself endorsed as the greatest of them all: "You must love the LORD your God with all your heart and soul and strength" (Deuteronomy 6:5; cf. Matthew 22:36ff.).

5. See above, p. 119.

There were other insights in Deuteronomy which proved invaluable for Josiah's era. In a way, it functioned to demote the king and the ark of the covenant, so soon to be swept away, and to promote the prophet. The prophet had all too often been persecuted and ignored; but Deuteronomy taught that Moses himself had foretold the succession of prophets like himself. This is the primary intention of the divine promise in Deuteronomy 18:18f.: "I will raise up for them a prophet like you, one of their own race, and I will put my words into his mouth. He shall convey all my commands to them, and if anyone does not listen to the words which he will speak in my name I will require satisfaction from him."

The king, on the other hand, had by Josiah's time been placed on a pedestal, so to speak. The Davidic covenant had become a static dogma to the people of Judah, as though the very existence of a king of David's line guaranteed their well-being. In Deuteronomy 17:14-20, however, we find in effect a critique of Judah's and Israel's kings as they really were — not always chosen by God, not always even of Israelite birth, proud, avaricious, despotic, and often utterly heedless of the laws of Yahweh. Josiah, by now, was the exception to prove the rule.

As for the ark of the covenant, it had for too long been credited with what we would call magical powers. Enshrined in the Jerusalem temple for long centuries, it had long acquired a mystique, and was thought to guarantee the presence of Yahweh, and all that implied, in his temple and city. But in Deuteronomy 10:1-5 the ark is very casually treated, as the mere wooden box which housed the Ten Commandments. The ark would soon perish for ever; but the Law to which it pointed, when properly interpreted, would survive the holocaust the Babylonians were soon to bring upon Jerusalem.

Deuteronomy has its omissions, to be sure; no missionary message is to be discerned there, nor does it offer the hope of life beyond the grave. But Josiah's era was better served by a book which stressed the truths which would bind God's people together and keep them distinct from other nations, and which offered the basis for a national rather than a personal hope. It was the nation's grave which loomed largest at the time, even if few were capable of perceiving the fact.

Josiah, we have said, "promulgated" Deuteronomy. Book publication as we know it was in the nature of things impossible, but Josiah did the next best thing. He "sent and called all the elders of Judah and Jerusalem together, and went up to the house of the LORD; he took with him the men of Judah and the inhabitants of Jerusalem, the priests and the prophets, the whole population, high and low. There he read out to them all the book of the covenant discovered in the house of the LORD; and then, standing on the dais, the king made a covenant before the LORD to obey him and keep his commandments, his testimonies, and his statutes, with all his heart and soul, and so fulfil the terms of the covenant written in this book. And all the people pledged themselves to the covenant'' (2 Kings 23:1ff.). Thus "the whole population" was introduced to the book, and obliged to subscribe to its teaching, not only by personal pledge but also in the activities which the king proceeded to instigate and enforce, which culminated in a joyous Passover celebration, kept in accordance with the prescriptions of Deuteronomy. Those rules (see Deuteronomy 16) make the festival very much a family affair, as it has continued to be in Judaism till this day. We may be sure that then, as now, youngsters were educated, in the context of the festal celebrations, as to the purpose and function and history of their faith.

Covenant documents were no new invention of Josiah's era, far from it; but there was nevertheless something new about the covenant to which his citizens pledged themselves. The norm was for a covenant document to record and bear witness to a covenant; in other words, the covenant itself preceded the document. On this occasion, however, the document came first, and the covenant was made on the basis of the document. Thus in the eyes of the king and all who treated his reforms seriously, Deuteronomy was a much more important document than any other; it was accepted as the unique basis of their faith and practice. With Josiah's promulgation of Deuteronomy, accordingly, we may fairly say that the story of the Canon of Scripture begins. We must emphasize again that parts of Scripture had of course been in existence long before the seventh century; but never before had a biblical document been used in such a fashion, and given such a position in the constitution of the faith. Josiah's promulgation of Deuteronomy can therefore fairly be compared with Luther's "rediscovery" of the Epistle of the Romans, and the subsequent creation of the Protestant churches on the basis of *sola Scriptura*.

Deuteronomy did not long remain the only book in the Old Testament Canon (a contradiction in terms!). It gave the signal and the impetus to bring together all "the words of God" then known to God's people, perhaps especially in the dark days of exile that so soon followed Josiah's reformation. Deuteronomy thus inspired the task of writing and recording, editing and collecting, copying and recopying. It was a task which was to continue into New Testament times, so that both Jews and Christians were one day to be known as "the people of the Book".

Apart from this general impetus which Deuteronomy's promulgation provided, there was another, more specific, consequence of no little importance. The Book of Deuteronomy offered its students a clear philosophy of history. Moses, Deuteronomy records, had advised Israel before ever they moved into the Promised Land, that their well-being in Canaan and their very tenure of it would be dependent upon their fidelity to the unadulterated worship of Yahweh and to his laws as embodied in the book. Apostasy would bring political disaster, as faithfulness would bring prosperity in its train.[6]

Whether or not such a philosophy of history appeals to twentieth century historians, it undoubtedly had a powerful and timely effect upon devout and thoughtful men in the Judah of the seventh and sixth centuries B.C. As the era of the Hebrew monarchies came to its sad and sorry end, such men took stock of their situation and of their nation's history, and it is to them that we owe the primary source material for this book — in other words, the Books of Samuel and Kings, and perhaps Joshua and Judges too. Much written material was available to them, of course, but the final editing of these books is "Deuteronomic", that is to say, dependent upon the teaching and even the language of the Book of Deuteronomy. For that reason, it has nowadays become commonplace to refer to Joshua, Judges, Samuel and Kings comprehensively as "the Deuteronomic history".[7]

It would seem, then, that we today are indebted to an accidental discovery by some ancient Judaean workmen for a substantial part of our Bible, if not for the whole concept of a Bible. A mere accident? Those of us who believe that God inspired the Bible's authors in the first place may well believe that he further acted in history in the case of its editors, scribes and transmitters of every kind, including thoughtful carpenters and pious kings.

The discovery and promulgation of Deuteronomy, then, had very profound and long-lasting effects for which we may still be grateful. In its own more immediate historical context, its importance was this: "It did not rescue Israel from the peril of political defeat and ruin, but it pointed to that realm of faith and of the spirit, where love and obedience mattered more than passing success or failure."[8]

---

6. Cf. Deuteronomy 4, in particular. The Books of Chronicles were written later, in rather different circumstances.

7. Both Ruth and Chronicles are separated from "the Deuteronomic history" in the Hebrew Old Testament.

8. R. E. Clements, *God's chosen people: a theological interpretation of the Book of Deuteronomy* (London, 1968), p. 119.

CHAPTER 27

The Future Perspective

"THROUGHOUT the Old Testament there is a forward look", wrote the late H. H. Rowley; "Israel believed that while there was a brief period of innocence and bliss at the opening of history, the real climax and crown of history lay in the future. She had a firm assurance that 'the best is yet to be', though that assurance, like every aspect of her faith, was rooted and grounded in God and not the mere expression of human optimism."[1]

All human beings, even in the most primitive society, seek to look into the future; all have their hopes and fears and aspirations. For Israel, the future was the point at which the words of God and the works of God met; for "the God who speaks" spoke of the future, chiefly through the prophets, and "the God who acts" must inevitably, by his very nature as Lord of history, continue to act in history future. From the very earliest period, accordingly, Israel exercised a future hope. We may go back to Abraham, for instance, and observe that the patriarchs were given a firm promise of the land of Canaan, though they did not live to see its fulfilment.

Once again, however, we must endeavour to restrict our attention to the period of the monarchy, and to trace how the expectations of Israel developed against the background of that era. Her hopes did not rise in an historical vacuum. The prophets were men of their time, and we may well believe that God spoke to them in and through their environment and circumstances. It is to the prophets we must turn primarily, because they were by their very nature men who spoke of the future. (If in the past too much stress was laid upon the predictive elements in their message, we must nevertheless beware of going to an opposite extreme; to say that they were "forth-tellers" rather than "fore-tellers" is to pose a false dichotomy.) But

---

1. H. H. Rowley, *The Faith of Israel* (London, 1956), p. 177.

we should remember that the predictive element is not lacking in other parts of the Old Testament. On the walk to Emmaus, Luke tells us, Jesus discussed "Moses and all the prophets", and explained to the two puzzled disciples "the passages which referred to himself in every part of the scriptures" (Luke 24:27). The "messianic psalms", as they have often been called, may serve to illustrate the point.

We have had occasion to mention Psalm 2 a number of times already; in the first place, it was a *royal* psalm, used of and by the reigning king in Judah. First and foremost, it referred to him. But if its historical setting and function had exhausted the meaning, then such a psalm might well have been rejected from Israel's liturgy once the exile began, and once David's dynasty came to its sorry end. However, it was *not* rejected; it was rather embraced all the more firmly and gladly as time passed. "Such royal psalms", writes J. H. Eaton, "from the outset . . . had a prophetic character: they included vision and oracle, and the purpose of God which they revealed far transcended the experience of the time. The destiny which they promised to the house of David seemed all the more removed from experience as time went on; like the Kingdom of God itself, it was a matter of faith, defying appearances on the strength of the divine promise."[2] The term "messianic psalm", then, is no misnomer.

It is possible, too, that the familiar expression, "the Day of Yahweh" took its origin from the temple ritual; some scholars have argued, in any case, that one day in Israel's festal year was specifically God's Day, perhaps a day when he was ritually enthroned. Others, like the present writer, prefer to think of the Day in terms of outstanding battles in Israel's history.[3] In Israel, it was customary to refer to significant battles of past history as "the Day of . . ."; Isaiah, for instance, recalled Gideon's victory over the Midianites as "the Day of Midian" (Isaiah 9:4). Similarly, the victory in the second century B.C. by Judas Maccabaeus over the Syrian general Nicanor became celebrated annually as "Nicanor's Day" (cf. 2 Maccabees 15:35f.); and among the Arabs, pre-Islamic and early Muslim defeats and victories were described by the same formula.

We might paraphrase Isaiah 9:4 with the words "the day of Midian's defeat", as does the New English Bible; by the same token, "the Day of the LORD" might well be rendered "the Day of Yahweh's victory". There is no wonder, then, that before ever a prophet discussed the Day of the Lord, a popular expectation had

---

2. J. H. Eaton, *Psalms: introduction and commentary* (*TBC*: London, 1967), p. 33.
3. For a brief discussion and useful bibliography on this much debated question, cf. H. H. Rowley, *op. ct.*, pp. 177ff.

arisen to the effect that another victory day was at hand, a day when Yahweh, the God of Israel, would again grant his people the miraculous sort of victories that they had experienced in the time of the Judges. When this popular expectation first grew we have no way of knowing, but we first meet it in Amos, in the first half of the eighth century. Probably it had gradually become prominent as the era of extreme Israelite weakness, at the end of the ninth century, had given way to the political recovery of Jeroboam II's reign; and the hope became a prop for Israel's faith when the Assyrians loomed on the horizon once again.

The interesting feature of Amos's discussion of the Day of Yahweh is that though he castigates the optimistic expectations of his contemporaries, he is far from denying that the Day of the Lord was certainly, unalterably, coming. "Fools who long for the day of the LORD", he proclaimed, "what will the day of the LORD mean to you? It will be darkness, not light. It will be as when a man runs from a lion, and a bear meets him, or turns into a house and leans his hand on the wall, and a snake bites him. The day of the LORD is indeed darkness, not light, a day of gloom with no dawn" (Amos 5:18ff.).

Amos, then, depicted the Day of Yahweh both as imminent and as a day of unrelieved gloom. But that is not the picture which meets us everywhere in the Old Testament, of course. We must bear in mind that days of battle were no rare event in Israel's history, and that "the Day of the LORD" had a variety of applications in the Old Testament writings. In Lamentations we read that the Day had already taken place;[4] but that was by no means the last word on the subject, in Old Testament or New.

A day of battle means victory for one party, defeat for the other, and as a rule escape or survival for a certain number of the vanquished army. These three motifs recur again and again in the prophetic writings, the commonest descriptive terms being "salvation", "judgement", and "remnant" respectively. The popular hope of Amos's day envisaged God as defeating Israel's foes and giving victory to his people; presumably the idea of a remnant played little or no part in their thinking. It was otherwise for Amos, who explicitly predicted not only defeat but "exile beyond Damascus" (5:27) for Israel, but at the same time offered limited hope to a remnant. "If you would live . . . if you would live, resort to the LORD", he counselled (5:4ff.). His remnant was in numerical terms startlingly small, however — "but ten men of Israel left", he declared (5:3). The number, though not the concept, contrasts with the promise given to Elijah nearly a century earlier, that the

---

4. Cf. Lamentations 1:12; 2:1; 2:21f. (The actual phrase used is "the day of Yahweh's anger".)

"Remnant" would be 7,000 strong (1 Kings 19:18). The phrase "the Day of Yahweh" does not occur in the latter passage, but the battle concept is implicit in the declaration that the "sword" of Hazael, Jehu and Elisha would kill very many people in Israel.

The predictions made to Elijah and by Amos alike came to their fulfilment, and proved in very truth to be days of darkness, bloodshed and calamity for the Northern Kingdom. Now the theme was taken up by the Judaean prophet Isaiah, whose very name signifies "the salvation of Yahweh" and who named one of his sons "a remnant shall return" (Shear-jashub); his other son was called by a name which vividly signified the nature of judgement, "speed spoil, hasten plunder" (Maher-shalal-hash-baz). The remnant motif betokened at the same time warning and promise, for "a remnant shall return" signifies that *only* a remnant will do so. For the Northern Kingdom, the remnant would be minimal, as pitiful as Amos's ten men — "two or three berries on the top of a branch, four or five on the boughs of the fruiting tree" (Isaiah 17:6). But Isaiah's contemporary, Micah, was less concerned with numbers than potential, when he depicted the remnant of Jacob as dew, and as a lion (Micah 5:7f.).

Towards the end of Isaiah's ministry, a day of Yahweh's anger descended upon the prophet's native Judah; and the prophet, looking back on the events of 701 B.C., could say, " If the LORD of Hosts had not left us a remnant, we should have been like Sodom" (Isaiah 1:9). History had fulfilled the word of God which had come to him at his call, that there would be a literal decimation, and then worse to follow, of his people's population (cf. Isaiah 6:11ff.).

Once again the same motifs were taken up, this time by a prophet of Josiah's reign, Zephaniah, whose short book is devoted to the major theme of the Day of Yahweh, "The great day of the LORD is near," he warned, "it comes with speed" (Zephaniah 1:14); and he describes it in the by-now familiar terms of darkness and battle. With this prophet, however, we find a more universal dimension than with his predecessors. The very opening words of his prophecy announce God's purpose to "sweep the earth clean of all that is on it" — even to "wipe out mankind from the earth". The broad sweep of his canvas may be seen again in the oracle of Yahweh in chapter 3, verse 8: "Mine it is to gather nations and assemble kingdoms, to pour out on them my indignation, all the heat of my anger; the whole earth shall be consumed by the fire of my jealousy." In Zephaniah's prophecy, then, we are confronted with the final Day of Yahweh; it is not the downfall of Jerusalem predicted by his contemporary Jeremiah that fills his vision, but the day when Yahweh will exercise judgement upon all the nations. Not that Judah will escape the holocaust; Yahweh's judgement will fall there too, and only a remnant will survive.

The themes connected with the Day of Yahweh were thus used and re-used by the prophets, first to describe imminent political events, and then to depict something of God's final purposes (though without losing any of the conviction of imminence). The gradual transition to an eschatological frame of reference was natural and logical; it stemmed from the prophets' insight that if Yahweh was indeed the Lord of history and the God of his elect nation, then he could not forever leave Israel on the treadmill of history; hc must ultimatcly rcscuc his pcoplc from wrong within and foes without. The monarchic period, as it had turned out to be, could not possibly be God's last word for Israel. All the prophets, therefore, however much some of them muted the note of hope, looked forward to a day when their God would bring Israel through to its final, its ultimate salvation. In the meantime, as successive Days of Yahweh passed, he always took care to preserve a remnant of his people.

The prophets saw, moreover, that this remnant consisted not of those who just chanced to escape the disasters of the day, but of those whom Yahweh specially selected to escape them. Isaiah described Yahweh's purpose thus: "Once again I will act against you (Jerusalem) to refine away your base metal as with potash and purge all your impurities" (1:25). It was the dross that was to be consumed. Zephaniah put Yahweh's purpose for Jerusalem into more specific terms: "Then I will rid you of your proud and arrogant citizens . . . But I will leave in you a people afflicted and poor" (Zephaniah 3:11f.). In similar vein Habakkuk prophesied: "as for the traitor in his over-confidence, still less will he ride out the storm, for all his bragging"; but by contrast "the righteous man will live by being faithful" (2:4f.).

In the remnant, then, lay the hope for the future; it would be the true Israel, fulfilling all God's hopes and intentions for his people. Several prophets emphasized that righteousness and holiness would be the keynote of the future people of God. Hosea, schooled by his own unhappy marital experiences, represented God as taking his people to himself in a second betrothal ceremony. "I will betroth you to myself for ever, betroth you in lawful wedlock with unfailing devotion and love: I will betroth you to myself to have and to hold, and you shall know the LORD" (Hosea 2:19f.). Jeremiah's teaching was very similar, but he preferred to use the imagery of the covenant, very probably because he had seen the failure of the covenant renewal sponsored by King Josiah:

> The time is coming, says the LORD, when I will make a new covenant
> with Israel and Judah. It will not be like the covenant I made with their
> forefathers when I took them by the hand and led them out of Egypt.
> Although they broke my covenant, I was patient with them, says the

LORD. But this is the covenant which I will make with Israel after those days, says the LORD; I will set my law within them and write it on their hearts; I will become their God and they shall become my people. No longer need they teach one another to know the LORD; all of them, high and low alike, shall know me, says the LORD, for I will forgive their wrongdoing and remember their sin no more.

(Jeremiah 31:31-34)

This famous passage offers the divine promise of the new covenant to both Israel and Judah, despite the fact that as a political entity Israel had long since ceased to exist. In the same way Jeremiah predicted not only the destruction of Jerusalem and the temple but also the rebuilding of the city, to serve the community of the future:

These are the words of the LORD who made the earth, who formed it and established it; the LORD is his name: If you call to me I will answer you, and tell you great and mysterious things which you do not understand. These are the words of the LORD the God of Israel concerning the houses in this city and the royal palace, which are to be razed to the ground, concerning siege-ramp and sword, and attackers who fill the houses with the corpses of those whom he struck down in his furious rage: I hid my face from this city because of their wicked ways, but now I will bring her healing; I will heal and cure Judah and Israel, and will let my people see an age of peace and security. I will restore their fortunes and build them again as once they were. I will cleanse them of all the wickedness and sin that they have committed; I will forgive all the evil deeds they have done in rebellion against me.

(Jeremiah 33:2-8)

The Jerusalem which fell in 587 B.C. had been characterized by idolatry and immorality; but the prophet, as this passage shows, envisaged a new Jerusalem, not merely rebuilt, but of a totally new character and quality. From now on the very name Zion came to signify the faithful people of the Lord, wherever they find themselves geographically located. In such a renewed condition, the future Jerusalem would be far more than just a minor capital city; it would have a universal role to fulfil. In their conviction that Yahweh was the Lord of history and of the whole earth, the prophets saw that the nations round about, so often hitherto the foes of Israel and so often fighting with each other too, could not forever continue thus in the purposes of God. In the future universal peace must descend; and that peace would be but one element in the universal scene of God's will done on earth:

> In days to come
> the mountain of the LORD's house
> shall be set over all other mountains,
>   lifted high above the hills.

All the nations shall come streaming to it,
and many people shall come and say,
'Come, let us climb up on to the mountain of the LORD,
　　to the house of the God of Jacob,
　　that he may teach us his ways
　　and we may walk in his paths.'
For instruction issues from Zion,
　　and out of Jerusalem comes the word of the LORD;
　　he will be judge between nations,
　　arbiter among many peoples.
They shall beat their swords into mattocks
　　and their spears into pruning-knives;
nation shall not lift sword against nation
　　nor ever again be trained for war.

(Isaiah 2:2ff.; cf. Micah 4:1ff.)

In the prophets' view of future history, then, Jerusalem had a new and immensely significant role to fulfil. It would be appropriately named "The-LORD-is-there", to use a memorable phrase from the last verse of the Book of Ezekiel. But not only so; it would also be the home of the Lord's anointed, the future Davidic King. Had human monarchy proved a failure? So it might often have seemed, but the prophets and many others besides could always cast their minds back to the era of David himself. His reign had been no utopia, but it proved for all time something of the concrete possibilities of royal achievement in Israel. What Israel needed, then, was not the abrogation of the monarchy but another and even greater David, whose realm would be of universal dimensions. Besides, had not Yahweh promised that David's throne should be established for ever (2 Samuel 7:16)?

We come finally, then, to the messianic hope of the prophets. It was a hope that had its antecedents, as in the rather cryptic oracle of Balaam (Numbers 24:17) and in the ambiguously worded blessing of Jacob (Genesis 49:10);[5] but it is in the books of the eighth century prophets that we first meet messianic predictions in plain language. In Hosea 3:4f. we meet a very brief statement to the effect that after many days without a king, the Israelites "will again seek the LORD their God and David their king". But what sort of king? In Hosea the theme is not elaborated upon. In Amos 9:11f., another short passage predicts the restoration of "David's fallen booth"; the word "booth" seems to betoken shelter and protection, so that it is implied that the second David would be a military protector to his people. Verse 12 goes on to predict the restoration of the Davidic empire; the reuniting of Israel and Judah is implicit in this

---

5. See the variety of possible translations offered by recent English Versions.

prophecy. Thus here we learn a little more about the role of the messianic King.

Micah 5:2-4 is the Messianic passage to which Herod the Great was introduced sadly late in life, it is recorded in Matthew 2:3ff. That king's interest centred on the one detail "Bethlehem"; but more significant in the passage as a whole is the prediction that the scion of Bethlehem would be both "a man of peace" and also one whose greatness should "reach to the ends of the earth".

But it is to Isaiah that we must turn for the fullest description of the messianic King. The famous Immanuel prophecy (Isaiah 7:14) does not in fact tell us very much; we are obliged to turn to the New Testament for the clear and unambiguous statement of a virgin birth, since so far as the limited evidence goes, the Hebrew noun used in Isaiah 7:14 (*'almah*), was not a term restricted to virgins (though it certainly included them): hence the rendering "young woman" in modern English Versions, including Roman Catholic ones. This fact need neither surprise nor distress us, for a careful reading of the context suggests that the primary fulfilment of Isaiah's prophecy was a contemporary one as a sign to King Ahaz — and nobody would wish to suggest that any birth in Isaiah's time was a virgin birth. It is just possible that the original reference was to Hezekiah; but even if so, the promise that "the LORD will bring on you, your people, and your house, a time the like of which has not been seen since Ephraim broke away from Judah" (7:17) seems, like the royal psalms, to be more appropriate for the ideal future king than for any historical king of Judah, even Hezekiah. The symbolic title "Immanuel", "God-with-us", is again more fittingly used of Christ than of Hezekiah.[6]

No such problems surround other passages in Isaiah, however. Isaiah 11:1-10 describes the essential ruling qualities of the Messiah, who is here called a shoot from the stock of Jesse — that is to say, a scion of David's house who would arise after the fall of the dynasty. This king, unlike so many of David's heirs, is described as equipped with "the spirit of the LORD", with its concomitant wisdom, righteousness and power. His reign will accordingly be reminiscent of Eden:

> Then the wolf shall live with the sheep,
>   and the leopard lie down with the kid;
> the calf and the young lion shall grow up together,
>   and a little child shall lead them;

---

6. The literature discussing the Immanuel prophecy is enormous. Very helpful despite its brevity is C. R. North in *IDB*, s.v. "Immanuel". A recent scholarly defence of a Messianic interpretation is that of J. Coppens, *Le Messianisme royal* (*Lectio divina* 54: Paris, 1968), pp. 69-76.

> the cow and the bear shall be friends,
> and their young shall lie down together.
> The lion shall eat straw like cattle;
> the infant shall play over the hole of the cobra,
> and the young child dance over the viper's nest.
> They shall not hurt or destroy in all my holy mountain;
> for as the waters fill the sea,
> so shall the land be filled with the knowledge of the LORD.

(verses 6-9)

Finally there is the well-known passage in Isaiah 9:6f.:

> For a boy has been born for us, a son given to us
> to bear the symbol of dominion on his shoulder;
> and he shall be called
> in purpose wonderful, in battle God-like,
> Father for all time, Prince of peace.
> Great shall the dominion be,
> and boundless the peace
> bestowed on David's throne and on his kingdom,
> to establish it and sustain it
> with justice and righteousness
> from now and for evermore.

The style of these verses is that of an annunciation, and it has often been thought that the words of the oracle have been adapted from another ceremony in the life of the kings of Judah. In other words, was it expected of each king of Judah in turn that he should come somewhere near the ideal posed in these verses? It may be so, but the suggestion can only remain a hypothesis. Be that as it may, the blueprint for the ideal Davidic King is here presented to us. His people's political needs would be met by one who was both God-like in battle and the very Prince of peace; the victory won, his people would find the inestimable solace of the one who was their Father for all time. And as the years stretched out it would be increasingly clear that here was a King who could be misled by no ill-advised counsel, for he himself was "in purpose wonderful".

Here we must leave our study of the prophetic hope — already so rich and full of promise, but not yet complete. The fulfilment could not come yet, for Hebrew history had not yet run its course. The dark days of exile and the difficult period of restoration which followed would have their own formative effects on Israel's faith and hope. The pre-exilic prophets had not said the final word of divine revelation; but they had laid a firm foundation on which the people of God would be able to build in the centuries that lay ahead.

APPENDIX

The Chronology of
the Hebrew Kingdoms

THE chronology of the kings of Israel and Judah presents us with a very vexed problem, the subject of a great deal of argument and discussion. The length of the reign of each king of Judah is indicated in the Books of Kings by reference to his contemporary in Israel, and vice versa; but unfortunately the figures given do not always match up, and other difficulties also arise. For instance, 2 Kings 3:1 states that Jehoram became king of Israel in the eighteenth year of Jehoshaphat of Judah; but 2 Kings 1:17 places Jehoram's accession in the second year of Jehoshaphat's son and successor.

It is always possible that some of the figures became altered in transmission; this seems to have happened in the case of Jehoram of Judah, who is credited with an eight-year reign by the Hebrew text of 2 Kings 8:17 (and hence the English Versions), but with a forty-year reign in some important manuscripts of the ancient Greek (Septuagint) translation. In this case the Hebrew may be accepted, but elsewhere it is always a possibility that the Hebrew and the Greek are alike inaccurate, due to a very ancient scribal error or alteration.

The present-day investigator is obliged to make sense of the data so far as he can, and also to link the biblical chronology with events in the history of nations outside Palestine, especially Assyria and Babylonia. Thanks to ancient records from Mesopotamia, a few fixed dates can now be supplied for the chronology of the Hebrew monarchies. Assyrian invasions of the Levant coast in 853 and 841 B.C. enable us to date Ahab and Jehu with precision; and the capture of Jerusalem in 597 B.C. by Nebuchadrezzar is beyond doubt. Slightly less certain are the dates of the fall of Samaria (either

723, 722 or 721) and of the destruction of Jerusalem (either 587 or 586).

Numerous scholars have wrestled with the relevant data and have offered a variety of solutions. An early and praiseworthy effort was by Archbishop James Ussher in the seventeenth century, whose chronological scheme (slightly revised) has graced many editions of the Authorized Version since 1701; but later information has made many of his findings untenable. There are three systems which are particularly influential nowadays, deriving from J. Begrich (1929), W. F. Albright (1945) and E. R. Thiele (1951) respectively; other independent schemes often produce results only marginally different from one or other of these three. Thiele's scheme accepts and makes sense of the biblical data to a greater degree than the alternatives offered by Begrich and Albright; he concludes that the evidence suggests two facts about the Hebrew kingdoms, firstly that the regnal years were for most of the time calculated on different bases in Israel and in Judah respectively, and secondly that there must have been a number of co-regencies. (A co-regency will for example solve the problem noted above, i.e. that Jehoram of Israel is said to have begun his reign at a time when both Jehoshaphat and his son Jehoram were ruling in Jerusalem.)

The three systems (with revised dates where these have been more recently adjusted by Albright and Thiele) are set out below in tabular form. It may be observed, however, that the differences between the three are generally of little consequence. The most important disagreements, it will be seen, relate to the date of Solomon's death (i.e. the date of the division of the kingdom) and to the period of Hezekiah's reign. It is to be hoped that further information will before long elucidate the problems; meanwhile the present writer feels that Thiele's scheme is on the whole the most satisfactory, and his dates have usually been followed in this book.

As regards the dates of Saul, David and Solomon, little can be said with certainty. The Old Testament does not supply us with the length of Saul's reign (see 1 Samuel 13:1, RSV); both David and Solomon are credited with forty years (as is Saul in Acts 13:21), but the problem here is that the number forty was often used in the ancient Near East as a round number, roughly denoting a generation, and nobody can be sure that in either case the number is intended to be exact. On the other hand, there is no evidence at present available which would rule out the possibility that these figures are precise. In the case of David, the data of 1 Kings 2·11 may suggest that the figure forty is to be taken literally. It is reasonably safe to assume that he came to the throne betwen 1010 and 1000 B.C.; it is generally thought that Saul's reign began no earlier than 1035 B.C.

The Kings of Judah

	Begrich	Albright	Thiele
Rehoboam	926-910	922-915	931-913*
Abijah	910-908	915-913	913*-911
Asa	908-872	913-873	911-870
Jehoshaphat	872-852	873-849	873-848*
Jehoram	852-845	849-842	853*-841*
Ahaziah	845*-844*	842*	841*
(Athaliah)	845-839	842*-837	841*-835
Joash	839-800	837-800	835*-796*
Amaziah	800-785	800-783	796*767*
Uzziah	785-747	783-742	792-740
Jotham	758-743	750-735	750*-732
Ahaz	742-725*	735-715*	735*-716
Hezekiah	725-697	715*-687	716-687
Manasseh	696-642	687-642	697-643
Amon	641-640	642-640	643-641
Josiah	639-609*	640-609*	641-609*
Jehoahaz	609*	609*	609*
Jehoiakim	608-598	609*-598	609*-598*
Jehoiachin	598	598-597	598*-597*
Zedekiah	597-587*	598-587	597*-586*

The Kings of Israel

	Begrich	Albright	Thiele
Jeroboam I	926-907	922-901	931-910
Nadab	907-906	901-900	910-909
Baasha	906-883	900-877	909-886
Elah	883-882	877-876	886-885
Zimri	882	876	885
Tibni	(Interregnum 882-879) -		885-880*

The Kings of Israel (continued)

	Begrich	Albright	Thiele
Omri	878-871	876-869	885-874
Ahab	871-852	869-850	874*-853*
Ahaziah	852-851	850-849	853*-852*
Jehoram	851-845	849-842*	852*-841*
Jehu	845-818	842*-815	841*-814
Jehoahaz	818-802	815-801	814-798*
Jehoash	802-787	801-786	798*-782
Jeroboam II	787-747	786-746	793-753*
Zechariah	747*-746*	746-745	753*-752*
Shallum	747*-746*	745	752*
Menahem	746-737	745-736*	752*-742
Pekahiah	736-735	736*-735*	742-740
Pekah	734-733	735*-732*	752*-732
Hoshea	732-724	732*-724*	732-723

(All dates B.C.)

N.B. These tables have been simplified. Since the Hebrew year did not correspond exactly with our year, many of the figures permit adjustment to one year *later* — e.g., Thiele gives the date of Rehoboam's accession as 931/930. An asterisk beside a date denotes that it is regarded by the scholar concerned as established with reasonable certainty. Note that co-regencies (or contemporaneous reigns) may be deduced where the figures overlap: see for instance the dates given for Uzziah and Jotham by all three scholars.

Bibliography

GENERAL AND PART I

Aharoni, Y. *The Land of the Bible* (ET London, 1966).

Aharoni, Y. and Avi-Yonah, M. *The Macmillan Bible Atlas* (New York and London, 1968).

Albright, W. F. *Archaeology and the Religion of Israel* (Baltimore,[5] 1956).

Albright, W. F. *The Archaeology of Palestine* (revised edition, Harmondsworth, 1960).

Albright, W. F. *The Biblical Period* (revised edition, New York, 1960).

Albright, W. F. *From the Stone Age to Christianity* (Baltimore,[2] 1957).

Anderson, G. W. *The History and Religion of Israel* (New Clarendon Bible: London, 1966).

Baly, D. *The Geography of the Bible* (London, 1957).

Bright, J. *A History of Israel* (Old Testament Library: London,[2] 1972).

Bruce, F. F. *Israel and the Nations* (Exeter, 1963).

Buttrick, G. A. (ed.), *The Interpreter's Dictionary of the Bible*, (4 vol., New York and Nashville, 1962; supplementary vol., 1976).

Douglas, J. D. (ed.), *The New Bible Dictionary* (London, 1962).

Grant, F. C. and Rowley, H. H. (eds.), *Dictionary of the Bible* (Edinburgh,[2] 1963).

Grollenberg, L. H. *Atlas of the Bible* (ET London, 1965).

Harrison, R. K. *Old Testament Times* (London, 1971).

Hayes, J. H. and Miller, J. M. *Israelite and Judaean History* (OTL: London, 1977).

Heaton, E. W. *The Hebrew Kingdoms* (New Clarendon Bible: London, 1968).

Heaton, E. W. *Solomon's New Men* (London, 1974).

Hermann, S. *A History of Israel in Old Testament Times* (London, 1975).

Jones, C. M. *Old Testament Illustrations* (Cambridge Bible Commentary: Cambridge, 1971).

Kenyon, K. M. *Archaeology in the Holy Land* (London, 1960).

May, G. H. and Hunt, G. H. *Oxford Bible Atlas* (London, 1974).

Negenman, J. H. *A New Atlas of the Bible* (ET London, 1969).

Noth, M. *The History of Israel* (ET London,[2] 1960).

Pritchard, J. B. (ed.), *Ancient Near Eastern Texts* (Princeton,[3] 1969).

Pritchard, J. B. *The Ancient Near East in Pictures* (Princeton, 1954).

Rowley, H. H. *The Teach Yourself Bible Atlas* (London, 1961).

Thomas, D. W. (ed.), *Archaeology and Old Testament Study* (Oxford, 1967).

Thomas, D. W. (ed.), *Documents from Old Testament Times* (London, 1958).

Thompson, J. A. *The Bible and Archaeology* (Exeter[2], 1973).

Wright, G. E. *Biblical Archaeology* (revised edition, London, 1962).

Wright, G. E. and Filson, F. V. *The Westminster Historical Atlas to the Bible* (revised edition, Philadelphia, 1956).

Yadin, Y. *The Art of Warfare in Biblical Lands* (London, 1963).

PART II

Bleeker, C. J. and Widengren, G. E. (eds.), *Historia Religionum,* vol. 1: *Religions of the Past* (Leiden, 1969).

Frankfort, H. and others, *Before Philosophy* (Eng. ed., Harmondsworth, 1949).

Frankfort, H. *Ancient Egyptian Religion* (Oxford, 1948).

Gray, J. *The Canaanites* (Ancient Peoples and Places: London, 1964).

Gray, J. *The Legacy of Canaan* (Supplements to *Vetus Testamentum* 5: Leiden,[2] 1965).

Habel, N. C. *Yahweh versus Baal: a Conflict of Religious Cultures* (New York, 1964).

Harden, D. *The Phoenicians* (Ancient People and Places: London,[2] 1963).

Harris, J. *The Legacy of Egypt* (London,[2] 1972).

Hooke, S. H. *Babylonian and Assyrian Religion* (Oxford, 1953).

Kitchen, K. A. *The Third Intermediate Period in Egypt* (1100-650 B.C.) (Warminster, 1972).

Moscati, S. *The Face of the Ancient Orient* (ET London, 1960).

Moscati, S. *The World of the Phoenicians* (ET London, 1968).

Ringgren, H. *Religions of the Ancient Near East* (ET London, 1973).

Roux, G. *Ancient Iraq* (London, 1964).

Saggs, H. W. F. *The Greatness that was Babylon* (London, 1962).

Unger, M. F. *Israel and the Aramaeans of Damascus* (London, 1957).

Vriezen, T. C. *The Religion of Ancient Israel* (ET London, 1967).

Wilson, J. A. *The Burden of Egypt* (Cambridge, 1951).

Wiseman, D. J. (ed.), *Peoples of Old Testament Times* (Oxford, 1973).
Zyl van, A. H. *The Moabites* (Leiden,[2] 1972).

PART III

Ellison, H. L. *Men Spake from God* (London,[2] 1958).
Ellison, H. L. *The Prophets of Israel* (Exeter, 1969).
Gottwald, N. K. *All the Kingdoms of the Earth* (New York, 1964).
Heaton, E. W. *The Old Testament Prophets* (revised edition, London, 1977).
Lindblom, J. *Prophecy in Ancient Egypt* (ET Oxford, 1962).
Rad von, G. *The Message of the Prophets* (ET London, 1968).
Scott, R. B. Y. *The Relevance of the Prophets* (revised edition, New York, 1969).
Vawter, B. *The Conscience of Israel* (London, 1961).
Winward, S. F. *A Guide to the Prophets* (London, 1968).

PART IV

Eichrodt, W. *Theology of the Old Testament* (2 vol., ET London, 1961-67).
Knight, G. A. F. *A Christian Theology of the Old Testament* (London,[2] 1964).
Payne, J. B. *The Theology of the Older Testament* (Grand Rapids, 1962).
Rad von, G. *Old Testament Theology* (2 vol., ET Edinburgh and London, 1962-65).
Ringgren, H. *Israelite Religion* (ET London, 1966).
Rowley, H. H. *The Faith of Israel* (London, 1956).
Schofield, J. N. *Introducing Old Testament Theology* (London, 1964).
Wright, G. E. *The Old Testament and Theology* (New York and London, 1969).

APPENDIX

Albright, W. F. in *Bulletin of the American Schools of Oriental Research* 100 (1945), pages 16-22.
Begrich, J. *Die Chronologie der Könige von Israel und Juda* (Tübingen, 1929; r.p. Nendeln, 1966).
Thiele, E. R. *The Mysterious Numbers of the Hebrew Kings* (Exeter,[2] 1966).
Finegan, J. *Handbook of Biblical Chronology* (Princeton, 1964).

Index of Biblical Passages

OLD TESTAMENT AND APOCRYPHA

NEW TESTAMENT

General Index

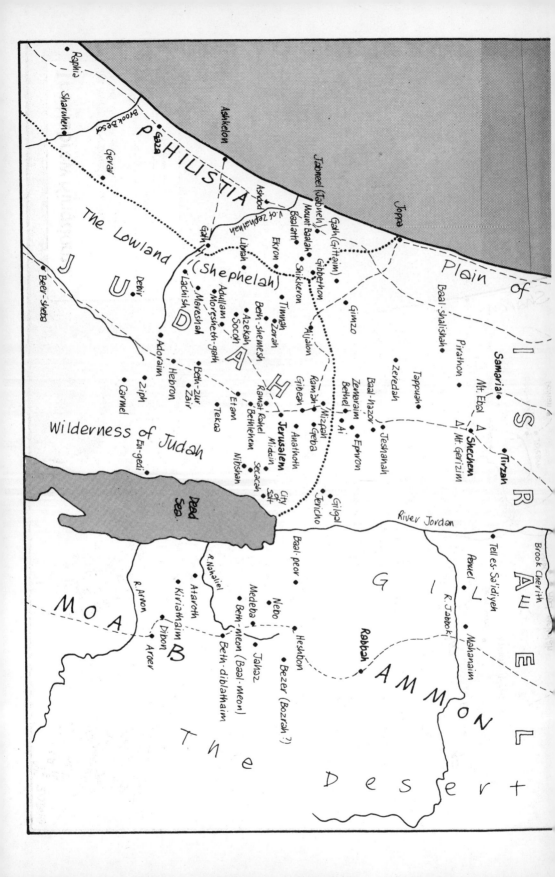

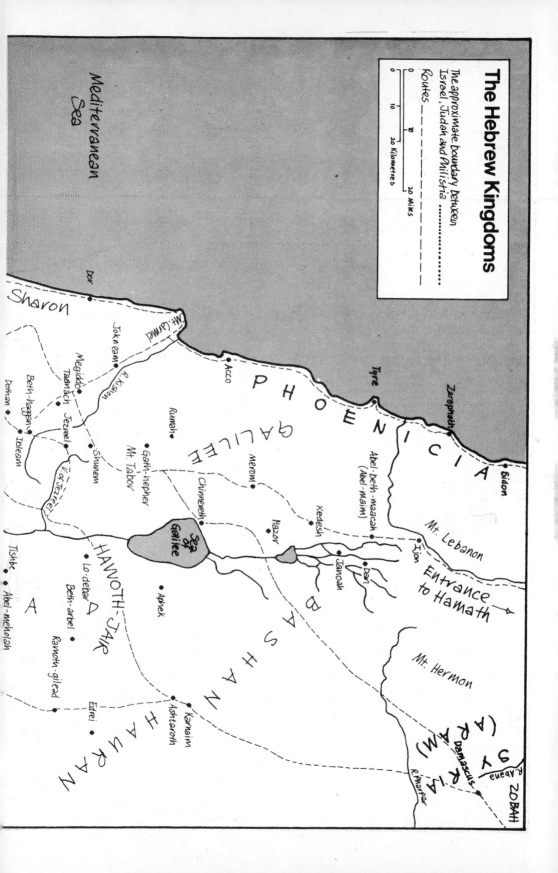

The Hebrew Kingdoms

The approximate boundary between Israel, Judah and Philistia

Routes

0   10   20 Kilometres

0   10   20 Miles

Mediterranean Sea

Sharon

Dor

Jokneam

Mt. Carmel

Acco

Tyre

Zarephath

Sidon

P H O E N I C I A

Megiddo

Taanach

Beth-haggan

Dothan

Ibleam

Jezreel

Shunem

V. of Jezreel

R. Kishon

Rumah

Gath-hepher

Mt. Tabor

Chinnereth

Merom

G A L I L E E

Abel-beth-maacah
(Abel-maim)

Kedesh

Hazor

Mt. Lebanon

Ijon

Janoah

Dan

Entrance
to Hamath

Tishbe

Abel-meholah

A

HAVOTH-JAIR

Lo-debar

Beth-arbel

Aphek

Sea
of
Galilee

B A S H A N

Mt. Hermon

Ramoth-gilead

Edrei

Ashtaroth

Karnaim

H A U R A N

Damascus

R. Abana

R. Pharpar

A R A M (A)

S Y R I A (M)

ZOBAH